THE MEN WHO FLEW THE
ENGLISH ELECTRIC
LIGHTNING

THE MEN WHO FLEW THE ENGLISH ELECTRIC LIGHTNING

MARTIN W. BOWMAN

Pen & Sword
AVIATION

First published in Great Britain in 2021 by
PEN AND SWORD AVIATION
an imprint of
Pen & Sword Books Limited
Yorkshire – Philadelphia

Copyright © Martin W. Bowman, 2021

ISBN 978 1 52670 564 8

The right of Martin W. Bowman to be identified
as the author of this work has been asserted by him in accordance
with the Copyright, Designs and Patents Act 1988.

A CIP record for this book is available from the British Library
All rights reserved. No part of this book may be reproduced or
transmitted in any form or by any means, electronic or
mechanical including photocopying, recording or
by any information storage and retrieval system, without
permission from the Publisher in writing.

Printed and bound in the UK by TJ Books Ltd.

Typeset in Times New Roman 11/13.5 by
SJmagic DESIGN SERVICES, India.

Pen & Sword Books Ltd incorporates the imprints of Pen & Sword
Archaeology, Atlas, Aviation, Battleground, Discovery,
Family History, History, Maritime, Military, Naval, Politics, Railways,
Select, Social History, Transport, True Crime, Claymore Press,
Frontline Books, Leo Cooper, Praetorian Press, Remember When,
Seaforth Publishing and Wharncliffe.

For a complete list of Pen and Sword titles please contact
PEN & SWORD BOOKS LTD
47 Church Street, Barnsley, South Yorkshire, S70 2AS, England
E-mail: enquiries@pen-and-sword.co.uk
Website: www.pen-and-sword.co.uk

Or

PEN & SWORD BOOKS
1950 Lawrence Rd, Havertown, PA 19083, USA
E-mail: Uspen-and-sword@casematepublishers.com
Website: www.penandswordbooks.com

Contents

Acknowledgements	vi
Preface: Tiger Or 'Pussycat'? - The English Electric Lightning	ix
Chapter 1: Flash of Fire - The First Fighters	1
Chapter 2: 'Tiger' Tales	16
Chapter 3: 'Firebirds', 'T-Birds' and 'Tremblers'	33
Chapter 4: Ab Initio	51
Chapter 5: The 'Fast Jet Fraternity'	99
Chapter 6: Tanking	113
Chapter 7: Quick Reaction Alert	141
Chapter 8: Tigers Fly East	171
Chapter 9: 'Linies'	180
Chapter 10: Lightning Strikes	194
Chapter 11: A 'Magic Carpet' Ride	223
Chapter 12: Last of the Lightnings	237
Appendix: Lightning Units	250
Endnotes	261
Index	272

Acknowledgements

J. Adams; Captain A. M. Aldridge; Brian Allchin; John Arnold; Diana Barnato Walker MBE; Rex Barrett; Group Captain Antony I. Barwood OBE; Richard C. Basey; Chris Bassham; Mike Baxter; Captain Martin Bee; Squadron Leader Dick Bell; Anthony 'Bugs' Bendell; John Bexfield; Ray Biddle MBE; AVM George P. Black AFC; Steve Bowes; Alan A. Brain; Roly Bray; Wing Commander John Bryant; John Brindle; Colin W. Brock; Ray Brooks; Flight Lieutenant Peter Brown; Trevor Brucklesby; Squadron Leader E. H. Bulpett; Wing Commander Ken Burford; *RAF Flight Safety Magazine*; Dave Bussey; A. G. Calver; Denis Calvert; Squadron Leader the late Brian Carroll; Edwin Carter; Mick Cartwright; Derek Chilvers; Martin Chorlton; John Church; Roger Colebrook; AVM Peter S. Collins CB AFC BA; Mike Cooke; Bob Cossey; Ray Cossey; Alec B. Curtis; Squadron Leader Dick Doleman; Tony Dossor; John Dunnell; Group Captain Ed Durham; Barry J. Dye; *Eastern Daily Press; East Anglian Daily Times*; J. Malcolm English; Kevin C. Farrow; Nigel Farrow; Daniel and Tony Fishlock; Mike Flowerday; Dave Freeman; D. E. Freeman; John Fuller, 432 (Woodbridge) Squadron ATC; Caroline Galpin; ACM Sir Joseph Gilbert; Ron Godbold; Tony and Brett Goodyear; Air Commodore Ken J. Goodwin CBE AFC; John Hale; A. L. S. 'Les' Hall; Joan Hammond; Ken Hayward; Peter Hayward; Ken Hazell; Group Captain Tim Hewlett; Mike Hillier; Group Captain Mike Hobson CBE; Del Holyland, Martin-Baker Aircraft Co. Ltd; J.R. 'Robbie' Honnor; Group Captain W. B. G. Hopkins AFC; AVM John Howe CB CBE AFC; Mike Indge; Mick Jennings MBE; Squadron Leader Jimmy Jewell; Ken Johnson; Robert Johnson; Ronald Johnson; the late Roy Johnson; Tony Kemp; Brian Knight, Prospect Litho Ltd; Douglas Knights; Jim Lilley; Paul Lincoln; Squadron Leader Jack Love; Barry J. Madden; Steve Masterson; Nigel McTeer; Alec Michael; Vernon Miller; Captain Bruce Monk; Squadron Leader Gordon Moulds MBE; Captain Ted J. Nance; Pete W. Nash; Group Captain Hans Neubroch OBE; Air Marshal

ACKNOWLEDGEMENTS

Sir John Nicholls KCB CBE DFC AFC; Flight Lieutenant R. E. 'Bob' Offord; Wing Commander George Parry DSO* DFC* OBE; Simon Parry; Tony Paxton; Gerald Pearson; Squadron Leader Henry Ploszek AFC; Bill Povilus; Pete Purdy; Richie Pymar; Wing Commander Alex Reed OBE; Richard Reeve; Jeremy Richards; Captain Mike Rigg; Ian H. R. Robins; Mike Rigg; Squadron Leader Derek Rothery; Ray Reed; Gary Revell; Graham Rollins; *Rolls-Royce Magazine*; Group Captain Dave C. Roome OBE MRAeS; Charles Ross; the Lightning Association Chairman and Secretary who amongst many courtesies, kindly obtained permission from Mrs Carroll for me to showcase her late husband Brian's fabulous stories, Squadron Leader Clive Rowley MBE; Adrian Savage; Group Captain Dave Seward AFC; Group Captain Mike J. E Shaw CBE; Kelvin Sloper, City of Norwich Aviation Museum; Patrick and Lionel Snell; Steve Snelling; Laury Squibb; Jean Stangroom; Peter Symes; Geoff Syrett; Air Commodore M. J. E. Swiney; Flight Lieutenant Andy Thomas; Eric Thomas; Hugh Trevor, Lightning Preservation Group, Bruntingthorpe; Vic Yorath; Graham Vernon; S. Wade; John Ward; Sid Watkinson; John Watson; W. H. Welham; C. A. Wheatland; David Williams; Peter Winning; Andrew Woodroof; Group Captain P. T. G. Webb OBE DL; Arthur Wright; Ian Wright, 222 (Broadland) Squadron ATC; A. Yates.

LIGHTNING! Yes, the mighty English Electric P.1B fighter - probably the most advanced interceptor now flying in the western world - 'was so christened by Marshal of the Royal Air Force Sir Dermot Boyle at an official naming ceremony held on 23 October. The choice of a name that has already graced a distinguished warplane of another nation has, as was to be expected, met with widespread criticism. We also would have wished to see a more original name allocated to the RAF's next fighter, but we must admit that, as the Lightning sizzles across our line of sight, its twin afterburning Avons trailing in their wake a thunderclap which stuns the aural sense for long after its originator has disappeared into the distance, the name is not inappropriate! Anyway, for better or for worse, Lightning it is and within little more than a year this tremendously potent weapon will be joining the squadrons of Fighter Command, its contours, possessing all the powerful ugliness of the veteran pugilist, contrasting sharply with the lithe, sleek lines of the Hunter that it supplants.

The single-seat Lightning will be joined during the early summer months by the first P.11, a two-seat trainer variant. Retaining the full range of operational equipment carried by the Lightning, the P.11 will differ principally in having a wider forward fuselage to accommodate two seats side by side. Precise performance figures for the Lightning naturally remain secret, but it may be revealed that during routine test flights speeds considerably in excess of 1,200 mph and altitudes greater than 60,000 feet have already been attained. The Lightning hardly transcends the heights of aeronautical elegance, but its powerfully ugly lines will become an increasingly familiar sight over the British countryside in the months ahead and who knows, it may yet be seen bearing the insignia of the Federal German Air Force now that the Lockheed F-104A Starfighter appears to have been ruled out of Germany's future plans.

**Lethal Voltage, RAF Flying Review,
November 1958.**

Preface

Tiger Or 'Pussycat'?
The English Electric Lightning

It was a Squadron reunion in June. The speeches had been funny and mercifully brief; the meal - first rate. The after-dinner gymnastics had produced no serious injuries (I was unbloodied) and the traditional piano-bashing competition, won by the mid-50s delegates, was now a mound of dying embers in the car park. I was listening spellbound to the survivors of the mid-40s delegation describing how to win a war with style, when the senior raconteur swung to face me, jabbed a war-worn trigger finger into my chest and said: 'Young man - you are sitting up-sun, with four of the other team cold turkey, three thousand feet below and in front of you. What's the first thing you do?'

'Call for help?' I proffered; more in hope than conviction that assistance would be more forthcoming in my war than in his.

'Stupid boy!' he retorted, 'Look for the other four. It's the ones you don't see that get you. Fortunately in my day, indiscretions were often survivable; there were no nasty, cowardly missiles to saw your aeroplane in half. Besides, the opposition's shooting was often no better than mine.'

Looking at the medals on his evening dress, I was unconvinced by his modest implication. Such ironmongery is in short supply and it is rare to see it on a living chest. However, I burbled something suitable into my beer and filed the point of airmanship away in my excuse for a brain.

Some months later, the squadron had moved overseas and after working up to theatre operational status, we were to join the local two-seater squadron in a major air defence exercise. One of our aircraft carriers (there was still a small selection) was due to pass through the area and the opportunity to attack a defended airfield had proved too good for them to miss. A profusion of signals, instructions and op orders laid the ground rules, which were very realistic indeed. The prospects of 'having at' the Navy under realistic conditions sent most of the squadron teetotal for days and tactics discussions squeezed the weekly 'aircraft systems' quiz off the lecture programme. The QFI was sent on leave and the squadron generally cleared for action.

On the first day of the exercise, both squadrons were brought to readiness a first light. Despite the exercise being scheduled to last three days and a suitable shift system being in force, it was amazing how many of our off-duty officers and airmen found urgent secondary duties demanding their presence at dispersal whenever a single-seater was scrambled. After a few hours of combat air patrol (CAPs) had yielded no sign of the enemy it was decided to revert to ground readiness and most of the spectators left. The duty Flight Commander dismissed the rest when he landed from his second sortie of the morning.

The first raid was, predictably, just before lunchtime. The Navy always seemed to organize these things around luncheon; quite properly, for this is one of the attacker's perks. Our ground alert was not alert enough; one-nil to Navy. The Squadron HQ filled with the secondary duties men and promptly emptied in the face of an apoplectic Flight Commander. 'Phone calls to and from the SOC compromised on some CAPs backed up by ground readiness and at this stage the 'first team' came on duty. I was allocated an aircraft and a wingman at ground readiness.

After an hour or so we were brought up to cockpit readiness for the CAPs had detected a low level raid and there appeared to be a running battle in progress about eighty miles south of us. The two-seater squadron had formed a quorum, backtracked along the enemy's attack path and were shooting-up the ship and anything trying to take off from it. Our own CAPs were mixed up with the enemy strike which was progressing, via move and counter-move, towards the airfield. We checked in on telebrief and in response the SOC crackled into life:

'Alert 2 Lightnings.'

'49 Alpha and Bravo,' from Base Ops. This was it; those were our call signs:

'49 Alpha and Bravo, vector 270, make angels one zero, call 'Stud 12.' Six plus Fakers heading north, fast and low.

TIGER OR 'PUSSYCAT'? THE ENGLISH ELECTRIC LIGHTNING

240-40 miles from you and mixed up with four chicks chicks. Your mission to intercept and exercise destroy. Gate, gate, scramble - acknowledge.'

Scramble start, check Bravo's canopy coming down, wave off the marshaller and watch him scuttling for the slit trenches. Pre take-off checks complete, take the far side of the runway and we're off. A check in the mirror and there is Bravo about 100 yards behind and left. After take-off, check right for ten seconds and reverse - there's Bravo in battle formation on the left.

'Weapons and cameras! "Stud 12" Go.'

'Bravo,' as he checked in.

'Loud and clear. Mission 49 - two chicks, gated angels ten. Tiger fast twenty.'

From the SOC: 'Roger left 250, your target's track 773, 11 o'clock twenty - heading North - reported line abreast one mile with escort five miles astern in a mix-up with chicks. I'll bring you in from the south, out of sun.'

Good planning! I hope we have plenty of overtake speed. Perhaps that's why we are at ten thousand. Then, from my wingman:

'Bravo - I hold 2 - ten left twelve miles, low, line abreast.'

'Roger - I hold them - going down - call visual and watch for the escort.'

Then I saw them, two dark grey banana shapes, intermittently merging with the sea:

'Tally ho - twelve o'clock 6 - only two, IN on the left one.' 'Bravo OUT - tail clear.' 'Alpha - they've seen us and are going right.'

Their smoke trail was now visible and thickened as they accelerated to avoid us. Then, again, from my number two:

'Bravo, your tail clear. Can I take the other one?'

Something stirred in the recesses of my mind:

'Negative, stay together, look for the escort.'

'Copied - no contact - your tail clear - wait one, two escorts three miles astern no threat yet, but closing in the turn.' I checked behind number two and called:

'OK Bravo, engage the escort and keep them off me. Your tail clear. Splash on my first target, going for the other.' Then silence for about a minute - too long. The second missile had seen and fired on the second target.

'Splash on both. North of you about 4 miles, 5,000 feet. Joining you in a right turn. Bravo - report.'

I yo-yoed out right, craning my neck for sight of the escort and my number two. Then I saw them; two different dark grey shapes in my 9 o'clock low, turning right underneath me. Bravo's g-strained voice huffed something about having the escorts tied up in a turning fight and my memory stirred again. Where is he? Forget the escorts for a moment. There he is! Filling my right windscreen. Break! Phew, too damned close. I was shaken and felt that enough was enough.

'Bravo, haul-off east, cover me.' He feinted at the opposition, who countered and ran off to the north, presumably to join their two charges. Realistic tactics, I suppose - we could argue their demise at the debrief. Breathing heavily, I advised SOC of the two that got away and they reassured me that they were now SAM targets.

Bravo and I reformed into defensive battle formation and went looking for the rest of the excitement. It was then that my mind started to clear and yielded up its stored memory. 'It's the one that you don't see that gets you.'[1]

Wing Commander Spry comments: The author of this particular 'I learnt...' story has certainly raised a topical issue. During the last 18 months alone, the Service has suffered seven mid-air collisions, which claimed 10 lives and 6 aircraft. In three of the cases, the aircraft concerned carried additional pairs of eyes as each carried two crew-members. With one exception, all of the collisions involved fellow formation members, who were well aware of the close proximity of each other's aircraft, but who probably failed to recognise the impending collision until it was too late to avoid it.

We can all learn about flying from this!

'Tiger or "pussycat"? That depended on whether you were flying it or being hassled by it. As a fighting machine it was surely a real tiger, as many opponents discovered to their cost. Its pure unadulterated power, the mind-numbing acceleration and the certainty that it would and could do anything you asked of it. As for its pussycat image, that too was true of this great aeroplane; it always conveyed a feeling of total reliability. It was sure-footed in every respect and having flown it in all the many variations of weather that one can imagine I was never in any doubt that it would take me home in good style. In fine weather with unlimited visibility you could just as easily have been in a Tiger, or should that be a Puss Moth, winging through the sky with consummate ease; equally I have brought it home in typical East Anglian weather, low cloud, rain, limited visibility and unfriendly crosswinds. In warmer climes, dust storms with equally poor forward visibility have never presented any problems that this thoroughbred could not handle.

'I recall one occasion when I was returning from RAF Germany with our junior engineering officer Flight Lieutenant Lloyd in the right-hand seat of T.4 XM994 on 65 Squadron. We had enjoyed a long weekend at Gütersloh and needed to be back at Coltishall early on the Monday morning. The UK weather was not the best but no particular problems were forecast so, having filed a flight plan, we took off for a routine trip.

'Cruising easily at around FL350 we were soon in contact with UK radar who cleared us into British airspace. Shortly after that we called up Coltishall for clearance to descend and join the ILS for an instrument approach and landing. We were maybe halfway into the let down, passing through 15,000 feet when Coltishall informed us that the weather was closing in with poor visibility and driving rain. All local diversion airfields were in much the same state so with nowhere else to go I continued our recovery to Coltishall. By the time I had levelled off at 2,000 feet, approach radar informed me that the airfield was now condition "Red".

'I cannot recall the actual visibility; suffice to say that it was well below minimums for my Master Green card but with nowhere else to go there was little choice but to continue. RAF Coltishall, like many other fighter units, was blessed with some of the best WRAF radar controllers and I elected at this stage to take a precision radar approach which I would couple with the ILS. My passenger was somewhat tense, having heard how poor the weather was; even so he decided to stay with me! (There was some other choice?). I asked him at this stage to concentrate on looking forward to picking up the runway lights and that as soon as he saw them to tell me exactly where they were, i.e. 100 yards to the right or left depending on the accuracy of the line up.

'By now a nice crosswind had developed, blowing at around 15 to 20 knots across the runway. The approach continued in increasingly bumpy conditions but, as always, the Lightning rode well and responded easily and promptly to the slightest input on the control.

'We were now getting very close to the airfield boundary when at about a quarter of a mile my attentive passenger shouted "contact" with the lights which were 150 yards to our right. I looked up from the instruments, jinked hard right and left and we were down, all in one piece and the final manoeuvre to achieve the touch-down point says much for the controllability of the Lightning. As I have mentioned previously it is so sure-footed in all stages of flight that it generates a significant degree of confidence in the pilots who fly it, knowing that it you treat it right it will do as you wish.

'I suppose the only criticism that I can muster about the Lightning is the fact that there was no chance to get up and wander around when on a long transit flight. I flew several of these over the years, Leuchars to Malta or Cyprus and once from Warton to Dhahran in Saudi Arabia. There were also many occasions when a scramble from QRA (Quick Reaction Alert) would result in long flights up to the Iceland/Faeroes Gap chasing 'Bears' (not the furry kind). These sorties could last for 3-4 hours, by which time the rear end was getting hot (and I do not mean the jet pipes).

'The long transit flights were not helped by the crews of accompanying tankers who could be seen having a meal, drinking tea and generally having a soft time of it. Meanwhile, we got by on a few Polo mints. Even so, none of us would have swapped our beloved Lightnings for anything else.

Close formation in the Lightning was another plus; the controls were balanced to a fine degree and coupled with the instant response from the engines, the aircraft could be held in position with minimal effort. Much different, at least initially from the F-15, which had engines requiring a day or so notice to spool up. Acceleration in both was impressive. The Eagle was almost as good and climb speed was rapidly achieved. Take-off roll is between 2,000 and 3,000 feet, depending upon military or maximum afterburner-powered take-off. The Lightning was quicker off the ground, reaching fifty feet height in a horizontal distance of 1,630 feet.[2]

'All this combined to make display flying relatively easy and I had my place in a number of display formations. One in particular was in Saudi in honour of a passing out parade of Saudi technicians at Dhahran. The King and his entourage were there, so everything was to be just so. Our American friends, who operated the F.5s, were also tasked with providing a four-ship team. The colonel in charge of the F.5 unit and I got our heads together, deciding on the exact format we would follow. His parting words were "Don't try and outdo our show" (as if I would!).

'Came the day and after several rehearsals the game was on. No height limits had been laid down so with everything to go for I led the "Lightning Four" into our planned display over and around the stadium. We never went below 100 feet so the noise was no more than a dull roar (back to the Tiger again) while the F.5s took the part of 'pussycats'. The whole display went off very well; word came back that His Majesty the King was more than delighted with the Lightning's performance, in spite of the fact that he couldn't hear much for a day or so!!

'The Americans' reaction was not quite so polite, though I did tell them that I kept our display "up a bit" to give them a chance. Vive la Lightning. As the saying goes "there's nothing wrong with b***** Americans, we should all have one".

'More on formation and the Lightning's turning ability was well demonstrated when we had a German detachment of Starfighters on a visit. We flew a considerable number of sorties with them, pairing a Lightning with a Starfighter as a fighting unit. These were all very successful until a recovery was started.

'To facilitate an easy recovery for our visitors, we always briefed for the Lightning to lead the return to base with the Starfighter flying in close echelon. This was fine until the Lightning applied more than about 35 degrees of bank at high level (above 25,000 feet) at which stage the Starfighter simply could not match the turn and fell out of position every time. Another plus for the Lightning's excellent handling. A similar profile was flown with a detachment of Swedish Saab Drakens. However, they were a different kettle of fish altogether and handled equally as well as the Lightning, staying in tight formation without difficulty.

'Tanking (air-to-air refuelling) was another of its good qualities and although it required a large degree of rudder and aileron trim to off-set the downwash from the tanker's wings, it was steady as a rock; a bit like fishing from a river bank, only we were catching the odd ton or so of fuel through the tanker's hose. The Victor was our usual supplier, though at one time we flew a trial with the American KC-135s. This was done initially during daylight and then at night. In each case it proved easy and we declined the offer from their hose operator to "fly the drogue on to our probe", as they usually (or perhaps always) did for their own air force.

'Sometimes, but not often, it proved impossible to get "plugged in". For me, this only happened once and that was on a return from a QRA scramble on the proverbial "Bear" Hunt 400nm north of Leuchars. The interception had been successful and my No.2 and I were en route for home and an RV with the tanker. We met up OK, only to discover that the tanker's wing hoses were not available. Only the somewhat larger and much heavier centreline hose was in use. Normally, this would not have caused any problem, though it would have been a first for me. Clear air turbulence, the like of which neither of us had ever experienced, joined in on the act so that the hose was moving vertically up and down over some 20-30 feet. I recall sitting behind the Victor for a little while, watching the basket whistle past my probe at an alarming speed.

THE MEN WHO FLEW THE ENGLISH ELECTRIC LIGHTNING

'Discretion dictated that we give this a miss. RAF Lossiemouth was within range on our internal fuel and the weather (typically Scottish) was superb, with unlimited visibility (well, 100 miles or so) and only about one eighth of cloud cover. An economic cruise and a glide descent put us on the runway with minimum fuel plus. It may surprise some of you to know that from, say, 36,000 feet with one engine shut down and the live engine at flight idle, the Lightning would glide for about 80nm, by which time the height would have reduced to 2,000 feet and the flight idle RPM increased to fast idle to keep AC supplies and the turbine on line.

'All in all, the Lightning was safe, fast and easy to fly and in all the hours I spent winging my way around the sky it never gave me a serious moment when I thought it would let me down. Every take-off was followed by a wheels-down landing and that says a lot for any aircraft.

'By now you may have gathered that I quite liked flying the Lightning and in that assumption you would be right. I first flew in it on 24 February 1966, but it was March of 1968 before I started the Lightning course at RAF Coltishall and from then on I continued to fly Lightnings until 1982, by which time I was about to complete my contract with BAe in Saudi as their Chief Flying Instructor, having managed to accumulate just short of 3,000 hours on type.

'Like all of you, my fingers and just about everything else are crossed in the firm hope that the CAA will come up with clearance to fly and we can all enjoy the thrill (yes, even me) of seeing and hearing the Lightning in the air (and that's where it should be) once again and again and again!'

Brian Carroll[3]
**All quotations by Brian Carroll are
by kind permission of the Carroll family.**

Chapter 1

Flash of Fire - The First Fighters

For many years, Norfolk and Suffolk (Coltishall and Wattisham respectively) were the hub of Lightning operations and many now opine that the only true 'Frightenings' were the natural metal-clad steeds, the ones that gleamed like polished silver. Reminiscent of knights in shining armour, their tailfins bedecked in tigerish yellow and black and Crusader red and white, their refuelling probe was their jousting lance, the pitot tube their foil, air brakes and wheel-well doors their 'shields'; and their weaponry, well, it was just evil! It is difficult for younger readers reared on the Typhoon and F-35 Stealth (Lightning II!) to believe that the Lightning was born of an idea in 1946 and that it progressed as a result of fifties and sixties airframe, engine and weapons technology - all of them British - into the thoroughbred that it is. If, during school holidays, in the far off, halcyon days of the sixties, you stood, like me, by the yellow crash gate to witness the last all-British fighter take off with full reheat, then you too would recall these times with affection. This was in the days before political correctness, when the sounds of the sixties were easy on the airwaves, the only foreign footballers came from Wales, Ireland and Scotland, car tyres were only £3 17s 6d in real money, a new 1968 Vauxhall Viva 90 (de luxe!) just £744 and your Morris Oxford Traveller came in Trafalgar Blue. A Lightning pilot, though, was earning over £2,750 per annum and in Norwich in 1968 a 'modern detached bungalow', just three years old, retailed at 'only' £3,350, while a 'spacious' detached house cost just £750 more. All right, so you were on £14 a week and probably you had to work for two or three months to buy a decent camera. Let us not forget that the Cold War years were dangerous years, too. No one though, can ever take away the vivid memories and the cacophony of sound generated by the twin Avon engines that reverberated around an airfield at take off time like a violent storm. The Lightning may be gone, but it certainly is not forgotten. There never has been and never will be; another aircraft like it. Without doubt it is the best of the best of British!

Martin W. Bowman.

'I first heard of the Lightning in 1953,' recalls Squadron Leader (later Group Captain) Dave Seward,[1] 'when a wing commander from the Central Fighter Establishment visited 1 Squadron at RAF Tangmere to give us a talk on fighter development. He discussed the problems with the Swift, the introduction of the Hunter and Javelin and then went on to describe the fighter of the future. At the time rumours were rife that we were going to get a jet-rocket fighter that took off on a trolley and landed on skids. To us this sounded too much like the Me 163 [a German Second World War rocket-powered interceptor] and we were not too enthusiastic. Also, this was the same time that the so-called 'moving runway' was in vogue. We reckoned that if you landed a bit too slow, the runway could be rotating too fast and you would end up through the windscreen. So, to get the real "poop" from the horse's mouth for a change was eagerly awaited.'

The 'poop' that Squadron Leader Seward and others like him received centred on a radical and revolutionary new design by the English Electric Company. It was the result of Experimental Requirement 103, issued by the Ministry of Supply in May 1947, for a research aircraft capable of exploring transonic and low supersonic speeds of up to Mach 1.5. A year earlier, in 1946, the de Havilland Vampire was entering RAF service and both Hawker and Supermarine were studying schemes for swept-wing jet fighters which would eventually emerge as the Hunter and Swift and which would be capable, just, of exceeding Mach 1 in a dive. At English Electric, chief engineer William Edward Willoughby 'Teddy' Petter began sketching possible fully supersonic designs.

One of the immediate problems was finding a suitable engine, even though Britain had established her jet pedigree as far back as 1937, when Frank (later Sir Frank) Whittle had run the first gas-turbine aero-engine in this country. Jet fighter development accelerated in the Second World War, not least in Germany, where the Messerschmitt Me 262, powered by Jumo 004-0 jet engines, became operational on 3 October 1944. Britain's first operational jet fighter, the Gloster Meteor I powered by centrifugal-flow engines, entered squadron service in July 1944. On 7 November 1945 a

Meteor F.4 of the High Speed Flight established a new world air-speed record of 606 mph. On 7 September 1946 the record increased to 616 mph.

In 1947 America seriously challenged Britain's world lead in jet fighter design for the first time. Early American jet aircraft had not proved successful, but in June 1947 America captured the world speed record when the Lockheed P-80R Shooting Star raised the record to 623.74 mph. The Douglas Skystreak raised it even further later that year, to 650.92 mph. Jet aircraft at this time were all of conventional straight-winged design, but then the results of German wartime research into high-speed aerodynamics became available and it was the American aviation and space industries which benefited most. German designers had explored ways of avoiding the problems of 'compressibility'. As an aircraft approaches the speed of sound, the air it displaces is compressed into a series of high-pressure waves that stream back in a cone from the nose. As these hit the wing, they cause the airflow over that part of the aircraft to break up and cause added drag. They also create extreme buffeting, with harmful effects to the structure of the wing. The German designers discovered that if they swept back the wing, this delayed the onset of compressibility problems and allowed higher subsonic speeds to be attained.

On 14 October 1947 Captain Charles 'Chuck' Yeager in the Bell X-1 became the first man to break the sound barrier, when he attained a level speed of 670 mph, or Mach 1.015, at a height of 42,000 feet. America's F-86 Sabre, the first transonic, swept-wing jet fighter to see service in the West, had flown for the first time on 1 October 1947 and on 15 September 1948 an F-86A established a new world air-speed record of 670.98 mph. By July 1953 the Sabre had increased the record speed to 715.75 mph. On 29 October 1953 the F-100 Super Sabre, the world's first operational fighter capable of supersonic performance, established yet another new world air-speed record of 755.15 mph. In the Soviet Union, the MiG-17, an updated version of the swept-wing MiG-15, also appeared in 1953 and was claimed to have exceeded Mach 1 in level flight three years before.

Britain could therefore be forgiven for the onset of despondency. She could also he accused of shooting herself in the foot. In February 1946, British technology was seriously jeopardized when, just as construction was about to start, the Miles M.52 supersonic research aircraft was disastrously cancelled; theoretically, this aircraft would have been capable of reaching 1,000 mph at 36,000 feet. By 1948 it was quite apparent that the lead in supersonic design had passed to America. John Derry in the de Havilland DH 108 made the first British supersonic flight on 9 September 1948, but only in a dive. Conceived in 1953, the delta-winged Avro 720, powered by an Armstrong Siddeley Viper engine and Armstrong Siddeley Screamer rocket unit, was theoretically capable of Mach 2 at 40,000 feet. It was cancelled in 1957 just as the prototype neared completion. Although her Canberra and Hunter aircraft established speed records in 1953 (the latter raised the world speed record to 726.6 mph on 7 September), it must have seemed that Britain had thrown away what could have been a world lead in supersonic research.

However, Specification 103, which had called for a high-speed research aircraft, had already prompted both the Fairey and English Electric companies to initiate design studies. Fairey was to respond with the delta-winged FD.z while at English Electric, Teddy Petter and his young, talented design team, started work on two prototypes and a third airframe for static test. In mid-1949 Specification F.23/49 was issued for a structural test specimen and two 7g research aircraft with guns and a sighting system 'to investigate the practicality of supersonic speed for military aircraft'. English Electric developed the P.1 supersonic day-fighter to meet it. The company had no direct research and experience to call upon. Indeed, English Electric's experience of aircraft production had been limited to producing Hampdens and Halifaxes in the Second World War and then Vampires after the war. But Petter's genius and the technical expertise of his team, already heavily engaged in bringing the EE.A1 jet bomber decision to reality as the Canberra, were ready to overcome all obstacles. They were helped greatly by data provided by the Short S.B.5. (WG768), a scaled down test-bed powered by a 3,500lb-thrust Rolls-Royce Derwent jet engine and fitted with a non-retractable undercarriage, adjustable for centre of gravity variations. The S.B.5 first flew on 2 December 1952. Various wing designs with a sweepback of 50, 60 and 69 degrees were tested and a variable-incidence tailplane positioned either at the top of the fin or on the rear fuselage was also experimented with by Short Brothers. Further data was provided by the installation at the Warton factory of both water and transonic wind tunnels (the first in Britain), including equipment capable of operating at Mach 4 and Mach 6. Fifty-one models were tested and in excess of 4,600 runs were made in the various wind tunnels. Even so, to produce an operational front-line fighter capable not only of sustaining supersonic flight, but also of reaching Mach 2, was a challenge so daunting that in 1949 it was akin to trying to be the first to put a man on the moon.

A decision was taken to use two Armstrong Siddeley Sapphire AS-Sa5 axial-flow engines. These had a lower frontal area than the centrifugal-flow engines that powered the older Meteor and Vampire and were each capable of providing 7,200lb dry thrust with no re-heat. By this method, less fuel would be used than with a single large engine combined with afterburning. If the two engines were 'stacked' one above and behind the other, double the thrust of a single unit could be obtained, while the frontal area was increased by only 50 per cent. Most Soviet and American designers had tried to design a fighter capable of achieving supersonic speeds in level flight without the use of afterburners, but without success.

Even more radical were the wings, with 60 degrees of sweep to minimize wave drag; had the trailing edge been continuous they would have been of delta form like those of the FD.2. Petter rejected the delta wing, however, because it would not provide sufficient control during certain flight contingencies and the positive control provided by a tailplane would not then have been available. A deep notch was cut into the trailing edge of the shoulder wings at about 50 per cent of each half span, with the ailerons being carried along the outer transverse trailing edge to the tips. To avoid pitch-up problems, the sharply swept-back, all-moving tailplane was mounted below the level of the wing (beneath the lower tailpipe) on the slab-sided fuselage. Advanced avionics, powered controls and a very clever retraction of the main undercarriage wheels into the thin wings were other notable aspects of the design. The wings, despite having a thickness/chord ratio of only 50 per cent, gave a very reasonable fuel storage area and kept the fuselage free of fuel tanks - a feature, which would hamper the Lightning in later years. However, in 1947 the RAF wanted only a short-range, rapid climb interceptor. Fuel was not then the main consideration.

WG760, the first prototype P.1 was powered by two 7,500lb static thrust Sapphires fed through the single nose intake, which was bifurcated, internally to each engine. It had a delta fin with a rounded tip and an uncranked wing leading edge. To minimize wave drag, the top of the hood was virtually flush with the upper line of the fuselage. In 1950 Petter left English Electric to join Folland Aircraft and responsibility for the design and subsequent development of the P.1 passed to F. W. (later Sir Freddie) Page.

The first indications that Britain had a world-beating design, which could catapult the RAF into the supersonic age, sparked understandable euphoria, as Squadron Leader Dave Seward confirms: 'It has an air intake right in the nose,' the wing commander from the CFE said. 'Wings swept so far back that the ailerons are on the wingtips and it has two engines - one on top of the other,' he added. 'Furthermore, it can climb to 36,000 feet in under five minutes and it flies at one-and-a-half times the speed of sound.' Then he said, 'It's so secret, that you should forget what I've told you.' Well, how could we forget such an aircraft when we were flying Meteor 8s, which could just about achieve Mach 0.82, almost out of control? The idea was to have a rocket pack fitted underneath the fuselage to give extra thrust for acceleration and combat. Thankfully, the rocket pack, which seemed to have a habit of blowing up no matter which firm made it, was dispensed with and a ventral fuel tank was installed in its place.

The P.1 prototype was finished in the spring of 1954 and was transferred by road to the A&AEE, Boscombe Down for its first flight on 4 August 1954 in the hands of English Electric's chief test pilot, Wing Commander Roland P. 'Bee' Beamont who reached Mach 0.85 on the first flight. On the third flight on 11 August WG760 became the first British aircraft to exceed Mach 1 in level flight, but it was not realized that this had been achieved until the following day when the aircraft's speed was accurately computed! On 18 July 1955 P.1A WG763, the second prototype flew for the first time and that September it gave its first public demonstration when it performed at the SBAC Display at Farnborough. The P.1A differed from the P.1 in having a pair of 30mm Aden cannon in the nose and American-style toe brakes. In the course of the development of the P.1 into the anticipated fighter, WG760 was re-designated P.1A, the fighter project becoming P.1B. WG763 was armed with a pair of 30mm Aden canon fitted in the upper nose decking and flew with her heading edge flaps fixed in place, as they had been found to be superfluous.

A decision was taken in 1954 to order three P.1B prototypes.[2] They would be powered by 200-Series Rolls-Royce Avons with four-stage re-heat and have provision for a Ferranti AI (Airborne Intercept) 23 (Airpass) radar and two de Havilland 'Blue Jay' (later 'Firestreak') infrared homing missiles. This brought about a complete redesign of the aircraft, although the general aerodynamic layout and concept were retained. The oval intake at the nose was changed to an annular design with a central shock cone; the airbrakes were modified; plain instead of area-increasing flaps appeared on the wing; and the cockpit canopy was raised. Handling trials revealed that a larger fin area was desirable for better stability and this was increased later by 30 per cent. The change to 200-Series Avons with re-heat nearly doubled the thrust available. An order for a pre-production batch of twenty P.1Bs plus three test airframes[3] came soon after and was followed, in November 1956, by an order for nineteen production aircraft, designated F.1 and a non-flying specimen. RAF plans for an all-weather heavy interceptor (OR.3Z9) capable of carrying two large radar-homing missiles (originally called 'Red Dean', later 'Red Hebe') never reached fruition and the RAF had to settle for the lightweight Lightning armed with clear-weather IR-homing missiles.

XA847, the first prototype P.1B, exceeded Mach 1 without re-heat on its maiden flight on 4 April 1957 from Warton with 'Bee' Beamont at the controls. Ironically that same day Duncan Sandys, the Minister of Defence, published the now infamous White Paper forecasting the end of manned combat aircraft (including a supersonic manned bomber) and their replacement by missiles! In part it said: 'In view of the good progress already made with surface-to-air missiles, the Government has come to the conclusion that the RAF is unlikely to have a requirement for fighter aircraft of types more advanced than the supersonic P.1 and work on such projects will stop.' The P.1 remained in being for the simple reason that supersonic interceptors were needed to protect the V-bomber force based in the United Kingdom. From now on, the role of Fighter Command was to be purely defensive.

In April 1958 the first deliveries of the pre-production P.1Bs began. The first (XG307) flew on 3 April 1958. On 23 October, the name 'Lightning' was bestowed on the P.1B at Farnborough. During the year the idea of installing a Napier Double-Scorpion rocket pack, as had been fitted to a Canberra to create a new world altitude record in 1957, was dropped. On 25 November 1958, XA847 became the first British aircraft ever to fly at Mach 2, bettering this achievement on 6 January 1959. The first P.1 production example flew on 30 October 1959. It had two Rolls-Royce Avon RA.24R 210 engines, each giving 11,250lb static thrust at maximum cold power and 14,430lb static thrust in full re-heat. With an all-up weight of 34,000lb, the 28,000lb thrust of the engines provided a very good power/weight ratio. It had two 30mm Aden cannon in the upper front fuselage and could have two more fitted in the lower fuselage in lieu of the missile pack. It had the Ferranti AI.23 Airpass radar in the nose shock-cone and carried two Firestreak infrared missiles, one on each side of the fuselage.[4]

There were no dramatic problems during the development flying stage with the P.1 series. However, on 1 October 1959 test pilot John W. C. Squier was fortunate to escape death after ejecting from XL628, the prototype T.4 two-seat variant, which Bee Beamont had first flown from Warton on 6 May. At 11.15am on the morning of 1 October Squier took off from Warton and climbed to 35,000 feet before accelerating to Mach 1.7 over the Irish Sea. His brief was to note engine data at every 0.1 Mach above Mach 1.0 to Mach 1.7, when he was to climb to 40,000 feet, stabilize and make a 360-degree roll to starboard using maximum aileron with his feet off the rudder pedals. This manoeuvre had previously been accomplished in single-seat Lightnings, but it had never before been tried in the two-seat version. Squier reached Mach 1.7 and twenty miles due west of St. Bees Head he carried out the aileron turn. A high-speed roll immediately developed and when Squier centralized the controls to halt it XL628 yawed violently to starboard in a manoeuvre far fiercer than had previously been encountered during maximum aileron rolls in the single-seat Lightning. Squier knew that a structural failure had occurred and the aircraft was now totally uncontrollable, yawing violently right and left and pitching. He had to get out, fast. He reached up, noticing as he did so that the pitot tube was bent right across the air intake and grabbed the seat blind; and the seemingly slow-motion ejection sequence was put in motion. The canopy was whisked away into the void and the Martin-Baker seat fired him out of the doomed Lightning. As he exited, Squier took a blow to his right elbow from the SARAH (Search and Rescue Homing) battery and both his legs from his knees downwards were badly bruised by the ascent. He tried to hold the blind to his face in the full force of the blast, which blew away his oxygen mask, but his arms were painfully wrenched away, almost out of their sockets. (Two compressed vertebrae were also diagnosed later.) Then the seat fell away but the parachute failed to deploy. Squier only became aware of this when he passed through cloud and could see that the sea was getting ominously close! Instantly, he pulled the manual override and at last the parachute deployed.

Squier plunged into the water and sank beneath the waves. He managed to inflate his life preserver and as he soared to the surface he became entangled in the shroud lines until he was able to disentangle himself and release the parachute. Fortunately, the dinghy in the PSP (Personal Survival Pack) had inflated and it now floated invitingly nearby. He managed to clamber aboard but it was full of seawater and in the absence of the bailer he had to use a shoe to scoop out the water. Then he rigged the SARAH homing beacon and its aerial, but, to his dismay, the apparatus failed to work - the high-tension battery, which was one week beyond its inspection date, was flat. For two hours Squier bobbed around on the sea before an amphibian approached. Squier managed to pull the pin on the two-star signal rocket, but it refused to fire and the aircraft failed to spot the tiny dinghy. Another hour passed and the aircraft returned, but again the signal rocket failed to work. Ironically, the third and final rocket worked perfectly, but by now the amphibian had departed.

Squier spent the rest of the day adrift on the sea and he must have begun to despair when darkness settled. He had still not been found the next morning when rain and bad visibility cloaked the horizon. However, he could make out what he thought must be the east coast of Ireland. (It was actually Wigtown Bay in western Scotland.) He tried paddling but all he succeeded in doing was going around in circles. A piece of driftwood helped and he eventually reached a point about 200 yards from the shore. Finally, after passing ships hour after endless hour had seemingly ignored his whistles for help, Squier berthed alongside a tower in a small inlet and eventually managed to reach the shore, from where he was able to stumble to the safety of a house. In the garden was a matron from an adjoining school who told Squier that she had seen the story concerning his disappearance in the newspapers. He had spent thirty-six hours on the surface of the sea. Squier was rushed to Stranraer Cottage Hospital where, the next day, four doctors from the Institute of Aviation Medicine at Farnborough, who diagnosed the two compressed vertebrae, examined him. His eyes and middle ears had also haemorrhaged and he became deaf after a week - fortunately only temporarily. Two weeks later, he was airlifted from West Freugh to Warton and was admitted to Preston Royal Infirmary, where he spent another month. The outcome of the investigation into the cause of the disaster found that the thickening of the forward part of the fuselage to accommodate the second seat had reduced the Lightning's stability, particularly with two Firestreaks attached. It would be eight months later before John Squier was able to fly again.

The Lightning entered service in December 1959 with the delivery to the AFDS (Air Fighting Development Squadron) at Coltishall of three pre-production P.1Bs. Prior to their arrival there were some concerns about the suitability of the Norfolk station to support Mach 2 aircraft. However, the runway had been extended to over 7,000 feet. The first three P.1Bs were followed in May-July 1960 by the first production F.1s for 74 'Tiger' Squadron, also at Coltishall. First to arrive was XM135, on 25 May. Squadron Leader John Frederick George Howe, an assured thirty-year-old South African born in East London, Union of South Africa on 26 March 1930 and educated at St Andrew's College, Grahamstown. He joined the South African Air Force immediately after leaving school. John Howe began his military flying career in the post-Second World War South African Air Force and learned to fly in Tiger Moths, Harvards and Spitfires. In 1950 he was posted to 2 Squadron SAAF 'The Flying Cheetahs' and deployed to Korea to fly combat missions as part of South Africa's contribution to the Korean War in support of the UN forces. During his first tour of duty in Korea he flew the Mustang F-51D fighter-bombers in front-line action.

A later second tour saw him serving with US Infantry units, as a ground based Forward Air Controller, operating in the thick of the fighting. He was awarded the US Distinguished Flying Cross and the US Air Medal for his service during these actions. When the political situation in South Africa became more difficult and extreme in 1954 he decided to resign from the SAAF and moved to England where he transferred to the RAF in the rank of Flying Officer to fly early types of jet fighters. He became a QFI on Vampires, later converting to the Hawker Hunter and serving the front-line North Sea interceptors on 222 Squadron at RAF Leuchars in October 1957 as a flight commander on promotion to Flight Lieutenant. During the Suez crisis in 1956 he had again operated as a Forward Air Controller and landed with the first invasion wave on the beaches with 40 Commando. After Suez John Howe returned to flying duties as a Flight Commander on 43 Squadron RAF during which time he was awarded with the Queen's Commendation for Valuable Service in the Air. Four years after the Suez debacle Howe was promoted to Squadron Leader in July 1960 and appointed as Officer Commanding 74 Squadron. He said at the time: 'We know that we can catch the bombers and going on past experience, we know we can outfight any fighter equivalent to the USAF Century series. The performance of the aircraft, coupled with the ease with which it is flown, gives the pilots confidence and the fact that it is felt to be the best fighter in operational service in the world today gives our Lightning pilots the highest possible morale.'[5]

F.1s, though, were slow to arrive and Lightning spares were almost non-existent. Although seven Lightnings had arrived by August, only one was operational. Then it was announced that the 'Tigers' were to fly four Lightnings each day during Farnborough Week in September! However, this helped speed up deliveries and these enabled the squadron to begin work-up at Boscombe Down late that summer. Then the aircraft were back in the hangars at Coltishall again for much needed maintenance so that they could take part in Battle of Britain commemorations. Ground crews worked right around the clock, dealing with constant electrical failures and myriad other complex teething troubles to keep six to twelve Lightnings on the line at one time. 74 Squadron would not become fully operational until the following year. Progress was one step forward, two steps back. Of the 339 Lightnings built, 109 were lost or written off by a combination of many things, including pilot error, undercarriage failure and fuel or hydraulic leak-related fires. In the late 1960s and very early 1970s, this became a disease known as 'LFS' (Lightning Fire Syndrome), which in 1972 reached epidemic proportions. One of the first instances of LFS occurred on 16 December 1960 when Flight Lieutenant Bruce Hopkins of the AFDS had a lucky escape in F.1 XM138.

'I was on a trial sortie from Coltishall with a Javelin as my target when suddenly there was a big thump. I felt it on the rudder bars. Then - nothing. I called the Javelin pilot to check me over. He looked and said he could see nothing wrong. I decided to abandon the sortie and recover to Coltishall. During the approach I had restricted elevator control so I knew something was wrong. I did a straight-in approach using elevator trim. The landing was normal. I was rolling out with the brake deployed when the 'Attention Getters' started clanging. One of the fire-warning lights was on. At the same time ATC told me I was on fire! I completed the landing run - what else could you do? I stopped, switched off everything, unstrapped, stood up in the cockpit, looked back and saw a conflagration; a great twenty-foot sheet of flame was spewing out! I hurriedly exited. Usually, you needed a ladder to climb down. I just leapt out onto the dummy 'Firestreak' and onto the ground in one bound. I ran! By which time, the fire engines had arrived. What had happened was that there had been a hot gas leak from the No.1 engine near the jet pipe and it had impinged on the fire extinguisher bottle. Of course the inevitable happened. It cooked it and exploded it. The blast had bent the elevator control rods and fractured a fuel pipe. The fuel had spilled all down the underside of the fuselage but the airflow had kept it from igniting, until, that is, I landed and slowed. This incident was very unusual and as a result, fire extinguishers were modified to include a pressure valve.'[6]

A few days after a three-day 'meet the press' event in February 1962, a serious Lightning fire hazard was discovered in the area between the ventral tanks and the No.1 engine and jet-pipe. As a temporary measure, the ventral tanks were removed for flight until the problem was solved by a manufacturer's modification. Finally, by the end of April, all 'Tiger' pilots had completed their conversion to fly the aircraft by both day and night.

Production of the twenty-eight improved F.1A version and twenty-one of its T.4 two-seat equivalent continued under the auspices of a new organization. In 1960 English Electric Aviation was merged with Bristol Aircraft, Vickers Armstrong (Aircraft) and Hunting Aircraft to create the British Aircraft Corporation (BAC). The F.1A had provision for a detachable in-flight refuelling probe under the port wing and improved windscreen rain dispersal. The other main difference was a UHF radio in place of the F.1's VHF. It also benefited from a general cleaning-up of the electrics and layout (strakes were added). Later, all F.1s were modified to F.1A standard. The T.4 was basically a side-by-side two-seat version of the F.1A. It looked awkward and bulbous, but its performance was only very marginally down on that of the single-seaters. On the squadrons it was classed as a front-line aircraft. All squadrons had one T.4 and the LTF (Lightning Training Flight), soon to become 226 Operational Conversion Unit (OCU), had eight initially. The first F.1A (XM169) flew on 16 August 1960 (the first production T.4 having flown on 15 July) and the first examples were issued to the Wattisham wing. 56 Squadron began receiving the first ones late in 1960 and 'Treble One' Squadron began receiving theirs in early 1961.

One of the very best kept secrets during the Lightning's service career was the very high loss rate, which some place on a par with that of the notorious Lockheed F-104 Starfighter.[7] Dave Seward comments, 'If you look at the numbers we lost, the numbers were not great, but you have to look at the total we had and the total number was also not great.' In 1962 six Lightnings were lost. Lightning test pilot George P. Aird cheated death when he was forced to eject from P.1B XG332 near Hatfield on 13 September after an engine fire. Aird had just completed a re-heat test up to Mach 1.7 off the south coast of England at 36,000 feet. All had gone well until during the return flight the test engine twice refused to relight. Aird's third attempt succeeded but fuel, which should have been vented, was retained in the rear fuselage by a blocked drain and eventually ignited via a small crack in the tailpipe. As Aird descended at 400 knots through 15,000 feet, 15-20 miles northeast of Hatfield, a 'double re-heat' engine fire warning glowed on the instrument panel. He weaved from side to side but was unable to confirm the extent of the problem. With the Hatfield runway in sight he decided to attempt a landing, hoping that it was only the fire warning light that had malfunctioned. He decided not to jettison the large ventral fuel tank as it could seriously injure anyone on the ground. Unfortunately, Runway 24, which was nearer, was not in use and Aird had to make for Runway 06, which proved a shade too far for the Lightning to remain airborne. Just ten seconds from touchdown the tailplane actuator anchorage, weakened by the fire, failed completely and XG332 pitched violently upward. Aird instinctively pushed the stick forward and was horribly surprised to find that, when he waggled it around between his legs, it appeared to be disconnected. Aird pulled the ejection seat face blind and was blasted out of the doomed Lightning. He landed in the middle of a large greenhouse by the St Albans road at Smallford. Although he suffered no lasting back injuries, both his legs were smashed.

The next stage of the Lightning's development was the introduction of the F.2, which externally resembled the F.1A and had the same radar and Avon 210 engines, but the latter with fully variable after-burning in place of the earlier four-stage system. It also incorporated a number of other refinements: a much improved cockpit layout, slightly better automatic flight-control system, all-weather navigational aids and liquid oxygen (LOX). XN723. The F.2 prototype first flew on 11 July 1961 and it was delivered to AFDS at Binbrook in November 1962. A month later, 19 Squadron at Leconfield became the first operational squadron in the RAF to equip with the F.2. It was joined late in 1962 by 92 Squadron, which received its first Lightnings in April 1963, the Leconfield Wing becoming fully operational that summer. At the end of 1965 both squadrons became part of 2nd Tactical Air Force in RAF Germany, later becoming the Gütersloh Wing.[8]

What was the performance like on these early aircraft? Dave Seward explains. 'If you look at the air intake of a Lightning, the radome forms a centre body, which offsets the effects of compressibility over the engines as the speed is increased into the supersonic range. Theoretically the Lightning could achieve Mach 2.4 or two-and-a-half times the speed of sound before the supersonic shock wave angled back into the air intake, which would cause the engines to stall and possibly flameout. This rarely occurred, however, because to achieve Mach 2.4 you would use an enormous amount of fuel and with the pointed fins, the 1, 1A, 2 and T.4 could lose directional control at very high Mach numbers if harsh control movements were attempted. So these early aircraft were restricted to Mach 1.7. To overcome the limitations of these early models, the F.3 was introduced in 1962. It had a larger, squared-off fin and bigger Avon 301 engines, each giving 12,690lb dry thrust and 16,360lb in re-heat. These aircraft were cleared to Mach 2. The F.3 had the upgraded AI.23b fire control system with greater range and better definition, together with a visual identification mode for interrogating targets [OR.946 with Mk.2 master reference gyro]. But, of course, you do not get anything for nothing and the extra circuitry for the radar, plus a liquid oxygen system, meant that the gun had to be dispensed with - an unfortunate move which was to be felt later.'

The F.3 made provision for two jettisonable overwing tanks, but these were never fitted. It also introduced the 'Red Top' (originally 'Blue Jay' Mk.4) missile, which was a development of 'Firestreak' but which allowed a head-on attack to be made on supersonic targets.[9] XP693, the first prototype F.3, flew on 16 June 1962 and production models entered service with the RAF when XP695 was delivered to the Central Fighter Establishment at

Binbrook in January 1964. 74 Squadron at Leuchars became the first front-line squadron to so equip, in April when it began replacing its F.1s, while 23 Squadron at the same station began replacing its Javelins with the F.3. Towards the end of the year both 56 and 111 Squadrons at Wattisham also began re-equipping with the F.3. Soon to join the F.3 in service was the T.5, a two-seat version of the F.3A.[10]

In 1963 four more Lightnings were written off. In 1964, another six were lost after in-flight fires, undercarriage failures and pilot- or fuel-related problems. In 1965 four Lightnings were lost. On 11 January XG335 was abandoned by A&AEE test pilot Squadron Leader J. Whittaker over the Larkhill Ranges in Wiltshire after the undercarriage had failed to lower. Whittaker ejected safely and the F.1 crashed at Woodborough. On 26 June Flight Lieutenant Tony Doyle on 11 Squadron ejected safely after XR712 shed pieces of tailpipe during the Exeter Air Show. The F.6 crashed near Padstow, Cornwall. On 29 September another 11 Squadron pilot, Flight Lieutenant Hedley Molland, safely abandoned F.3 XP739 on approach to Wattisham after a double engine flameout.[11] Earlier, on 22 July XM966, a T.4 used to test the Microcell air-to-air rocket pack was lost over the Irish Sea when its fin disintegrated during rolling manoeuvres at Mach 1.8 at 35,000 feet with the rocket pack extended. English Electric test pilot Jimmy Dell was able to slow the T.4, hoping to recover it to Warton. Graham Elkington, the Flight Test Observer (FTO), ejected without any order to do so from Dell, who had his seat adjusted to the highest position and was thus exposed to high air blast as his head was above the top of the windscreen frame. His eyes were severely air-blasted but his subsequent ejection was normal.

Lightnings were always very tight on fuel, especially the F.3 and T.5, which had the more powerful engines and the small ventral tank. To overcome this, the F.6, essentially an F.3 but with modifications for extra range, was introduced. (Originally the F.6 was referred to as the F.3* or F.3A, or the interim Mk.6 or jokingly 'Fuel for six minutes'). In addition to the 600-gallon ventral tank, provision was made for overwing 260-gallon ferry tanks and it had an extra crank in the leading edge to give better control throughout the speed range. XP697, the F.6 prototype which flew for the first time on 17 April 1964, was, like the first production series F.6s, an early build F.3 in F.6 configuration. All had the flying characteristics of the new mark, but initially these were not fitted with the arrestor hook for runway cable engagements. (This modification, which entailed re-designing and strengthening the rear fuselage, was introduced later, in 1967, after it was found that the conventional arrestor barriers tended to ride over the Lightning cockpit and rupture the spine, often setting fire to the AVPIN-isopropyl nitrate starter fuel). The first of the sixty-two F.6 production models went to AFDS in November 1965 and shortly afterwards entered front-line service on 5 Squadron at Binbrook. In September 1966 74 Squadron at Leuchars began converting from the F.3 to the F.6 and in 1967 23 Squadron, also at Leuchars, followed suit. On 1 April 1967 11 Squadron at Leuchars began to equip with the F.6 and on 1 May 29 Squadron at Wattisham became the last Lightning squadron to form, when it equipped with the F.3. In August 1967 the final Lightning F.6 for the RAF came off the production line.

By now all UK front-line squadrons had either F.3s or F.6s and the F.1As and T.4s were used in the OCU at Coltishall, together with F.3s and T.5s. It was then decided to convert all F.3s to F.6 standard, although in the end only enough aircraft were modified or produced to equip four squadrons (5, 11, 23 and 74). The remaining F.3s were eventually passed to the OCU, as they were an embarrassment to the squadrons due to their poor range endurance compared to the F.6. So the F.3, with its very short range, remained in service. It was decided, however, to rebuild thirty-one of the RAF Germany F.2s and give them the larger, 600-gallon ventral tank, large fin and cranked leading edge, while retaining the smaller Avon engines and the upper guns. These aircraft were redesignated F.2A. They were very popular with the pilots and many reckoned that they were the most versatile of all the Lightnings.[12]

Dave Seward concludes: 'In 1970, it was decided to fit two Aden cannon into the front of the ventral tank of the F.6s, reducing its fuel volume [by only 640lb] to 535 gallons [because some fuel was carried in a compartment formed in the gun pack]. The F.3, however, remained without the guns. [For peacetime policing sorties, guns can be used to fire warning shots to deter intruders and in war the gun is the only weapon which is unaffected by electronic or decoy jamming. It is also a very useful thing to have in close combat]. We also fitted drop tanks to the Mk.6s to extend the range but, because the long undercarriage retracted outwards, putting them under the wing was impossible; so overwing tanks were installed. Only we British could defy the laws of gravity and prevent fuel from flowing downwards; the cases of non-feeding tanks were legion. Essentially they were a ferry tank and with them fitted the aircraft was limited to subsonic speeds; but some squadrons put them on more less permanently in the quest for more flying hours.'

Chapter 2

'Tiger' Tales

It was a dull Tuesday morning and I was resigning myself to yet another spell of boring duty in the Tower when 'Supermate' (our euphemism for OC Ops) called me to his office. I crammed on my cap and entered his office wondering how Supermate had found out about the previous day's illicit hassle. I put on my best downcast expression in anticipation of a rollocking.

'Jak, I've got a little job for you, mate,' says OC Ops.

'Super,' says I, inwardly groaning (not Mess Entertainments again!).

'Your old squadron at Leuchars is due for a shock tomorrow and we have been tasked with providing four high flying, supersonic targets - I want you to lead it, mate.'

'Super,' says I, brightening visibly and thinking of all the trouble I could cause at my old squadron's expense.

Wednesday dawned with me, chalk akimbo, delivering a punchy brief to three other experienced guys - 'Lippe to Dutch Mil, over Amsterdam at FL 360, turn North, over to Buchan on safety frequency, turn West on their orders - each to be two miles abreast, Mach 1.5 at FL 450 and watch 'em cock it up - AAR just off Newcastle and home boys. Give 'em stick! Task time is important, so get out to the jets early and use the spare if required.'

Four pilots walked out to four Lightnings and the fun began. My aircraft was us on start-up so I took the spare. Ten minutes to take-off - Pas de Sweat. Radio a bit poor, never mind, probably because we're still in dispersal - press on. Radio OK now and four jets lift off on time into perfect battle formation in clear skies. Top of climb - you guessed it - poor radio - change to Dutch Mil - very poor radio. Abort? Never! Hand over lead? Shame! Possible diagnosis - dirt in the PEC

(Personal Equipment Connector). OK, time to spare, so clear straps out of the way, take deep breath (oxygen comes through same connector), unplug the PEC, clean terminals with sweaty flying glove finger-end and replace PEC. Easy, but the PEC wouldn't clip back - Panic, hypoxia, hyperventilation? Who knows. Descend! Throttles back, airbrakes out, perfect battle formation follows - damn! dropped a 'boom,' level at 10,000 feet, feel OK now, replug PEC. Where are we? Overhead Amsterdam! Blast! Big strobe lights on that DC10-10, thank goodness. DC10-10? Amsterdam Control Zone! 'Reheat go,' radio now OK (no height encoding altimeters then), back up to FL 360, still in approximate battle formation.

'Bingo 1,' calls Number 4.

'Cancel Reheat,' says I.

Damn, now behind time, set max dry power (just subsonic), fuel now becoming critical. Bright idea! Cut the corner - save time and fuel - turn 45c to starboard. Must call Buchan. Call frequency change, perfect battle formation reduced to a shambling 'same way, same day', but on time, on fuel at the start point.

Inelegant certainly, unprofessional definitely, but ready on task as requested. We turn West, plug in the reheat again, accelerate to Mach 1 5 and climb to FL 450. Buchan launches the Leuchars Wing and the game is on. Halfway down the target run, on comes FIRE 2. Shut down engine, slow down, descend, easy meat for fighters, PAN and divert to - where else? - Leuchars. Tedious journey back to Germany courtesy of Pembroke and MT.

Incident report reads: 'No 2 engine fire on routine target task, divert Leuchars.' The whole story? Certainly not! Could the engine fire have been related to my total disregard of the engine limitations - 15 minutes per sortie at max stroke? I had had all those jets at full power for at least 40 minutes.

This incident came to mind after a 40-minute range sortie in the new-fangled BAC product I now fly. It needs max dry (with occasional bursts of reheat) most of the time on range, is equipped with a poor radio and is limited to 30 minutes per sortie at max power.

Have I learned about flying from that? Have I!

I learnt about flying from that.

Christmas came early for the Central Fighter Establishment in 1959. At the morning briefing at Warton on 23 December, Squadron Leader John Nicholls, an RAF liaison pilot and a member of the test-flying team, had been told that XG334 would be ready to fly to the AFDS at RAF Coltishall, Norfolk. The first of the twenty development batch aircraft for delivery to the RAF would be used for service handling trials. Aware that his Christmas present would perhaps be better delivered with him wearing a Father Christmas outfit, John Nicholls rang around to get one. A Santa suit was duly found and he took off with it for Coltishall. As he taxied in at the famous old Battle of Britain station, all and sundry who had gathered to welcome the momentous arrival could not fail to notice that the pilot was wearing a red hood round his shoulders, a huge white heard and a broad grin! John Nicholls then got a shock, as he recalls: 'I expected that the station commander, Group Captain Bird-Wilson and a few others would be there, but as I taxied past I noticed this 'area' of gold braid! Where had they all come from?! I quickly stuffed all the Father Christmas gear into my very early post-war flight suit, which I was wearing and climbed out. All the top brass was there, from the AOC and his SASO to 'Birdie' and others. Thankfully, nobody mentioned the Father Christmas outfit. I had a cup of coffee and waited for the Meteor 7 that was coming to take me back to Warton. However, one of them asked me how long I had been at Warton. I said, 'About a year, Sir.'

'Where were you before that?' he enquired.

'I said, 'Fighter Command HQ, Bentley Priory.' (Where I had been Project Officer for the Lightning Simulator.)

'He winked and said, 'Oh, you're a serving officer then?'[1] Obviously, he had not noticed my rank tapes on the shoulder of my flying suit, which perhaps looked more like a rubber Mac!

'I'd done quite a lot of Lightning flying by that date. I'd been at Warton since May 1959 and had done about forty flights by then. I quickly discovered that flying the Lightning was hugely exhilarating. It was comparable to the F-104 which, as well as the F-100 and the F-86L, I had flown in the USA in 1958. The Lightning was a real kick up the behind, a terribly impressive aircraft for its day. There was never anything quite like it in that respect, as far as I was concerned, until I got a chance to fly the F-15.'

Later that month XG336 became the second P.1B delivered to the AFDS at Coltishall and on 4 January 1960 the LCS (Lightning Conversion School) was formed at the station. Its job was to train Lightning pilots for the front-line squadrons in Fighter Command. At first, only the more experienced jet pilots with 1,000 flying hours or more were selected to fly the new aircraft and some of these were retained as instructors before the qualifications were relaxed to include younger pilots on their first squadron tour. The initial training was accomplished with various systems aids and a flight simulator and because the LCU had no Lightnings of its own they were borrowed from AFDS and later 74 Squadron.

Flight Lieutenant Bruce Hopkins was the last of the original group to join the AFDS at Coltishall, at the beginning of February 1960. He recalls: 'The CO was Wing Commander David Simmonds and Major Al Moore, an American on exchange, was the A Flight commander. The group also included Flight Lieutenant Peter Collins, an ex-Javelin pilot and Flight Lieutenant Ken Goodwin and Flight Lieutenant Ron Harding, who were ex-Hunter men like myself. There were only three Development Batch Lightnings at this time.[2] Our role was to carry out trials to develop tactics and procedures for the aircraft and its weapon systems. We had Hunter 6s for target and chase work and a Meteor 7 for OR.946 instrumentation (later fitted to the Lightning F.2), which AFDS was mailing for the CFE. We also had two Javelin FAW.Mk.6 aircraft for target work. My first Lightning solo was in XG336 at Leconfield (the runway at Coltishall was being re-surfaced) on 16 May 1960. The Lightning was an awesome aircraft, totally different to the Hunter. For a Hunter pilot like me it was a long climb to the cockpit. On my first two trips I had difficulty in keeping the nose up high enough to get the right climb angle to climb at Mach 0.9 (400 knots to begin with). The performance was out of this world.

'On the early sorties we were chased by the Hunter, whose pilot would get airborne, then orbit at 10,000 feet waiting for the Lightning to take off. It took the Lightning just 3½ minutes (with re-heat, under 2½ minutes) to reach 36,000 feet, easily passing the Hunter in the climb! At height the Lightning pilot would watch the Hunter still climbing underneath. (The Lightning climb angle was 22 degrees without re-heat or 40 degrees with re-heat.) Once in position the Hunter, who was there to observe and to help out in an emergency, would chase the Lightning. As the Lightning accelerated to Mach 1.6 (our maximum cleared speed at that time because of the problems of directional stability) the Hunter got left behind, of course and we would pick him up on the way back. We would then recover and land.

'We developed intercept techniques. Don't forget that the Lightning was the first RAF single-seat aircraft with intercept radar. We would film the radarscope pictures and the navigators on the AFDS Javelins would advise us on the radar techniques. The radar handgrip controller had fourteen controls, so it took some time getting used to it. Radar profiles were practised in the simulator. Another important consideration at this time was fuel. Every time we fired off into the blue in this aircraft, which had so little fuel, we became so fuel-conscious. How could we minimize the fuel use? As far as possible we did not use re-heat.

'Then we got five F.1s[3] for 74 Squadron - delivered to us at Leconfield. I flew XM135 on 13 June 1960. On 11 July I flew XM165 to Coltishall, where it became the first 74 Squadron aircraft with the four other AFDS F.1s. When I arrived I was directed to the 74 Squadron flight line in this shiny, brand new aircraft. After I had climbed down the ladder there was no 'Thank you'. Their only comment was, 'Is it serviceable then?' There was little difference between the DBs [Development Batch aircraft] and the F.1s. They just cleaned up the cockpit a little. The first re-heat take-off was quite an experience. The performance was incredible. Reheat, though, was not necessary. The take-off performance was perfectly adequate, so we didn't use it as a rule.'

Early that July the conversion team at Coltishall had the task of converting 74 'Tiger' Squadron, the first front-line Lightning squadron. Pilots had to undertake a five-day aviation medicine course at RAF Upwood. On their return to Coltishall, a further seven days of lectures on such subjects as aircraft systems and emergency drills were followed by the simulator phase.

'At this point,' recalls Ken Goodwin, 'I had nearly thirty hours on type; Squadron Leader John Robertson [who now commanded the team] had one or two and the remainder almost nil. However, we did have a set of those multi-coloured display boards, pilots' notes from English Electric and the confidence of the blind leading the blind. The conversion process consisted of lectures for a month. This was followed by a first solo (there were no two-seaters) which included a good brief before the instructor got airborne in a Hunter chase. Having wound on about 500 knots and timed a pass over the field nicely with the student's brakes off, the instructor kept the two aircraft in near proximity up to about 25,000 feet. Thereafter, with much corner-cutting and help from Neatishead radar, we could join company again for the descent.

'I suppose the main objectives of the chase were firstly to tell the convertee if his nose-wheel was still down after selecting gear up - a fairly commonplace occurrence with new pilots being a little behind the rapid acceleration after take-off, thus allowing aerodynamic pressure to out-do the hydraulics. Secondly, to advise generally from close proximity (better psychologically than a remote ground station) on the unexpected or unfamiliar and lastly, to offer an opinion on fire warnings - we had frequent spurious and spurious real warnings. Having done a good job on 74 - they flew a 'Diamond Nine' with yours truly as No.9 and the solo aeros spot at the 1961 Paris Air Show - our little team and its boards went to Wattisham to convert 56 and 111 Squadrons.'[4]

Anthony 'Bugs' Bendell reported to the Air Fighting Development Squadron (AFDS) at RAF Coltishall in mid-July 1960: '74 Squadron, the resident front-line squadron and the first to re-equip with the Lightning, was due to receive its aircraft in August. But the AFDS - the trials unit responsible for developing new fighter tactics and for the operational evaluation of armament - had already taken delivery of four Lightning F.1s. The Lightning presented a major challenge. It was the RAF's first supersonic, night/all-weather interceptor. In speed alone it doubled the performance of the Hunter. But more than that, with its combination of AI.23 (airborne interception radar) and 'Firestreak' air-to-air guided weapons the Lightning had a genuine interception capability against high-performance bomber aircraft. The F.1 was also fitted with two 30mm Aden cannon, mounted at shoulder level aft of the cockpit. Alternative weapons packs, consisting of additional guns or unguided air-to-air rockets could be fitted in place of 'Firestreaks'. At that time opinion within Fighter Command was sharply divided as to the need for gun armament on modern fighters. Missile aficionados claimed that only guided missiles would be effective in future air combat, while those who supported the gun - rightly, in my opinion - insisted that it was still the best short-range, multi-shot weapon available. But for the time being, the main thrust of the Lightning weapons' development was limited to the 'Firestreak' ... With the introduction of the Lightning, air defence was at last being given an appropriate degree of priority. Many fighter experts thought that this was long overdue.

'At Coltishall I spent eleven hours in the simulator before flying my first Lightning sortie. There was no dual Lightning, so the first flight was also a first solo and thus it was very exciting. Even at idling power I had to ride the brakes to curb the acceleration. The main tyre pressures were a rock-hard 350lb psi but the long-stroke undercarriage smoothed out the bumps. In the Lightning F.1, it was not necessary to use re-heat for take-off; even in cold power, nose-wheel lift-off at 150 knots occurred well within ten seconds of brake release. As one wag on 74 Squadron was later heard to comment, 'I was with it all the way, until I released the brakes on take-off.'

'As the first RAF station to be equipped with the Lightning, the morale at Coltishall was sky high and the mess provided a lively social centre.

The Norfolk Broads are very attractive, with many historic inns; few officers at Coltishall will ever forget the best pint of draught Worthington 'E' in Norfolk, served at the 'Fruiterer's Arms', just off the market square in Norwich. It was a hard-drinking, high-living, fast life.

'In December 1960 56 Squadron received its Lightning aircraft. Treble One's first Lightning F.1A (XM185) was delivered in March 1961. The F.1A's performance was similar to the aircraft at Coltishall, but it had several worthwhile refinements. Instead of two ten-channel VHF radios, the F.1A was fitted with the latest UHF radio with nineteen preset channels and with nearly 2,000 manually dialled frequencies available. Another valuable addition was a rain-removal system: hot air tapped from the engines could be blown in front of the windscreen to keep it clear of precipitation. The F.1 also had the necessary plumbing for flight refuelling, although refuelling probes were not fitted to our aircraft until February 1963.

'The black livery of our Hunters was inappropriate for the Lightning, so we had to redesign the squadron markings. There were several suggestions, but my proposal for a stylised bolt of black lightning outlined in yellow was eventually chosen for the fuselage. The boss decided that the motif on the fin, consisting of crossed sword and seaxes superimposed on a yellow Cross of Jerusalem, should be copied from the official squadron badge.

'The squadron's re-equipment was a long, slow business. Lightning aircraft were delivered at the rate of one a week, so it was mid-July 1961 before we reached our full complement of twelve aircraft. The equipment was not helped by the loss of XM185 on 28 June 1961. Following a services hydraulic failure, 'Pete' Ginger was unable to lower the undercarriage and since a wheels-up landing was definitely not recommended, he had no choice other than to bail out. The Mark 4BS seat was capable of safe ejection from ground level at 90 knots, but Pete wisely decided to climb to 8,000 feet before making a copybook ejection. A few moments later, hanging in his parachute, he was pleased too that one of the chaps had come to see if he was OK. The pilot seemed to be cutting things a bit fine, though - in fact he was going to pass uncomfortably close. Pete then noticed that the passing aircraft had no cockpit canopy and no pilot - it was the aircraft he had just abandoned. After three more close encounters with XM185, Pete finally landed. His aircraft eventually crashed in a field near Lavenham. That evening a group of squadron pilots was having a drink in the 'Swan' when they overheard one of the local farmhands shooting an incredible line about dropping tools and running to avoid this aircraft before it crashed on top of him. It seemed an unlikely tale, but it was enough to keep him in free beer for the rest of the evening. Some days later the RAF salvage team dug up the ventral tank, which marked XM185's first contact with terra firma, to reveal the farmhand's hoe buried beneath it.'[5]

The Lightning first appeared on the aerobatic stage in 1960 when the 'Tigers' on 74 Squadron led by the CO Squadron Leader John Howe introduced their routine of formation aerobatics. As from July only four aircraft were available and by the end of August the squadron had increased its Lightning complement to seven, but the 'Tigers' were soon training hard for their new role, as John Howe recalls: 'We started flying high-speed, low-level runs (just subsonic, at about 200 feet) in formation, but this put the Lightning airframe under more than normal pressures. One day during that summer, 'Lefty' Wright was leading a box formation at Coltishall when the fin came off Jim Burns' aircraft. I watched from the tower as bits sprinkled to the ground. Jim now had no fin and no radio either, so I told 'Lefty' to close in and try to tell Jim of the problem. Should Jim now eject or land? The weather was perfect and the wind straight down the runway so he was cleared to land. He did and without any problems. Thereafter he was always known as 'Finless Jim'.[6] Unfortunately the C-in-C now ruled out high-speed, low-level runs in formation so we flew high-speed, low-level in battle formation (spread out).'

Incidents still occurred, however. On another occasion Flight Lieutenant Tim Nelson's drag chute failed to deploy on landing. Mindful of the restrictions on braking, he put the Lightning into full afterburner to go around again. Just as he rotated, the chute deployed and it was immediately engulfed by the re-heat. As every Lightning pilot knew, landing without a brake chute was a hazardous undertaking that often would result in the brakes being burned out, but this time Coltishall's long runway and the close support of the Fire Section carried the day and Nelson was able to land safely.[7]

The 'Tigers' performed before the public for the first time at Duxford on 14 August, at Little Rissington on the 28th and at Stradishall on the 31st. By the end of August John Howe for instance had just eight hours on Lightnings in his logbook! Beginning on 5 September he led his formation of four in fly-pasts at the Farnborough Air Show each day, except one when the weather was too bad and the team finished the month with a Battle of Britain display at Coltishall on the 16th. Before each display or rehearsal, the CO would brief the pilots who were to fly in the formation and explain the programme. For example, when the four-aircraft display was given: 'Tiger Black', four aircraft to do formation aerobatics over the airfield, R/T checks will be on 'Four Romeo', 'India' and 'Four Quebec', followed by a drill start-up. Taxi at 100-yard intervals and line up on the runway in echelon. We'll use 80 per cent rpm holding on the brakes and roll at three-second intervals for maximum re-heat take-off. Aim to use the same pull-up point for an 80-degree climb. I'll call cancelling re-heat and use 82 per cent rpm to give us 300 knots at 6,000 feet, join up in box. The display will start with the fly-past in 'Swan' with wheels and flaps down. We shall clean up the aircraft in front of the crowd to move into the rest of the display. No.4 remember to call 'Clear!' for the change into line astern and Nos.2 and 3 guard against dropping low in the very steep turn. Rejoin in box for the run in and two-way break; we shall fly synchronized circuits leading to the ten-second stream landing. Any questions?'

With such a radically new and complex aircraft as the Lightning, there was a corresponding change in the technique of formation flying: the physical and mental strains imposed on pilots flying high-speed aircraft in close formation are intense. With a power/weight ratio of roughly 1:1 there was an immense reserve of power and the team leader had to use it with discretion, bearing in mind that the rest of the formation must from time to time use more power to maintain their position. Although the Lightning was a Mach 2 aircraft, aerobatics in close formation, only five or six feet apart, could be flown at 450 mph - about one-third of the speed which the Lightning would achieve in level flight on an operational mission. Like the Hunter, the Lightning was an extremely manoeuvrable aircraft and despite its great size and weight was capable of astonishing low-speed turns, even when the re-heat of the two Avon turbojets was not being used. The tight turning qualities of the Lightning permitted a display to be given in a small area of sky, so that the public could have no difficulty in keeping the formation in view.

The two engines of the Lightning caused greater jet wash than the single engine of the Hunter and in formations the aircraft had to be stepped down to a slightly greater extent to avoid interference. The rapid rate of rotation in a turn meant that the pilot at the rear at the rear had to fly a slightly longer flight-path to avoid the jet wash and still hold his place. In a tight turn the Lightning was put onto its side, the power stepped up and the nose pulled back to increase lift; and the aircraft would go round smoothly.

At higher speeds an aircraft like the Lightning is surrounded by an envelope of disturbance which must be avoided by other aircraft in the formation. The 60-degree swept wing of the Lightning made it a little more difficult for the pilot to maintain accurate formation than the Hunter, because he could not see his own wingtips. Accordingly, when flying in echelon, he lined up on the trailing edge of the aileron of the adjacent aircraft. Judgement of lateral separation comes only from experience and constant practice is necessary before pilots can hold their aircraft in a tight and accurate formation. Each man lines up a point on his wing leading edge with a point on the fuselage of the next aircraft and after lengthy practice can accurately estimate his distance. The leader has no fixed point on which to fly. He concentrates on placing his aircraft in the best possible position to let the crowd see the show, timing to a split second each stage of the flight and the rest of the team watch him constantly and are alert for his radio instructions ('Pulling up for wing-over starboard. Pulling more G. Taking off bank and relaxing back-pressure. Pulling up for roll to port and rolling - NOW!')

The year 1960 proved to be auspicious for 74 Squadron in more ways than one. When John Howe discovered that an old friend from the Korean War, Lieutenant Colonel Ed Rackham, was commanding the 79th Tactical Fighter Squadron - the 'Tigers' - at Woodbridge, they got together to form the first of the now famous 'Tiger meets'. The 'Tigers' finished their first year as the Lightning aerobatic display team with a fly-by over all the fighter stations in East Anglia on 13 December.

In the New Year, 1961, the 'Tigers' received more Lightnings - enough for a 'Diamond Nine' formation, a solo aerobatic display pilot and spares - and work-up began in earnest for the Paris Air Show scheduled for 3 and 4 June. By the end of April all of the 74 Squadron pilots were operational on the Lightning and cleared to fly both by night and day. During that summer operational training had to be combined with displays and publicity events, as the RAF was eager to introduce the new aircraft to the public. John Howe's team of 'Tigers' was a mixture of youth and experience. Flight Lieutenant Maurice J. Williams (30) and Flight Lieutenant Alan W. A. 'Lefty' Wright (30) were the two flight commanders. The two deputy flight commanders were Flight Lieutenant 'Finless Jim' Burns (26) and Flight Lieutenant Jeremy J. R. Cohu (24). The son of an air vice-marshal, Cohu had converted to Lightnings in 1960 after flying Hunters on 74 Squadron at Horsham St. Faith. The rest of the team comprised Flight Lieutenants Tim Nelson (25) (the adjutant), George P. Black (Z9), Edward J. Nance (25), Jeremy E. Brown (25), Martin Bee (23) and Michael J. Dodd (26). The Flying Officers were David Maxwell Jones (27); Jacques W. Kleynhans (33), who, like his CO, was a native of South Africa; Peter J. Phillips (24); Thomas Vaughan 'Vorn' Radford (23), an admirer of Picasso and used to do the illustrations and cartoons for the Fighter Command *Flight Safety* magazine; Graham Sutherland, whose ability to paint abstracts in oils was put to good use between flights, painting the squadron crest on the main hangar; and Mike S. Cooke, who had converted to the Lightning in June 1960.

The solo slot was flown by Flight Lieutenant Ken Goodwin of the LCU, whom John Howe rated as one of the most fantastic low-level aerobatic pilots he'd ever seen. The 'Tigers' performed wing-overs with nine F.1As, the largest number ever seen publicly together and rolls with four. Between times Ken Goodwin, having detached himself at the end of the nine-man demonstration, put in solo aerobatics, which included Derry turns and low inversions. It was all a stunning success. Back home again, the 'Tigers' displayed at Farnborough in September. *Flight* reported: 'Nothing in the show exuded more sheer power than the three-second interval stream take-off by the nine Lightnings on 74 Squadron, beating down the runway in a sustained blast of brown dust and stomach-shaking noise. As the rear machines were taking off, the leaders were climbing an invisible, vertical wall over Laffans Plain. All were airborne in 35 seconds. [After the sixteen blue Hunters on 92 Squadron] the Lightnings were on stage, smoking in towards the airfield in arrowhead formation, changing to Diamond nine and including wing-overs and [in tight formation] a roll in their programme. A split into three echelons preceded the final run-in and break for landing.' More displays followed, on Battle of Britain Day at Biggin Hill and Coltishall and at Cranwell on 21 October. Two days later, at Leconfield, they performed for the Queen Mother and on the 24th John Howe brought his team back to Coltishall to bring the curtain down on a highly successful season. Persuaded to land first he was surprised and then delighted, to see the other eleven Lightnings fly over him in 'H-Howe' formation!

In December 1961 John Howe left to take up a new post at Fighter Command HQ at Bentley Priory[8] and on the 12th Squadron Leader Peter G. Botterill assumed command of 74 Squadron. He did not get to fly a Lightning, however, until 26 March 1962, because the early Lightnings had all been grounded pending modification and all pilots had to use the flight simulator before being permitted to fly a Lightning again. By early May sufficient Lightnings were modified and that same month an advanced party left Norfolk for Scandinavia to demonstrate the Lightning at the trade fair and at other locations. (The 'Tigers' visit paved the way for eight Drakens from two wings of the Swedish Air Force based at Norrkoping and Uppsala to visit Coltishall on a five-day exchange in 1961.) On their return the

'Tigers' began work on their full display routine, because 92 Squadron's Hunters began converting to the Lightning and the 'Tigers' became the only official Fighter Command acrobatic team. Work-up began for a full aerobatic display with five Lightnings at Upavon on 16 June.[9] At Farnborough the team brought down the curtain with an unforgettable diamond fly-past of seven Lightnings and sixteen Hunters.

Flight Lieutenant Mike J. F. Shaw joined 74 Squadron in 1962. 'The Lightning F.1 had replaced the squadron's Hunter F.6s in June 1960 and had rendered all other European fighters obsolete; it was twice as fast and had more than double the rate of climb of anything else in service. This was brought home to me when I first saw a stream rotation take-off of five F.1s at three-second intervals. The technique was something that could not be applied safely to any other aircraft. Namely, to lift off at 175 knots, retract the undercarriage, push forward firmly to prevent too rapid a gain in height, then, at 220 knots IAS, to pull the stick right back until the attitude reached seventy degrees. Provided both burners were still going, this gave a climbing speed of 190 knots and a feeling to the pilot of ascending vertically, as the ejection seat rails were inclined at 23 degrees. At 3,000 feet the Lightning could be rolled onto its back and the nose gently pulled to the horizon before rolling out erect and cancelling re-heat at about 250 knots. At that point the nose wheel, which retracted forwards, would finally lock up! To be anywhere in such a stream take-off was an unforgettable experience.

'At first all the two-seat flying was done in two Hunter T.7s; beautiful aircraft to handle but which had no resemblance to the mighty Lightning. Pilots were trained for that in the F.1 simulator, which had no freedom of motion but was more than adequate for the job, including radar interception work. So good was it that on one occasion, descending through 10,000 feet when I felt a twinge of toothache, I remember thinking, 'Oh, it'll feel better when I get down to a lower altitude.' Pretty convincing simulation, obviously!

'There were some downsides to flying Lightnings. First, there was 'practice death': being thrown into the sea at RAF Mountbatten. Pilots were towed behind a pinnace and had to release their harnesses when a whistle was blown, to haul in their dinghy packs, to inflate and then board their dinghies. After about an hour a Whirlwind would appear, pick up a few 'survivors', disappear again, then come back and eventually retrieve all the hobbling sea-sick aviators - often closer to the rocks off Plymouth Hoe than they would have liked. Next, there was decompression training at RAF Upwood. The chamber took us up to 56,000 equivalent pressure altitude, requiring us to 'pressure breathe'. Bulging necks and arms full of stagnant blood, a squeezing mask, pressure jerkin and G-suit. Awful. Worse with the Taylor helmet - up to 60,000 feet.

'Then there was the drag across the airfield at RAF North Luffenham behind a rig on a three-runner. This was to simulate being dragged by a parachute. Great. I was one of the first students to undergo a course on the Lightning Conversion Squadron (LCS) at RAF Middleton St. George, where new T.4s had just been delivered. (The OC was Wing Commander K. J. 'Ken' Goodwin with, inter alia, flight lieutenants Pete Steggall, Roly Jackson and a huge navigator, Donaldson-Davidson, on the staff.) As I was to be 74 Squadron's QFI, it was important that I had some feel for the T.4, a model (XM974) which provided two-seat Lightning training for the first time and was not wholly welcomed by the largely self-taught squadron pilots. I found, however, that all the pilots flew Lightnings very much in the same way thanks, presumably, to the flight simulator and its staff.

'The Lightning was incredible. It climbed, initially, in cold (i.e. non re-heat) power at 22 degrees attitude at 450 knots LAS and, if a positive re-trimming was not done at about 20,000 feet, would slip through Mach 1 in the climb. It took quite a strong pull at that altitude to counter the nose-down effect of the rearward shift of aerodynamic centre when 450 knots became Mach 0.9. With its beautifully made airframe, ingenious main wheel retraction geometry, first-class engines and superb handling, the Lightning was a truly remarkable aircraft. It may have had a thirst for tyres and had operating costs far higher than those of its predecessors, but in the 1960s it was the queen of the European skies and its pilots knew that nothing could match it. If they kept their eyes open - and watched the fuel gauges - nobody could ever get close to them. It's not surprising that Lightning pilots were the most confident (and nauseatingly cocky) that could be found anywhere - with good reason!

'What the Lightning did lack was fuel. It carried only 7,400lb at start-up, including a 250-gallon ventral tank. The contents of this tank usually exhausted a few minutes after levelling off at 36,000 feet, where most of the standard Practice Intercepting (PIs) took place - near the normal tropopause. Recovery was usually through a 'dive circle', a circle centred on a point eighteen nautical miles out on the duty runway, with a radius in nautical miles equal to the height of the Lightning in thousands of feet. This gave a comfortable descent at 350 knots at idle/fast idle (the No. 2 - top - engine was kept at a fast idle setting to provide sufficient bleed air to drive the alternator fast enough to keep the aircraft services on line) for a feed into ILS, GCA, or visual rejoin. Further, the fuel used was only about 400lb from each wing, allowing a dive circle descent with 1,200/1,200lb to be completed to landing with the laid down minimum of 800/800lb. That gave a reserve, to tanks-dry, of little more than ten minutes - enough to cause an airline captain to have a heart attack. Indeed, he would have collapsed before take-off!'

After being associated with military aircraft during the 'golden era' of the 1950s and 1960s - both fighters and bombers - Dave Betts' fondest memories were of the three years spent with the Mk.1 Lightning. 'Being a mere 20-years-old and very impressionable, my four years spent on 74 Squadron from 1959 to 1963 was a great period in time to be around. 1959/60 saw the rundown of the Hunter Mk.6 from 74's inventory and June 1960 saw the arrival of the first Lightning F.1 looking shiny and bright in its all metal finish. I do not remember the name of the pilot who delivered that first Lightning; however, I did once see 'Bee' Beamont over in the line office! Life became very busy in the hangar and over on the line. Several of the technicians went to Warton on familiarisation courses. Many busy months were spent training both aircrew and ground crew to a peak of excellence. If my memory serves me correctly, most of the mishaps with our shiny new Lightnings were due to 'chute failures. The occasional barrier engagement usually caused severe damage to the spine area just to the rear of the cockpit, causing a further heavy workload for the technicians.

'1962 was the year that 74 Squadron was nominated as the official aerobatic display team by HQ Fighter Command. About this time, several good detachments were on offer, including a trip to Scandinavia. May 1962 saw the squadron on its way to Vasteras in Sweden. The outbound leg was routed through the Danish Air Force base at Karup. I was detailed to be at this staging post to assist with turn round and maintenance. The Lightnings arrived in pairs and several of them unfortunately developed technical faults - a curse on the F.1 at this time. Apart from the usual fuel leaks, one of the commonest faults was caused by the hydraulic lines being routed too close together, which resulted in chafing and leaks. We spent many hours putting in extra cleats on the lines, a task which was only possible after removing the engines and jet pipes! This was subsequently remedied on the F.1A. Fortunately, the faults were usually quickly remedied and the aircraft on their way again. The only real delay was the despatch of a spare part, which was delivered from Coltishall courtesy of the Squadron Hunter T.7! The Hunter itself had a mishap on one landing when one of the main wheels hit a landing light, cutting the tyre to the cords. With no spare Hunter main wheel available, it was marvellous what we could do with a tube of tyre dough. The Swedish military were impressed with the eight Lightnings which the Squadron brought. Plenty of noise and some nice tight close formation flying - destined to become the hallmark of the Lightning. The Lightning certainly put the Swedes' new Draken aircraft in the shade! Next stop, Gardermoen in Norway for a military airshow. Several other leading NATO countries were there and displaying their latest types of machinery. The Americans had their Century-Series fighters there. On one occasion the pilot of a Starfighter had an embarrassing moment when the afterburner cut out as he thundered down the runway and he had to abort the take off! Following this came the eight Lightnings on 74 Squadron for a stream take off. Afterburners blazing - and no failures! The Lightnings thundered down the runway following with a near vertical climb to several thousand feet. What a show! The crowd loved it and 74 stole the show; we certainly earned the applause that day. However, all too soon the detachment was over!

'September was Farnborough show time. 74 and 92 Squadrons put on a joint display. What a sight; seven Lightnings and sixteen Hunters performing a superb aerobatic routine. Remembering the day twenty-five years later on television, Bernard Braden said that the boys flying the Lightnings at Farnborough that year were told to tone down their show, as complaints of broken windows were coming in from householders all around the locality!'[10]

'In 1964,' continues Flight Lieutenant Mike Shaw, '74 Squadron was posted from Coltishall to Leuchars to help 23 Squadron Javelins to cover the northern part of the UK Air Defence Region and shortly thereafter, re-equipped with the F.3. This had Avon 300s in place of the 200s and an increase in the fin area. The radar was improved. Provision was made for 'Red Top' IRAAM and the guns were deleted. The aircraft was cleared to Mach 2 (the F.1 was limited to Mach 1.7 for reasons of stability, not thrust) and all the pilots did at least one run to that speed. The fuel content was not increased, however and the bigger engines were even less economical, so the practical use of this top speed was doubtful. Provision was made for in-flight refuelling and the flight instruments were to [RAF standard] OR.946, including a strip (harder-to-read) airspeed indicator cum machmeter. Further, the air intake was not really large enough for the Avon 300s and the cockpit floor would vibrate on take-off as they gasped for air. Overall, the F.3 was not the advance that we had hoped for, although it still flew nearly as well as the F.1 but with a CG (centre of gravity) which was noticeably further aft (heavier engines, no guns?).

'My average length on a sortie on the Lightning F.1 was forty-two minutes. During my tour on 74 Squadron I flew just over 350 sorties, about a quarter of them at night. We lost two aircraft during the period. One F.1 (XM142) on 26 April 1963 indicated a double power controls failure after an inverted check during an air test and its pilot, Flight Lieutenant 'Jim' Burns, ejected successfully over the North Sea. The second loss [on 28 August 1964] was an F.3 (XP704) which failed to complete a loop overhead the airfield at Leuchars, killing the pilot, Flight Lieutenant G. M. 'Glyn' Owen.

'I had two anxious sorties myself, both due to the fact that our T.4 was really an F.1A rather than an F.1 and was fitted with UHF radio, as opposed to VHF. The squadron had all twelve F.1s and its T.4 at Farnborough in 1962 and on its return it was decided to fly VFR at low-level to Coltishall. We settled at 2,000 feet AGL initially, with four vees of three, plus me in the T.4 with Flying Officer Peter Clinton, the Junior Engineering Officer, tagging along behind, unable to hear any of the VHF transmissions. We flew over a town (Northampton) under a lowering cloud base, then over Lakenheath at a rather alarmingly low altitude, but it was a Sunday and nothing else was stirring. Then I saw the vic ahead of me begin to climb, so I joined in as a No. 4. We reached 30,000 feet before we broke cloud. Nobody was talking to me on UHF and I held on tightly to the No. 2. The airbrakes extended, so mine went out too and we went downhill until we broke cloud at 800 feet, Coltishall in sight. I landed behind the other three in the sub-formation, still without any R/T contact. The other nine were still airborne but appeared very shortly afterwards. The mission had not gone according to plan, but we were all safely home!

'My next UHF problem was at night, when I was flying with a pilot who was not a Lightning man in the right-hand seat of the T.4. All went well until recovery, when Coltishall did not answer my call on UHF and the station's TACAN was off the air. An adjoining station's TACAN was working, so I positioned overhead Coltishall using that and began a teardrop (out-and-back, turning homebound at half the initial altitude plus 4,000 feet) let-down. When we broke cloud at about 3,000 feet, we were over land. But the TACAN had broken a lock during the inbound turn (not surprisingly, as the beacon was twenty-five nautical miles away) and I could not see Coltishall, who spoke to us for the first time when I requested clearance to land straight in. We touched down, vibrated badly and stopped in 700 yards. The main wheels had not rotated at all. It later was proved that the Bowden cable from the right-hand control column had not released when the pilot on that side had retracted the wheels after take-off, so the brakes were still firmly on. My fault, of course - I should not have let an unqualified (though very experienced) pilot take-off. But there was no clue in the cockpit that the brakes had not released. Sometimes, you can't win.

'My next contact with Lightnings, after a tour in exchange with the US Marine Corps, flying McDonnell Douglas Phantom F-4Bs, was on RAF Handling Squadron at A&AEE Boscombe Down in 1966-1968. As the pilot responsible for the writing and or amendment of the Lightning Pilot's Notes and Flight Reference cards, I had the opportunity to add the T.5, F.6 and lastly, the F.2A to my tally. The T.5 was an odd aircraft, based on the F.3, but with throttles (unlike the T.4) on the right-hand cockpit console for the right-hand seat. This meant that the stick had to be controlled by the left hand, the only fighter where this had been the case. Odd.

'The F.6 was a Mk.3 with a long belly tank, non-jettisonable. It had extended leading edges, which increased the wing area, improved the camber and compensated for the extra weight. It could also carry overwing fuel tanks, which would catch your eye and until their presence was accepted, prove rather distracting. For ferry purposes only, these tanks made a great difference to endurance.

'The F.2A was, in my view, the best of the lot. It retained two guns in the nose (the F.6 could carry two in its ventral pack, with the loss of some fuel), had the old Avon 200s, which were much smoother than the 300s and had the F.6-type long ventral tank and extended leading edges. The long tank deadened some of the sound of the No. 1 (forward, bottom) engine and increased the start-up fuel to over 10,000lb. It still had the old AI.23 radar, but that was quite good enough for the job. When the F.2A was released to the RAF I collected the first one from the English Electric factory at Warton, flew in to Boscombe Down and then, as was my brief, took it to the edges of its cleared flight envelope. It was a beauty, handling exactly as expected. Then, in January 1968 I had to take it to RAF Gütersloh and hand it over to 19 Squadron. It was not fitted with TACAN or IFF; that was a task for Gütersloh. For the first twenty minutes I could see the ground, but the Continent had solid cloud cover and, oh dear, Lippe radar didn't answer my calls. I knew that I had a 90-knot tailwind and being anxious not to plunge into the Air Defence Identification Zone just to the east of Gütersloh, decided to forget Lippe and call Gütersloh direct. They identified me, to my relief, twelve miles to the south after I had set up a prudent triangle. The subsequent let-down and recovery was immaculate and the squadron CO, Squadron Leader Laurie Jones, later Air Marshal, intercepted me on the final approach. And that was the last time, as I knew it would be, that I ever flew a Lightning.'[11]

Chapter 3

'Firebirds', 'T-Birds' and 'Tremblers'

The aeroplane was superb to fly, a bitch to maintain and always short of fuel. In hindsight we probably wouldn't have wanted it any other way.
Squadron Leader Dave Seward.

Beginning in December 1960 the Lightning F.1A, which was fitted with a port-mounted probe for in-flight refuelling, was issued to 56 and 111 Squadrons at Wattisham.[1] In 1961 a joint RAF/USAF exercise was held to demonstrate the compatibility of the Valiant tanker with American fighters and fighter-bombers and of the American KB-50J tanker with Valiant, Vulcan, Victor and Javelin receivers. Although the Lightning F.1As did not participate, the valuable close co-operation between the two nations did have benefits for the Lightning force the following year, as Squadron Leader Dave Seward, OC 56 Squadron recalls: 'Now, when the F.1A first entered service, each squadron was given various development tasks to perform. On 56 Squadron we were ordered in December 1961 to develop air-to-air refuelling techniques for the Lightning force using Vickers Valiant tankers. The timetable directed that during January-July 1962 we would work up six pilots in the AAR role and in July send two Lightnings to Cyprus with tanker support. Full squadron deployment to Cyprus was scheduled for October 1962.

'This sounded OK, but over the period August-December 1961 we experienced odd, unpleasant happenings with the Lightning. You would be flying along in cruise power when the re-heat fire warning lights would illuminate without having re-heat selected. As the only method of extinguishing re-heat fires was to select re-heat and shut down the engine, it was rather thought-provoking if both re-heat lights were on without being in re-heat and the only alternative seemed to be to become a glider! Some pilots shut an engine down and in some cases the fire indication went out. To their cost, others hoped it was a spurious warning. We lost one of the AFDS (Air Fighting Development Squadron) aircraft when the back end burned off and in another incident, all was revealed when an aircraft landed with the re-heat area on fire. The cause was traced to hydraulic pipes (which were aluminium rather than high-tensile steel) chafing inside the fuselage, causing the hydraulic fluid to pour back along the inside of the rear fuselage and swirl around the back of the jet pipes where it caught fire in the re-heat area.

'Thus in January 1962 it was decided to replace and re-route the hydraulic system in all aircraft and at Wattisham 56 Squadron and 11 Squadron and 74 Squadron at Coltishall were modified. It was going to be a four-week job for the lot, six weeks at the outside; so plans were made to have the air-to-air refuelling ground school in January and start flying in February. Unfortunately, the hydraulic modification was not completed in four weeks, but dragged on for sixteen weeks. However, Fighter Command was adamant that two Lightnings had to be at Akrotiri, Cyprus, in July and that the squadron would be there by October!

'It was purely fortuitous that at Wattisham we had a social relationship with the American 55th Tactical Fighter Squadron, 20th Tactical Fighter Wing, at RAF Wethersfield. Over drinks one Friday I mentioned our problems to their commanding officer. I remarked that the flight refuelling system on their F-100F Super Sabres, although being on the opposite side (starboard) to the Lightning (port), was basically similar and what a good idea it would be if we learned our flight refuelling on the F-100. Things must have been desperate, because on the following Wednesday we had permission from both Fighter Command and HQ USAFE for six pilots on 56 Squadron to fly flight-refuelling sorties in the F-100 using the KB-50J Superfortress tankers [of the 420th Air Refuelling Squadron]. Although the KB-50 flew at 180-200 knots indicated and probes on the Lightning were angled to squarely hit a Valiant basket, the refuelling went remarkably well. From Aldburgh to the Humber we did dry, then 'wet' proddings. The USAF would have a KB-50 on station off Aldburgh flying a racetrack pattern and would listen out on a particular frequency. When a chap needed fuel he would call using his call sign and 'book in' and the fuel was then attributed to the squadron. In the half hour to go before the KB-50 had to dump excess fuel, refuelling during this time was free. They'd all come in then because the squadron would not get charged for the fuel.

'Two of us were up one day on PIs and I heard this guy say that he had half an hour to go and was throwing away the fuel. We gave the call sign for Wethersfield, which was 'Trout, Three-Five and Three-Six'. 'Roger, you're clear in astern,' he replied. He asked, 'What type of aircraft?' We said [untruthfully] 'Foxtrot 100'! He said, 'Roger'. We flew in, lowered the flaps and took on the fuel from the KB-50. Thinking about it afterwards, we knew we were taking on JP4 and our Avons were not tuned for AVTUR, but we kept that to ourselves (our engineers were worried about the lubrication of the fuel pumps, but we had no problems). We each received six tanking sorties in the F-100 (needless to say, the Americans all had trips in the T.4 Lightning), before starting our tanking with Valiants on 13 June.

'The method we used, as recommended by both English Electric and the USAF, was to position the Lightning about thirty yards behind the Valiant and synchronize speeds, with the Valiant at about 250 knots indicated, at 30,000 or 36,000 feet. We then set the No. 1 throttle at about 94 [per cent] and set up an overtake speed of about five knots, using the No. 2 throttle to vary the speed. You lined up with the basket and edged forward, not looking at the basket, which is going up and down about 3 feet, but getting what is called a 'sight picture' of the Valiant and flying steadily in. As the basket passes the nose of the Lightning it is 'trapped' and if your line-up has been good, your probe goes into the centre of the basket and you make a good contact. You then move forward into a close formation line astern, keeping a slight bow in the hose and when contact and positioning is confirmed by the tanker, he passes the fuel to on. Fly too low and the hose becomes taut and the probe could break. (You could also break the probe by being too far left or right.) You could also break a probe having too high an overtake speed and thus hit the basket too hard. On the other hand, if you are too cautious and hit the basket slow with too low an overtake, you will get a soft contact and end up being sprayed with fuel or, in extreme circumstances, have your engines flameout with fuel pouring into the intake. A trick in getting at least the vertical position right was to fly in with the fin tip just 'burbling' along the bottom of the Valiant's jet efflux - a technique that we were to regret somewhat later. Still, all went well and the schedule was met. We simulated the trip to Cyprus by going twice around the UK and got the first two aircraft (myself and John Mitchell, attached from AFDS) to Cyprus on time, flight refuelling to Akrotiri on 23 July (exercise 'Tambour').'

The second detachment, 'Forthright One', involving six other 56 Squadron pilots, went ahead on 6 October 1962, as Flight Lieutenant Bob Offord recalls: 'We went in pairs, three tankers per pair and I flew XM153. Jerry Cohu and I flew at Mach 1.7 until Crete, where we carried out our seventh and last refuelling. In Cyprus the Turkish inhabitants took one look at our red aircraft and thought, 'Hooray, here comes the Turkish air force!' We spent about eight weeks in Cyprus, carrying out low-level PIs, one against one and the odd Canberra at 60,000 feet from Akrotiri's four resident squadrons. We'd pull up to 36,000 feet and zoom up to in excess of 50,000 feet. The radar stations at Cape Gata and Mount Olympus also aided us. We could not do low-level work in the UK but the Mediterranean is much calmer than the North Sea and the radars could better see. The AI.23 was good for its day but at high level it was difficult to see the Lightning beyond 25 miles on radar and even worse at low level, where it was down to just five or six miles because of the sea returns. Most days we worked in the mornings and swam in the afternoons. These were the best days of Lightning operations. We returned to the UK in April and then spent the summer exercising and tanking, part of it at Coltishall for three to four weeks while Wattisham's runways were repaired.

In February 1962, meanwhile, Flight Lieutenant 'Bugs' Bendell finally got his chance to work up a solo Lightning display. 'Les' Swart on 56 Squadron and Ken Goodwin of the Lightning Conversion Squadron, who had provided demonstrations in 1961, had moved on. 74 Squadron was still providing the formation aerobatic team, but the solo Lightning slot was now vacant. I always believed that solo demonstration flying required thorough professionalism. Any fool could beat up an airfield in a high-performance aircraft, but it needed practice and precise judgment to put together an impressive demonstration ... It was easy to impress people with the Lightning but the show had to be repeatable. Maurice Williams, a potential Lightning display pilot on 74 Squadron, once lost control while attempting a Derry turn at 1,500 feet over the airfield and flicked into a flat spin. Maurice immediately engaged reheat - there was usually a three-second delay before they lit up - and more by luck than good judgment Maurice just managed to recover control before hitting the ground. The aircraft was so low, the flames from the re-heats set fire to the grass on the airfield.

'In June I was one member of a three-man board of inquiry into a fire incident on an aircraft [XM176] flown by Squadron Leader John Rogers - OC, 56 Squadron. The Lightning's fire and overheat warnings were displayed on a standard warning panel, which also triggered klaxon bells and flashing red attention-getters. There was never any question of missing a fire warning; in fact, the pilot's first action was usually to cancel the klaxon bells before dealing with the emergency. Unfortunately, the Lightning had gained a reputation for fire warnings, both real and spurious.

The fire sensors, running through the engine bays and jet pipe areas, would detect any local increase in temperature, caused either by fire or simply by a hot gas leak. When the source of heat was removed, the warning light would extinguish and the system would automatically reset. Attempts to find the cause of warning often disturbed the engines and in the process, destroyed the evidence. But in John Rogers' incident [on 14 February 1961] the fire had re-ignited in dispersal, indicating a genuine fire rather than an elusive hot gas leak. An expert investigator from the accident investigation branch at RAE Farnborough eventually proved that excess fuel trapped on top of the ventral tank had been sucked back through fuselage drain-holes on the hot jet pipe, causing an intense but fortunately brief fire. This positive finding did little to restore confidence in the Lightning's warning system and we continued to experience fire warnings, often for no apparent reason.

'September [1962] was a busy month. To mark the anniversary of the Battle of Britain I flew displays at Biggin Hill and Wyton. Then on 18 September I did a show at Wattisham for the first half of a Royal College of Defence Studies visit. The weather was poor, with a thick layer of haze reducing the horizontal visibility to less than a mile. But, as is so often the case in fog, the vertical visibility was better and I managed to do a complete display. The spectators were hard-pressed to keep sight of the Lightning. I landed from a high visual circuit, much to the chagrin of a pair of 41 Squadron Javelins that had been obliged to land off a GCA approach.

'Two days later I was scheduled to repeat the performance for the remainder of the course and a visiting group of officers from the RAF College of Air Warfare. No problems with weather on this occasion - there had been a complete change of air mass and it was a much colder day. I usually concluded my show with a high-speed run in front of the crowd. With both engines at maximum re-heat, the Lightning's silent approach, followed by a thunderous departure with flames issuing from the jet pipes, all made for an impressive finale. There was just one small problem. In the F.1A, re-heat ignition could not be guaranteed at speeds above 350 knots, although once they were lit the re-heats were stable throughout the speed range. Because of this I always started my high-speed run from a high wing-over, engaging re-heat at about 300 knots. When the burners lit up I would dive for the runway and level out fifty feet or so above the ground. The Lightning accelerated extremely rapidly. It was not possible to monitor the instruments closely at an altitude of fifty feet, but my speed abeam the tower was usually about 600 knots. On this particular day, because of the low ambient air temperature, the engines were more efficient than usual and the local speed of sound was relatively low. The aircraft was moving very fast as I went past the tower. I thought Air Traffic Control was joking when they called on the R/F to say that they no longer needed air conditioning. But after landing the boss met me at the aircraft and told me to report immediately to OC Ops - with my hat on. I was in deep trouble. Apparently my high-speed run had caused extensive damage to the tower and surrounding buildings.

'Wing Commander Bill Howard's office was in a single-storey prefabricated building alongside the tower. It appeared undamaged from the outside, but that was deceptive. Actually, the roof had been lifted a fraction and the walls had been nudged sideways. All the internal doors were hanging askew and the pictures hung away from the walls rather than on them. The office was lit by neon tubes, normally suspended from the ceiling on chains, but now all the chains had jumped off their hooks and the lights dangled on the ends of their electric flex. I had to part these pillars of light to get in. Bill was sitting behind his desk, covered in white dust, a ghost of his former self. The only blue thing about him was his hat, which had been in a desk drawer when I flew over.

'He looked up as I came in and with a perfectly straight face, said with a nasal twang 'I suppose you think that's funny!' I had to admit that I did. But apologies were in order; and he suggested I start with local control. The tower was a shambles, at least six huge double-plate-glass windows had been shattered and there was a stiff breeze blowing across the controller's desk. The staff, who were busy sweeping up, were taking it all in good spirits.

'Next I went to apologize to the duty met man, whom I found sitting huddled on a stool in one corner of the Met office. The room looked as dusty and dilapidated as Bill Howard's office. The Met man appeared to be suffering from battle fatigue.

'I served throughout the war,' he said, 'and I have never been so frightened in all my life. And what about my barograph?' He pointed to the sensitive pressure instrument that traces a record of the barometric pressure on a rotating drum. The drum was still rotating but the pen was bent up against the top stop. 'In sympathetic tones I suggested that the Queen would probably buy him a new one. 'Maybe,' he snapped, 'but she won't buy me a new raincoat.' The coat in question had been hanging on the back of the door; but now it was pinned in place by a large splinter of glass. I apologised profusely and returned to the safety of the squadron crew room. It was not long before another message came from on high. I was to change into best blue and be 'on the mat' in the station commander's office, immediately if not sooner. This was getting serious - the station commander, Group Captain Simmonds, was my old boss from the AFDS. I had always got on quite well with him before, but this promised to be a rather one-sided interview. And so it proved. After a stiff haranguing which seemed to go on forever, he ordered me to report to the Air Ministry the following day - the implication being that I would be immediately posted. He finished by demanding. 'What do you think about that?'

'Now a staff tour in London was just about the worst fate I could imagine and frankly I thought it was uncalled for. So I let fly, pointing out all the reasons for it being unfair. David Simmonds burst out laughing and explained that I was being called forward for briefing prior to an exchange tour with the USAF at Nellis Air Force Base in Nevada.

'That evening in the bar they told me how the high-speed run had appeared from the ground. The pilots who had been watching from outside the squadron knew that something was amiss when they saw the grass on the airfield being flattened behind my aircraft. A high-ranking army officer had been heard to comment, as he dusted glass splinters from his uniform and surveyed his badly cut toe-caps, 'I will say this, when the Air Force put on a show they don't spare any expense.'

'In addition to the damage sustained by the tower, two other prefabricated buildings alongside were rendered unfit for habitation. Overnight I became something of a celebrity among the local schoolboys, who would point me out, 'That's Bugs - he's the guy that broke all those windows ...'

On 5 February 1963 'Bugs' Bendell went to Buckingham Palace for an investiture and was presented with the AFC by Her Majesty Queen Elizabeth the Queen Mother. Later that month the squadron started flight-refuelling training on the Valiant tanker.

'For me, air refuelling was a unique experience. In simple formation flying the pilot must at all times avoid the other aircraft, but with flight refuelling he deliberately makes contact. I flew one sortie on the Valiant, which was all useful experience for my forthcoming tour in the States, but the bulk of the training was reserved for the other members of the squadron who were due to deploy to Cyprus.

'In March I flew tactical checks with the pilots on 'B' Flight. The Squadron's first two-seat Lightning T.4 had been delivered in October and had since been involved in acceptance checks. My last flight on 'Treble One' was a dual low-level aerobatic demonstration for the benefit of Alan Garside, who had volunteered to take over the solo aerobatic slot. Some months later Alan was tragically killed during a display. My tour on 'Treble

One' had lasted twenty-seven months; during that time I had accumulated barely 270 hard-won hours on the Lightning. On any other aircraft this would have accounted for little, but Lightning flying was special. The experience I gained on 'Treble One' would stand me in good stead throughout the rest of my flying career.'[2]

Meanwhile, 56 Squadron had been selected as the new Lightning aerobatic team for the 1963 season. Squadron Leader David Seward, the 32-year-old CO, had first got wind of his squadron's new role in mid-October 1962, as their second detachment in Cyprus came to a close. 'We began to pick up rumours that 74 Squadron were starting air-to-air refuelling and 56 Squadron were to become the next RAF formation aerobatic team. This was indeed confirmed a week later. The first thing was to get ourselves a name. We chose 'Firebirds' because of the 56 Squadron badge: the phoenix rising from the ashes and we devised a paint scheme. We painted the spine and fin red and we rounded this off with the leading edges of the wings and tail-planes red also.

'We started the leaders doing individual aerobatics and in choosing the leaders and deputy leaders I went purely on seniority in the squadron. In other words, I was the formation leader; the 'A' Flight Commander, 27-year-old Flight Lieutenant John M. Curry, led the rear formation; the 'B' Flight Commander, Flight Lieutenant Jeremy Cohu, was my deputy leader; and the deputy 'B' Flight Commander was the deputy rear formation leader. Four of us had experience in formation aerobatics. [Curry had flown in the 229 OCU aerobatic team before March 1960 saw him with 'Treble One' Squadron at Wattisham, flying with the 'Black Arrows', while Cohu (and Mike Cooke) had of course flown with the 'Tigers' acrobatic team before joining 56 Squadron in October 1962.] I had dabbled in the 1950s in Meteors and on T-33s, Sabres, F-102s and F-106s whilst on an exchange tour in America, but not really seriously. As luck happened, all the leadership choices fitted in. We also had one or two queens who fancied themselves, but who really had no experience. We had fifteen pilots on the Squadron. So that was ten in the team plus an airborne reserve. The solo man ['Noddy' MacEwen] made twelve and the commentator/manager [Flight Lieutenant Robert F. 'Bob' Offord, a QFI who had flown Meteors and Sabres on 66 Squadron before converting to the Lightning] only left two on the squadron as spares.'

Apart from those already mentioned, the other pilots were all equally first-rate Lightning men. Flight Lieutenant Henry R. Ploszek (27), the No.3, had flown Hunters before converting to the Lightning and had been on 56 Squadron since September 1960. His father had been a major in the Polish Air Force and joined the RAF in the UK in 1940, serving as an engineer officer during the war. After the war he joined the RAF, retiring as a wing commander. Ploszek and his mother came to Britain in 1946. (In the 1980s, Henry, now a squadron leader in his early fifties, managed the world famous Red Arrows team for several seasons and he also flew the team's spare aircraft, 'Red 10'.) The rest of the squadron comprised Flight Lieutenants Robert J. Manning (26), Timothy Francis Haughton Mermagen (25), 'Terry' R. Thompson RCAF (31),[3] Ernie E. Jones (30), Malcolm J. 'Mo' Moore (30), Peter M. 'Jimmy' Jewell (29) and Richard Cloke (24). Wing Commander Bernard H. Howard (39) was team manager and Flight Lieutenant Brian J. Cheater (25) was the adjutant.

The real work of building up the team began on 1 March 1963. Dave Seward continues: 'The only guidance we were given was that the main formation was to be a nine-ship and for the display we were to provide continuous aerobatics so that something was going on in front of the crowd all the time. There were to be no gaps. We decided, therefore, that we would start the show with a stream take-off and the very steep climb. As we joined up in formation, a solo Lightning would perform solo aerobatics, clearing as we came round in a 'Diamond Nine' to do the odd roll and loop before splitting into two formations of five. We had a tenth man airborne to link up with the rear formation after the first bomb-burst away from the nine. We then would do manoeuvres in two separate fives, with the solo man interspersing with bomb bursts and join-ups when a gap appeared. [In a bomb burst the aircraft break formation sharply and fan outwards.] We also devised a means of making smoke. The Lightning had fuel in the flaps. We isolated the port flap tank, ran a copper pipe from the tank along the inside port spar strake on the fuselage (the starboard strake carried all the electrical wiring looms and the left-hand one was a dummy strake to balance it up) to a small nozzle above the bottom jet pipe. Then an electric pump was connected to the gun trigger. We filled the flap tank with diesel fuel, selected 'guns', pulled the trigger and we had instant smoke. Now, we did all this ourselves by self-help, at very little cost, but I got a telling off from Fighter Command engineers for being too 'enthusiastic'.

'So there we were: a name and a paint-job and smoke on demand and four of us reasonably proficient in aerobatics. We then worked up in pairs doing steep turns and wing-overs and then loops and rolls, progressing to five-ship formation changes doing all the various aerobatic manoeuvres and formation changes. This was 'arrow formation' and we called this 'Fork'. We used to do these various changes during a roll, loop, or wing-over.

We then worked up into the full nine doing rolls, loops and wing-overs. Unfortunately, we then hit a snag. The tail fin-tips started to work loose. The aerobatics were blamed and we were banned from doing rolls or loops in the 'big nine' formation, so we had to step our line astern position down lower. I was suspicious from the start, as my aircraft, which had always been the lead ship, was one of the ones to have a loose fin tip. By coincidence, it was the one which had done the most flight refuelling in the Valiants' jet efflux. But despite our protestations, the powers that were would not lift the ban on aerobatting the nine ship so we were restricted to level turns and formation changes with the nine formation before splitting into the two five-ship formations. We then did semi-synchronized manoeuvres with the two fives and the solo man, ending up with the lead five bomb-bursting down and the other five bomb-bursting up through the smoke. We then joined up in a big 'vee' formation, with the airborne reserve and the solo man in as well for a simultaneous 'vee' peel off and rapid landing, followed by a formation taxi in.'

At first all practice had been carried out at an altitude which would have given pilots enough time for recovery if any snags were encountered. After the 'threes' had achieved a reasonable degree of skill, Squadron Leader Seward had added two other aircraft to fly 'fives'. Soon after this he was confident enough of his pilots' ability to ask for clearance to operate down to 1,500 feet. This was granted and a short while later was followed by another clearance down to 500 feet and finally clearance was approved down to just 200 feet, one of the lowest clearances ever given to an RAF aerobatic team.

On the morning of 13 May 1963 Geoffrey Norris of the *RAF Flying Review* was privileged to fly a forty-minute sortie with the 'Firebirds' in T.4 XM989, as the team began their work-up to show standard. He wrote: 'With Flight Lieutenant Bob Offord at the controls, we took off as number six behind a section of five. This may have been only a practice sortie, but all the excitement of a real show was there. The six aircraft taxied along the perimeter track, staggered with alternate aircraft left and right. At the end of the runway we lined up in position, our aircraft almost struggling to go as the brakes held it against full throttle.

'The Section Leader was Flight Lieutenant John Curry. When we were all set he announced that he was rolling and his aircraft accelerated rapidly down the runway at Wattisham. At three-second intervals the others followed. By the time it was our turn to go, the runway had almost disappeared in a haze of swirling fumes and just before Offord released our brakes, Curry's Lightning suddenly leaped skywards like a runaway rocket at the other end of the runway. This steep, afterburner take-off had become an accepted part of Lightning aerobatics and the 'Firebirds' have proved they can do it as well as any others. It certainly is most exciting to watch; it is breath-taking to actually do it.

'As soon as we had started rushing the acceleration was patently obvious. Then Offord cut in the afterburners and there is only one word for it - we simply belted down the runway. Glued firmly to the back of my ejection seat, I watched the ground flash past and at regular intervals, the aircraft ahead of us shot upwards. Then we were airborne with our wheels up. For a few seconds Offord held the aircraft level at about thirty feet to let the speed build up.

'By roughly three-quarters of the way down the runway we had 250 knots showing. Then Offord pulled the stick back smartly into his stomach. The ground disappeared as if by magic and I sank into my seat as the sudden upwards turn gave us 3½g - not much by modern standards, but quite something at such an early and critical part of the take-off. But perhaps the biggest sensation of this dramatic take-off technique is the frightening loss of apparent speed. One second you are roaring down the runway with trees and hangars blurring in the distance and the next you are almost on your back in the rear cockpit, looking straight up at the clouds with seemingly no speed whatsoever. A reassuring glance at the air speed indicator showed, however, that we still had 230 knots and the Lightning, which, with full afterburner, has almost as much thrust as its weight, could maintain this attitude and speed for a long time. Still with the afterburners on, we trailed the five aircraft ahead, which were already forming up. As we broke through the clouds, Curry in the leading Lightning eased off the climb and announced that he was coming out of afterburner. There was a short breathing space while we looked for a clear area in which to practice and then, over a large break in the clouds below, we started. Curry calmly announced rolls, wingovers and loops and the formation changes while the team followed. As we brought up the rear in the T.4, making all the manoeuvres with the team, the sky and the ground ceased to mean up or down. Our reference point became the five aircraft ahead and the Suffolk countryside and the horizon whirled over and around us unceasingly as the section of five flew smoothly through their practice. At no point were we straight and level for more than a second. The accelerometer showed peaks of up to 4g and most of the time we were between 2 and 3g. Our speed remained fairly constant at 350 knots.

'Keeping station within the 'Firebirds' as we were, one could appreciate their faultless station keeping and the smoothness of their manoeuvres. It was almost like putting a work of art under a microscope and still finding it flawless. Watching the team in action like this it was difficult to realize that, only a few months previously, hardly any of the pilots had experience of formation aerobatics. That they have achieved a standard of perfection is a tribute not only to the general calibre of the average RAF pilot today, but to the work of Squadron Leader David Seward.

'Although the 'Firebirds' display is, in every way, a team effort, right through from pilots to the equally essential and highly skilled ground crew, there is little doubt that Dave Seward is the man who can make or break a show. One of the great assets of the Lightning for formation aerobatics - apart of course, from its excellent handling characteristics - is the great amount of power which pilots can call on if necessary. This means that the pilot on the outside of a turn should have no difficulty in keeping his station. This excess power does, however, pose problems for Seward. He must concentrate on flying a course which pilots in all parts of the large formation behind him can follow. If he allows too much power to build up in a turn he could well cause embarrassment to a pilot on the outside of the formation.

'We stayed with Curry's section at practice for twenty minutes. Although Offord had not flown as close to the formation as the other aircraft were close to each other (the view from the T.4 is a little restricted for close formation aerobatics) he had to concentrate closely on the movements of the aircraft ahead of us. Obviously, the pilots who were literally flying only a few feet apart were concentrating even harder. Back on the ground I asked several of them whether they found this concentration tiring. They did not seem to take their task as anything particularly out of the ordinary. 'You have to concentrate pretty hard anyway when you are flying a Lightning,' one said. This applies whether you are flying formation aeros or making a radar interception.

'But one thing is certain. Although the pilots might say that their job is not particularly out of the ordinary, by the end of this summer many people in various parts of Europe will have had an opportunity to judge for themselves how 'out of the ordinary' their show is. My guess is that the 'Firebirds' will he adjudged one of the best yet.'

'However,' continues Dave Seward, 'before we really got going, 'Noddy' MacEwen, the solo man, was posted and promoted, so Flying Officer Alan Garside the 11 Squadron solo aeros man joined us. [In April 1963 Flight Lieutenant Brian C. Allchin (25) joined 56 Squadron. 'Alch' had flown Hunters in 92 Squadron and in the Blue Diamonds aerobatic team in 1961 and 1962.] Everyone then became involved after we had a mid-air collision.'

'FIREBIRDS', 'T-BIRDS' AND 'TREMBLERS'

The collision occurred during a formation horizontal bomb burst over Wattisham airfield on 6 June. 'The day before,' recalls Mike Cooke, (the No.3, (left of centre in the five-vic formation, in F.1A XM179, behind Gerry Cohu) 'Squadron Leader Seward had given us a 'pleasant ear-bashing' to smarten up the horizontal bomb burst because of the 'slack' bomb burst at the end of the sequence. We did a practice. On one roll I must have been low because I saw rather a lot of trees near the airfield at Wattisham. We were then coming in, each Lightning, 6-7 feet apart as usual and Gerry Cohu ordered 'Bomb Burst, Bomb Burst ... GO!' 'Mo' Moore, the No.5 and the No.4 went straight away. One second later it was my turn and that of the No.2. I made a very sharp turn and at the same time I pulled the stick to make it 'slicker'. You then didn't normally look too far over to the left. We were about to reassemble and I looked ahead for the leader, took off the left bank coming out of the left turn to go right.

'Suddenly, I felt a bump. [His port wing had touched the under fuselage of XM171, 'Mo' Moore's Lightning, knocking the starboard 'Firestreak' missile off. Moore managed to land safely at Wattisham.] Immediately the aircraft carried on rolling to the right, despite full left aileron and full left rudder. I couldn't stop it. I remember that the height was 500-700 feet AGL. In a few milliseconds I realized I'd have to eject. At that height I could eject onto the ground, so I had reflex - 'Go for the handle!' I used my left hand to pull it. Glancing at the ASI I saw that it was around 400-500 knots and rising. I pulled. It seemed an age before something happened. The canopy went. I waited for the 'nip' in the back of the neck (previously I had done two training ejections in a static ramp), but it did not happen.

'The next thing I remember was that I was coming down in the parachute and into a green field. I could not move my arms or my legs. I couldn't breathe either. Because of the whiplash effect caused by a malfunction in the ejection seat sequence, the parachute had opened at too high a speed (called a hangman's deployment). The whiplash effect had broken my neck (actually, my fifth and sixth vertebrae had been severed), although I did not know this until a few days later. (A 'hangman's deployment' is so-called because we breathe though the diaphragm and when someone is hanged on the scaffold the noose breaks the neck and breathing stops. This is what had happened to me when the parachute had deployed.) I came to on the ground. I still had my facemask on. I could not breathe too well. I thought that this was because I was lying on my breathing apparatus. Two labourers came over. I said, 'Mask off, Mask off!' They said, 'He's still alive' and answered back. Overhead, another Lightning circled, pin-pointing my position presumably. A crash crew arrived with an ambulance and a very uncomfortable ride ensued. I was taken to hospital in Ipswich and later that day I was helicoptered to Stoke Mandeville.'

Professor Sir Ludwig 'Poppa' Guttmann CBE FRS (3 July 1899-18 March 1980) a German-born British neurologist who established the Paralympics Games in England, oversaw Mike's treatment. 'He was a German Jew who had fled to Britain in 1937 and had become world-renowned in the treatment of spinal injuries at Stoke Mandeville. He is considered to be one of the founding fathers of organized physical activities for people with a disability. His technique was to permit the patient good, basic nursing to avoid potentially dangerous bladder and kidney failures later and so prolong the patient's life span. (At one time, the normal prognosis for spinal injury patients was only ten years.) I had a tracheotomy to improve my breathing and my head was put in traction for three months after a harness was bolted to my skull. The first night I couldn't move and I was more occupied with coping with the present effects of my accident than thinking about what the future now held. Stoke Mandeville was something of a culture shock after RAF station quarters. The wooden huts had nicotine-stained ceilings and it was so cramped, you could touch the patient's bed next to you on both sides. The food wasn't at all good. Everyone, though, was in the same boat. Recovery, if you do recover, comes after six weeks. At the time of my accident my wife Patsy was five months pregnant and she was understandably very upset. All told, I spent seventeen weeks in bed. Gradually, my arms got a little movement. My first day's outing on 23 October coincided with the birth, at RAF Bicester, of our son, Simon.'

Mike Cooke's RAF career was finished; he was just 26 years old at the time. Incredibly, he did not qualify for compensation (under Section 10 of the Crown Proceedings Act of 1947, he could not sue the MoD), nor a pension; he had not been in the RAF long enough. Without a trace of bitterness, he says: 'The RAF is there to fight wars, not look after the injured.' The RAF Benevolent Fund also was unable to help the pilot, who was now a paraplegic. However, Sir James Martin at Martin-Baker had told Patsy Cooke that if there was anything Mike needed he could have it. In 1968 Martin-Baker provided money to enable the Cookes to buy a Citroen Safari and to have it specially adapted for his use. Mike used it for twelve years and Martin-Baker then provided another £10,000 for him to replace it with a Nissan Prairie.

Flight Lieutenant Peter Symes, recently arrived at Wattisham from Cranwell, remembers: 'After 56 was given the aerobatic commitment it was fascinating to see them gradually working up into shape. When they began to display at lower level over the airfield, almost everybody used to stop to watch. Eventually we became accustomed to their routine and they just became a noise in the background. However, on 6 June 1963, in my office on the upper floor of SHQ facing the back of the hangars, I noticed an unusual WHOOMPH as the formation did its horizontal bomb burst head on to the hangar line. Glancing out of the window I saw an airman outside the guardroom looking to the sky above SHQ in obvious amazement and I noticed something glinting as it tumbled down into the Airmen's Married Quarters. Realising that something had gone wrong, I dashed up onto the roof in time to see a mushroom cloud of smoke starting to drift downwind - then a Lightning starting to orbit at low level. Shortly afterwards the wife of the Discipline Sergeant came into SHQ to see her husband. She was in a very distressed state. XM179 had thundered into a field of peas only about 50 yards from the narrow road on which she had been driving towards the station and it had seemed to be heading straight for her.'

Dave Seward, who had been filming the formation from the ground, now had tough decisions to make: 'Sad though it was, I had a job to do and suddenly, you have to fight back the tears, harden it and get on with the job. Not a pleasant thing. You've got to tell the relatives. The station commander asked me what I was going to do. I said, 'We carry on.' It was the only way. This was one of the times when you had to make a hard decision. You're not the most popular guy. Then again, you're not running a popularity poll. We had a Queen's birthday flypast the next day and not only that but we were scheduled to lead it. I'll give Mo Moore his due. I said, 'This accident has shaken you up boy. What are you going to do?' (I counselled him and told him he had done nothing wrong). He said, 'I'll carry on.' We needed all the aircraft so Edwin Carter and his engineers changed the missile pack on 'Mo' Moore's aircraft and hammered the dents out and put it in the air.'

Although the 'Firebirds' gave most of their displays with synchronized aerobatics from two sections of four or five aircraft, each show that summer of 1963 was opened by the full formation of nine with, sometimes, an extra solo performance thrown in. On 18 July 1963 Flying Officer Alan Garside was killed when he became disorientated in cloud during an aerobatic presentation at RAF Wittering and so Sam Lucas, the 11 Squadron solo aerobatic pilot, took Garside's place in the 'Firebirds' for the rest of the season. Seward recalls that, 'Lucas was an 'ad libber' who would get 'bored' with his show and throw in some unannounced routines. On one occasion

I saw him enter the fog at Biggin Hill inverted and I never expected him to come out alive, but he did!'

On 12 June the 'Firebirds' flew to France to perform at the Paris Air Show at Le Bourget. The *Flight* correspondent wrote: 'The programme at Le Bourget proved that Dave Seward was fully aware of the showmanship part of his job as he was of his airmanship. The French crowd was treated to a dazzling display of colour and spectacle, but, above all, one of precision, which began as soon as the pilots strapped themselves into their cockpits. If there was to be a full take-off of ten Lightnings, the onlooker would be treated to the sight of ten canopies closing as one on Squadron Leader Seward's orders. Next, the immaculately white-overalled ground crew would march smartly forward in line abreast as the aircraft prepared to move off. This move was not just 'bull'. Each airman was there to marshal one of the Lightnings from its line-up position and to give it a last-minute visual check. The aircraft moved off in two sections of five and again on their Squadron Leader's command, each aircraft in each section of five would check its brakes at precisely the same instant after it had rolled a few feet. The effect was almost that of a gracious bow towards the crowd. 56 Squadron's pre-take-off manoeuvres were, certainly, a fitting prelude to the precision which was to follow in the air.'

Unbeknown to the *Flight* correspondent, things did not go as smoothly as hoped, as Dave Seward explains: 'We were pushed for time (the Greek Air Force had already been diverted for overstepping their slot). We only had something like twelve minutes from take-off to landing. (Normally, we timed ourselves from the time the first aircraft (mine) started to roll.) The French said that our start time was as soon as I taxied out.' Dave Seward was also the man who faced the last-minute decision on what type of show was to be given: 'Despite Met reports it is sometimes impossible to know exactly what flying conditions are like until you are in the air. Basically, we planned for three different types of show to meet all eventualities. If the clouds were above 4,000 feet we would give the complete show. We had another display which we could use if the ceiling was lower and a final bad weather show with which we operated within a radius of two miles with a 500 feet ceiling. For Paris we would do a loop in a 5,000 feet cloud base. However, it was a murky day and so I had sent Bob Manning, the spare, up to see what the cloud base was. He said, 'No clouds below 6,000 feet.' I told John Curry, 'OK, we'll do the full show.' Up we went - straight into cloud at 2,500 feet! We did the whole loop in cloud using the attitude indicator (a nasty little instrument with no 'aircraft' mounted on the artificial horizon) and came out at 2,500 feet. It was a 'dodgy' time but we all stuck together - I'll say that for the team. So then the rest of the display was the flat show. Afterwards, I asked Manning why the hell he had told me there was no cloud below 6,000 feet and he said, 'Well Boss, you've been practising the loop for so long now, that I thought you wouldn't want to miss it!' After we came down we went into the BAC tent. [Air Marshal Sir Desmond] 'Zulu' Morris, the C-in-C Fighter Command, had a face as black as thunder. I could see him looking at me and saying, 'What about that loop?' He was not that happy anyway that a front-line squadron had been taken out of the line for aerobatting. (It did not make economic sense using a front-line squadron like us when you're trying to maintain a watching brief in a Cold War situation.) I explained to him that we'd been given the wrong weather forecast and that was it. He was just starting to get to the awkward question when Bill Bedford suddenly dropped the P.1127 Kestrel right outside the judges' tent! The crash took me off the hook and with other things now on his mind, 'Zulu' Morris never mentioned it again!'

Geoffrey Norris' prediction that the 'Firebirds' would be adjudged one of the best yet was proved true and they became the last squadron formation aerobatic team to display. The following September a team of five yellow-painted Gnat T.1 trainers from 4 Flying Training School led by Flight Lieutenant Lee Jones performed at Farnborough 1964. The 'Yellowjacks' success led, in 1965, to the world-renowned Red Arrows, whose first public performance was at Biggin Hill in May that year. The rest, of course, is history.

The year 1966 was another bad one with seven Lightning losses. The one on 5 January was fatal. Flying Officer Derek Law on 56 Squadron was piloting XR721 when it suffered an engine flameout. Law, a Rhodesian pilot whose tour in the UK was almost up, tried to eject, but the system malfunctioned and his canopy would not separate after he pulled the ejection seat-panhandle. With no option but to try to belly land, a procedure which was normally out of the question in a Lightning, he skilfully put his crippled F.3 down in a ploughed field at Helmingham, near RAF Bentwaters in Suffolk, after avoiding high-tension cables. XR721 shed its tail and careered out of control across the fields before clipping a tree on the B1079 Helmingham-Otley road. However, the young pilot was then ejected through the branches of the tree and was killed, his Lightning coming to a halt barely a yard from the front door of Elm Tree Farm Cottages on the other side of the road.

Group Captain Antony J. Barwood of the Institute of Aviation Medicine at Farnborough explains what probably happened. 'The cockpit canopy jettison system had fired when Law initiated ejection but one lock or shoot bolt had failed so that the cockpit canopy could not lift from the front and it had remained held by that shootbolt. Law would then have had no option but to attempt a crash landing. The ground impact was sufficient to shake the cockpit canopy off and thus to remove the interdictor. It would have required a further seat-pan or face-blind pull to extract the ejection gun sear after the interdictor had been removed by the separating cockpit canopy. Law may have realised that the canopy had separated and that he could now eject or he might have retained a pull on a handle throughout the incident but this is unlikely as he was flying the aircraft so successfully to effect his crash landing. An unlikely alternative was that it was an impact ejection - the seat being forced up at ground impact, breaking the top lock to allow the sear to move up, displacing the sear to fire the gun, but we had no reported evidence of this.'[4]

Dave Seward, Law's commanding officer, recalls his loss: 'It was part of the bloody game I'm afraid. He did everything right. Somehow, against all the things in the book, he made a copybook wheels-up landing despite having two dead engines and seized up controls. It was a great shame. He was a great pilot and a lovely lad who had great potential.'[5]

Chapter 4

Ab Initio

For a young Air Traffic Controller in the early 1970s there was no finer place to be than the Lightning OCU at Coltishall.
Flight Lieutenant Dick Doleman.

Initially, before two-seat Lightnings became available, the trainee 'Frightening' pilot would begin his introduction to the aircraft by spending three days at ground school at Middleton St. George, followed by a week in a simulator at his front-line squadron station, where he would make twelve 'flights'. It was therefore expected that on the student's momentous actual first flight he would be able to perform starting procedures and pre-take-off vital actions perfectly. Later, when two-seat Lightnings became available, the student was subjected to an intensive syllabus consisting of thirteen and a half hours' dual and six hours solo - plus one and a quarter hours, spare for dual or solo as required - on the Lightning T.4 or T.5.

The first conversion exercise would be a familiarization sortie and was given to the student on the very first day that he arrived at the OCU. He would be a passenger only, the instructor flying the aircraft from the left-hand seat and no attempt would be made to give any flying instruction. This sortie proved to be of great value in that it whetted the appetite and helped to make the ground instruction that much easier to absorb. However, if the weather was unfit for flying on the first day of the course, the sortie was normally lost and no provision was made to give this exercise at a later date.

Pre-take-off vital actions would be performed in dispersal on the first sortie. When the student carried them out whilst taxiing, he was reminded not to commence until the aircraft was well clear of the dispersal area. Taxiing the Lightning caused difficulty during the first sortie. The student would be unaccustomed to being high off the ground and to the considerable force needed to operate the rudder pedals. In the T.4, full rudder deflection was required to produce full differential braking, whereas in the single-seater, only half rudder was needed. With the throttles set at idle/fast idle, the Lightning would easily accelerate whilst taxiing and braking against the power was essential. This would result in a tendency to taxi too fast and towards poor directional control due to under-controlling of the rudder pedals. (At idle/fast idle, fuel consumption would be 55lb per minute and approximately 400-500lb would be used to get to the take-off point. Students were therefore instructed not to delay on the ground!)

When clearance to take-off had been obtained from ATC (Air Traffic Control) and the intention to taxi signalled to the marshalling airman by flashing the taxi lights, the aircraft would taxi to the runway for a cold-power take-off (the re-heat take-off was practised to show to the students the full performance and capability of the aircraft).

First, the cold power take-off (i.e. without re-heat). The aircraft would be lined up along the centreline of the runway in between the Bomber Command start markers with the nose-wheel straight. From this starting position, a good acceleration check could be made during the roll. Throttles would be paralleled and power increased to 100 per cent. Acceleration would be rapid and if the aircraft had not been lined up correctly it could lead to difficulty during the early part of the take-off run. The rudder would become effective at about 90 knots. Once the nozzle position, JPTs (Jet Pipe Temperatures) and RPMs (Revolutions Per Minute) had been checked, the ASI (Airspeed Indicator) had to be monitored closely. Under normal take-off conditions, the control column would be moved back at 125 knots to bring the nose-wheel off the ground by 135 knots. Once the nose-wheel was raised, a forward movement of the control column would be made as required to hold the correct attitude. At 160 knots, a further smooth, progressive, backward movement of the stick would lift the aircraft off the ground at 170 knots. Violent backward movement of the control column at the unstick speed had to be avoided as the tail bumper could strike the runway.

Once airborne with the undercarriage selected and locked up and at a safe climbing attitude, a turn onto the climbing heading could begin. When the speed reached 420 knots, the angle of climb was then increased to eighteen degrees to maintain 450 knots. Once the aircraft had been trimmed, small adjustments only would be required to maintain the correct climbing speed. After settling down in the climb, the post take-off checks would begin.

Due to the high fuel consumption when re-heat was used and the consequent reduction in total endurance, only one dual and one solo re-heat take-off and climb were carried out during OCU training. Students had to be reminded that fuel used on a re-heat climb only exceeded that used in a cold climb by a small margin; time and range covered to height would be markedly reduced, though overall range was hardly affected. (Distance to height on cold power was twenty-eight nautical miles and sixteen nautical miles on reheat, while time to height was 3¾ minutes on cold power and 2½ minutes on reheat.) In the Lightning T.4 when the throttles were pushed forward into the full re-heat position, the undercarriage 'up' selector button was difficult to reach. (During the left to right pre-start cockpit checks it was considered advisable to pause at the TTC (Top Temperature Control) light check and let the student sort out for himself how he could best select 'wheels up'.)

On take-off, re-heat ought to be selected as soon as the JPTs had stabilized at 100 per cent cold power. This allowed time to take the necessary action should one or both afterburners not light and it was most important that this eventuality was covered during the briefing. If, after selecting re-heat, one or both nozzles went into pre-open only and the re-heat did not light up, re-heat could be cancelled and re-selected again when the JPTs had once again stabilized. If No. 1 reheat failed, the 'piano-keys' on the runway would have to be used. Only two attempts at selecting reheat could be made. If unsuccessful, the take-off had to be continued in cold power. If a light up occurred normally but then failed with the nozzle in the fully open position, only fifty-seven per cent cold thrust was available and the JPT would be very low. In this case, re-heat had to be cancelled immediately and the take-off continued in cold power. If a re-heat malfunction resulted in a cold power take-off, re-heat could be re-selected when safely airborne so that the exercise could be completed.

With re-heat lighting up normally after the first selection, the increased acceleration was marked and the ASI had to be watched closely. Speeds for raising the nose-wheel and getting airborne were as for the cold take-off. There was even more danger of the tail-bumper striking the ground if harsh control was used during a re-heat take-off. If the wheels were not selected 'up' as soon as the aircraft was safely airborne, the acceleration was such that the nose-wheel would not retract forward against the airflow. If this happened, in order to get the nose-wheel undercarriage light out, re-heat would have to be cancelled and speed reduced, but reheat could be re-applied once the undercarriage was completely retracted. Once the undercarriage was locked up and a safe climb away initiated, a hard turn ought to be made onto the climbing heading. At 420 knots the angle of climb then ought to be increased to about thirty degrees on the attitude indicator. As in the cold take-off, once the aircraft had been trimmed, small adjustments of the angle of climb maintained the climbing speed of 450 knots. It was important to attain the correct climbing speed early, since, if the student's reaction was slow, the speed would rapidly accelerate beyond 450 knots and in order to get the correct speed, large alterations in the angle of climb would be necessary and he would probably not settle down at all.

Because of the increased performance and greater rate of climb, the post take-off checks would really be left until Mach 0.96 was reached. The student may have noticed the fuel gauges going down during the climb, but this was normal since the engine demand was more than could be supplied from the slipper tank alone. Four thousand feet would be allowed for levelling out. As the aircraft passed through 30,000 feet, the angle of climb would be progressively reduced and re-heat cancelled.

On a cold-power take-off the transition from 450 knots to Mach 0.9 occurred at approximately 16,000 feet and poor instrument scanning would usually cause it to be missed on early sorties. Above 30,000 feet, the angle of climb would have to be reduced slightly in order to maintain the speed. During the climb to altitude, particular attention had to be paid to the rudder trim since the small slip indicator might get hidden behind the student's right knee. The level-out from the climb would ideally be commenced as the altimeter passed through 32,500 feet to level out at 34,000 feet. There would be a considerable 'dead-band' in the throttle movement and they needed to be brought back a long way in order to bring the nozzles into the cruise position. While the power was being reduced, the nose had to be eased down to maintain the speed and once flying level, the power could be adjusted to maintain the required cruising speed with the nozzles remaining at cruise and the aircraft trimmed.

Handling the aircraft at Mach 0.95 was practised during the first conversion exercise and would normally consist of the student getting the feel of the controls. A speed of Mach 0.95 was chosen as this was the best subsonic manouevring speed. (During normal handling, the aircraft was flown at Mach 0.9.)

During this short period of subsonic general handling the student would get used to the slow action of the tailplane trim, which was considerably slower than in other aircraft that the student may have flown previously. He could also practise turns, noting the apparent difference when turning left and right while sitting in the left-hand seat. Once settled down, turns to the buffet, maintaining the speed at Mach 0.95, would be practised. During these turns, the student would be asked to note the increase in power required to maintain the speed. As the bank was increased and the power increased to 100 per cent, the student would be asked to note the angle of bank (about 60-65 degrees) and the reading (about 2-2½ g) at which buffet occurred and be aware that the speed dropped, even though full cold power was being applied.

Before accelerating to supersonic speeds, clearance had to be obtained from the controlling authority. Clearance to fly supersonic speed was normally given on an easterly heading. It was essential, while flying at high speed, to constantly monitor the fuel gauges and TACAN position, since fuel consumption was so very high. (It was essential that the student be taught the use of TACAN at a very early stage in his training and made to use it at every available opportunity from then on in order to induce a flexible mental approach to the operation of the Lightning.)

The acceleration to supersonic height was termed 'precision acceleration' and this was stressed from the start since it would form part of the instrument rating test at a later date. During the acceleration the 'cobblestone' effect would be noticed at about Mach 0.97. This is caused by the breakaway of airflow from different parts of the aircraft and could be mistaken for slight clear air turbulence. As the aircraft further accelerated, at about Mach 0.99 the pressure instruments would become unreliable until the shock wave moved back past the static vents (at about 1.04 TMN (True Mach Number)). At this point the altimeter would 'jump up' approximately 1,800 feet, the RCDI (Rate of Climb 6 knots Descent Indicator) would show a high rate of climb, the ASI (Air Speed Indicator) would show an increase of about 30 knots and the TMN would settle at about Mach 1.04. For this reason, the aircraft would be eased into a gentle dive during the initial acceleration so that it lost 1,800 feet in height. When the 'jump up' of the altimeter occurred, the height would be back to 34,000 feet. During this transonic period when the altimeter and RCDI were giving false readings, attitude would normally have to be maintained by reference to the attitude indicator. Trim changes throughout the acceleration were only moderate. At Mach 1.3, power could be reduced to that stage of re-heat required to maintain the speed. The instructor would emphasize the need to check directional trim and possible over-pressurization.

The high rate of fuel consumption limited handling at Mach 1.3 to a turn each way and the turns had to be completed before the aircraft was positioning towards land when within thirty-five miles of the coast. On the first turn it would be shown that the maximum angle of bank could be reached whilst maintaining Mach 1.3 and on the second turn, that the aircraft should be pulled to the judder with consequent speed reduction. It could then be pointed out that the first turn was the more efficient method. Approximately seventy degrees of bank and 4g could be obtained at the judder. Entry would be the same as for the Mach 0.95 turns, except that apparent increased sensitivity of the RCDI would be noticed at Mach 1.3.

The precision deceleration is the exact reverse of the acceleration, the intention being to decrease the height by approximately 1,800 feet during the initial deceleration so that when the 'jump up' occurred at Mach 1.04, the altimeter again finished at 34,000 feet. To decelerate, the power would be reduced to idle/fast idle and a gentle climb commenced. The student would maintain the attitude obtained as the RCDI passed 1,500 feet/minute. At the point of 'jump-down', the aircraft would have considerable climb inertia and the change in attitude required to maintain level flight at 34,000 feet would be marked and had to be anticipated. Air brakes were not used. As soon as the 'jump-down' occurred, power had to be increased to hold the required subsonic speed and the aircraft trimmed for straight and level flight.

Once subsonic speed was obtained, the recovery to the descent point could be commenced, either under GCI control or by pilot navigation using TACAN fixes. The ILS (Instrument Landing System) approach aid was new to many pilots converting onto the Lightning and though the approach pattern may have been practised to a limited extent in the Lightning simulator, its use had to be thoroughly briefed and not taken for granted. Being essentially a pilot-interpreted aid, it would not involve a different scan pattern to that used for the more normal GCA approach and in order to get this practice, ILS approaches had to be carried out whenever wind direction and serviceability allowed. The base QFE would be obtained and set on the altimeter before reaching the dive circle. After the deceleration, any out of balance fuel state would have to be corrected by using the wing-to-wing transfer system during the cruise to the dive circle and descent made by using differential throttle.

The return to the dive circle was carried out at 36,000 feet and might be under GCI control, or by TACAN, during which period the student would practise fuel and time calculations. To save fuel, it was the instructor's job to make him aim directly for 'Point Alpha' (if on a direct approach), or 'Point Bravo' (if approaching to the opposite end of the runway), so long as the course did not take him outside the limits of the dive segment. It was important that the descent should be commenced as soon as the dive circle was reached, since a small error in the speed during the descent would make a considerable difference to the rate of descent. If the rate of descent was found to be insufficient, the power would have to be reduced to idle/idle maintaining the speed. If the rate of descent was subsequently still found to be insufficient, speed had to be increased. If, during the descent, the rate of descent was found to be excessive, then the air brakes had to be selected 'in'.

Point Alpha (or Bravo) would ideally have been reached at 3,000 feet, at which height the aircraft could be levelled off and speed reduced to 240 knots. The aircraft would be trimmed as the speed reduced and then descended to 1,500 feet upon GCA permission being received. The talk-down controller should be asked to stop talking when the aircraft reached two miles from touch-down on the very first approach practised, so that the instructor could take over control and demonstrate the final stage of the approach and the overshoot, to demonstrate the approach angle and engine handling technique and speed control.

The overshoot action could be taken just before the wheels touched and the Lightning would climb away easily with ninety per cent power so full power was unnecessary. As the power increased, airbrakes could be selected 'in' with the same movement and the climb angle set. Wheels could then be selected 'up' followed by the flaps at 180 knots. When the speed reached 240 knots, power was then reduced to eighty-five per cent to maintain this speed during the climb to the downwind leg. If a further instrument approach was to be flown, the instrument overshoot procedure would be used. To overshoot into a visual circuit, a minimum of 50 degrees of bank would be used, commencing at a safe height. Power would be reduced progressively to roll out on the downwind leg at 240 knots. Once straight and level seventy-five per cent power would normally be sufficient to maintain the speed.

Circuit work commenced right at the beginning of the conversion course, each pre-solo dual sortie finishing with the different types of circuit being practised. The flapless circuit was practised in order to demonstrate to the student the approach pattern in the event of a landing without the use of flaps or airbrakes. (Although a flapless landing was never practised, the instructor had to brief fully on the flapless landing technique.) The systems failure was assumed from the overshoot from a normal circuit and the student was required to perform the complete circuit with the flaps and airbrakes inoperative. It was strongly emphasized to the student that if he had to overshoot with a known failure of this nature, he must not raise the undercarriage. A flapless landing run would be about 200 yards longer than for a normal landing.

The single-engined handling of the Lightning presented no difficulty and the circuit pattern, approach and landing were carried out at the normal speeds. However, when practising on No. 1 engine, this would be throttled to idle after touchdown along with No. 2. Due to the poor engine response from this RPM an overshoot would be hazardous; therefore, all single-engined landings were treated as precautionary landings. The downwind R/T call would be, 'C/S Downwind Practice Single-Engine Precautionary Landing.'

To maintain the normal circuit pattern with one engine throttled back to idle, approximately 8-10 per cent extra in RPM was required on the other engine. The approach on one engine would present no problems if accurate speeds were maintained. The normal approach RPM was 90-92 per cent. If the speed was allowed to fall off, the increase in power required to regain it may well move the engine nozzle to the 'closed' position with a subsequent increase in thrust. If this occurred, it had to be remembered to re-open the nozzle, otherwise speed control would be difficult during the final stages of the approach.

The final approach and landing would be exactly the same as for the normal circuit, but it was even more important on one engine that power was not reduced too much before touch-down, or the aircraft would sink rapidly and land short. This was particularly important in strong and gusty wind conditions. On the overshoot, 100 per cent cold power had to be applied initially and the airbrakes retracted immediately. The undercarriage must not be retracted until the aircraft was safely away and the flaps would be raised at the normal speed of 180 knots.

Before flying his first solo, the student would be briefed on the crosswind technique for take-off and landing in a Lightning (crosswind landings in a Lightning, with its slab-sided fuselage and enormous tail fin, could prove particularly terrifying for the unwary and even for the most experienced pilot, especially on a wet and dark night!). Before starting-up in strong crosswind conditions, careful note had to be made of the condition of the tyres and the student had to be conversant with what was acceptable under these conditions.

Initial take-off actions were normal, but as the aircraft started accelerating down the runway, it might be necessary to keep straight initially by differential braking and then by use of the rudder when it became effective. The rotation method was then used. This involved keeping the nose-wheel on the runway until 150 knots and then lifting it and then the aircraft, off the runway at 170 knots with one smooth, backward movement of the control column. The effect of maintaining the nose-wheel on the runway until the higher speed was to provide extra stability against the cross-wind and reduce main wheel tyre wear; however, care had to be exercised not to over-control when moving the control column as under these conditions the pilot ran a greater risk of scraping the tail. As the aircraft became airborne, the downwind wing might drop and would have to be levelled.

The 'crab' technique was recommended for approach and landing. A sufficiently long final approach should be flown in order to assess the drift. Normal approach speeds were used and drift kicked off as the aircraft was rounded-out; aileron might have to be used to counteract roll if there was much drift to remove. The student had to be told initially to keep the ailerons neutral after touch-down; latterly, he might be shown the effect of using downwind aileron. As the brake parachute was deployed, he had to be prepared to use downwind rudder to prevent excessive weather-cocking, particularly at the moment of deployment. The tendency of the aircraft's nose to weather-cock would gradually become more pronounced as the aircraft speed reduced, when differential braking might have to be used; this in turn might lead to a longer landing roll. If the weather-cocking became excessive and directional control difficult, the brake parachute would have to be jettisoned, though use of downwind aileron would effectively delay the point at which control could no longer be maintained. The student would be told that if he allowed the nose of the aircraft to yaw too far, there might not be sufficient rudder available to regain directional control.

It had to be borne in mind that gusty conditions are frequently associated with strong crosswinds. Therefore, care had to be exercised in throttle handling as the aircraft was landed. If necessary, some power had to be left on until touch-down; the more drift to be removed, the more important did this point become. By the same token, large fluctuations in wind speed could also be encountered. It was therefore essential under these conditions to ensure that low speeds were never used on the approach and in the severest turbulence it might be necessary to increase the approach speed slightly.

The student would also have been thoroughly briefed before his first solo on the technique of carrying out a precautionary landing, where he was committed to stopping 'come what may' and all the circumstances under which he would perform it. As soon as possible after first solo, he would carry out a dual practice; subsequently, he would be made to decide whether or not such a landing should be made and any disinclination to use the precautionary technique would be immediately curbed. The overriding factor as to the necessity for a precautionary landing was circumstances dictating that, even if the brake parachute failed, the pilot would not overshoot the aircraft; with this in mind, the student would more readily remember the technique involved.

The occasions when a precautionary landing was mandatory included: after overshooting following a brake parachute failure; when the fuel remaining would be below 800/800lb on touchdown; below any higher fuel minima as laid down by the DOCFW; when to overshoot would constitute a hazard to the aircraft; when weather conditions were 'Yellow Two' state or worse; and when practising a single-engined landing. (A fuel state of '800/800lb' means 800lb of fuel in each side of the aircraft.)

The intention to make a precautionary landing would be announced with the downwind R/T call, or when appropriate on an Instrument Approach. A normal touch-down would be made, engines throttled to idle/idle and the nose-wheel lowered. Maximum wheel braking was then to be applied at the same time as the brake parachute was deployed. If the brake parachute operated, a normal landing was to be completed and the aircraft returned to dispersal. If it failed, hard wheel braking was continued and one engine shut down. After the runway had been cleared, the aircraft would be turned into wind on the ORP and shut down and a towing vehicle requested.

Most students found that good landings followed from good approaches. Landings had to be made with a minimum of 800/800lb of fuel and a decision made before landing on the action to take in the event of a brake parachute failure. Final approach speeds altered according to all-up weight. Up to 1,500lb/side fuel load required a final approach speed of 175 knots and a one knot increase for every additional 200lb/side beyond this load. The over-shoot into the circuit pattern was difficult at first, since the aircraft accelerated quickly once power was applied and circuit height would soon be reached.

As soon as the aircraft settled on the downwind leg, vital actions (VAs) would be commenced. The sooner they were completed, the more time there would be to concentrate on the circuit pattern. There would be an attitude change, not experienced in the flight simulator, once the flaps were lowered and unless it was anticipated it would result in a sudden gain in height of 200-300 feet. Once the vital actions were completed, speed would fall off quickly and at 200 knots power would have to be increased to approximately eighty-three per cent in order to maintain 190 knots.

The turn onto the final approach would start at about one runway's length from the end of the runway. If the wind was down the runway, approximately thirty-five degrees of bank would be sufficient and a rate of descent of about 1,000 feet/minute would be aimed for. The throttles were extremely sensitive over the range of RPM being used and very small throttle movements would give comparatively large increases in percentage RPM and equally large changes in thrust. The RPM gauges were obscurely positioned on the right-hand side of the cockpit in the T.4, so most students had considerable difficulty in making accurate power adjustments; these would only improve with practice.

If a student tended to over-control the throttles, he would be advised to set No. 2 throttle and adjust his power on No.1 only. During the final turn the airbrakes would be selected 'out' when appropriate. As the bank was gradually taken off, speed would be reduced to 185 knots, further reducing to 175 knots when lined up with the runway. At this stage, a V/1 degree glide-path would be intercepted with a Red/Pink indication from the VGPIs (Visual Glide Path Indicators), but at half a mile the aircraft would be descended below this glide-path and the nose raised slightly. Approaching the lights, the speed would be reduced to 170 knots and from here on the speed would be reduced constantly to achieve 165 knots at the runway threshold, which would be crossed at an approach angle of about half a degree. Under normal wind conditions, the power should at this stage be about eighty per cent.

As the aircraft approached the runway threshold, power could again be reduced slightly (but not taken completely off) and the nose-wheel raised still further. At the threshold, which was probably the last time that the airspeed would be checked, the speed should be 165 knots. As the threshold was crossed, power could be progressively reduced and the control column brought back to what appeared at first to be quite a high nose-up position. Normally, power was still being used at touchdown and therefore, as the wheels touched, power ought to be reduced to idle/fast idle. If too much power was reduced too early, the aircraft could drop and even hit the ground before the threshold. At this stage, the overshoot could be initiated if required.

Touch-down speed would be about 155 knots. As soon as the aircraft was on the ground the control column would be eased forward to bring the nose-wheel down and at 150 knots the brake parachute would be deployed. As soon as the deceleration was felt and it was most marked, power would be reduced to idle/idle. Little or no braking would be required initially, but brakes needed to be checked and used as required to reduce the speed. When stabilized at about 100 knots the aircraft would be moved to the turn-off side of the runway and at approximately ten knots the parachute could be released. Once released, the SWP (Standard Warning Panel) would be tested and No. 2 engine moved to the fast idle position. Hydraulic pressures could be checked and No. 1 engine shut down when the aircraft had cleared the runway.

If the runway was wet, the braking effect could be greatly reduced and would depend directly upon the amount of water on the runway surface. Generally, under wet conditions, it was recommended that light braking action be commenced once the aircraft was firmly on the ground and the wheels had had time to spin up. The brake application could then be progressively increased and could be held continuously as the speed fell off. When maximum wheel braking was necessary, its effectiveness could be increased by progressive backward movement of the control column as the speed reduced, thereby transferring more weight to the main wheels. Care had to be taken to ensure that this movement was not started at a speed high enough to raise the nose-wheel from the runway. If a slip or skid was suspected, the pressure had to be released momentarily and re-applied gradually.

Once clear of the runway and with No. 1 engine below ten per cent power, flaps and airbrakes would be selected 'IN' and all the non-essential switches turned 'OFF'. It was important to check the recovery of the services hydraulic pressure, thus ensuring that both pumps had been checked.

All students would have covered the full dual syllabus before their first solo, whatever their previous experience. Few students failed to achieve the standard required on schedule, but it need hardly be said that the instructor had to be in no doubt as to the ability of the student to safely operate the aircraft before he was allowed to fly solo. Many factors would enter into this, some of them beyond the control of the student and particularly close (personal) supervision by the instructor would be needed with regard to weather conditions, though this situation was to a certain extent relieved by the requirement for the student to complete a dual ride on the same day as his first solo.

At 150 knots the pilot would deploy the brake parachute. This provided good retardation when the energy levels were high and the brakes would handle the phase when the parachute became fairly ineffective, below about 100 knots IAS. A chute failure was always a bit exciting, as the brakes could not really absorb all the landing energy and would often weld solid if they had to do all the work on their own. As soon as the deceleration was felt and it was most marked, power would be reduced to idle/idle. When stabilized at about 100 knots the aircraft would be moved to the turn-off side of the runway and at approximately 10 knots, the chute could be released.

Apart from the straightforward sortie brief, the student had also to be thoroughly briefed on the crash diversion procedure, action in the event of a brake parachute failure and the precautionary landing technique, as well as the reasons for a precautionary landing. He also had to know the technique for flapless and single-engine landings (the circuits for these having been demonstrated and practised) and the crosswind technique for take-off and landing.

The start-up would be supervised by the instructor from the right-hand side of the T.4 or T.5 and the student would be told to carry out pre-take-off VAs in dispersal. The instructor would then be in the control tower for the duration of the student's sortie. Subsequent solo sorties would, wherever possible, be carried out in the F.1A.

As soon as possible after his first solo, the student would be introduced to variations to the dive circle recovery where it was required to conserve fuel. An important aspect was that the student was being encouraged to think all the while in terms of fuel economy, even though the amounts saved may not have been very large. The first method was the one flown at Mach 0.9 (250 knots). This had a 'height loss/range relationship' of two nautical miles/1,000 feet (300 metres) compared with the SOP (Standard Operating Procedure) descent of one nautical mile/1,000 feet and consequently twice the range could be achieved for the same height loss. The fuel saved was only of the order of 75lb but this might, nevertheless, prove valuable under certain circumstances. The increased time taken to descend must also be considered as to its desirability, along with the fact that the aircraft was at height for a longer period at a low speed and so was vulnerable to strong winds. The descent was entered by throttling back to idle/idle and lowering the nose to maintain Mach 0.9 and full windscreen de-mist had to be used to obtain de-misting at the reduced power. A careful check had to be kept of height and range and rate of descent altered if necessary either by increasing the speed or the power setting. The IAS could not be allowed to fall below 250 knots, for the sharply increasing drag would increase the rate of descent. Due to the low windmilling RPM below 20,000 feet, gradually increasing throttle would be required on one engine in order to keep the A/C power on line.

Should there be reasons why the slower descent was not practicable, a good method which lay between this and the SOP was to descend at Mach 0.9/375 knots with airbrakes 'IN'. This configuration would give a descent rate of one and a half nautical miles/1,000 feet and height/range corrections could be made by increasing or decreasing the airspeed. A range of forty-five nautical miles from Point Alpha would be allowed for this and although under ideal conditions the fuel saving would not be as much as for the slow rate of descent, there would be tactical advantages which might outweigh this consideration.

The student, having already flown up to Mach 1.3 in previous exercises, would fly the T.4 to its airspeed and Mach number limits of 650 knots/ Mach 1.6 (or 600 knots/Mach 1.6 when 'Firestreaks' or 'Red Tops' were fitted) to investigate the handling at these maximum speeds. As the speed increased beyond Mach 0.9 there would be a slight nose-up change of trim and buffeting (the 'cobblestones') at about Mach 0.97. The nose-up change in trim increased during the transonic region up to approximately Mach 1.1 and from Mach 1.2 to 1.6 there would be a nose-down change in trim. Between Mach 1.2 and 1.6, JPTs, cabin altitude, directional trim and position had to be constantly checked. Above Mach 1.2 the student had to remember that the airbrakes must not be selected. The acceleration was normally carried out on one heading, but should a change of heading be necessary which would result in G being applied above Mach 1.2, the handling characteristics might then change appreciably, particularly when carrying missiles. In this speed region, application of aileron might then induce a pronounced adverse yaw, causing reduced roll response and a feeling of control heaviness and difficulty might be experienced in accurate lateral trimming. Therefore, throughout the acceleration up to Mach 1.6, correct rudder trimming was important.

When Mach 1.6 was reached, the aircraft might be some considerable distance from base and a maximum rate turn using full re-heat could be commenced towards the dive circle once clearance to do so had been obtained. Bank would be applied and gradually increased while the turn was pulled tighter until 4½g was being pulled. Although the limitation was 5g, 4½ was normally used in training. This ensured that the fatigue meter did not record a 5g loading and thus helped conserve the fatigue life of the aircraft.

An exercise was flown whereby the student would climb to service ceiling on cold power and re-heat to investigate the climb performance of the Lightning. (The service ceiling was defined as that height above which the rate of climb became less than 1,000 feet/min.) A normal cold power climb was carried out and continued at Mach 0.9 as far as possible on one heading, until the rate of climb on the RCDI fell to 1,000 feet/ minute. Reheat was then selected and the climb continued until the RCDI again fell to 1,000 feet/minute rate of climb. It was pointed out to the student that when re-heat was applied, the aircraft would be very close to the boundaries of the Lightning's performance envelope. The approximate heights of cold-power and re-heat service ceilings were 42,000 feet and 47,000 feet (T.4).

The student had to be made aware that if the exercise was to be of any value, then accurate climbing speeds were essential. If possible, no turns should be made until the ceiling was reached. This necessitated constant checks of fuel and position. Under certain conditions 50,000 feet, the limiting altitude of the aircraft with its current oxygen equipment without a Taylor high altitude helmet, could be reached before the re-heat service ceiling. In that event, the climb had to be discontinued and the aircraft levelled off.

When height was reached, a turn was made to show how little bank could be applied before speed reduced and the aircraft started to judder. The rate of turn was low and it would be noted that the IAS was below 250 knots at Mach 0.9 and therefore the aircraft was on the wrong side of the drag curve. The operational implications were that in order to be manoeuvrable at height, the aircraft must be at a higher IAS in order to overcome the aerodynamics problem and also provide better engine performance due to ram effect of air entering the intake. The acceleration to this higher speed was carried out at the tropopause, where the aircraft performed most efficiently. This then would lead into the energy climb (see below), which was performed during the same sortie.

The energy climb, or 'zoom climb', was the operational method of reaching the Lightning's maximum operational height (50,000 feet, the maximum height with the Mk.20 oxygen regulator and P/2 type mask) and entailed an acceleration to Mach 1.5 at the tropopause, followed by a zoom at a fixed angle of climb until height was reached. Using an attitude of 15 degrees for the zoom, a speed of Mach 1.5 at the tropopause was sufficient to reach 50,000 feet at Mach 1.3. To avoid exceeding 50,000 feet, the level-out had to be commenced at 47,000 feet. If the student commenced the level-out later than required, he had to avoid over-controlling on the pitch forward due to the possibility of illuminating the HYD (Hydraulic) alarm in the AWP (Auxiliary Warning Panel). Full re-heat had to be kept applied and the aircraft turned level at the maximum angle of bank to maintain speed. The rate of turn and the angle of bank would be compared with those which were attained when demonstrating the re-heat service ceiling, then the bank was increased to the judder to note how quickly the speed reduced to a figure too low to operate at.

The fast descent would be carried out at Mach 1.1 until 450 knots - airbrakes out and engines at idle/idle. Due to the high rate of descent it was most important that full de-mist was set at the commencement of the descent and maintained until after the aircraft had been stabilized at low level. At 10,000 feet the power would be set to idle/fast idle. Height was lost very quickly during this type of descent, the distance from 50,000 feet to 2,000 feet being approximately twenty-five miles and the time taken, approximately three minutes. The fast descent therefore had to be commenced close to the dive circle and care had to be taken that the aircraft was initially heading away from land. The student had to allow approximately 5,000 feet for the level-out. Within the context of the actual sortie, it was suggested that a descent to 20,000 feet would be sufficient to demonstrate the most important points while still leaving the aircraft in a reasonable height/range position relative to base for the remainder of the recovery.

During the conversion phase students would complete instrumentation flights using full instrumentation and the standby instruments. The Interim Integrated Flight Instrument System was fitted in the T.4 and F.1. It gave accurate indications of pitch and bank attitude on the attitude indicator. The G.5 compass virtually eliminated all turning errors and gave completely 'dead-beat' indications of heading. The Mk.22C altimeter reduced considerably the lag experienced in older designs. In addition, the information provided by the attitude indicator, altimeter and, in the T.4, the compass was all duplicated for the second seat, giving the pilot full instrumentation as long as electrical power lasted. Nevertheless, the same principles applied for accurate instrument flying: a good instrument scan pattern, smooth control movements and accurate trimming.

Instrument flying would culminate in the instrument rating test which covered the climb, acceleration, supersonic precision turns (at Mach 1.2 at 60 degrees) and subsonic precision turns (at Mach 0.95 and 50 degrees), recovery on the standby instruments and GCA and ILS approaches down to break-off height. The instrument flying sorties included certain parts of the recovery being conducted using the standby instruments and though full instrumentation was available, difficulty would be experienced due to the different scan patterns required, particularly in the case of the Lightning T.4. The Mk.6H standby horizon presented no problems, but the altimeter had a presentation, particularly above 10,000 feet, that was difficult to read accurately and changes in height were difficult to notice. When using this instrument the student had to rely on the RCDI more than he had done previously. Unlike the Lightning T.4, the F.1 did not have a standby direction indicator system fitted. Consequently, timed turns, using the E2 compass only, were practised. For these turns to be accurate, E2 readings had to be taken only in steady flight with the wings level and a constant speed being held. Timing had to commence after the bank had been applied and had to stop only when the wings were level again. Throughout the turns the angle of bank had to be held constant.

GCA and ILS approaches presented no difficulty in the Lightning and were simple to fly accurately, providing that the corrections were made positively and promptly. At speeds below 200 knots the aircraft had a large nose-up attitude in level flight and the RCDI played an important part in maintaining height. Extremely accurate speeds and rates of descent could be maintained providing that the aircraft was correctly trimmed and power corrections were not over-controlled. During dual instrument flying sorties, approaches could be flown to well below the recommended break-off heights.

Before carrying out aerobatics in the Lightning, the student had to be briefed on a few points. The Lightning was a heavy aircraft and it therefore had a large amount of inertia. If the nose were allowed to drop too much below the horizon during manoeuvres, a considerable height loss resulted. Manoeuvres such as loops, barrel rolls and wing-overs used up a large amount of sky. Therefore, a very good lookout had to be maintained during these aerobatics. It was also very easy to over-stress the aircraft unless a careful eye was kept on the airspeed and accelerometer. Without missiles it was difficult to hold the nose of the aircraft above the horizon when inverted. For this reason, slow rolls were best performed at 370 knots until the pilot was reasonably experienced. Slow rolls were not to be performed at less than 350 knots.

With the Autopilot Master Switch 'OFF', it was possible to lose one degree of tailplane movement. The AMS was therefore always 'ON' during aerobatics, but the Pitch and Roll/Yaw switches were 'OFF'. Loops were started at a speed which required re-heat for completion of the manoeuvre. Speeds were therefore at least 450 knots with or without re-heat until experience was gained. A minimum speed of 200 knots was aimed for at the top of the loop, but if the speed was less the back pressure was relaxed and the aircraft allowed to fly round the manoeuvre until the speed had built up to at least 270 knots on the descent. Loops were never started at less than 400 knots. Hesitation rolls were forbidden.

Students were given the chance to gain experience in flying the Lightning at low level, a cross-country being included in the OCU syllabus to be flown at 500 feet AGL. This was comparable to the lowest height at which operational flying would be carried out on a squadron. The legs of the cross-country were flown at different speeds, thus providing experience in operating the Lightning at both range (i.e. most fuel-economical) speed and at the maximum which would be used during PI. In the same way, turns would be flown at different angles of bank.

The AFCS (Automatic Flight Control System) had also to be mastered and the student learned the differences between the T.5 and the T.4. They were basically similar, although once the engines were started the student would find that the JPTs at idling RPM would be higher on the T.5 than on earlier marks and when taxiing, the higher idling thrust would require more use of the brakes. The take-off would not normally present any difficulty, providing that the student had been briefed on the greater stick force required to raise the nose-wheel when missiles were being carried.

Flying the F.3 after, say, the T.5 carried some minor, but important differences that the student pilot had to familiarize himself with. On take-off the F.3 had a much lighter nose and much lighter controls all round. It also accelerated faster than the T.5, was much noisier, particularly when accelerating after take-off. The 'cobbles' would start with less warning and were more intense. The student would quickly note, too, the improved visibility from the cockpit and the fact that the approach was easier to fly, but that the lighter tailplane might lead to a high round-out. Equally, the brake parachute would pull the nose-wheel off the runway if it was streamed with the stick not fully forward.

After learning to fly the Lightning well, basic and advanced radar courses, using Canberras as targets, would follow. The basic course (when night flying would be carried out as well, with two additional handling sorties (one dual, one solo) and at least one solo Rad-ex) involved a total of fourteen hours' dual and five and a quarter hours' solo. On the advanced radar phase, nine hours, forty minutes (consisting of eight hours' dual and one hour, forty minutes' solo time), would be spent learning to use 'Red Top' and automated and pilot-interpreted AI radar. Additional sorties, probably one dual and two solo, would be flown starting with an ORP scramble and using targets.

Then and only then the embryonic Lightning pilot was posted to a front-line fighter squadron or, as in some cases, it was off to MU as a test pilot, or to OCU as an instructor. Whatever his destination, he could be sure of a thrilling, sometimes dangerous, experience in the hot seat of the 'Frightening' Lightning!

The LCU had moved to Middleton St. George in August 1961 and become the Lightning Conversion Squadron (LCS). Group Captain Freddie Rothwell was Station Commander, Wing Commander Charles Laughton OC Ops and Squadron Leader Ken J. Goodwin Commander of the LCS. The LCS was without aircraft until December 1961 when their first T.4 came, only to leave almost as quickly as it had arrived. It returned six months later after a major rework of the hydraulic pipes in No. 1 engine bay. The LCS continued to borrow Lightnings, now mainly from 56 and 'Treble One' Squadrons. Usually, only a single aircraft for a few days at a time could be spared, but nevertheless the LCS was responsible for the successful conversion of several squadrons to Lightnings. Not until 27 June 1962 did the LCS receive its own aircraft, when T.4 XM970 was delivered to Middleton St. George and was coded 'G'. By the end of July the number of T.4s had risen to four. One of the LCS's first students was AVM 'Tubby' Clayton, AOC 12 Group, who was sent solo after only five dual rides. By the end of October the LCS had eight T.4s on strength. On 12 December 1962 XM993 ran off the runway at Middleton St. George after landing while returning from Chivenor and turned over. Fortunately, Al Turley of the LCS and his student, Wing Commander G. M. Gibbs, escaped before the aircraft caught fire and burned out.

On 1 June 1963 the LCS was re-titled 226 OCU (Operational Conversion Unit) and shortly afterwards it received seven ex-74 Squadron F.1s, via 60 MU (Maintenance Unit), where they had been overhauled. In August the OCU introduced a red and white livery which was based on the St. George's Cross and reflected the unit's 'shadow' identity, which was adopted during the many Fighter Command exercises that would follow and in time of crisis.

Ken Goodwin was posted to Bangkok in October 1963. That same month, Squadron Leader Dave Seward arrived from 56 Squadron to be the Chief Ground Instructor in the ground school. 'Already,' he recalls, 'Geoff Steggall and Roly Jackson from the EQS had developed an effective organization. I was sent to Coltishall in February 1964 to set up the OCU there prior to their move in April. [Middleton St. George had been sold, for just £340,000, to become Teesside Airport and on 13 April 226 OCU and its fourteen Lightnings flew to their new home at Coltishall.] 74 Squadron had moved to Leuchars and we had Coltishall to ourselves, save for the search and rescue helicopters. Setting up the OCU at Coltishall went very smoothly and the station personnel, from the CO, Group Captain Roger Topp, down were all very enthusiastic to receive the new unit.[1] The plan was to provide the OCU with three squadrons. No.1 would be responsible for ab initio conversion to the Lightning, the course length being around seventy hours, split between the T.4 and solo hours on the F.1A. No.2 would give basic radar training on the AI.23 (and AI.23B for pilots going to F.2 and F.2A squadrons in RAF Germany), while No.3 would provide advanced radar training on the AI.23B for students joining UK F.3 and F.6 squadrons and Cyprus. Occasionally it would operate Interceptor Weapons Instructor (IWI) courses for the RAF Germany Lightning squadrons and be responsible for advanced weapons training, including the AI.23B/'Red Top' missile system. (Later, 3 Squadron operated only T.5s and what little solo flying there was on this final part of the course was completed in the two-seat aircraft.) During 1964 Les Davis, OC 3 Squadron was away with the front-line squadrons and OC 2 Squadron had not yet converted, so the OCU operated essentially a two-squadron organization. Students were a mixture of ex-Hunter and Javelin pilots, including Flying Officer (later ACM Sir,) 'Bill' Wratten, Paul 'Humpty' Holmes, Al Morgan and Gerry Crumbie and various staff officers.

The OCU was not without incident, as Dave Seward recalls: 'An accident on 11 September 1964 involved a bail out by Squadron Leader Terry Bond, the Unit Test Pilot. He was flying an F.1 on a post-Minor air test when he could not get the starboard undercarriage leg fully down, as it had suffered a serious hydraulic failure. The secondary system also failed and after a series of low, slow flypasts, it was obvious that there had been a sequence valve malfunction and the gear was stuck partially (almost halfway) down on both sides. It was therefore decided that he would eject. A runway landing was considered, but advice was that the aircraft could cartwheel. Terry Bond ejected as near to the coast as possible to ensure the aircraft went into the sea, but he hoped to keep his feet dry. In the event, he landed about twenty yards off the shore just south of Bacton with the helicopter virtually waiting for him. I had worked out his ejection area using met winds to 10,000 feet and he was quite annoyed that I'd played it just too close. He was unhurt and quickly returned to flying status. There was one other accident, which was really an incident that was very well handled by the student, Ian MacFadyen. He had a nose wheel stuck in the up position and landed on the runway keeping the nose up until the last moment, causing only minimal damage to the aircraft.

AB INITIO

'In 1965 the OCU began to expand to its full strength and during this period we received the first ab initio students straight from Training Command. On the first of these courses were John Ward, Dickie Duckett (who would later lead the Red Arrows) and Doug Aylward, who all did exceptionally well on the Lightning.' Aylward, who was from Darlington, went to Durham School and had planned a career as a vet, but, attracted by the adventure and challenge of flying, he applied to join the Royal Air Force and was accepted in December 1961. In mid-1965, Wing Commander Mick Swiney took over the OCU as chief instructor and OC Flying Wing. On 20 April XS419, the OCU's first T.5, arrived. By now the F.1s were being replaced with F.1As from 56 and 11 Squadrons.

XM135, which had been the first F.1 assigned to 74 Squadron in 1961 and which joined 135/226 OCU on 12 January 1964, was assigned to 33 MU Lyneham on 12 January 1965 for modification for target facilities duties. On 22 July 1966 XM135 hit the headlines for all the wrong reasons, as 'Taffy' Holden a RAF Engineer Branch officer and the CO of a civilian manned aircraft storage unit recalls: 'XM135 was being prepared for despatch to a Target Facilities Flight, but over a period of weeks, it had been giving no end of trouble. Each time it was being flight tested, the pilot found that on the initial few yards of a take-off run, the inverter, supplying power to the primary flight instruments, would cut out and the stand by inverter would have to cut in, clearly an unsatisfactory state of affairs. Electricians were using every trick in their trade to establish the cause, each time thinking that they had removed, replaced and tightened every likely component. With nothing out of order, they would seek another test flight. It was a Boscombe Down pilot who next attempted to fly the aircraft, found the same problem persisting and refused to fly until a more positive explanation could be determined.

'Back to the drawing board, electricians decided to devise some tests which might isolate the fault and indicate roughly where and which component was at fault. They intended to ask the next test pilot to switch in and out parts of circuits, using trailing wires from the likely circuits to temporary switches in the cockpit and to do these electrical switchings before and after each few yards of a simulated take off run, when the fault was manifest. The temporary wires from internal circuitry required the cockpit canopy to be removed and in this state the aircraft was made ready for another air test. Being a pilot, it was easiest for me, as CO, to request the services of a qualified test pilot, from wherever I could find one, but for the next test on XM135, no pilot was available for at least another week. With my unit closing down, many civilians being made redundant, a timetable of clearance being upset with this 'rogue' aircraft, there was much tetchiness and irritation amongst my staff. The intended Boscombe Down pilot, knowing I was a pilot, suggested I might try the test myself.[2] He suggested using an out of use runway (Runway 36) as I would only be using thirty or forty yards at a time. He suggested using a Land Rover to communicate with Air Traffic Control and to get their clearance for each movement of the aircraft. However, there was one remaining minor problem. I had only sat in a Lightning cockpit once before and I had no idea how to start its two Rolls-Royce Avon engines! The foreman of engine trades gave me a five minute briefing on how to do this and XM135 was towed out to Runway 05 on 22 July for my electrical tests.

'It was by way of extraordinary good fortune that my engine foreman explained that, although I would not be needing reheat, that reheat needed the throttles to be pushed past a reheat 'gate' and one had to feel for the gate keys, behind the throttle, to unlock. My only other knowledge of the Lightning was what I could remember from pilot's notes. At each test flight by the qualified pilot, I would be in ATC with a copy pilot's notes, should he need any aircraft figures to be relayed to him. One or two figures stuck in my mind, namely that the undercarriage had a maximum speed before it should be retracted and I had an even vaguer figure of about 150 knots for a landing speed. Some extra knots would be required for each 1,000lbs of unused fuel, but I did not need to bother with any such figures for the test, which I was to undertake.

'I was correctly strapped into the cockpit (seated on the in situ parachute and ejection seat) and after starting the engines and holding the aircraft static, on the brakes, I did the necessary preliminaries for the electrical checks in the cockpit, checking the notes I had scribbled on a notepad which lay on the coaming in front of me. All seemed ready for the first test and I indicated to the Land Rover to obtain ATC clearance for use of the short 30 or 40 yards of runway. Holding the brakes I gradually opened the throttles to about 90%. My feeling at the time was the unexpected heavy vibration of Avon power held against the brakes. I did a quick check of the temporary electrical switches and circuitry lights, then released the brakes. That initial punch from the thrust was quite remarkable and I moved the expected 30 to 40 yards before I throttled back and applied the brakes. So far so good. I made some notes, altered some more switch positions, noted the on/off lights and prepared for the next test. This was done in a similar fashion and I was leaving the 'fault' diagnosis to my electrical staff who would have to interpret my notes. I needed to do one more test and ATC had noted that I had only used about 100 yards total, so they were quite happy to clear me for a similar short distance. ATC had also been holding up a fuel bowser and trailer with 3,600 gallons of AVTAG for awaiting C-130 aircraft refuelling; they decided to allow the bowser to cross the runway. On opening the throttles for that final test, I obviously pushed them too far, misinterpreting the thrust, because of the unexpected heavy vibration and they got locked into reheat. Yes, I did use some expletives but I had no time to think of getting out of reheat, because in front of me, the bowser and trailer had just crossed the runway, from right to left, so my thoughts were to make sure I was missing them by sufficient margin. No, I couldn't steer to clear them; reheat takes you in a straight path like a bullet out of a gun. The time between finding myself in reheat and just missing the bowser was less than half the time I have taken to write this sentence.

'Before my thoughts could again return to getting myself out of reheat, I was gathering speed and about to cross the main duty runway, where a Comet had just passed on its take off run. I then had no time to look for reheat gate keys, my eyes were on what next lay ahead. Two things, the end of the short runway 07 and just beyond was the small village of Bradenstoke which I just had to miss. There was no chance of stopping, none whatsoever. I had gained flying speed (that is what reheat is for, short sharp take offs) and I had no runway left. I did not need to heave it off the runway, the previous test pilot had trimmed it exactly for take-off and only a slight backward touch on the stick and I was gathering height and speed. Then my thought was to get my speed back in case I should damage the undercarriage. Incidentally, I could not have raised the undercarriage; the ground servicing locks were in place for safety reasons. With only clear blue sky in front of me, I could then search and feel for those gate keys. Yes, I found them and thanked my lucky stars that my engine foreman had quite incidentally told me of their location and I was soon able to get the speed back to (I am guessing now) about 250 knots. My next thoughts were to keep Lyneham airfield in sight and where had the Comet got to, the one I had missed a few seconds ago? Then I asked myself, should I eject and where and when? No, I could not; the safety pins were in the ejection seat and safe for servicing, not for flying. My only alternative then was to attempt a landing, but how does one interpolate or extrapolate Tiger Moth, Chipmunk, Harvard flying to a two engined, 11 ton, beast like the Lightning?

'After regaining my bearings, a little composure and simply by observation, making sure that the Comet had been warned away, I decided I should attempt a landing on the duty runway and direction. I was trying to combine all my limited flying experience into a few minutes of DIY flight 'training' on a Lightning. It wasn't easy, but I must admit that some of the elementary rudiments of my proper flying training and flight theory were coming in useful. I needed to get the feel of the aircraft, if I was to get it back on the ground. My first approach was ridiculous, I could tell that my speed, height, rate of descent, even alignment wasn't correct and my best plot was to go round again. This time making sure that my throttles would be well below reheat position. A second approach was no better. I had some aspects better, but as the duty runway 25 is on the lip of an escarpment, with a valley floor beyond, my rate of descent took me below runway height and I found myself adding power to get back to the right level. More power also meant more speed and I was trying to get to something like 150 knots for landing, but the uncoordinated attempt was becoming a mess so I abandoned it, took myself away on a very wide circuit of Lyneham and decided to land in the opposite direction. This I thought would give me more time to get the 'feel' right and if I made a mess of the landing, I would overrun the runway and just drop (crash) into the valley beyond. In that direction, with a messed up landing, I would have no fear of crashing into Lyneham village.

'The long final leg of this approach gave me the thinking time that I needed and I gradually got the feel that speed, alignment, rate of descent, height and approach angle were better. I plonked it down at about the right position off the runway threshold, but just forgot that I was in a nose wheel aircraft and emulated my best three wheelers in a Chipmunk or Harvard. The result was that I crunched the rubber block which encases the brake parachute cables. However, I had got down, but I then had to stop. I obviously knew the Lightning had a brake parachute, but where was the chute lever, button or knob? There, I found it marked 'Brake Chute' and I pulled it and I could then look ahead and concentrate on keeping straight and somewhere near the centre line. I hung on to the brake lever, I wasn't slowing as much as I would like, so I just kept up my hand pressure on the brakes. I had about 100 yards of runway left when I stopped and even then, I didn't know that the brake parachute had dropped off as soon as it was deployed, because the cable had been severed as a result of my super tail wheel three pointer.

'XM135 was towed back to the hangar and I was taken to see the medical officer who gave me some pills to calm my nerves. I felt reasonably calm because I had almost killed myself on five occasions in that twelve minute flight, yet I had miraculously survived. What is more, I would see my wife and young family again. Two or three times in that same twelve minutes,

I thought I would never ever see them again. My only priority was to save my own skin, I was not thinking about the non-insured loss of a Lightning 1A aircraft. The minor damage to the aircraft was repaired with a new set of brake shoes and a new rubber chute block.

'Although the tests I did and the ensuing flight did not immediately provide a reason for the initial electrical fault, my electrical staff, with additional assistance from English Electric, Samlesbury eventually did. Apparently, in early versions of the Lightning, there was to be a ground test button fitted into the standby inverter circuit. It was never fitted to the Mk.1A but the wires were left in the looms. It was one of these redundant wires which shorted on to the UHF radio as it moved on its trunnions when the aircraft nudged forward on take-off. Who would have thought I should risk my life to find it, in the way I did?

'There was a subsequent Inquiry to find out what had happened and why and to make recommendations for it never to happen again. As I was the Commanding Officer of the Unit, I was responsible for my own as well as the service actions of all my staff. I was not acting against any orders in the Flight Order Book which I religiously kept up to date. But those orders did not cater for engineering officers doing investigative type checks on Lightnings. They were later amended. After the Unit Inquiry I had to go up in front of the Commander-in-Chief. That was when I thought my career would be placed in jeopardy. I even thought that my coveted 'wings' would be taken from me; I had no idea how the incident was being regarded by Command or indeed Air Ministry. But as I stood in front of Air Marshal Sir Kenneth Porter he read the proceedings, asked me if I agreed with his view that "With the limited flying experience that I had the test would have been better left to an experienced and current Lightning test pilot." I agreed of course. He then told me to remove my hat, sit down and proceeded to tell me some of his unfortunate flying incidents in Mesopotamia in the Middle East. I was thankful that nothing more was to become of the incident and that I still had a job to do back at 33 Maintenance Unit, Lyneham.

'I coped with all the official communications regarding the incident, but what I was unprepared for was the release of the story to the public. I had had very little experience of working with the press, certainly none with radio, TV, national and world press. I had no training in how to deal with their quest for news. My Command Headquarters suggested I went away on leave before press releases were made by Air Ministry. This I did and took my family off camping to Jesola, in Italy. Imagine my complete surprise when, on the first day of camp, on my way to find some ice, someone shouted

"Hello Taffy, I've just been reading about your Lightning flight!" The world seemed a very small place. On returning to the UK I was overwhelmed to find that the incident was still front-line news. People wanted to write articles in newspapers, books, magazines, interviews on TV and radio and underhand attempts to hear my account of what had happened. Having admitted that I had made an unwise decision to do the ground tests, I decided that the unwanted publicity that I had attracted was in no way going to be for financial gain. I steadfastly refused offers although for a two page article in the Sunday Express, I requested the editors to make a contribution to the RAF Benevolent Fund. Despite prompts, no moneys were ever handed over and I became very disillusioned with all publicity media. Some friends thought I had gained reward for an article in *Mayfair*; it was written without my knowledge and authority, but, because it was factually correct, I had no redress from the Press Complaints Board. Nonetheless, I was extremely annoyed.

'Some years after the incident, my hidden fears of high speed flight came to the surface and I had to spend two periods in hospital. I had not come to terms with the emotional side of the event. To return to my wife and family after five close encounters with death, was indeed a miraculous experience, but I had not been honest with myself, to accept it as such, so I needed psychiatric help. I could recall the technicalities of the flight without any hang-ups, but was unwilling to talk about that emotional side of the ordeal until I was placed under medical drugs to bring those emotions to the surface. That was a rewarding experience and it gave me a much better understanding of people who might need that same kind of help, after similar unfortunate occurrences.'

By the late 1960s 226 OCU at Coltishall had forty-two Lightnings on its inventory, divided fairly evenly between the three versions, to which eight F.3s were added in June 1970. Some of the F.1As were now periodically operated as targets, in much the same way as the Target Facility Flight (TFF) Lightnings, with the AI.23 radar replaced with a Lüneberg Lens to create a larger radar 'signature'. Along the way there were a few accidents at 226 OCU at Coltishall. In 1966 three Lightnings were lost, though all three pilots were uninjured. On 15 March Captain Al Peterson USAF safely ejected from XM190 after an ECU fire and the F.1A crashed into the North Sea off Cromer. (On 6 May F.1A XM213 veered off the runway on take-off from Coltishall and hit a fence when the landing gear retracted prematurely during take-off.) CFI, Squadron Leader Paul Hobley, who was unhurt was flying the F.1A. 'As CFI,' recalls Flight Lieutenant Alex Reed, his flight commander who authorized the flight, 'Paul could only fly on a "grace and favour" basis. SCT (Staff Conversion Training), though, was required. I was coming back from lunch through the hangar. By then I knew there had been an accident. Paul had done a normal take-off, but he took the gear up too quickly and sat it down on its ventral tank. Guys who saw it said they saw a great stream of flame going down the runway and off onto the grass, thirty yards short of a brick building. He was very lucky to walk away. Paul just looked at me. *Sorry Alex, I just f—ed it!* was all he said. "Don't worry," I said, 'there but for the grace of God...'[3]

On 1 July Flying Officer Geoff Fish, who was on his first T.5 solo in XS453, suffered an undercarriage failure on the down-wind leg in the circuit. At the end of runway zero-five Wing Commander Mick Swiney was waiting to start his instrument rating test with Don Oakden in a T.4; Swiney recalls: 'Fish flew by the tower at 500 feet and we could all see that the young South African was in trouble. He was told by Pete Van Gucci, the DOCFW (Deputy Officer Commanding Flying Wing), to re-cycle the undercarriage. I decided we could go up and see what was what. We formated close behind his tail and could see quite clearly that there was a 'hugger's muddle'. The sequencing of the oleos and the undercarriage doors had gone wrong. A 'D' door had closed prior to the undercarriage leg being retracted. It was quite clear that he was not going to get that aircraft down on the ground. Fish would have to eject. We stayed with him the whole time. SAR were alerted and positioned over the sea off Happisburgh. Fish seemed very calm, although his fuel was now running out. Flight Lieutenant Jimmy Jewell in the tower had the presence of mind to tell Fish to check that his straps were done up tightly – they weren't as it happened. He had failed to insert one of the harness lugs properly during strapping-in prior to start-up. Coolly, Fish undid and then reconnected them. By now his No. 1 engine had flamed out and he had to go now while he still had a modicum of control provided by the No. 2 engine. At about 3,000 feet he ejected perfectly. His chute opened, as it should have. From my cockpit it all seemed to happen in slow motion. Then, to our great alarm, the Lightning started to head back towards land! Essentially, though, it nosed into the sea. Fish was picked up so quickly he hardly got his feet wet.'

On 24 October 1966 Flying Officer Roger J. Colebrook on 226 OCU, who at that time was undergoing conversion as a 'First Tourist', was flying T.4 XM968 for his first solo on type. Whilst climbing at 450 knots with full cold power set, 'FIRE 1' illuminated as the aircraft was passing through 6,000 feet. Full fire drill was taken during the turn back towards base, but the light remained on until the ventral was jettisoned into the sea one mile off shore. Colebrook recovered to Coltishall and he attempted to join downwind but was too fast. A wide single-engine circuit was made, followed by a precautionary landing. The brake parachute was slow to deploy and the No. 2 engine was shut down on the runway. The T.4 was steered onto the ORP (Operational Readiness Pan) and stopped; the brakes were then released to prevent them welding on. The pilot's reactions to the emergency were copybook and he was awarded a 'good show' in the December issue of the *Flight Safety Review*.[4]

Roger Colebrook recalls: 'I was well aware that all was not well, as my total fuel remaining was decreasing at an alarming rate on the fuel gauges. I was not aware that it was being pumped overboard by the aircraft system, owing to the fact that the seal that was designed to keep the fuel in was not carrying out its design function. I landed with about 400lb total fuel remaining, having been airborne for only ten minutes! As I climbed out on to the ORP after shutting down, fuel continued to run out of the ventral fitting, much to the consternation of the fire crew as the wheel brakes were red-hot. If I had carried out a missed approach, the aircraft would have run out of fuel and become a total loss on that occasion! As this was my first solo my instructor, Flight Lieutenant Michael J. Graydon[5] was in the control tower. He debriefed me after the flight and commented that the observers in the control tower had seen what they thought was smoke coming from the underside of the aircraft, as I passed downwind. They decided, however, not to tell me at the time, in case I panicked!

'Following my debrief I made myself a coffee in the crew room and recounted my dice with death to others on the course, who wanted to know what had happened. While this was going on, several different instructors came in and engaged me in rather forced conversation, or peered in the door at me before returning to their previous duties. Later, I discovered that a heated debate was going on in the operations room as to whether my nerve had gone and that my next flight should be with an instructor, or whether I was considered sane enough to fly an aircraft solo immediately to complete my first solo exercises. The various instructors had been sent to make an appraisal and report back to the flight commander! I am pleased to say that I was considered normal and launched off a short while later on my second First Solo!

'The debate as to whether I needed to fly with an instructor or solo almost led to a second incident when I got airborne on my next flight. Whichever way the decision went, I was to fly in a T.4. Initially, the line engineers were told that an aircraft was to be prepared for a dual flight. This necessitated the activation of the right-hand seat, where the instructor sat. Harness straps were made ready for their occupant and critically, the liquid oxygen for that seat had to be turned on. Subsequently, after it had been decided that I should fly solo again, the line engineers were given new instructions. The right-hand seat was now to be de-activated! As a result, a harness-restraint apron was fitted to the right-hand seat, to ensure that loose straps and connectors did not flail about during manoeuvres and, critically, the liquid-oxygen supply to that seat was now turned off! Shortly after commencing my take-off run, as I hurtled down the runway in afterburner, the centralised warning system activated to alert me to a problem. This was exactly the same system that had alerted me in the fire on my first solo. Although it covered all critical aircraft system failures, it used exactly the same audio alert to draw the pilot's attention to the panel, where an appropriate caption illuminated to advise the pilot of the particular failure he had experienced.

'After my experience on the previous flight, my adrenaline level was probably higher than normal as I roared down the runway and when the alarm bells sounded, I found I had instinctively cancelled the afterburners as I glanced down at the system warning panel. I suppose I had expected to see another fire warning; however, the 'OXY 2' light was illuminated. Realizing my mistake, I pushed the throttles back through the afterburner gate and continued with my take-off, lifting off quite a bit further down the runway than normal.

'I expect the line engineers were only notified of the change to 'solo' configuration at the last minute. Consequently, the line pressure in the instructor's oxygen system had started to leak away when the system was turned off. The time at which the system activated the low pressure warning, (OXY 2), just happened to coincide with my take-off and could have resulted in an aborted take-off, or an excursion into the Safeland Barrier, due to my inexperience.

'Despite my parlous introduction to the Lightning, I enjoyed every minute on the aeroplane. So much so that, when I was posted to Central Flying School to become an instructor at the end of my tour, I protested that I wanted to stay in the air defence role. In doing so, I presumed I would be posted to another Lightning squadron, as this was the only air defence aircraft in service with the RAF at the time. Unbeknown to me, a decision had been taken to decommission HMS *Eagle*, the Royal Navy's secondary aircraft carrier. Consequently, its complement of Phantom FG.1s was in the process of being transferred to the RAF for the formation of an air defence squadron, with a secondary role of fleet defence. The intention was to back up the Royal Navy's only air defence Phantom squadron on HMS *Ark Royal*. The Air Member for Personnel accepted my request for a change of posting and I found myself posted to 43 Squadron, operating the Phantom FG.1 from RAF Leuchars, in Fife. Having protested once I did not feel I could object to this new posting. I accepted my fate and became a WIWOLA! (Wish I Was On Lightnings Again).'[6]

Flight Lieutenant Alex Reed recalled another occasion, on 2 January 1967 when he was coming back from lunch ('these things always seemed to happen after lunch!') and he bumped into Squadron Leader Terry Carlton, OC No.2 Squadron. Reed recalls, 'I was surprised because I knew he should be airborne. He said, looking across the airfield at a plume of smoke, 'That's my aircraft!' Carleton had been on a dual radar sortie in XM971 with his student, Flight Lieutenant Tony Gross, when, on the climb-out shortly after take-off, there was a very expensive noise internally and an immediate loss of power. (The radome had come loose and the engines had ingested the debris.) Assuming control, Carlton throttled back and commenced a recovery to Coltishall. On a high downwind leg, he applied throttle to check his descent, but found that he had no power. Gross ejected first, Carlton going at about 800 feet and the aircraft crashing at Tunstead. A Whirlwind helicopter from the SAR Flight on 202 Squadron on the base recovered both pilots, each of whom suffered minor spinal injuries.'

Carlton was involved in another incident, on 12 September, returning from working up on Red Section in a four-ship formation. Alex Reed was flying No. 3: 'We carried out an echelon starboard break into the circuit and Terry called "Downward for the formation". As he came round on finals at the far end there was a "twinkle, twinkle, boom!" Obviously, an aircraft had crashed! Terry saw this as well and as we had all broken and fanned out bethought his No. 4 must have crashed. Terry called, "Check in!" and we all did. I was just coming off the runway as the crash vehicles were heading for the column of smoke, 200 yards off the runway. Well, we were all here. Puzzled, we wondered, "Where did that come from?" 'Flight Lieutenant Jock Sneddon, a Wattisham TTF pilot, had experienced a cockpit fire in XM136. Sneddon ejected safely and he landed at Scottow, close to RAF Coltishall. The F.1, which had begun its career with 74 Squadron at Coltishall, seemed to know its way home because the wreckage landed on the airfield boundary!'

During the afternoon of 7 March 1967 there occurred another incident at Coltishall, the first in a series to plague the T.5 Flight Lieutenant Mike Graydon and his instructor, Flight Lieutenant Bob Offord. They were at

English Electric chief engineer William Edward Willoughby 'Teddy' Petter. In 1950 Petter left English Electric to join Folland Aircraft and responsibility for the design and subsequent development of the P.1 passed to F. W. (later Sir Freddie) Page.

P.1A WG760 being flown by English Electric's chief test pilot, Wing Commander Roland P. 'Bee' Beamont. On 11 August 1954, on only its third flight, Beamont broke the sound barrier making the English Electric Britain's first truly supersonic jet, capable of exceeding Mach 1 in level flight.

P.1B/F.1 XG331 which first flew on 14 May 1959 and T.4/P.11 XL628, the prototype T.4 two-seat variant, which Bee Beamont had first flown from Warton on 6 May 1959 and was abandoned by Test Pilot, J. 'Jimmy' W. C. Squier on 1 October 1959 over the Irish Sea when he was fortunate to escape death after ejecting from XL628.

P.1B/F.1 XG308 which was first flown on 16 May 1958.

On 4 April 1957 the first prototype P.1B (XA847) exceeded Mach 1 without reheat on its first flight in the hands of Bee Beamont.

Bee Beamont piloting XR754. This aircraft went to the Handling Squadron/A&AEE at Boscombe Down on 3 December 1965 and was issued to 5 Squadron on 2 February 1967. That same year it was modified to F.6 at Warton and went on to serve on 23, 11 and 5 Squadrons, flying for the last time on 24 June 1988. It was then used on BDR (Bomb Damage Repair).

Last minute adjustments to a pilot's helmet prior to flying B.1B XG336/C on the AFDS at RAF Coltishall. XG336, which first flew on 25 August 1959, was the second P.1B delivered to the AFDS at Coltishall. On 1 September 1959 the AFDS (Air Fighting Development Squadron) was formed at Coltishall under the command of Wing Commander Jimmy Dell after moving from West Raynham, whose runways were unsuitable for Lightning operations and on 4 January 1960 the LCS (Lightning Conversion School) was formed at the station. Its job was to train Lightning pilots for the front-line squadrons in Fighter Command. (via Tony Aldridge)

Squadron Leader John Howe climbs out of F.1 XM135 after his flight. XM135 first flew on 14 November 1959 and was issued to the AFDS (Air Fighting Development Squadron) and at Coltishall it was loaned to 74 Squadron and coded 'R'. It is now on permanent display at the Imperial War Museum (IWM), Duxford, since being flown there on 20 November 1974. (AVM John Howe Collection)

F.1 XM145/Q during reheat-runs at Warton, one of which caused severe damage to the rear fuselage. This Lightning first flew on 18 March 1960 when it was piloted by 'Dizzy' de Villiers and completed 17 flights prior to delivery to the 'Tigers' on 14 May 1962. It joined 226 OCU on 3 June 1964 and later, Leuchars TFF, on 26 April 1966. On 24 January 1972 XM145 made its last flight when it was flown to 60 MU Leconfield for store. It was declared a NEA (No Effective Airframe) on 30 November 1973 and used for spares before being placed on the RAF Leconfield dump by June 1974 and it was reduced to scrap late that same year.

Jacques Kleynhans, born in South Africa in 1928, poses on the ladder of XM146/L his 74 'Tiger' Squadron F.1 Lightning. From early on all young Kleynhams wanted to do was fly aircraft. However his father, who was a practical man, said that was fine but he must first of all get himself a proper career. So Jacques qualified as an accountant and found himself a young wife, Desiree, who was from the Port Elizabeth area of South Africa. Jacques never practised as an accountant, but immediately applied to the RAF and was offered a twelve year commission. On completion of his initial training this was raised to sixteen years which he was delighted to accept. His first posting was to 74 Squadron and he was there when they converted onto Lightnings, a huge thrill for him. He had the honour of being the first member of the 'Tigers' to fly solo at night on the type.

74 Squadron pilots with Squadron Leader John Howe.

74 'Tiger' Squadron Lightnings on the line at RAF Coltishall, where the squadron was the first to equip with the Lightning in the summer of 1960.

74 'Tiger' Squadron
Lightnings on the line at
RAF Coltishall in 1961.

Squadron leader (later AVM)
John Howe, commanding 74
'Tiger' Squadron.

Above: F.1 XM139/C on 74 'Tiger' Squadron armed with Firestreak missiles. This Lightning was first flown on 12 January 1960 and was delivered to the 'Tigers' on 21 June 1960. It joined 226 OCU (as '139') on 21 April 1964.

Left: Flight Lieutenant David Jones on 74 'Tiger' Squadron poses for the camera in front of the Squadron's F.1s at RAF Coltishall in 1961.

Lightning on re-heat take off.

On August Bank Holiday Monday in 1962 as Flight Lieutenant Ernie E. Jones on 56 Squadron taxied out for his display at RAF Upper Heyford his F.1A caught fire but prompt action by the USAF fire crew minimised damage to the aircraft.

Squadron Leader (later Group Captain) Dave Seward, commanding 56 Squadron.

In 1963 56 Squadron was selected as the Fighter Command squadron aerobatic team and the 'Firebirds' adopted scarlet fins, spines and leading edges to wings and tailplanes.

T.4 XM993 on the LCS, which was written-off after over-running the runway at Middleton St. George on 12 December 1962. A1 Turley and student, Wing Commander C.M. Gibbs escaped before the aircraft caught fire and burned out.

F.1A 'S' on 56 Squadron, one of only twenty-four built and the first Lightnings to be fitted with a production in-flight refuelling probe closes in to refuel to tank from Vickers Valiant in January 1964. In 1965 the Valiants were scrapped following metal fatigue problems. The F.1 had the necessary plumbing for flight refuelling with the provision for a detachable flight-refuelling probe under the port wing and it became the responsibility of 56 Squadron to pioneer flight-refuelling in the Lightning squadrons. Squadron Leader Dave Seward and his pilots began perfecting the art of air-to-air refuelling in 1962. At first they trained on USAF F-100Ds with Boeing KC-97s as tankers, before air refuelling in earnest in 1962 with Vickers Valiant tankers. The loss of the Valiant tanker fleet in 1965 resulted in a rapid conversion of Victor B.1 bombers to K.1A in-flight refuelling tankers, the first flying on 28 April 1965.

T.4 XM973/T on 111 Squadron at RAF Wattisham. This T-bird, which was first flown on 17 May 1961, operated on 'Treble One' from 1 January 1964 to late July 1964.

Squadron Leader (later AVM) George Black on 111 Squadron with RCAF exchange pilot Flight Lieutenant Robert Chisholm at Wattisham on 8 April 1964 after a flight in T4 XM973/T. F1A's 'K' and 'H' are the other aircraft in the photo. Chisholm, an exchange pilot on 111 Squadron for three years, later became a Major General in the CAF. (Canadian Forces Joint Imagery Centre, Ottawa)

On 22 July 1964 T.4 XM966, which was used to test the Microcell air-to-air rocket pack was lost over the Irish Sea when its fin disintegrated during rolling manoeuvres at Mach 1.8 at 35,000 feet with the rocket pack extended. English Electric test pilot Jimmy Dell was able to slow the T.4, hoping to recover it to Warton. Graham Elkington, the Flight Test Observer (FTO), ejected without any order to do so from Dell, who had his seat adjusted to the highest position and was thus exposed to high air blast as his head was above the top of the windscreen frame. His eyes were severely air-blasted but his subsequent ejection was normal.

19 Squadron's F.2s ready to leave Yorkshire on 23 September 1965 for the flight to their new posting at Gütersloh in West Germany. 92 Squadron's F.2s also left Leconfield, for Gelsenkirchen, three months later to join them in RAF Germany.

F.1A XM171 which first flew on 20 September 1960 and went to the A&AEE for evaluation and handling tests. Later, on 7 April 1965 it went to 226 OCU (pictured) and operated on the Operational Conversion Unit until 28 November 1968 when it was declared Cat.3. It was SOC as scrap on 29 March 1974.

F3 XR721 on 56 Squadron which Flying Officer Derek Rollo Law (24) crash landed at Helmingham, Suffolk on 5 January 1966. Law, who was originally from South Africa, had served at RAF Khormaksar in Aden on 43 Squadron and he had taken part in the 16 aircraft flypast in honour of Sir Winston Churchill's funeral in 1965. XR721 had taken off from RAF Wattisham on the morning of 5 January, Law having been briefed to fly a training mission over the North Sea but after takeoff and climb out he discovered that his radar had failed so he elected to carry out some continuation training with an instrument-only approach into RAF Bentwaters only 25 miles away from Wattisham. On the approach to Bentwaters one engine failed causing him to abort and head for the safety of Wattisham. On flying over the Suffolk countryside his second engine failed. He pulled the ejection handle but the canopy would not release trapping him on side the aircraft and he was forced to make an emergency landing into a ploughed field with no power and landing gear in the up position. He brought the aircraft almost to a dead stop at the wall of a small roadside cottage on the Otley Road just yards from overhead electrical cables. The wing of the aircraft had struck an oak tree and this caused the canopy to release causing the ejection seat to fire and propelling Flying Officer Law into the outer branches of the tree and onto the tarmac road beneath. He suffered fatal injuries and died at the scene. He had suffered only a few minor head injuries and a broken wrist on the impact with the ground while still in the aircraft but it was concluded in the inquest that if he had ejected into open land that he may have survived the crash. Flying Officer Law is buried at Ringshall Church, one mile from the end of the runway at Wattisham airfield.

T.5 XS454/T first flew on 30 August 1965 and arrived at Leuchars on 8 October 1965. It went to 226 OCU at RAF Coltishall on 12 January 1966 where it suffered an undercarriage collapse on the runway on 7 March 1967. Flight Lieutenants Mike Graydon and Bob Offord emerged unhurt. This Lightning made its final flight on 11 June 1975 and was then used as decoy until September 1987 when it was scrapped.

F.1A XM173, pictured on 226 OCU at RAF Gaydon on 16 September 1966, is now on display at RAF Bentley Priory, Greater London.

A seven-ship formation of 74 'Tiger' Squadron's F.6s early in 1967. F.6. XS921 was issued to 74 Squadron on 21 December 1966 and became 'M'. After 74 Squadron's disbandment, it was transferred to 56 Squadron in September 1971. On 19 September 1985 this Lightning crashed into the North Sea fifty miles off Flamborough Head, Yorkshire after Flight Lieutenant Craig Penrice ejected following loss of control due to malfunction of the aileron powered flying control unit, probably caused by a foreign object jamming one of the four aileron input levers. Penrice pulled the handle at 19,000 feet, 0.98 M or 540 knots and suffered a broken elbow and broken knee and 22 pieces of metal were needed to fix broken joints and he joked that he needed a nerve transplant. He did not return to flying until 11 months later.

5 Squadron F.6s and T.5 XS454 on 74 Squadron (in the foreground) at Luqa, Malta during the night phase of the October 1967 Air Defence Exercise (Adex) scramble as part of the night-phase in exercise 'Forthright 67' when ten of 5 Squadron's Lightnings deployed to Malta. T.5 XS454/T first flew on 30 August 1965 and arrived at Leuchars on 8 October 1965. It went to 226 OCU at RAF Coltishall on 12 January 1966 and made its final flight on 11 June 1975 before being used as decoy until September 1987 when it was scrapped.

AB INITIO

the end of a Rad-ex in XS454 and alighted on Runway 22, when suddenly, despite three greens showing on the instrument panel, the main undercarriage collapsed! The nose wheel, however, stayed down. Bob Offord recalls: 'The drag chute hit, then the wheels went. Because the levers were on his side, I told Mike Graydon to shut down the engine and open the canopy. We had no control. It just went straight in and then veered off to the right and stopped. I said, "Get out!" and I went over the side. I didn't know at this stage what had happened. You can imagine the looks we got!'

Peter Hayward, a technician at 226 OCU, explains: 'The landing gear failures affected only the T.5. The leg(s) would fold towards the end of the landing run when the aircraft was rolling relatively slowly. So, apart from the pilots' injured pride and a somewhat scraped wingtip, little damage was done. Many investigations were carried out and many theories put forward. One theory was that the pilots were inadvertently operating the "gear up" lever instead of the brake chute lever – on the T.5 the two levers were quite close to each other. This was immediately rejected by the pilots, who pointed out that with the aircraft on the ground with weight on the landing gear, the gear select lever is locked in the down position and a positive override action is required before it can be selected 'up'.

'The theory that pilots were inadvertently operating the landing gear lever led to an unexpected bonus for the ground crews. 'Joy trips' for technicians in the right-hand seat of a Lightning were highly desirable, but, because of the training commitment at Coltishall, were rare occurrences. When the above theory was first mooted, the decision was taken that whenever a T.5 had to be flown solo (test flight, conversion pilot's first solo etc.), the right-hand seat would be occupied by a ground technician so that the brake chute could be deployed by him from the lever in the right-hand side of the cockpit. There was no shortage of volunteers.

'On some flights the opportunity arose for a member of those technicians to join the 1,000 mph Club. I achieved it during a flight with Flight Lieutenant Henry Ploszek. Two other flights I had as a passenger are indelibly recorded in my mind. One of these was a low-level PI with Flight Lieutenant 'Oscar' Wild. Low-level PIs consisted of flying at 50 to 250 feet above the sea and intercepting 'enemy' aircraft (usually another Lightning). Interceptions were carried out under instructions from ground control and using the information supplied by the aircraft's AI.23B radar. This meant that the pilot had his eyes glued inside the radar visor and the aircraft was flying on autopilot in the altitude hold mode. Now, this may sound perfectly normal. But if you are a passenger sitting in the right-hand seat and have got nothing to look at other than the whitecaps of waves or North Sea rigs and shipping flashing past below you at close range and perhaps if you do not share the pilot's blind faith in the technology that is supposed to prevent you flying into the sea, then a feeling of being in the wrong place can overcome you.

'Similarly, a formation let-down with a USAF exchange pilot at the controls led to a feeling of wishing I was back in the crew room enjoying a cup of coffee and a cigarette. There were perhaps four aircraft in the let-down. Above the clouds in the bright sunlight everything looked easy and was most enjoyable, but then we entered cloud and remained in formation. The separation from the other aircraft was maybe ten or fifteen feet and the only visual contact I had with them was the flash of the anti-collision lights on the wingtips. Then the lights would disappear again in the gloom. It was like driving in thick fog with candles for headlights. The relief, when we finally broke cloud, was immense. It was after this flight that I realized why pilots are called 'steely-eyed'.

'BAC sent a team of specialists to assist the RAF. Test equipment was installed on a single T.5 and even a movie camera was mounted in the airframe to take a film of the behaviour of the landing gear during the landing. However, as is often the case when you want something to happen, it never does and no incidents occurred on the test aircraft. So, nothing was proved conclusively and it was decided that stray voltages induced into the wiring to the landing gear control unit were the most likely cause of the problem and that the routing of the wiring would be modified. This involved approximately two days' work on each side aircraft and the Coltishall T.5 fleet (which included four T.55s belonging to the RSAF) was completed in the record time of three weeks.'[7]

Coltishall's association with Norwich stretches back to the Battle of Britain in 1940, the days of Douglas Bader and Bob Stanford-Tuck. A most notable event in the station's calendar in 1967, therefore, was the Freedom of Norwich flypast on 6 April, held to mark twenty-seven years of RAF association with the fine city. Group Captain Mike Hobson selected Wing Commander Mick Swiney to lead the formation flypast. This would comprise no fewer that twenty-seven aircraft (made up of twenty-four Lightnings and three Spitfires from the Battle of Britain Memorial Flight), the largest Lightning formation ever to take-off from and recover to its parent station, as Mick Swiney recalls.

'No other station could produce so many Lightnings from their own resources. I had forty-two. Also, I had enough instructors to fly them in boxes without turning a hair, so I decided we would fly in boxes of four, all in line astern, behind the three Spitfires. Flight Lieutenant Gil Pink (37), a Canberra PR.7 navigator and an old acquaintance from my Laarbruch days, was on a ground tour at Coltishall and he helped plan the route and calculate the precise timings needed. A brilliant navigator, he also loved flying. He flew two recces with me in the T.4. Our first practice was with twenty-four Lightnings on 3 April and on the auspicious day the weather intervened and I took just a token box across the city to coincide with the parade outside city hall, together with three Spitfires. On 27 April I led sixteen Lightnings in formation for the AOC's parade. In the meantime, 23 May was chosen to re-stage the mass flypast over Norwich and this time I was able to mount the whole show. We could not get twenty-seven aircraft onto the runway at once, so I led twelve Lightnings off in three boxes and Squadron Leader Brian Farrer, OC 3 Squadron, with twelve in the second lot, would fall in behind. I led Red, Blue and Green boxes off, did a wide, right-handed circuit, turned in over the coast and ran up the runway at 1,000 feet. Brian Farrer's formation took off and pulled in behind. I did not want our entire formation to snake, so, to avoid any changes in direction, we had a long run in point. (I got one of the SAR Whirlwinds to drop a smoke float at a precise point in the sea.) Ahead of us were two Spitfires (a third developed engine trouble after take-off and had to return so Flight Lieutenant Alex Reed, the 'whipper-in', replaced it to make up the magic twenty-seven). We lined up and led all twenty-five Lightnings straight to Norwich, aiming for the cathedral spire. The Spitfires flew at 180 knots, the Lightnings at 360 knots. I am happy to say that it was a DCO [Duty Carried Out] exercise. I sent Brian Farrer's lot in to land first, as they were slightly thirstier aircraft.'[8]

In October 1967 Wing Commander George P. Black AFC arrived at Coltishall to take over command of 226 OCU/145 Squadron and the added responsibilities of CFI/Wing Commander Flying. Having already accumulated 1,000 hours on the Lightning, he was given a brief conversion course consisting of one dual and three solo sorties to initiate him in his new post! Being the main operator of two-seat Lightnings, 226 OCU's T.4s and T.5s were in great demand in 1963-74 to fly VIPs and other notables at speeds greater than 1,000 mph. This would qualify them to be members of the 'Thousand Miles Per Hour Club', otherwise known as the 'Ten-Ton Club', complete with scroll and special tie. On 2.6 August 1963 226 OCU had made it possible for Diana Barnato-Walker, a famous flyer and wartime Air Transport Auxiliary pilot, to become the first British woman to achieve the distinction when she was accompanied by Squadron Leader

Ken Goodwin the CO in XM996. Diana clocked Mach 1.65 (1,262 mph) which for a short time was an unofficial women's speed record, beating that of Jacqueline Cochrane of America and Jacqueline Auriol of France. It was also around this time that a Guinness toucan bird, stolen from a pub in Newcastle, was flown to 1,000 mph membership and became a jealously guarded trophy held for short periods variously by 19 and 92 Squadrons and the LCS. Amid all the publicity, Guinness threw a celebration party at the Park Royal Hotel in London, but the festivities were brought to an abrupt end after the Park Royal tower clock disappeared.

By 1968, appropriately the RAF's fiftieth anniversary year, the club's membership now included well over 900 members, from royal personages such as King Hussein of Jordan and the Shah of Iran, to people of more humble origins. On 27 February Mr. Hastings, a member of the Norwich Observer Corps, became the 999th member of the club when Group Captain Mike Hobson flew him at 1,066 mph! 1968 being a leap year, the station commander considered it appropriate that a woman should be the 1,000th member to achieve the distinction of membership to the Ten-Ton Club. Nineteen-year old WRAF, Pilot Officer Vivian Whyer, a flight-control officer at Coltishall was the lucky candidate, on 29 February. (The three safety equipment workers responsible for packing their parachutes were all women.) 'However,' recalls Mike Hobson, 'the weather was appalling and all flying was cancelled, but the press and the TV were there in force so we couldn't really back down. It was all right to take off and I could always land elsewhere if necessary, so off we went in the T.4 (XM970). Only problem was, once Neatishead said that the high-speed run could begin, I could only get one engine to re-heat, so to reach the magic 1,000 mph, I had to put the nose down over the North Sea!'

Colonel Akbar Khan, chief of staff to the C-in-C of the Royal Afghan Air Force, who had just presented the RAF with a Hawker Hind as a fiftieth anniversary present,[9] became a member of the Ten-Ton Club on 12 June 1968 when he flew in XM974 with Mike Hobson. 226 OCU also flew Colonel Cesar Rohon, the Ecuadorian Chief of Staff, as Mike Hobson recalls: 'He duly received his tie but he did not receive his certificate. An opportunity to correct this came late in 1969. I was now DD Ops at MoD and was one of the team sent to Ecuador with BAC when it looked like the Ecuadorians were going to buy Lightnings. I sent Rohon's certificate to the Air Attaché in Quito, only to be told that he had been kidnapped! About five days later he was found dumped by the side of the road and a few days after that, he was placed under arrest. He never did get his certificate!'

AB INITIO

Meanwhile, in 1968 Fighter Command had made way for Strike Command and at Coltishall twenty Lightnings (in four boxes of four, plus reserves) were required for the fiftieth anniversary flypast at Abingdon on 1 April. Fuel requirements for the flypast dictated flying from RAF Wyton so most of the Coltishall Wing was deployed there for almost two weeks. Wing Commander George Black recalls: 'I led the formation in a T.5 and behind the Lightnings were four boxes of four Hunters led by Wing Commander Nigel Price, 229 OCU. The exciting bit was the join-up and on one of the rehearsals the Hunter Wing overcooked the join-up and came in at a very interesting angle. I graciously let them have the lead! On the very last day we could not get all the way around the route safely and chose to come back to Coltishall; we really had to land at Wyton. But we had tremendous confidence in the aircraft and the systems, so we devised a somewhat unusual plan for the recovery. Once we had completed the flypast a code word was given and we all shut down one engine! Once overhead Coltishall every single engine was re-lit without a problem and we did two flypasts at Coltishall before landing. It was shortly after this that we had to produce twelve aircraft for the demise of Fighter Command.[10] The flypast was not as spectacular as we were involved in Abingdon and we also had aircraft in the Queen's Birthday Flypast.

'Another significant incident during my reign was on 21 June 1968 when Squadron Leader Arthur Tyldesley taxied in with no brakes and buried the aircraft in the side of No.1 Hangar. Both engines jammed at about 80 per cent and the Rolls-Royce rep did a splendid job going underneath to the engine bay and eventually managing to stop the engine. It was a horrific sight as the intake sucked in the bricks and mortar (and much of Bob Lightfoot's and Nick Galpin's desks), chewed them up and then hurled stones and gravel at ATC; there was a brown column of dust about 200 feet high. Arthur Tyldesley climbed out of the cockpit onto the roof of the hangar offices and was an amusing sight running around as though his hair was on fire.

'Our recent formation flying proficiency was remembered and I was persuaded to put up a Diamond Sixteen, which had never been flown by Lightnings before, in the September Battle of Britain Open Day at Coltishall.'

First, a rehearsal was flown and then, at the beginning of Battle of Britain Week, Monday 9 September, the formation flew over the city hall. All this activity placed a great strain on the ground crews, as Peter Hayward recalls: 'Preparations were pretty hectic. This was always a joint effort between the two flights of 226 OCU. (One flight alone did not possess sixteen aircraft.)

It was often said that to get one Lightning serviceable for a flight was a pretty remarkable achievement, but to get thirty-two Avons started in quick succession (the most infernal noise imaginable) and see sixteen aircraft off without any major problems bordered on a miracle!' Problems, however, did arise on the Saturday during the Battle of Britain Day show, but it had nothing to do with the Lightnings, as George Black explains: 'We had twelve to fourteen aircraft landing, following the convention of the time landing left-right-left etc., when a Hunter landed and called, "No brakes!" The pilot somehow "threaded the needle beautifully", took the lead from me and went straight into the barrier in front of me. An unfortunate end to what had been a great occasion. It was a year of interesting flypasts that interrupted the OCU training but ensured that everyone on the OCU worked extremely hard. As a result, we even managed to get the courses out on time.'

On 19 September 1970 the Battle of Britain air show at RAF Coltishall included a 'diamond sixteen' fly-past which ended in disaster. The week prior to the open day T.4 XM990 was undergoing checks to solve control problems which added to the already high workload the maintenance engineers were under preparing sixteen-plus Lightnings for the flying display. After an air test and practicing the formation, XM990 was ready to be crewed by Flight Lieutenants John Sims and Brian Fuller on 226 OCU, as a reserve for the diamond-sixteen formation display. XM990 was called into the centre of the box. However, XM180 piloted by Flight Lieutenant Bruce Hopkins burst a tyre on landing and blocked the Coltishall runway. Brian Fuller tells what happened next. 'For the landing the formation split into four sections of four aircraft and we were in the last section to land. Unfortunately, the last aircraft of the previous section [XM180] blocked the Coltishall runway so our section was diverted to Wattisham. We re-fuelled there and put in new brake-chutes and then waited for the return to Coltishall once the rest of the display had finished. It was after the 'break' into the circuit on the return from Wattisham that the problem arose. Flight Lieutenant John Sims found that he needed more and more right aileron to hold the wings level going downwind. Eventually it was obvious that we would have to depart the aircraft so he let the aircraft roll under and got me to eject as it passed the upright position. He then let it roll again and ejected as it once more passed the upright position. However, as soon as he let go of the control column the rate of roll increased. Also the canopy had gone when I went out so he missed the top ejection seat handle when he initially went for it. By the time he managed to pull it the aircraft had rolled considerably to the left.

AB INITIO

Thankfully he got out safely although he did suffer a minor fracture to one of his vertebrae which necessitated some time at Headley Court.'

XM990 had lost aileron control when a bolt dropped out and the aircraft began corkscrewing and losing height with every revolution. To people on the airfield it seemed that the single Lightning was treating them to an impromptu air display! Mike Baxter, a local man in the large crowd who had enjoyed the open day and the flying, highlighted by the 'Diamond 16' formation recalled: 'It was early evening before Coltishall became operational again and '990' approached the airfield. Suddenly and without any warning the Lightning started corkscrewing, losing height with every revolution. Swiftly assessing the situation, the pilot applied power and pulled the aircraft up at the top of each corkscrew, gaining precious height. To people on the ground it appeared that the pilot was staging an impromptu display of his own, but the crew of Flight Lieutenant John Sims and Flight Lieutenant Brian Fuller knew differently – they had lost control!'

Eye-witnesses watched as something appeared to fall off the plane; it was, in fact, the canopy, followed by one of the crew ejecting. The pilot had to time his ejection on the next upward corkscrew, which by now was getting very close to the ground (Sims ejected at 1,500 feet and 220 knots). As he left the aircraft it had time to complete only one-and-a-half more turns before crashing inverted into a small wood bordering the A140 Norwich to South Walsham road very close to the village of Little Plumstead. Part of the tail unit was hurled across the road, inches in front of a car driven by 28-year-old Michael Howard who, with two friends, was returning from an unsuccessful fishing trip.

Standing by his car a few minutes after the crash, Mr. Howard recounted: 'Suddenly there was a hell of a screech and a shrieking noise. I glanced up to the trees on the right-hand side of the road – they were almost overhanging the road – when I saw a white flash going into the top of the trees. The plane hit a big oak tree and burst into a mass of flames right in front of my eyes. The tailpiece crashed right across the road a few feet in front of me. The next thing I knew I was right in a mass of flames from the trees where the rest of the plane was burning. It was all over in a flash. Then we were OK. I thought that the whole road was a ball of flames as we drove through it. We were all in one piece and the car was all right.

'Local people hurried to assist the crew. One had parachuted into a wood. He was located in a small clearing, having removed his helmet and lifejacket and complained of pains to the back of his neck. His parachute was hanging about ten feet up a tree. He was concerned about the other crewman and also about where the Lightning had crashed. He said he had had only seconds before the crash to eject and asked them to tell his wife he was OK. As he was speaking, the other crewman came into the clearing looking for him and upon seeing each other they both looked greatly relieved. The Coltishall SAR Whirlwind soon arrived and took them to hospital, one of them on a stretcher. The crash site was cordoned off for nearly a week while the wreckage was examined by the RAF before it was removed, along with tons of topsoil: even today you can see the depression.

'The inquiry, following the crew's evidence, concentrated on the controls and control surfaces. Helped by the lack of a major fire, it was found that one of the aileron linkages had not been securely fitted and had vibrated out with the aileron movement causing loss of control. Fortunately, the crash of XM990 did not result in any loss of life or any great damage to property.

'My interest was stimulated by the plane crashing some two miles from where I used to live and only 600 yards from my brother in law's bungalow. He thought his time had come when he saw the jet heading straight for him until it veered away on its last corkscrew and hit the trees. Apart from this connection, it was only later during the Manx Grand Prix on the Isle of Man racing motorcycles that I found out that my friend Tony Martin was stationed at Coltishall and worked on the Lightnings on 226 OCU. He even declined a flight in a T.4. He reckoned it was too risky and this from a man who has finished fourth in the MGP on a TZ350 Yamaha!'

'For a young Air Traffic Controller in the early 1970s,' recalls Flight Lieutenant Dick Doleman, 'there was no finer place to be than the Lightning OCU at Coltishall. You did not have to be a pilot to enjoy the aura or potency of this magnificent beast and I never tired of watching it. The Lightning seemed to attract or develop pilots of a certain character. For me this character was epitomized by the leadership team that came together about a third of the way through my tour. A finer bunch of larger-than-life characters you couldn't wish to meet: Group Captain Joe Gilbert (station commander); Wing Commander Dave Seward (OC OPs Wing); Wing Commander Paul Hobley (OC 2(T) Squadron), an ex-Junior 'Mr Midlands'; and Wing Commander Murdo MacDermid (OC 65(F) Squadron) – the 'gang of four'! They were all immensely likeable people with totally different but complementary characters and a great pleasure to work for and with.

'The instructors on the OCU were an equally impressive and unforgettable bunch of personalities. These included Derek 'Furz' Lloyd; Pete 'Chappie' Chapman, whose spectacular solo display was never bettered; and 'Oscar' Wild, whose premise that a fighter circuit meant no levelling of the wings before the threshold resulted in some spectacular approaches and one-wheel touchdowns. Sometimes, it was rumoured that to achieve the objective required the judicious use of burner in the final turn! Others were 'Taff' Butcher, Rick Peacock-Edwards, 'Thumbs' Gosling, 'Duk' Webb, 'Jimmy' Jewell, Dave 'Quingle' Hampton,[11] 'Jonx' Kendrick, Ian Sanford (later killed in mid-air between Gnats while instructing at Valley), Rick Groombridge, John Spencer, Bob Turbin, 'Jack' Frost, Dicky Duckett, Trevor 'McDoogle-Boogle' McDonald-Bennett and Rory Downes, to name just a few.

'Coltishall was a very busy OCU and like all OCUs each conversion course was a mixed bag of both experience and rank. The description of a Lightning as an "aluminium tube with a frightened teenager strapped inside" was not altogether strictly correct as it could sometimes contain a frightened group captain! From a controller's viewpoint, work at Coltishall was always interesting and very often demanding. Student inexperience, weather, aircraft speed and shortage of fuel often combined to make for some very 'interesting' moments; adrenaline was never in short supply. Considering the prodigious fuel consumption of the Lightning and the limits to which it was operated, it has always surprised me that we never lost an aircraft due to lack of fuel. However, it was mighty close on many occasions and flameouts on the ground were not unheard of. As Captain Ed Crump, a USAF exchange officer and Vietnam veteran succinctly summarized: "With that kind of endurance, I don't call take-off, I call PAN!"[12] Another tribute to the OCU at Coltishall is that, so far as I am aware, there was never a fatality and the aircraft attrition rate was surprisingly low compared to my experience at other fighter bases operating more modern types of aircraft.

'There were so many memorable controlling incidents that it is very hard to pick out the outstanding moments. Some memories, however, seem more vivid. Rory Downes (2.(T) Squadron) launched on a very foggy Friday. It was his last day in RAF service and he needed the flight to achieve the coveted 1,000 hours on type. No pressure to fly of course! Unfortunately, his exodus spurred the otherwise dormant opposition (65(F) Squadron) into instant action and a mass launch. A pair on the runway baulked Rory's minimum fuel instrument recovery. With only fuel for a visual circuit, he completed this in the fog using only vertical visibility to position himself onto finals. An ambition only just achieved in more sense than one.

'A further incident occurred around one of the AOC's [AM Sir Ivor Broom] inspections early in my tour. As part of the occasion, it had been decided to fly a 'Diamond Nine' [led by Wing Commander John McLeod, who had taken over as OC OPs Wing and Chief Instructor (although not a QFI) in October 1969] and a solo aerobatic display. Unfortunately, the weather once again had its part to play. Before the planned take-off, we had been tracking a truly large thunderstorm on radar which was heading directly for the airfield. Despite our best advice, it was decided to launch. The arrival of the formation and the thunderstorm coincided perfectly and chaos soon ensued. The radar was now completely weather cluttered and unable to help. The frequency became frenetic with all kinds of join-up calls being made as the broken formation tried to re-establish contact. In the middle of this chaos, the solo display pilot ran in fast at low level, hotly pursued by one of the formation who assumed he had found part of his section. The subsequent manoeuvre seemed to take him completely by surprise! The first landing on the by now flooded runway resulted in aquaplaning and the aircraft overrunning and entering the barrier [safety net at the end of the runway]. The wind had now changed direction as the storm passed overhead, necessitating landing in the opposite direction. Calls of "Land over me" from the pilot in the barrier went unheeded as the various elements diverted off to Marham, including one aircraft having declared 'Mayday'. I'm not sure whether the AOC was impressed or not!'[13]

Brian Carroll recalls the initial impact that operating a Lightning in realistic operational conditions had on one trainee pilot who was about to start his conversion flying on the OCU at RAF Coltishall.[14] 'The unit in question was the LXV Fighter Squadron (VI et Armis), whose prime role was to carry out conversion training for pilots just out of Hunter flying at Chivenor. At that time we operated the T.4 trainer along with the F.1s and F.1As. We were also tasked as a front-line squadron. As such, we were subject to alerts and TACEVALs (Tactical Evaluation Exercises) in just the same way as the full-time front-line squadrons. To set the scene, the time was late 1971 and we had recently received a new intake of pilots. They had completed their initial ground school programme of lectures and were reasonably conversant with the Lightning's systems and operating procedures. They had also started flight simulator sorties and all had been airborne on Exercise I. This was by way of being an 'Instructor's Benefit' sortie, during which the full potential of the aircraft was demonstrated! All manoeuvres, needless to say, were within the approved flight envelope.

'We were just into the third week of October when a TACEVAL was called at 0300 hours. The weather was cold and wet with steady rain that had been falling all of the previous day and was to continue for the next forty-eight hours. Cloud was extensive, the lowest as I recall being around 800 to 1,000 feet and going all the way to 30,000 feet without a break – just the weather that fighter pilots dream about (well maybe on a bad day). Within a very short time, the squadron was a hive of activity. The ground crews were working at a feverish pitch, pre-flight inspections were being completed as rapidly as possible and aircraft were then positioned in their pre-determined slots, ready for the pilots to mount up. Weather and exercise briefings for the aircrews were all well under way, emergency and other procedures were all covered and we then awaited the first call from the operating authority to start the ball rolling. Meanwhile, the new course of students was being kept busy with routine jobs in operations and the coffee bar. Operating, as we did, a number of two-seaters, it was decided that we would fly as many of the new course students as possible in the right-hand seats to let them see what operating a Lightning as a weapons system was all about. They had, of course, no knowledge at this time of the radar, so it was left to each instructor to attempt to brief on that aspect during the sortie.

'Word finally came through to bring a number of crews to cockpit readiness. I had been allocated a T.4 and so had a student with me. I had already carried out my own pre-flight inspection, so we were able to climb straight into the cockpit. Strapping in took but a few moments, helmets were plugged into the telebrief, ground power was on line, radio frequency selected, flight instruments erected, weapons checked and we were all ready to start engines as soon as scramble instructions were received. We had only been strapped in a few minutes when instructions came to scramble. "Eagle 04' (my call sign) vector 120, make flight level 220, contact when airborne on 'Stud 7', SCRAMBLE."

'Three minutes later we entered the active runway, applying full power and accelerating as only the Lightning could. The rain was still falling and the runway lights blurred as we raced into the darkness – now airborne, gear retracted, radar scanning, a hard turn onto our designated heading of 120 degrees and into a standard climb out as we changed frequency to 'Stud 7'. Now snug and warm in what I called my 'airborne office' (it was nice to be out of the rain), I explained briefly what the radar picture was showing, though I doubt that my passenger was able to make much of the orange scene displayed. Less than two minutes had passed since we entered the runway when we levelled off at 22,000 feet.

'Our target was said to be at 25,000 feet some forty miles away and crossing our track from right to left. To this day I do not think that my student actually saw the contact on the radar even though I talked the attack right through to the kill. We were, of course, in thick cloud, so never made contact with the hostile intruder. As I broke away from this interception, new instructions were passed from ground control to take another target. This one was at a high level and closing fast. Reheats were engaged and a rapid climb made to 36,000 feet, speed was increased to Mach 1.3 and weapons rearmed. As we closed from astern I pulled the aircraft into a steep climb in an attempt to scan the target on radar. A good contact was achieved and the target was splashed (killed) at 47,000 feet.

'Back to cruise power and a gentle descent to 35,000 feet, briefly enjoying a clear sky above, well spattered with stars but no moon. The night was really very dark. I was beginning to think we would now be allowed to recover to base when another target was allocated. (They did actually ask whether we had sufficient fuel for one more – we did!). This next one was at low level, apparently bent on attacking our base, so a rapid descent was required. Back on the power to idle/fast idle, air brakes extended and with gravity on our side, we were soon plunging into the cloud layer at 30,000 feet – levelling shortly after at 2,000 feet to start the search for our third target. We were vectored towards the intruder and finally caught him at 500 feet, still some fifteen miles from the coast. This had to be a 'guns' kill as I had used the available missiles on the first two interceptions. Closing in with a degree of care, I finally made visual contact at around 200 yards – success number three. We were now cleared to recover to base.

'Briefly back to 3,000 feet to intercept the Instrument Landing System (ILS), we were cleared into the approach pattern. We were now getting low on fuel and had to make the first approach count. Rain was still falling as we broke out of the overcast at around 800 feet. The runway lights, a welcome sight as always, came into view and fifty minutes after rolling we touched down. Taxiing back to dispersal I asked the student what he had thought of the sortie. He was remarkably quiet for some time. Eventually, as we were walking back to the operations building, he looked at me, shook his head and said there was no way he could ever do a sortie like that. From take-off to recovery he reckoned not have caught up with what was going on, even though I told him as much as I could, bearing in mind the fact that my work load was high and I had little time to chat. I did make the point that he would not undertake a mission of that nature for quite some time to come, but it would give him some food for thought as he progressed though the course. Some months later, he successfully completed the conversion and weapons course and finally arrived on his first operational squadron. That sortie did, I think, make quite a significant 'first impression'.'[15]

In November 1971 Wing Commander John McLeod left for HQ 11 Group and was succeeded by Wing Commander Dave Seward, who filled the posts of Chief Instructor and OC Ops. For operational reasons it was decided to declare the Lightning F.1A element of the OCU to SACEUR (NATO) as an operational squadron. No.1, with F.1A and T.4 aircraft, now became a front-line squadron, taking the 'numberplate' of 65 Squadron. No.3 was absorbed by 2(T) to become a full training squadron and postgraduate course using F.3s (and F.6 systems) and T.5s. Wing Commander Murdo MacDermid became OC 65 Squadron, which was declared to NATO as such with its war base at Coltishall. OC 2 Squadron, Wing Commander Paul Hobley, became known as OC 2(T) Squadron and in war either would operate from Coltishall, or disperse its aircraft and personnel to support other front-line squadrons.

'We had, therefore,' recalls Wing Commander Dave Seward, 'an OCU with a wing commander chief instructor, who was also OC Ops Wing RAF Coltishall and two wing commander squadron commanders, one of which had a front-line number plane. Personally, I have always thought this to be distinctly unfortunate as it really split the thing into two. Before this, we were one identifiable unit with a single reserve squadron number, which engendered a true unit spirit. If it were imperative that No.1 Squadron should become 65 Squadron, I felt that 2(T) Squadron should have retained the reserve number plate of 145 Squadron. Then at least we would have had parity in squadron identification, but just one squadron number plate for the whole OCU would have been preferable.

'In the event, the running of the unit required careful handling and demanded the utmost co-operation of the three wing commanders in carrying out the OCU training I task as well as maintaining operational efficiency to front-line squadron standards. 'I started my refresher conversion course on No.67 Course in January 1972. I had hoped to refresh on the full long course with both squadrons, but in the event it was decided that I should be in post by the end of April 1972 when Coltishall's runway I was to be complete.[16] For me the course was reduced to three months, half with each squadron. Thus, for four months the OCU was dispersed. 65 Squadron went to Honington, Suffolk and then back to Norfolk, to Marham and No.2 (T) to Binbrook. The Battle of Britain Flight went to Wattisham. Due to an attempted takeover bid by Ken Goodwin to retain the historic aircraft at Wattisham, I was dispatched there for most of the detachment to ensure that it returned to Coltishall. I therefore managed to get some hours on the Lightning in those four months, but had a veritable feast on the Hurricanes and Spitfires. 226 OCU returned to Coltishall on 1 September 1972, much to the surprise of some new homeowners in the area who had purchased their property believing that all flying had ceased. We had a few months of complaints and visits to local councils and organizations plus several parties visiting the station to see for themselves, but by Christmas all was relatively serene.'[17]

In December that same year one aircraft-mad enthusiast received an early Christmas present. Brian Stiff was a young man with an ambition in the 1960s. Like hundreds of others, he wanted to fly in a Lightning. His story began in the 1960s, when, as a teenager living near RAF Coltishall, he began to develop an interest in the Lightning as it entered service with 74 Squadron. Throughout the 1960s he spent hours watching the aircraft movements from the perimeter fence, determined that one day he would fly in a Lightning. A job promotion meant moving to North Wales, where his determination to achieve his ambition became even stronger. In the autumn 1969 he wrote to the commanding officer at RAF Coltishall, seeking his permission for a flight. Of course, he could not sanction his request, but he did invite Brian to tour the facilities at Coltishall. He did and he flew the Lightning simulator. Fired with an even greater desire to fulfil his dream of flying in a Lightning, Brian hit on the idea of approaching the editors of the Chester and Liverpool newspapers to ask if they would be interested in publishing his story if he ever achieved his ambition. To his delight both editors agreed, so with their blessing he wrote to Headquarters Strike Command seeking approval for a flight in a Lightning. Brian was ecstatic when on 29 May 1970 he received a letter from Strike Command informing him that he would be offered a flight in the not too distant future. It was not until the autumn of 1972 that he heard again from Strike Command, when he was given details of what his schedule would be prior to flying from RAF Coltishall. Brian Stiff recalls:[18]

'Firstly, I would visit RAF Cosford where I would undergo a stringent medical. From there I would go to RAF North Luffenham for a decompression test and two days of instruction on aspects of the Lightning's functions and survival training. On 7 December 1972 my dream became a reality when I flew in Lightning XS413 on a sortie with 2T Squadron. After my most memorable experience I wrote the following story for the press: A long line of blunt-nosed, gleaming Lightning jet aircraft faced me as I stepped from the crew room onto the tarmac of RAF Coltishall, Norfolk. I was about to have my first flight in this 1,500 mph RAF fighter – a rare privilege for a civilian. Having already undergone a stringent medical decompression test, lectures on safety and survival and a fully clothed dip in a swimming pool to see how I coped with survival equipment, I was passed fit to fly. Fully briefed, I was to accompany Liverpool-born Flight Lieutenant Christopher Coville on a routine patrol. At 27 he is an Instructor on No. 2 (Training) Squadron at RAF Coltishall, having had experience of flying other types of jet fighter.

'We reach our aircraft and I climb up the ten-foot ladder, slide down into the tiny cockpit. Outside there is feverish activity as our ground crew prepare for 'firing up' the two mighty Avon Jets which can catapult the Lightning up to an altitude of nine miles in 60 seconds. In the cockpit I fumble with the countless straps which anchor every part of my body to the seat ... on with the helmet, clamp on the oxygen mask, remove pins 1, 2, 3 and 4 – ejector seat primed. Beside me, Chris is already working hard – No. 1 engine running ... No. 2 engine running. The cockpit canopy clicks shut. We begin to taxi. Line up on runway 22. A final methodical check of the masses of instruments and dials.

'"Clear for take-off," rasps a voice in our earphones. Engines run to 85%.

'"Rolling ... Rolling ... GO!" calls Chris.

'"Brakes off. Reheat on." A terrific thump in the kidneys as the 33,000lb of thrust blasts us along the runway. Airborne at 200 mph. The undercarriage slams home. The Lightning shudders. We streak over the perimeter at 350 mph, bank left and bore up into the clear blue sky. My arms and legs are pinned down by the force. I can just about move my head. We level out at 35,000 feet. The speed reaches 700 mph, the acceleration gradually decreases and I am able to move my limbs again. Below, the North Sea and to the right the Dutch coast. We are cruising "on station". The headphones crackle, "OK, you fly it, Brian."

'I take the controls. Still shaken by the rapid take-off and climb, I am content to fly a straight and level course, enough for me to feel, however, just how responsive the Lightning is.

'Suddenly, a new voice breaks through the routine chatter. It's from the Ground Control Interception station, part of the radar stations networked over the UK, warning us of an unidentified aircraft approaching from the north east, about to penetrate British airspace. Chris grabs back the controls. Am I about to witness an 'international incident'? With data provided from the ground, Chris pushes buttons, flicks switches. The aircraft with its two air-to-air missiles slung beneath the wings, is ready to strike.

'Again the phenomenal thrust as the re-heat cuts in. Mach 1 – smoothly through the sound barrier. Guided by a voice from the GCI station, we swing northwest. I'm riveted to my seat, barely able to open my eyes, head forced between my shoulders. Mach 1.4, Mach 1.5, 1.6 – that's 1,200 mph (Liverpool to London in ten minutes!)

'"Tally Ho!" yells Chris as the target appears on our radar.

'Fifty miles away and closing at a combined speed of 2,000 mph. Another numbing turn as we climb onto an attack vector. Chris makes a split second speed and fuel calculation (at these speeds the engines consume 50 gallons a minute).

'"Missiles gone!" – Well, that could have been the situation had this been a genuine interception, but not on this routine training exercise. Reheat off, throttle back and there's our target, a sister aircraft from Coltishall still four miles away. We turn for base. The nose dips toward the North Sea. We lose height gradually. An air traffic control station remote from Coltishall guides our initial approach. Ten miles out, the home station's own precision radar controller takes over and talks us down until we sight the runway. Panel lights indicate wheels down and locked. A slight jolt as we touch down at 201 mph.

'Out comes the brake chute and we are home. We had been airborne 35 minutes and the metal beast had devoured enough fuel to drive a mini around the equator. The aircraft had reached a speed of 1,200 mph, considerably less than its maximum and I had been initiated into the 'Ten Ton Club', exclusive to those who have handled the controls of a Lightning at speeds in excess of 1,000 mph.'

'1973', continues Wing Commander Dave Seward, 'was an exceptionally busy year. We had a very vigorous TACEVAL and incidentally won the TACEVAL Trophy.[19] On 27 July we had a Royal visit by His Royal Highness the Prince Philip, Duke of Edinburgh, which was very successful and training continued at an intensive rate. In addition to the long and short Lightning conversions and refreshers, we ran the Interceptor Weapons Instructor (IWI) courses. During my period of office, we had three accidents. Two were bail-outs and one an aborted take-off. The first bail-out [14 December 1972] was due to the break-up of an engine when [T.4 XM974] the target aircraft was acting as a high-speed, low-level target for the IWI (Intercept Weapons Instructors) course. In order to maintain 650 knots, re-heat was engaged and shortly afterwards the engines rapidly exited the rear end of the aircraft in a plume of thick black smoke. The crew, an instructor and a student who had finished his course and was awaiting posting [Squadron Leader John Spencer and Flying Officer Geoff Evans respectively] both ejected.'

At 1,000 feet near Happisburgh and flying at 600 knots XM974 developed an ECU/re-heat fire. Spencer pulled up to 9-10,000 feet and put out distress calls. At 270 knots and one minute after the critical emergency, Evans ejected first, followed by Spencer. Both men were picked up after eighty-five minutes (thirty of them in the dinghy) by helicopter. By then Spencer, who was wearing too small a girth of immersion suit and totally inadequate insulation, was hypothermic. Evans, on the other hand, in his Bunny suit and Mk.10 coverall, was reported to be warm and dry.

'It is possible,' continues Seward, 'that somehow medical records may have been inexplicably switched because the student, looking exceedingly healthy, was kept in hospital and the instructor, with his head sagging to one side, was returned to duty. I seem to recall that he was posted to RAF Germany as a flight commander and was very rapidly sorted out in Wegburg [RAF Hospital in Germany]. He also went on to complete a very distinguished career and achieved air rank.

'The aborted take-off was a singularly unfortunate occurrence. The F.6 used flap for take-off in order to give more positive lift off during the take-off roll. It is interesting that due to not having inter-connected flaps, the F.2A did flap-less take-offs without any difficulty. Higher authority decided that all re-heat take-offs by F.3s and T.5s would also be with flaps down. This was a very uncomfortable manoeuvre and was considered by the OCU to be unnecessary. We were overruled. The case [31 January 1973] involved an instructor, [Captain Gary Catren] a USAF exchange officer, on an SCT [Stall Continuation Training] sortie in a T.5 [XS420] with a student [Flight Lieutenant George Smith] as ballast. During the re-heat take-off at night the lower re-heat failed to ignite and with flap down, the resultant force of the upper re-heat did not allow the nose-wheel to be raised. The whole affair was settled when the instructor uttered an expletive, *Sheeeet George,* which the student interpreted as 'Chute George' and he promptly deployed the drag-chute. Although it rapidly burnt off, the deployed chute scuppered any chance of take-off and the aircraft took the barrier with it into the overshoot. Of course the instructor took the blame and when I tried to take the matter up with the Wing Commander Training at HQ 11 Group, he had already progressed to better fields; but I seem to recall that flaps were no longer used for re-heat take-offs in F.3s and T.5s.

'The second bail-out occurred [on 5 June 1973] when the student [Wing Commander Chris Bruce on 74 Squadron, in a solo sortie in T.4 XM988] pitched up when carrying out a hard diving turn from supersonic to subsonic. He hit the transonic cobbles and lost control, causing a violent pitch up, which became uncontrollable. [Bruce, who was just twenty-three minutes into his flight, called 'Mayday' during the descent, the Lightning spinning to the left; nose down and out of control.] At just above 10,000 feet he ejected using the SPH [Seat Pan Handle] and landed in the North Sea, suffering from a few cuts and bruises. After forty-five minutes in the water (which was 10 degrees C) he became hypothermic, but after being picked up by helicopter and once back at Coltishall a hot bath restored matters. Bruce was unhurt and continued with his distinguished career as a senior officer.)

'By the end of July 1974 the writing was on the wall for the Lightning OCU; the F.1s and T.4s were disposed of to various airfields as decoys, crash, rescue, etc and I flew my last Lightning sortie on 29 August. Jaguars were now at Coltishall and those Lightnings to be retained were flown to Binbrook, where the LTF continued to serve the remaining Lightning squadrons. I found the task of running 226 OCU during the period 1972-1974 to be challenging and extremely satisfying. I am sure that we had a first-class team at Coltishall and produced for the squadrons a very high calibre pilot. Most of these young men went on to give excellent service and many distinguished themselves in their future careers.'

In September 1974 226 OCU was disbanded and many of its Lightning F.1As and T.4s were withdrawn from service and scrapped.

Chapter 5

The 'Fast Jet Fraternity'

'Binbrook, this is Neatishead. Alert Southern QRA ... Scramble ... Scramble ... Scramble.' In the Quick Reaction Alert shed at the take-off end of the runway the fighter controller's voice on the telebrief, a mini-speaker on the wall of the pilots' ready room, is measured and unemotional. Flight Lieutenant Tony Paxton, 30, curses, spills his coffee, grabs his helmet and, hurtling through the open doorway, thumps a bell-push to scramble the ground crew. A bell starts ringing insistently as though the whole world is on fire. It is 1100 hours, about the time when, in the summer of 1940, the scramble bells sent the 'Few' of the Battle of Britain running to the cockpits of their Hurricanes and Spitfires as the Luftwaffe sought air superiority over southeast England.

'Forty years on the inheritors of the role (Strike Command 1980 has two Lightning and five Phantom squadrons as against Fighter Command's 33 Hurricane and Spitfire squadrons at the beginning of the Battle of Britain) are scrambling regularly from the east coasts of England and Scotland to intercept and investigate prowling Soviet reconnaissance bombers. It is peacetime, but in a period when East and West watch out suspiciously for any hostile move the approach of an unidentified aircraft is treated very seriously indeed at RAF Binbrook, just south of Grimsby.

'Within two minutes of the alert Tony Paxton's single-seat supersonic Lightning (maximum speed 1,500 mph at 40,000 feet) was screeching down the runway then climbing steeply towards the North Sea, leaving behind it the neat and ordered barrack blocks and quarters, named Mannock and Bishop after First World War flying aces.

'The 0830 after-breakfast briefing would be familiar to any addict of war films. The Station Commander and his Wing Commander Ops pass sandbagged strong points, walk in briskly and take their seats by a vast screen. Some of the airfield names on it are reminiscent: Manston, the Kent coast Battle of Britain airfield, is there in large letters.

'In the hangar area across the airfield from the isolated Quick Reaction Alert, or Q shed, Wing Commander Doug Aylward, Commanding Officer of 11 Squadron, one of the RAF's two Lightning fighter squadrons, walks into the crew room.'

'"Unidentified blip. 'Pax' (Tony Paxton) was 'Q,' says Squadron Leader Stu Gosling, a flight commander and adds: 'Coffee, Boss?' Excepting formal occasions, the CO is Boss, an easy-going form of address, which respects Wing Commander Aylward's true authority while bridging the gap between the familiarity of Doug and the disciplinary overtones of Sir.

'Outside, where the Lightning jets stand on the line, it is rain. Visibility is poor: the Met man has got it right.

'The boss sips his coffee. His thoughts are 800 miles away on Tony Paxton, flying a fully-armed supersonic fighter, perhaps making contact with an inquisitive Soviet aircraft nosing across the skies with a big red star on its tail.

'Wing Commander Aylward acknowledges that the squadron bears an enormous responsibility; Paxton is alone out there, a finger trigger that can release two heat-seeking missiles and fire two 30mm cannon. In a pocket just above his left knee is a green reference book marked SECRET, readily available for reference in case hostile action seems imminent.

'Taking another look at the weather the Boss checks with Gosling on alternative landing possibilities: a Strike Command air-to-air refuelling Victor tanker is also available. Out in the North Sea, British and US warships are exercising and Soviet aircraft are seizing the opportunity to attempt electronic surveillance. Like the rest of Strike Command the squadron is short of operationally trained pilots and serviceable aircraft. Paxton could remain airborne for five or six hours, refuelling every 35 to 50 minutes.

'Flying Officer Chris Allan from Dundee is the new boy of the squadron. At 24 he is the youngest pilot, married and well

THE 'FAST JET FRATERNITY'

on the way to qualifying for the coveted responsibility of Q. He will then be subjected to a boisterous initiation ceremony. A king-size tankard, the Limop Pot (Chris will have qualified for Limited Operations) is filled with three pints of beer and handed to the pilot who, standing on a chair in the mess bar and surrounded by his fellows, must drain it in one go.

"Steve is Q2, Boss," announces Gosling, confirming that Flight Lieutenant Steve Gunner has taken Paxton's place in the Q shed. Steve scrambled yesterday morning. Now it is his turn again to sit out the day within yards of a Lightning with his name on the fuselage, all ready to go.

'Squadron Leader Mike Champion, Stu Gosling's fellow flight commander – as Devon schoolboys they served together in the Air Training Corp's Exmouth Squadron and then he did an exchange tour with the US Marine Corps – is intoxicated with the opportunity as he puts it, "to turn and burn and fight". This enthusiasm has withstood considerable pressure to return to the West Country and take his place in the family chemicals business.

'Steve and Pax and Mike are the sort of pilots to be seen in the glossy advertisements for RAF officer air-crew – products of a campaign to appeal to a young man's yearnings for the elitist role of an interceptor pilot.

'In 11 Squadron the burden of its share of Q is the prime cause of its heavy workload and the frequent condition of 'Zorbin' – last minute changes. But as I training and secondary duties have to be fitted in as well and with only six other fighter squadrons defending Britain, some of the pressures on a young Lightning pilot can be appreciated.

'At times this summer Strike Command interceptor scrambles totalled as many as seven in one morning. Unlike fighter sorties of 40 years ago – never lasting more than an hour or two – today's scramble, often interrupting a spell of 24 hours sleeping, eating and waiting in the Q shed, lasts almost as long as an office working day. Such long periods airborne may be undesirable but shortage of pilots and aircraft make them necessary and the facility of air-to-air refuelling make them possible.

'Of course the zenith of a mission for each member of 11 Squadron is to be on the tail of a Soviet military aircraft and for

all the assistance he receives from fighter control, achieving it remains a taxing business for a single-seat interceptor pilot.

'The phone rings. "Six taken off from Murmansk and coming round the top. 'Badgers' and 'Bears'. Hodge has scrambled." No one, least of all 27-year-old Flight Lieutenant Pete Hodgson, really expects that on this sortie he will be lucky enough to notch up his first meeting with a Soviet aircraft. As he heads north of Scotland, his eyes on the radar and instruments, he grabs a crew-room sandwich from the packet under the canopy.

'Danish radar on the Faroes and a Shackleton early warning aircraft help to point him at two blips moving through the Iceland gap. Today there is no need to depend on the cockpit radar for there, 450 miles north of Scotland, 700 miles from base, dead ahead at 30,000 feet, contrails advertising their presence, cruise huge Soviet 'Bear' reconnaissance bombers.

'They Inherit The Skies: Are Britain's front-line fighters as ready as they were 40 years ago?'
Telegraph Sunday Magazine, 27 July 1980.

During the summer of 1969 at RAF Leeming Tony Paxton was learning to fly the Jet Provost with 3 FTS; the last aircraft that he wanted to fly on completion of his training was the Lightning! Paxton obtained a Private Pilot's Licence when he was 17. He had dreadful air sickness problems, which had to be ironed out by RAF doctors. To help him they had to use a device known as a 'spin table'. If there was a common denominator among the Lightning pilots it was the determination to succeed in this lonely, quick-thinking, quick-reaction profession; the 'press-on' quality, as his predecessors would have described it, discovered while at Biggin Hill Officers and Aircrew Selection Centre where graduates were assessed for the three years of training. The selector would also be looking for mental agility, physical coordination and an ability to take the stresses of flying: in short, as the RAF says, 'flying aptitude'. Generally, graduates will have had pre-entry training – flying solo in university air squadrons. Those entering straight from school will probably have belonged to local ATC squadrons. So, by the time he reaches RAF College Cranwell for initial officer training, the future fighter pilot may well have flown solo and will already know a great deal about the service and what it expects of him. There followed 100 hours basic flying training in the Jet Provost to wings standard and for all his ambition to become a fighter pilot it

THE 'FAST JET FRATERNITY'

is not until the young officer has qualified for his wings that he moves for advanced training into what is known as the 'fast jet stream'. For fledglings this meant training in the Gnat. 'The staff at the flying training schools can influence their students with enthusiasm, or lack of it, for their old role or aircraft. When I went through Leeming there were no ex-Lightning pilots on the staff. Also the Harrier and Phantom were just about to enter service so mud-moving was the popular goal. As students our view of the Lightning then was a steep climb to 40,000 feet, fly around for twenty minutes with one's head buried in a radar scope, rapid descent and land from a GCA; where was the fun in that? I was to find out! By the time that I had done most of my Gnat course at Valley I had decided quite definitely that my overriding wish was to fly single-seat and at the time that meant Harrier or Lightning. There were seven of us on my course and only two fast jet postings; I came second on the course and was posted to Lightnings.

'The Lightning OCU was 226 at RAF Coltishall in Norfolk and like any other OCU started with four weeks or so of ground school. However, to whet the students' appetite, day one of the course included a trip in the famous 'aluminium tube'; it was not an instructional sortie, just a marvellous incentive to get down to work in the ground school.

'During their early time on a Lightning squadron most pilots took right-seat rides to watch the more experienced hands operating the aeroplane and its weapons system. The Lightning was an easy aircraft to fly. It had to be. The task of operating the radar by day and night in all weathers was quite demanding enough without having a tricky aeroplane to fly as well. So every opportunity was taken to allow the junior guys to watch the combat-ready pilots do their stuff. Inevitably, there would be a chance to fly the aircraft from the right seat. Realising the problems involved, it was obvious that the in-flight refuelling probe could not be seen from the instructor's position. However, there was a well-kept secret about tanking from the right seat. If the angle made by the windscreen centre strut and the coaming was used as a reference point and the aeroplane flown forward so that the tanker's hose passed behind the reference point, the pilot flying from the right seat could not miss making contact with the basket! Many a junior Lightning pilot has been struck with awe and admiration when, after the instructor has uttered those words with a resigned tone, "I have control," he has then made contact smoothly at the first attempt and condescendingly given control back to the hapless learner who knows that the newly revered demigod in the right seat can't even see the probe or basket!

'All military fast jets are controlled by a stick in the right hand and throttle(s) in the left. The trainer versions are generally configured in the same fashion and indeed the T.4 was. However, the T.5 was different. For the right seat occupant the throttles were mounted on the right-hand side of the cramped side-by-side cockpit and the flying controls were operated by a stick with the left hand. This arrangement could cause some coordination problems during certain phases of flight, particularly formation flying and landing. During my course to become a weapons instructor, known in the Lightning force as an IWI or Interceptor Weapons Instructor, but later standardized as QWI (Qualified Weapons Instructor), I remember very well my conversion to the right seat of the T.5. I had coped pretty well with flying the aeroplane "back to front", but I had been concentrating very hard. The time came to return to Binbrook during my first right-seat ride in control. I was determined to fly a good approach and touchdown so I was concentrating very hard to send the correct messages to the appropriate hands.

'All went well during the initial phases of the instrument approach; air speed 175 knots with the aircraft stabilized on the descent in the landing configuration. Approaching the runway threshold a slight reduction of power to cross the end at 165 knots; then a further reduction of power and a slight increase in back pressure on the stick to flare and touch down at 155 knots. I was delighted; an almost perfect landing. However, then I relaxed; big mistake because I reverted to instinct. Because of its high approach speed the Lightning used a braking parachute to shorten the landing roll. The brake chute is stowed under the lower jet pipe at the extreme rear of the fuselage. To prevent damage to the canopy the nose wheel must be firmly on the ground before the chute is deployed. Therefore the after-landing actions are to lower the nose wheel quickly onto the runway by pushing the stick forward, simultaneously reducing the power by pulling the throttles rearward. Yes, you've guessed it, after my near-perfect touchdown I 'lowered the nose wheel' with my right hand and 'reduced the power' with my left. The result was that we rocketed skyward because in my 'relaxed' state I had, much to the amusement of my instructor in the left seat, engaged re-heat and pulled the stick back! Much chastened I flew a reasonable circuit with an acceptable touchdown and managed to carry out the correct actions to bring the aircraft safely to taxi speed. I bought a few beers that evening.

'The Lightning was designed as a high-level, fast response interceptor because that was the perceived threat at the time. As a result the aeroplane's guns pointed up by a few degrees, an angle which was exacerbated by the increased angle of attack if flying at a low air speed. The idea was that the Lightning would manoeuvre into a position astern of the target by using the information from the AI.23 onboard radar. The aircraft would then close into gun range keeping below the target's slipstream. However, the actual threat during the service life of the Lightning was predominantly low level and if a low-level target had been engaged as previously described, the Lightning would have hit the ground or the sea long before achieving a gun firing position. The solution was a quite terrifying manoeuvre called the low-level guns attack. The complete intercept was carried out above the target and once astern; the Lightning closed the range maintaining 1,000 feet above and a track slightly to one side. The range continued to close until visual contact was almost lost because the target appeared to be disappearing beneath the Lightning. The technique then was to roll inverted, pull the gunsight through the target and rapidly roll upright again. By this stage the aeroplane was in a quite steep dive with the gun sight behind the target, now pull the sight onto the 'baddie', squeeze off a short burst and carry out whatever manoeuvre was necessary to avoid hitting the ground. Of course, the whole procedure relied upon the enemy holding a steady course throughout – which was highly unlikely. Even if he had I think the chances of success would have been minimal.

'The pressure instruments – that is those flight instruments operated by changes in the atmospheric pressure surrounding the aircraft – were subject to varying degrees of 'pressure error'. By far the greatest error was with the altimeter, which underfed by a significant amount at subsonic speeds, but was accurate once the aeroplane was flying faster than Mach 1. The rule of thumb to correct for pressure error to the pressure altimeter was that the instrument under-read by the Mach No. 2 x 100 feet. Therefore if flying at Mach 0.7 at 500 feet above the sea the altimeter would read zero! The rule of thumb was valid up to Mach 0.8 and then the error rapidly increased until just before Mach 1.0 it was 1,250 feet; as the aircraft accelerated through the 'sound barrier' the altimeter would suddenly wind up 1,250 feet to read accurately. The error could be quite disconcerting at night or in marginal weather conditions. If one were flying at 450 knots (Mach 0.75 at sea level) to fly at 300 feet above the sea the altimeter would be showing 99,750 feet having wound down 250 feet below zero and believe me there is a strong psychological baffler to flying around with that sort of indication.

'The Lightning had a fast landing speed (155 knots) and not very effective wheel brakes. Because of these characteristics the aeroplane was fitted with a brake parachute which was stowed in a housing below the jet pipes at the very rear of the fuselage. It was mandatory to use the chute for all landings and a landing without it was a minor emergency. If the tail chute failed to deploy the standard procedure was to apply power and go around for a 'chuteless' landing. If returning to base with the minimum fuel reserves then a special landing technique was employed so that the aeroplane would stop on the available runway if there was no chute deployment.

'One very fresh winter's morning I was airborne in the T.5 with a new pilot to the squadron. We had finished the exercise that we had taken off for and were in the circuit at Binbrook. It was time to land; the ground was covered in snow with small snow banks either side of the runway which was clear with a dry surface. After touchdown the brake chute failed to deploy so power was applied and we turned down wind for a 'chuteless' landing. It was a beautiful day and from the downwind position I could see our brake chute lying in the middle of the runway. It had come out of the housing, but for some reason hadn't remained attached to the aircraft. The position it was lying in would cause a hazard to us on our second touchdown so I asked ATC to request the fire section to remove it from the runway before we landed.

'Our fuel was now down to minimums so it was time to make plans. The diversion airfield was Waddington, about twelve miles to the South West. No problem, because they were used to Lightnings arriving suddenly and short of fuel so I was not unduly concerned. As we made our second orbit of the airfield the fuel situation was becoming critical and because of the snow banks along the runway edges it didn't look as if our 'dead' chute would be removed soon. Best to make an early decision so I declared to ATC that we would be diverting to Waddington. I shut down one engine (standard procedure) and started transferring fuel so that it would all be available to the functioning engine. We headed towards the diversion airfield on one engine, with a minimal amount of fuel and our braking parachute lying on the runway at Binbrook. No problem, all in a day's work for a Lightning pilot and after all it was such a beautiful, sunny day. We call Waddington ATC and they are expecting us; we are cleared straight in to Runway 21, no other traffic (it was about 0830). Then the bad news! Braking action moderate to poor. This is indeed bad news because we are committed to landing at Waddington. We have no fuel to go anywhere else.

'Our brake chute is back at Binbrook and the normal landing ground roll is extended by 60 per cent on a wet runway. Suddenly we have all sorts of problems but no choices, we are on final approach the speed is good but I reduce it to give us a slower touchdown speed and hopefully, a shorter ground roll. As we cross the aerodrome boundary I can see that the runway is completely covered in a white shining frost but there is nothing for it, we are going to land. I cross the threshold 15 knots slower than normal and 'plant' the aircraft down in the first 100 feet of runway, the nose wheel goes down immediately and I apply full braking (the aeroplane's maxaret units will ensure that the brakes do not lock and cause a skid). We are down safely; all we have to do now is stop! Waddington's 9,000 feet of runway is being rapidly used up and I become dubious about our ability to come to a halt before the end. As the end of the tarmac approaches it is obvious that we are going to go off the end, very slowly, but off the end. The only option is to try and steer onto the taxi way, the aircraft responds with agonising lethargy but we eventually come to a halt with all three wheels still on paved surface and clear of the runway. The engine is shut down and we open the canopy. The silence is deafening. Then I hear the 'Da-da ... Da-da ... Da-da' of an approaching fire engine and we sit spellbound as 'Crash One' from the Waddington fire section slides gracefully under our left wing in a four-wheel skid. The tension is released and we both start giggling. Eventually a very embarrassed crew leans a ladder up against the side of the aeroplane and we climb down to terra firma. However, it is very difficult to stand up on the frosty surface and we realize how lucky we are not to have gone cross-country in a totally unsuitable vehicle.

'Flying the Lightning is a pleasure which every pilot who has had the good fortune to do will always savour, but I was soon to learn that flying the aircraft was something that had to become second nature very quickly. The Lightning is, essentially, a very easy aeroplane to fly; where many pilots have failed is in not having the spare capacity to fly the aircraft and operate its weapon system effectively. The radar hand controller had fourteen separate controls all to be operated by the left hand while the pilot interpreted the radar scope, responded to GCI instructions and flew the aircraft accurately on heading, height and speed.

'So, was I spending my days rushing around at 40,000 feet? Far from it: during the Coltishall course we covered a lot of low-level exercises, one of which I remember was particularly exciting. The Lightning was designed as a high level interceptor and so the guns were mounted to point slightly upward so that the aircraft could be flown behind and below the target clear of its slipstream. Imagine a target flying at 50 feet; a normal gun firing position would result in the Lightning flying into the sea or ground. So, to achieve a low-level guns kill the following manoeuvre was taught at Coltishall. We flew slightly to one side of the target's track with overtake and about 1,000 feet high; as the target started to disappear from view behind the fuselage we rolled inverted, located the target and pulled the nose down through it, rolled upright and the gunsight would be pointing behind the target which was at a range of about 600-700 yards. The Lightning was by now in a fairly steep dive at about 500 feet and accelerating. We started firing the guns and pulled the sight up through the target hoping to get some hits; then increased the pull to avoid flying into the sea or ground. This may seem rather haphazard but every round from an Aden 30mm cannon is effectively a hand grenade, meaning that just one hit on a wet wing could bring the target down. It was obvious that life on a Lightning squadron was going to be very different from my original idea at Leeming.

'I arrived at RAF Gütersloh in West Germany on 28 October 1972, exactly four years after I had joined the air force. I was posted to 19 Squadron and about to start three years of the most enjoyable flying I have ever done.

'The Gütersloh Wing was equipped with the Lightning F.2A which I would say was the best Lightning ever built. The F.2A was an extensively rebuilt version of the F.2; externally it resembled the F.6 with the large ventral tank, enlarged square-topped fin and extended and cambered leading edge to the wing. Why was it the best? The Rolls-Royce 211 series Avon engines, although less powerful than the 302 series of the F.6, were somehow better matched to the airframe and intake. The harmony between engines and airframe gave a very economical performance and required fewer ancillary intakes and projections along the fuselage which made the F.2A more slippery than the later mark. On a medium to high level practice interception (PI) sortie it was not uncommon to fly for 1 hour 40 minutes, which is not dissimilar to the sorties flown in the Tornado F.3.

'The F.2A retained the top guns of the early marks with the option of replacing the Firestreak missile pack with a further pair of Adens. Firing the guns was quite an exciting event. They were mounted 2 - 3 feet behind the pilot with the barrels one each side of the cockpit at about thigh level; when they were fired all hell broke loose in the cockpit. Bulbs would fall out, dust flew around, everything was shaken and there was a strong smell of cordite. Quite often the main flight instruments would fail. This was because the shaking and rattling of the guns firing could cause the push-pull switch for the master reference gyro to vibrate to the pull/off position; no problem if you realised what had happened but most disconcerting the first time it was experienced.

THE 'FAST JET FRATERNITY'

'There I was on my first Lightning Squadron tour; were my fears from Leeming to be realised? Certainly not; the flying was quite superb and after the six months of training, to become fit to hold Battle Flight (Germany QRA) can only be described as licensed hooliganism. Most of our radar work of PIs was flown on the night shift. The day flying was largely low-level CAP (Combat Air Patrol) or ACT (Air Combat Training). The rules for engaging other aircraft in Germany were simple and flexible. If one encountered another fast jet at low level you could 'have a go'; if he reacted the game was on, if he waggled you off he was left alone.

'The Lightning's navigation kit was not marvellous, designed to use radio and TACAN beacons which were not available at low level; our radar was next to useless at low level over the land so we were effectively a supersonic Spitfire. If we had to chase a target at low level there was no chance to look at a map so the navigation technique was quite simple. As you left CAP you started the stopwatch and noted the heading; once the kill had been achieved, turn on to the reciprocal heading and fly back for the same time as you had been chasing. Once in the general vicinity of the CAP you were bound to recognise some ground feature or other.

'In 1975 I was posted to 5 Squadron at RAF Binbrook in Lincolnshire. Flying in the UK was different but still nowhere near my fears from Leeming. 5 Squadron was equipped with Lightning F.6 and F.3s, the only difference between the two being the large ventral tank and cambered leading edge of the F.6. These marks carried an improved radar am front hemisphere 'Red Top' missiles giving an increased capability over the F.2A.

'The Lightning's job in the UK was similar to Germany but the environment was very different. We still flew a lot of low level but it was mostly over the sea and quite a bit of it was at night. The radar performance at low level was reasonable over the sea and with 'GO' control many successful intercepts were carried out. During these low level PIs at night the workload became really high particularly if the task was to identify the target visually. The Visident procedure required continual monitoring of the radar scope whilst flying level and accurately on heading which had to be adjusted by 2° or 3° at a time along with very small speed adjustments to position the aircraft for the best chance of visually acquiring the target. A short lapse in concentration could quickly lead to a descent and acceleration towards the sea. We had no radar altimeter and therefore no low height warning. The pressure altimeter suffered from large pressure errors such as that at Mach 0.9 the altimeter under-read by 700 feet; it was very disconcerting to fly along with the altimeter reading less than zero!

'Navigation in the UK Lightning force was not a major problem; we were generally under GCI control when not overland and even if not, a quick sweep of the coast on radar was sufficient to determine one's position.

'The UK Lightnings had a head-on capability with their 'Red Top' missiles and setting up the correct geometry for the firing could be quite tricky. The final stages could be exciting too because at missile launch the fighter and target aircraft were on a collision course with a closing speed of around thirty miles a minute. The breakaway manoeuvre was a rapid roll to inverted and pull to avoid the debris after missile impact.

'In both the UK and Germany the Lightning was kept at a permanent state of high readiness. In Germany it was known as Battle Flight. In the UK the readiness state was ten minutes and in Germany it was five minutes. That meant that from the alert, normally a bell or a siren, one or both of the aircraft in the alert facility had to be airborne within the prescribed time by day or night and in all weathers.

'The Lightning pilots on the Germany squadrons (19 and 92, latterly at Gütersloh) would be rostered to hold the Battle Flight duty for a 24-hour period every week or so. It was a popular duty because one was almost certain to get a training scramble during each period and always had the next day off. The reason for the frequent training scrambles was that five minutes really is not very long to run to an aeroplane, climb the ladder, strap in, start engines, taxi to the runway and take off. If one were asleep when the bell sounded the time allowed was even tighter. Of course there were several live scrambles each year; they would normally be because of East German/Soviet activity near to the border, unidentified radar contacts or even suspected aerial smugglers.

'Very early one summer Sunday morning in the early seventies I was fast asleep in the Battle Flight 'shed' at Gütersloh when a loud ringing noise penetrated through my dreams. Because of the very short reaction time we used to sleep in full flying kit including anti-g suit and boots. The life jacket was hanging over the Firestreak missile on the aircraft and the flying helmet was plugged into the oxygen hose and radio lead and perched on top of the canopy arch. Once the full meaning of the bell ringing in my ears had sunk in I was up and running, colliding with the ground crew, in various stages of undress, who were also running to perform their tasks to get the Lightning airborne in the shortest possible time. I arrive at the aeroplane and after donning the life jacket I do up a couple of buttons as I scramble up the ladder. Once I am in the cockpit with my helmet on, one of the lads is right there handing me the straps as my hands move around the switch panels, readying the aircraft for start. I check in on the telebrief (a secure landline communication to the base operations and the sector controller) and declare myself 'On State'. I am strapped in, the ground crew has removed the safety pins from the ejection seat and the canopy, the ground power is plugged in. The mighty Lightning is sitting there, fully armed with all the electrical systems running. We are just awaiting the order to launch. That order comes immediately: "Vector 070, climb angels 10. Contact 'Crabtree' on xxx.x SCRAMBLE! SCRAMBLE! SCRAMBLE!"

'Even before the sector controller has said the word scramble one engine is running and the second is already winding up as I acknowledge the instructions. The aircraft rolls forward and the external power leads pull out of the aircraft sockets automatically as I lower the canopy. The taxiway is just long enough for me to complete the pre-take-off checks before pointing the great machine straight down the mile-and-a-half long runway, lighting the re-heats and thundering into the sky. As soon as we are airborne I retract the undercarriage pull into a tight climbing turn and look at my watch. Oh my goodness, 0545. I bet I'm popular down there on the ground. However, just now I have more important things to worry about. Apart from anything else, my eyes won't stop streaming. It must be a reaction to the sudden awakening. Upon my return I discover that I went from fast asleep to airborne in a Lightning supersonic fighter in just three minutes and 45 seconds!

'Climbing to 10,000 feet I contact 'Crabtree', which is the code name for an air defence radar site manned by the German Air Force. They vector me towards an 'unknown'. At least they vector me towards the last position that they saw the unidentified blip because it has since faded from their screen. As I approach the area I descend to about 1,500 feet, my eyes still will not stop streaming and I have to wipe them constantly. After patrolling the area for a while I see a small twin-engined jet taxiing on a small airfield. Crabtree ask for the registration. This could be fun! I make a low pass, about 200 feet and must startle the pilot somewhat as it is still just after 6.00 am on a Sunday morning. I get most of the letters on the first pass but have to go down again to confirm that I have the correct details. I pass the full registration and the aircraft type and colours to Crabtree. It was a Cessna Citation all over white with a green stripe along the fuselage.

'The controller acknowledges the report and vectors me to a border patrol CAP (Combat Air Patrol) at 20,000 feet. I fly around the large racetrack pattern as the sun rises ever higher in the sky and welcome what is going to be a glorious summer Sunday. When I get back to Gütersloh there will just be time to refuel and service the aircraft, put it back on state and have breakfast before I am relieved. The way the day is developing, I think we may spend the day by the pool and light the barbecue to cook the evening meal. However, now the fuel is getting down to recovery levels so I point the aeroplane back west towards Gütersloh.

'Of course there is no other traffic about so I'm cleared straight in for the run and break at base. I keep the power well back all the way to minimize the noise as it is still very early on a Sunday morning and only advance the throttles to stabilize the speed around finals at 175 knots. I reduce power as the runway comes up so that I cross the threshold at 165 and touch down at 155. Stream the chute and clear the runway at 0700. What a great start to the day!

'Back in the 'shed' I speak to the controller on the telephone. The Citation was taxiing for take-off when I found him; so he was not our 'unidentified' contact. It may have been a false radar blip, it may have been a flock of birds, or even smugglers in a light aeroplane; we'll probably never know. However, the air defence alert system has been exercised again and all has worked as advertised.'[1]

Squadron Leader Tony Paxton has flown every mark of Lightning in RAF service, flying the aircraft with 226 OCU, Nos. 5, 11 and 19 Squadrons and the LTF. As he said, 'I had a marvellous time flying the Lightning. The F.2A was certainly my favourite and that has gone forever anyway.' He then did two operational tours on 'bombers', flying Tornado GR.1s with Nos. 9 and 31 Squadrons before returning to the air defence role via a conversion course on 229 OCU. This was a prelude to joining 5 Squadron at Coningsby flying the latest Tornado F.3s, where he was one of the unit's most experienced pilots and is now a Flight Commander with 23 Squadron flying Tornado F.3s from Leeming. Apart from initial pilot training, all his flying career has been within the 'fast jet fraternity', where he has notched up well over 2,000 hours on Lightnings and more than 1,200 on Tornadoes.

Chapter 6

Tanking

'We had no simulators then and no twin-seaters. It was all a bit of an adventure'. The words were those of Wing Commander Stewart 'Stu' Nance, OC 11 Squadron as he reflected upon his own conversion to the 1,500 mph Lightning from the 700 mph Hunter when he was at Coltishall in 1960 as a member of 74 Squadron, which became the first operational unit to re-equip with Lightnings. Since those days he taught at Cranwell (where he himself received his flying training) and completed several tours, including one at Randolph Air Force Base, Texas, where he trained USAF instructor pilots on T-38s. We then discussed one of these developments which has become an everyday art for the Lightning pilot – in-flight refuelling, by day or night, in or out of cloud. How do pilots acquire the necessary expertise? 'They begin by attending ground school at Marham, the Victor tanker base and at Binbrook before the first practice 'dry prodding' - putting the probe in the 'basket' (drogue) which is streamed from the tanker. Initially this is tried from a dual-controlled Lightning T.5. 'It's a knack...it's not easy to do the first time', explained Wing Commander Nance. 'My first reaction when I did it was quite alien to me, because you're naturally cautious, but this rapidly becomes a routine matter and confidence and skill levels rise rapidly until it becomes a bread and butter operation'. The Lightning's probe carries a light which illuminates the nozzle during air-refuellings at night or in cloud, while the drogue has peripheral lights and 'the overall lighting on the tanker has been thought out pretty well'.

**There's A Lot Of Life In The Lightning
by Roger Lindsay, writing in 1976.**

THE MEN WHO FLEW THE ENGLISH ELECTRIC LIGHTNING

When in January 1965 92 Squadron's turn to fly a detachment to Cyprus came, the requirement unfortunately coincided with the withdrawal from service of all Valiants after dangerous metal fatigue had been discovered in their airframes in August of the previous year. Flight Lieutenant Alex Reed, one of the four pilots in 92 Squadron at Leconfield who would still fly the trip, explains how it was carried out, now that the Valiants were unavailable:

'We were going to 'puddle-jump' our way to Cyprus, four of us, in two pairs. We took off from Leconfield on 9 January (I flew XN792), made our first stopover at Geilenkirchen in West Germany before going on to Istres in southern France, then crossed the Mediterranean to load at Decimomannu, Sardinia, before stopping the night at Luqa on Malta. Next day we took off for El Adem in Libya, the last stop before Akrotiri. We thought before we went that this sounded a pretty good trip and it was. We had a ball. At each stop we did a quick run in and break and we all received glowing tributes!

'While on the detachment on Cyprus, we flew PIs or 'Profit Sorties' against Canberras of 360 Squadron. Unlike in Britain we had the added benefit of the radar station on Mount Olympus to help us. We would be scrambled off, go out and find the target, 'fire' two missiles and then, after the targets were 'splashed', we would break off and cream our way back to Akrotiri. Back on the airfield again we would go straight unto the ORP, ready to scramble again. This was the most exciting operational flying I did! I averaged twenty-three minutes per sortie (we did four sorties each). We were flying the Lightning to its maximum operational capability. Mind you, it was under optimum conditions, but tough work in the hot sun. Then Squadron Leader Les Hargreaves, our CO, decided we would do low-level interceptions at night. Les said, "I'll lead the first pair. We don't want to push it." (Low-level PIs on a black night using AI.23 left a lot to be desired.) Les added that we would have the target at 1,000 feet so we'd have plenty of room. It was pitch black. He came back, looked at us and said, "Right, we'll put the target at 1,500!" The rest of us heaved a big sigh of relief.'

It was in Cyprus that Brian Carroll had his first encounter with the Lightning, as he recalls: 'One's actual thoughts at the time of flying the Lightning for the first time are now difficult to re-crystallize. Nevertheless, I intend to try and cast my mind back to those heady days when I first flew the better part of eighteen tons of highly polished metal, projected by 32,600lb of thrust. My first encounter with the Lightning was at a

TANKING

time when I was flying the Gloster Javelin Mk.9, also nicknamed the 'harmonious dragmaster' (an aircraft designed to prove that drag can overcome thrust), in 1963-65 at Nicosia and then Akrotiri in Cyprus. A UK-based Lightning squadron had arrived there for a month's detachment and was sited just a few yards from our dispersal, so we were very much aware of the noise, if nothing else. One particularly clear memory from those days was, "What an ugly aircraft. I wouldn't wish to fly one of those." I hasten to add that my opinion changed totally once I got my hands on one but that was not to be for another three years, until March of 1968. Well, even that is not totally correct. I did have a passenger ride in a T.5 on 9 July 1965 and another in December of the same year. I think that it would be true to say that one has a terrific loyalty to whichever aircraft one is currently flying. In spite of somewhat derogatory remarks that have been made about the Javelin, it was a great aircraft to fly.'[1]

'As Lightning enthusiasts,' recalled Brian Carroll, 'we are all aware that fuel was never an excess commodity. It was not that we didn't carry a lot; it was simply the rate of usage. I do, however, recall one particular occasion when I really did have fuel to spare. At the time I was stationed in Scotland (no prizes for guessing where), we were in the midst of a night flying phase and I was scheduled to lead a pair for a mixed sortie of PIs (Practice Interceptions) followed by a high level cross country.

'In order to achieve this we were fitted with overwing tanks. They were fuelled with a nominal load on the ground, just a couple of hundred pounds to prove the transfer system prior to take off. I briefed the sortie and in due course the pair took off in stream for a climb to 30,000 feet and a RV with the tanker after we had carried out a couple of PIs. The RV was achieved forty minutes after takeoff, at which time the tanker captain informed us that only one hose was available. This posed no problem, as we both had plenty of fuel and we were quite close to base.

'Night tanking always added that extra bit of interest to the sortie. My personal preference was for the tanker to leave its floodlights off (when used they lit up the under surface of the tanker's wings and ruined night vision). This left just the tanker's navigation lights and the small triangle of blue lights on the basket. In some ways tanking was easier in the dark, as one was not supposed to look at the refuelling probe when trying to engage the basket. In the dark you couldn't see it anyway, so it was one less thing to be concerned about.

'As lead, I elected to take the hose first, filled to capacity and standing off, called my No.2 in. He too successfully engaged the hose only to discover that his aircraft would not take on any fuel. Hose contact was broken and remade three of four times but all with the same result. I had little choice then but to send him home while I decided what to do with some 14,000lbs of fuel. The tanker captain invited me to stay with him for a while as he started his run for home base, so that once I had used some of my fuel I could engage the hose again just to make sure that the tanker feed system was OK. This I did, but only took on a few hundred pounds as I already had more fuel than I knew what to do with.

'The time was now approaching 0030 hours and I had a comfortable two and a half hours of fuel to use up. I then had a brain-wave (well that's what I thought it was). My aircraft had a radio compass fitted, so with the DME working well I was equipped to fly airways (one has to have two separate systems of fixing position in civil airways). So, sorting through my in-flight documents I placed the required doc on the aircraft coaming while I tanked for the second time, proving that the tanker systems were OK, then bidding farewell to the tanker. I informed military radar of my intentions and changed over to a civilian frequency to call London Airways in order to file an in-flight flight plan.

'This proved to be a little more difficult than anticipated for, having selected the required document to extract the necessary information for joining airways, I had placed it on the coaming while I was testing the tanker system for the second time. I had not considered the fact that these documents were of the type that have a glued spine. Yes, you may have already guessed what comes next. The aircraft heating system had melted the binding and I was suddenly presented with a loose leaf version. The majority of the pages were now in full flight around the cockpit. A few wild grabs secured the bulk of them and as luck would have it, I actually found the right pages, all this action taking place whilst I carried on a calm conversation with London Airways control. (If only they knew!)

'Eventually all was in order and I was able to inform London Airways of my requirements and intentions. I advised that I wished to join at Clapton Beacon and then transit across to the west coast, fly up to Prestwick and then return to military control, all this to be carried out at FL150. This would use my excess fuel up quite nicely. The London controller was more than a little surprised when I called him up and took some convincing that I was a 'fast jet' (we never gave out our type of aircraft) though my speed finally made him realise that I really was.

'The flight was something of a one-armed paper hanging act, using the radar to keep an ever watchful eye out for other aircraft, tuning the radio compass to the required frequencies (none of the modern digital kit, what was known as 'the coffee grinder type', usually better at picking up Radio 2 than the navigation beacon) but the DME was particularly good, locking on every time at the first attempt and to make life really easy, the auto pilot was put to good use. Just as well, bearing in mind my unique edition of the in-flight document. All of this coupled with a fairly continuous conversation with London Airways control ensured that I stayed wide awake. It was quite a relief to finally exit from civil control and to return to the relative sanity of military radar.

'Now in the Prestwick area and back at a more civilised height of 35,000 feet, I still had fuel to spare, so popped off to Lossiemouth for a practice diversion, shot a couple of approaches there and finally returned to home base. None of this very exciting, but it was a good demonstration of how long and how far the Lightning would and could go once at height and fitted with overwing tanks. I finally completed the sortie, having been airborne for nearly three and a half hours, not as long as some; I recall flying from Warton to Jeddah in five hours 40 minutes, but that's another tale.'[2]

Meanwhile, the conversion of Victor B.1 bombers to K.1A in-flight refuelling tankers was speeded up. The first to fly was XFT620, on 28 April 1965. 55 Squadron, which had become non-operational as a Medium Bomber Force Squadron at Honington on 1 March, moved to Marham on 24 May 1965 to operate in the in-flight refuelling role. The Squadron's first two Victor K.1A two-point tankers[3] arrived the following day and two more arrived at the end of May.[4] (These interim, two-point tankers severely limited long-range operations, as they were unable to permit Victor-Victor refuelling operations and would be withdrawn and be replaced with three-point tankers at a later date.) 55 Squadron's full complement of six Victors would not be reached until October but, like the 7th Cavalry, the Americans again came to the rescue. Arrangements had already been made with the USAF for the use of three KC-135s over a six- to nine-month period so that much-needed in-flight refuelling practice could commence immediately. Two SAC KC-135S from the 919th Squadron, to be stationed at Upper Heyford, would begin in-flight refuelling with 23, 56, 74 and 11 Squadrons' Lightnings in the UK while another, from the 611th ARS, to be based at Adana, Turkey, would operate with 29 Squadron's Javelin FAW.9S at Akrotiri.

Operation 'Billy Boy' as it was called began on 5 April with 1½-hour sorties with 23 and 74 Squadrons' Lightnings, refuelling with 3,000lb of fuel each sortie. Pilots discovered that the KC-135's rigid refuelling boom, to which was attached a seven-foot flexible hose and drogue, called for a much different receiver technique to that used on the hose and reel-equipped Valiant. Flight Lieutenant Bob Offord, now on 23 Squadron, who did his first 'bracket' with a KC-135 on 5 April, recalls: 'This caused us no end of problems because we were not set up. On 7 April I became the first pilot in the squadron to break a probe, which cost me a barrel of beer! However, my probe breaking was the first of many. [Of the twenty-two conversion and twenty-five continuation training sorties flown, the loss of probes on 15 per cent of these sorties was 'unacceptably high'.] On the end of the KC-135 boom was a basket, which went into an Omega shape and this put more stress on the connection. Our weak-link safety device just behind the nozzle in the probe (which broke off in emergency) was too weak to mate with the KC-135.'

Initially, 23 Squadron's pilots, 75 per cent of whom had had previous experience of in-flight refuelling, had the lion's share of the KC-135s (by the end of April only nine pilots in 'Tiger' squadron had completed a minimum of three in-flight refuelling sorties). However, the CO, Squadron Leader John Mcleod, admitted that it had also 'broken the largest number of probes – a weakness which would be largely eliminated by a current modification'. Bob Offord confirms, 'We had to have our probes 'beefed up' (the weak link was made stronger). From the on, the Americans would ask during tanking if we had a 'beefed up' probe.' Pilots on 11 Squadron at Wattisham, however, reported that initial contacts in the 'boomed' KC-135s proved relatively easy compared with the Valiant tanker. However, the CO, Squadron Leader George Black, wrote that, 'the kinking and shortness of the KC-135's hose and drogue (seven feet) [had] proved more strenuous in probe rivets' and that remaining in contact for prolonged periods of up to five minutes had been 'more exacting and tiring than Valiant refuelling'.

Then, in May, several sorties were flown with the flight profile being one hour with the KC-135, followed by forty minutes on PIs. During 24-28 May, preparatory to their deployment to Cyprus, 56 Squadron at Wattisham, which had just converted from the F.1A to the F.3 in April, began their 'Billy Boy' refuelling practice with five tanker missions involving three pairs of Lightnings being allocated to each tanker. However, one sortie was cancelled owing to Lightning unserviceability and two were lost when the KC-135 was forced to return to base with a probe end stuck in the drogue. Four probes in total were lost in the twenty-seven sorties achieved.

When a Tanker Training Flight was formed at Marham in July, 55 Squadron could get on with the task of training pilots in 74 Squadron.

Nine successful sorties were carried out with nine pairs of F.3s. 74 Squadron's need was urgent, as four pilots would fly the receiver aircraft in the forthcoming in-flight refuelling exercise 'Forthright 22/23' to Cyprus in August. This would be the first occasion that the Victor tanker was used for an operational overseas deployment. The F.3s left Leuchars for Wattisham on 13 August and took off from the Suffolk station the next day, in-flight refuelling to Akrotiri. All four Lightnings arrived on schedule after an average flight time of four hours ten minutes. In the meantime, six pilots from 19 Squadron at Leconfield converted to high-level in-flight refuelling and then carried out low-level in-flight refuelling trials from five of the K.1A tankers in preparation for 74 Squadron's return to the UK in August. Low-level tanking was possible but extremely difficult and was best carried out over the sea, where conditions are relatively smooth. The Victor's wing was prone to flexing in turbulence and the whip effect at the basket end of the drogue was quite frightening if a Lightning was not on the end to tone it down. Dave Seward agrees:

'You had to refuel cross-controlled because the vortex coming off the Victor's wing always forced the Lightning's wing down. (We always used the Victor's wing positions, the rear central position only being used by the bigger aeroplanes.) So, if you were going in on the starboard side, you had to feed in using the left rudder and right aileron to keep your wings level and keep yourself from being thrown out of the wing vortex. If you went in on the port side you got the same sort of problem, but it was exacerbated in that your probe, being on the left-hand side, meant that you had to be between the Victor's pod and his fuselage. You didn't have much room to play with if you started to buck up and down. People just got used to it. The problem came when we would demonstrate flight refuelling to a student using a T.5. Flying it from the right-hand seat when you were on the left wing of the Victor trying to get between his pod and the fuselage was difficult, especially since you flew the T.5 with your left hand and you had your right hand on the throttle! It worked but you had to work hard at it. You became more confident with practice but after becoming proficient at flight refuelling you got into a few bad habits. I for instance started off by religiously not looking at the basket and kept a general sight picture, but as you got more used to it once I had trapped the basket I would automatically have a quick look at the probe and nudge it in.

'At OCU the instructors were all flight commander material, but they did not practise flight refuelling at night so no one was current. For this reason, 11 Group said that we couldn't be used operationally at night.

However, we went up and did prods at night using a Victor until everyone was night qualified. When we told them, 11 Group demanded to know how we had become night qualified. I said we just went up and did it. How else did they think we had become proficient? It was rather like in the 1950s when you couldn't land at Gibraltar unless you had landed at Gibraltar before!' Just how difficult tanking could be was tragically brought home on 27 April 1964.

Flight Lieutenant George Davie had been the last on 92 Squadron's Lightnings to take his turn at air-to-air refuelling practice with Victors over the North Sea. Davie repeatedly failed to take on fuel and eventually had to abort. Unwisely as it turned out, he chose not to divert to nearby Coltishall, but decided to try instead to return to base with the rest of his squadron, which had now departed. He reached Binbrook, but on finals his cockpit canopy failed to de-mist and he was prevented from making a visual approach. As Davie entered the circuit for a GCA approach, his Lightning crashed out of fuel, at Beelsby near Binbrook, too low for him to safely eject.

By October 1965 the Lightnings were able to use all six Victor tankers. During the month four F.3s on 74 Squadron at Akrotiri in Operation 'Donovan' were refuelled all the way to Tehran and back, where on 17 October they took part in an IIAF (Imperial Iranian Air Force) Day. That same month a 23 Squadron detachment was made to Cyprus to take the place of 29 Squadron's Javelins, which, when UDI (Unilateral Declaration of Independence) was declared in Rhodesia, were sent to the troubled region. For Flight Lieutenant Bob Offord it meant a return to the island he had last visited while on 56 Squadron. 'This time we stayed three months, with crews rotating back and forth to the UK during this period. One of my interceptions, on 24 November was against Turkish Air Force RF-84Fs, who as soon as they realized they had been intercepted, turned and headed for home. Little did they know it but my radar was u/s. The Turks were always friendly. In fact they would hold up a map and point to indicate that they were going home.'[5]

At the beginning of December 1965 55 Squadron had been joined at Marham by 57 Squadron minus their Victor K.1/1As.[6] In 1966 56 Squadron was tanked to Malta by 55 and 57 Squadron Victors to take part in 'Adex 66', the Malta air defence exercise. In February 1967 exercise 'Forthright 59/60' saw F.3s flying non-stop to Akrotiri and F.6s returning to the UK, refuelled throughout by Victor tankers from Marham. In April 56 Squadron moved to Akrotiri to replace 29 Squadron's Javelins, a posting which would last seven years (May 1967-September 1974). The Lightnings' journey from

TANKING

the UK to Cyprus involved six in-flight refuellings for the fighter versions and ten for the T-birds, which were often taken on detachment to Cyprus to familiarize new pilots on target interception.

In-flight refuelling from Victors also became a feature used often on QRA (Quick Reaction Alert), 74 Squadron sharing the northern IAF (Interceptor Alert Force) defensive duties at Leuchars with 23 Squadron's F.3s (the Lightning's operational range and endurance being improved from August 1966 by the introduction of the F.6). Of course, intercepts were carried out at night and these posed some added considerations to take into account, as Brian Carroll[7] recalls: 'Night tanking always added that extra bit of interest to the sortie. My personal preference was for the tanker to leave its floodlights off (when used they lit up the under surface of the tanker's wings and ruined night vision). This left just the tanker's navigation lights and the small triangles of blue lights on the basket. In some ways tanking was easier in the dark, as one was not supposed to look at the refuelling probe when trying to engage the basket. In the dark you couldn't see it anyway, so it was one less thing to be concerned about.'

In June 1967 11 Squadron had practised in-flight refuelling and on 29 November, Flight Lieutenant Eggleton had established a record, of eight-and-a-half-hours' flying, refuelling five times, flying 5,000 miles.[8] In May 1968 four F.6s on 5 Squadron at Leconfield flew non-stop from Binbrook to Bahrain in eight hours, refuelled along the 4,000-mile route by Victor tankers from Marham. In August 1968 two Lightnings on 23 Squadron, fitted with overwing tanks, were required to fly the Atlantic to Canada non-stop to enable RAF solo display pilot Tony Craig to take part in the International Exhibition at Toronto. He would use one of the Lightnings for his solo display – the other was a spare in case of problems with the first Lightning. On 26 August Squadron Leader Ed Durham and Flight Lieutenant Geoff Brindle on 23 Squadron took off in XR725/A and XS936/B respectively and rendezvoused with their first tanker off Stornaway at 0800. Geoff Brindle, however, could not take on fuel and his overwing tanks were venting. Both pilots aborted and it was decided to re-mount the operation the following day after repairs to Brindle's aircraft. At 1140 hours on 27 August Squadron Leader Durham and Flight Lieutenant Brindle set out again with their supporting Victors. The first bracket went well, but at the second bracket, about 300 miles west of Stornaway, Brindle again could not take on fuel. Ed Durham continues:[9]

'We decided to carry on. Geoff would just have to refuel more often. I refuelled seven times across the Atlantic. Geoff Brindle did more like twelve or thirteen! The flight took seven hours twenty minutes. Apart from the refuellings and bad weather at Goose Bay, it was otherwise bloody boring. Craig took XS936 back with me in XR725 on 3 September and he had trouble with the overwing tanks on the first refuelling bracket! I said, "We force on". If a tanker did not get airborne we could always divert to Goose Bay. The Victors did arrive every time and after several tankings we reached Scotland again safely.'[10]

On 6 January 1969 exercise 'Piscator', the biggest in-flight refuelling exercise so far mounted by the RAF took place. Ten Lightning F.6s on 11 Squadron, refuelled by Victor tankers on 55, 57 and 214 Squadrons at Marham, deployed to RAF Tengah, Singapore, (staging through Muharraq and Gan) and back, a distance of 18,500 miles. During the two-way journey, 228 individual refuelling contacts were made during which 166,000 imperial gallons (754,630 litres) of fuel were transferred.

Twelve months later, in December 1969, exercise 'Ultimacy' was mounted. Ten F.6s on 5 Squadron this time flew to Tengah for joint air-defence exercises with 74 Squadron and RAAF Mirages there before exchanging some of their Lightnings for those of 74 Squadron, which were in need of major overhaul. Flight Lieutenant F. Stewart 'Stu' Rance recalls:[11] 'Ultimacy' provided an apt name for the deployment over Christmas 1969 of 5 Squadron's Lightnings to the Far East. Building upon previous deployment successes, the 'planners' had this time done us proud – for only one stop was involved, at Masirah in the Persian Gulf. Deployment time was to be kept to a minimum, too, with less than five days from first aircraft leaving the United Kingdom to the last aircraft arriving in South-East Asia. The detachment was to last for about a month, air defence exercises taking place in co-operation with 74 Squadron, the resident Lightning 'outfit' at our host station RAF Tengah. For the return home, starting the second week in January this year, the more leisurely 'scenic route' was to be made available, with stops at Masirah and Akrotiri a major planning concession to the pilot's anatomy. The last aircraft was to arrive in the UK by 16 January. It sounded good and anyone who had flown with the tanker force before knew that No.1 AAR Planning Cell at Bawtry would calculate and cosset us, Victor tankers metering fuel with slide rule precision. "We can hack it" and other such detailed planning epitaphs emitted as we studied our 'World Mercator' atlases. Where was the Far East anyway? The Squadron Navigation Officer, a serious-looking first tour flying officer, looked pained. No one else had liked the sound of the job! He was eventually heard to say did we "realise that Singapore was nearly 8,000 miles away, that each leg required some eight-and-a-half hours in the air and that some of it was at night?'. Even the sturdiest 'fighter jock' blanched, as a general realisation that "we'll set off on about one-five-oh degrees", just wouldn't do.

'Still, nothing that about a fortnight in the Planning Section didn't fix and on schedule the first wave of aircraft left the Binbrook runway in the pre-dawn and foggy hours of 8 December 1969. For those of us leaving on the third day, the knowledge that a first pair was already enjoying the sun in Singapore hastened the desire for departure from the ever-deepening fog machine that is North Lincolnshire in winter. An 0345 hours rendezvous in the dark with the Victor tankers over East Anglia and we were on our way. South across a clear France, slipping by a brightly lit Paris, we coasted out over a dawning Riviera at Nice. Italy went by at equal pace and soon a snow-blown but still smoking Mount Etna heralded the turn east along the Mediterranean and the rendezvous with more Victor tankers North of Cyprus. It is perhaps the almost monotonous precision of these link ups with tankers out of 'parts foreign' which visibly impress to the pilot in the air and speak for the standard of support from the planning and operations organisations on the ground. We were to be impressed in the same way many more times. More hours went by as in the sun we meandered on our way east, before a final crossing of the Muscat and Oman, which looked sandy enough to make even the most frugal consume the last of his pre-supplied orange squash – a tricky, technical feat in a small cockpit. Masirah at last and our friendly Ops Officer: "Is it serviceable? Sign in – hurry up or you'll be late for tea!" Tea? I still hadn't had lunch. As the sun slid immediately below the horizon, I felt vaguely cheated.

'I was woken at ten the following morning. Had I heard the news? A tanker man had backed away from a snake up the road and trod on a scorpion. I checked my boots warily before putting them on and repairing to the mess for breakfast. Much to my surprise it was still available and heartened by a staging post that obviously catered for staging, I spent the afternoon greeting the newly arrived aircraft from the UK for upon their serviceable arrival depended our own successful early departure. All was well and again a pre-dawn launch. This time into 4,000 miles of ocean, South-East to Gan and then due east to Sumatra. Being brave single-seat men, we braced ourselves to the task, ignored the water and concentrated upon the navigation – even if this did consist mainly of reciting the names of the diversion airfields to ourselves for the first couple of hours or so. We made our through connection with the Victors out of Gan on schedule and so came to the greenery of Singapore – a welcome escort being provided in the latter stages by 74 Squadron aircraft. A warm welcome awaited. With Christmas just around the corner, it was necessary to get cracking. First priority was an umbrella, second a briefing and third a flight around the local area. Of the fifteen pilots participating, twelve had not visited Singapore before and were unfamiliar with the problems of operating in the Far East theatre at the tail-end of the monsoon season. We soon got wet and the message.

'On 18 December exercise 'Antler' took place and together with 74 Squadron and 63 Light Anti-Aircraft Regiment, 5 Squadron aircraft helped provide the Singapore Air Defence Force against an enemy force comprising 45 and 81 Squadron Canberras, 20 Squadron Hunters and 75 Squadron Mirages of RAAF Butterworth. Victor tankers were also available to provide tactical air-to-air refuelling in the battle against targets at both high and low altitudes. A useful and rewarding exercise. Following the exercise, there was Christmas and more Tengah hospitality, both individual and general, for the squadron personnel. With our stay in the Far East now rapidly sliding by, only the New Year was left and it was time to refit our ferry tanks for the long homeward journey.

'With pairs of aircraft leaving Tengah daily from 8 January onwards, Masirah rapidly became the focal point of our operations on the route home. The planning called for a build-up of aircraft at Masirah before moving on to Akrotiri. It was here therefore that our 'man on the ground' became vital to the efficiency of the recovery. Acting as co-ordinator with the operations rooms thousands of miles away in the UK, meeting and despatching aircraft, looking after accommodation and messing and the arranging of briefing and transport all make for a busy day. They are essential tasks, however, in taking the 'staging load' off the route pilots and in ensuring their adequate rest. During our week's operations in the Gulf every assistance was provided for Lightning and Victor operations by the station permanent staff. It was perhaps only fortuitous that Masirah managed its first serious rainfall for nearly six years during our short stay!

'Leaving at first light on 11 January, it was on to Akrotiri for the staging aircraft. After an overnight stop, enjoying friendly hospitality and co-operation of the resident Lightning Squadron, it was homeward bound for a wintry recovery into the United Kingdom. Ah! The welcome sight of the Marham-based tanker who had come out from the UK to take us on the last stage of our journey back to Binbrook. Four days later, with all ten aircraft in the UK, it was all over. The successful conclusion of the most ambitious Lightning deployment yet, which had demonstrated our flexibility to operate in the Far East after short notice. The route experience gained had been immense. Now, with only fast-fading suntans as a reminder, we study the maps again. Perhaps they'll send us to Cyprus this year ...'[12]

In February 1971, 23 Squadron tanked from Victors to Cyprus, to take part in practice air defence of the island and ACM (air combat-manoeuvring exercises). On 25 August that year 74 Squadron disbanded at Tengah, Singapore and 56 Squadron acquired all of the Tigers' remaining F.6s. Starting on 2 September these were flown over the 6,000-mile route, a 13-hour trip, to Akrotiri. They staged through Gan and Muharraq and completed seven air-to-air refuellings with Victor tankers. 56 Squadron was relieved in June the following year by 11 Squadron, which deployed to Akrotiri for a one-month detachment, enabling 56 Squadron to fly to Britain to complete MPC (Missile Practice Camp) at Valley before returning to the island. Cyprus featured high on the agenda again in 1974. In January six F.6s were sent to the island, where on 15 July a Greek-led coup by the Cyprus National Guard overthrew President Makarios of Cyprus. Five days later, Turkey invaded the northern part of the island. After two days of fierce fighting, the United Nations arranged a cease-fire. The coup led to a dramatic increase in Turkish air activity around the island and Lightnings of 56 Squadron flew over 200 sorties, 20-27 July, none of them fully armed battle sorties, to protect the Sovereign Base Areas.

'It was in 1974, when HAS sites were unheard of and Lightnings were silver and ruled the roost,' recalls Mick Cameron. 'The then premier Air Defence Squadron – 11 of course – was deployed to Cyprus, as a spot of bother had broken out: people were starting to panic. We were told that half of the squadron would be going fairly sharpish and would be away for about six months and then the other half would take over from us. At the time I was a young, scrawny, immature SAC (not a lot has changed!), but had a lot of first line experience, so I was definitely on the list. Things out there were fairly hectic, especially as we were permanently on QRA and the armourers were used to one week of days, a week of nights and a week on 'Q'; plus I couldn't hold my Keo! We used to have three lads on days and two on nights and our SNCO was Sergeant Al Young. We were looking after six aircraft and one of them was XR762/H. As an experienced SAC, I was given special authorization to fit safety equipment for the duration of the detachment – this was normally the remit of 'fitters'. I had fitted safety equipment to Hotel sometime in the previous six months, but couldn't really remember when, but, as I was to find out, the RAF NEVER forgets.

'Our shift was off at the time when we were all called back into work. Rumours were rife, "The Turks have invaded" and, "We're going home early!" were but two of them. The main one was, however, 'Kite's gone in work we found out that 'Hotel' had crashed into the sea and the SAR was looking for the ejected pilot – beer for the armourers, we thought. I recall that 'Hotel' was part of a two-ship, the other pilot being Flight Lieutenant Joey Gough and that XR762 had spun in during a 1 v 1 combat. As it happened, the pilot [Squadron Leader Dave 'Quingle' Hampton on 11 Squadron] unfortunately drowned and the detachment took on a gloomy atmosphere.

'About a week later, yours truly in tatty KD shorts, bondu boots and a suntan was summoned to the Station Conference Room. "Shall I change?" said I. "No, go as you are," came the response. I was ushered in and confronted by so much brass that I realised this could only be a Board of Enquiry – witch hunt! They produced the F720s on which I had signed to say the fitting of the safety kit was satisfactory (the RAF never throws anything away) and would I care to describe to the panel how, when and where I had fitted the equipment to 'Hotel'? To the uninitiated, the fitting of safety equipment looks like a mess of straps and buckles with nowhere to go. In fact it is all fairly straightforward, except, of course, when it has to be described verbally, with one's career hanging on every word and not a friendly face in the house! In the end, I came out of it with a pat on the back. From what I understand the pilot had cut away the seals on his immersion suit in an attempt to remain cool. Upon entering the water his suit had filled causing him to drown.'[13]

In Germany in 1974 when Flying Officer (now Squadron Leader) Clive Rowley was flying F.2As from Gütersloh with 19 Squadron, he was photographed with this tanker hose coiled like a snake. Clive explains: 'We didn't get much tanking practice as Germany-based squadrons – spookily enough the tankers were only available on Fridays, meaning that the crews had to stop at the weekend! On about my sixth ever tanking-sortie (with gaps of several weeks between each) I think I was probably getting overconfident about this 'tricky' skill. When I attempted to connect with the hose trailed from this particular Victor tanker I used all the wrong techniques, including looking at the basket just before connecting. Seeing that I was going to miss to the right I put on a large 'bootfull' of left rudder to slide my probe into the basket. Unfortunately the probe tip 'rimmed' the basket, didn't engage and pushed it sideways. As I backed off I was surprised and horrified to see a very large lateral 'whip' develop in the tanker hose, which grew as it snaked towards the HDU (pod) and grew further as it snaked back towards me.

Next thing my Lightning was clobbered by this hose with a life of its own. There was a loud bang as it hit me somewhere on the intake and my aircraft was tipped 90 degrees of bank towards the Victor's fuselage – rather frightening! I levelled the aircraft to straight and level and having achieved this and averted any collision risk I was appalled to see that the hose – 55 feet of it – had fallen off over Germany! I transmitted, "Tanker Call-sign, your hose has fallen off!" This didn't go down well! A visual inspection by my leader reported possible damage to the intake.

'After a slow-speed handling check I landed back at Gütersloh safely. Unfortunately the stainless steel double skin of my intake had been dented and the skins squashed together. They were talking about several months to repair it. I was not popular. Meanwhile, I spent the weekend worrying about the tanker hose. Had it, for example, caused a multiple pile-up on an autobahn with significant loss of life? No news was good news, but the aircraft damage was still threatening the previously good relationship with the boss. BAe Warton sent an expert panel beater called Ted and his expertise saved the day (and my bacon). My 'punishment' was to buy Ted lots of beer, present him with a framed picture of the aircraft and have my photograph taken with a Victor hose wrapped around me. The hose was found some weeks later in a German farmer's field and returned to us – unfortunately! So you see it was a punishment!'[14]

The night of 26 November 1974 was a busy one for Derek 'Furz' Lloyd.[15] 'HMS *Glamorgan* was sailing in the Iceland/Faroes gap as the capital vessel of a Surface Task Group (TSG) taking part in a joint maritime exercise in the North Atlantic. Leuchars-based Lightnings and Phantoms were providing air defence and Vulcans, Buccaneers and Canberras were attacking the TSG. It was a Tuesday night of the second week of the exercise and I had already taken part during day-flying the previous Friday. The daylight mission had been in support of HMS *Hermes* as she sailed north abeam Aberdeen. This night mission was with Air-to-Air Refuelling (AAR) and involved manning a Combat Air Patrol (CAP) in 'Q' country, way up north of our normal operating area, where we would usually be intercepting Bear Deltas on their way to and from Cuba.

'Unlike the day mission, I was launched as a solo fighter direct to the tanker. All went well with the take-off and climb but the radar dropped off line as I levelled at height. I had just topped out at Flight Level (FL) 340 having climbed all the way up through thick cloud. The left front console dimmer was still distracting and I eventually decided to turn it off altogether. It was a clear moonlit night above the weather system, but I knew I would probably have to descend back into cloud to refuel. Therein lay the first problem: a tanker join in the weather with no radar. I toyed with the idea of asking the Victor to climb to attain Visual Meteorological Conditions (VMC) above the cloud. But relations with the tanker force were not at their best during this period of air defence operations in the UK and I would probably stand more chance of getting blood from a stone. At least I had time to think about it as I trawled north recycling the radar.

'The next problem was an intermittent feed from the ventral. This was relatively unusual in an F.6 and I didn't notice it until both flaps had fed and the mains had dropped a little. It wasn't until a full fuel check somewhere off the coast by Buchan that I realised I had about 800lb trapped underneath, both flaps empty and a slight imbalance in the mains. Selecting Flight Refuel 'ON' and 'OFF' seemed to help, but I had to continually attend to this as I monitored the fuel feed until the ventral emptied. So now I had no radar and a suspect ventral feed. Alarm bells started to ring because I was going to be operating in an area where diversion airfields were a long way away and a problem with ventral feeding would be less than desirable. However, previous experience suggested that my action of periodically depressurising the system would see me airtight and I pressed on northbound – still recycling the radar.

'I had to start thinking about the tanker join. The brief was for silent procedures and Buchan had been as discreet as expected on my way north. I was still flirting with cloud tops but the weather seemed to be getting better. As I turned onto a north-westerly heading the Victor turned port about and faced up for a 180-degrees intercept. I picked the Victor up on radar at about twenty-five miles as it came onto the screen from the right. I looked out and saw a set of lights in that direction. I mentally relaxed knowing I would be able to join visually. It seemed as if I was sliding down the top of the clouds as they fell away during my descent. Clear of the weather, there were now only scattered layers of cloud around me and by the time I was behind the flying 'Blackpool Illuminations', I was clear of all cloud with only patchy areas well below.

'I may as well not have bothered to set up the cockpit. The lights were so bright on the Victor that all adjustment for night vision was well destroyed before I got close to it. Cleared by the captain to join directly behind, it was with some trepidation that I realised that there were no hoses – at least no wing hoses; only the centre hose trailing out the back.

'In well over 1,000 hours flying in the Lightning I had never tanked from the centre hose at night. I had no problem coming to terms with this; after all it should be easier without the potential distraction of the very slight 'leans' which were common to flying on the wing without a visual horizon at night or in the weather. However, I had no idea what visual cues to use when closing in and this could be quite adventurous. I carried out the pre-refuelling checks and motored on in.

'The size of the Victor only really became apparent within a hundred yards or so and then during the latter stages of a join-up there was a definite sense of being overwhelmed by the graceful lines and 'crescent' wings. Turbulence from the disturbed air started to interfere with flight within about fifty yards or so and if joining on a wing station increasing amounts of aileron and rudder trim had to be used to maintain straight and level flight. At night, there was the annoying distraction of rotating anti-collision lights but fortunately, by approaching from directly behind and underneath. There was not a problem on this occasion. With great satisfaction I made contact at the first attempt and started to take on fuel.

'With a clunk, I disengaged and the basket rocked away as I backed off. Full to the brim, I quickly turned to take up a vector the navy had been pestering me to do whilst I was still in the process of topping up. Passing the 'Gate' of the TSG's defences in excess of Mach 1, I was rather pleased this was only a peacetime exercise. They appeared to be making a real hash of the procedures they should have been using and I was being steered over the fleet at high speed towards the threat. Without cast-iron identification I would not have done this in war!

'Soon I was able to pick up a faint contact which closely resembled the air picture being described by the fighter controller on board *Glamorgan* and I called 'Judy'. Now in control of the intercept I adjusted the geometry to lag the target in the stern and set myself up for a shot. I never identified the 'blip' but at about two miles I got a good acquisition and fired about a quarter of a mile later before breaking away starboard.

'I switched off the Master Arm Selector (MAS) and carried out a set routine of checks. I was not surprised to notice the same problem with the fuel and I depressurised the ventral. Whether it was because I was now far away from home at night or perhaps a genuine lack of reaction to my 'switchery' but I was under the profound impression that no fuel was transferring. I watched the gauges for a little longer but was immediately distracted by a pairing to another target. I judged that I didn't need to worry too much about it at this stage; after all the tanker was close by and if necessary I could top up early to ensure that I had enough reserves for a safe transit south.

'I don't remember this second intercept but I do remember my concern when the radar dropped off line again. The A/A TACAN was clicking away with random indications, the fuel was well and truly imbalanced with about 800lb trapped in the ventral and the navy had stopped talking to me. Now I had a problem. I turned roughly in the direction I thought the tanker would be and ferreted around in the left leg pocket of my immersion suit for my IMC 'aide-memoire'. The very small, reduced photocopy of several hundred frequencies used by the RN is easy to read in a crew room or briefing room but in the extremes of a poorly lit cockpit even my 'alleged' 20/20 vision was not coping too well. Inevitably I read the first collector frequency incorrectly and spent what seemed like hours talking to no one before I realised that something was wrong. Then the clips of my green aircrew folder popped open as I turned the page and the list of frequencies was lost on the cockpit floor forever. I fortunately remembered the initial contact frequency and tuned into that once more. Across the airwaves I could hear the other controller with verbal diarrhoea chatting away to the tanker and with some relief I waited for a break in the conversation. Within minutes the fuel seemed to have sorted itself out; I had topped up to full from the tanker. The radar was working; the cockpit had that warm and cosy feeling again and I was back in business.'[16]

In 1976 visiting pilot Dagmar Heller flew on CAP on 11 Squadron: 'Flying on CAP (Combat Air Patrol), or 'Capping' as the pilots term it, we started our search for the 'enemy' aircraft that were being slung at the UK shores. It was the second day of 11 Squadron's involvement in exercise 'Cold Fire' and the tempo was mounting as the day progressed.

'Following a racecourse pattern, Flight Lieutenant Paul Adams, the pilot of our T.5, had little time to relax. A few minutes on one heading, a change of course and back track, all the while searching his radar, computing his course, keeping track of his position, checking his fuel/time chart and obeying instructions from Boulmer SOC – the Sector Operations Centre master-minding Binbrook's participation in this NATO exercise.

'No wonder Lightning pilots have to be top quality, or as some maintain the elite of the RAF today. Alone, without a navigator or second-generation navigation equipment, their work load is indeed high and continual stick-hand changes are needed to operate the radar, the navigation equipment and other instruments located on either side of the instrument display.

'"Binbrook - stand all aircraft to readiness." This order at 0800 hours over the tele-line from SOC Boulmer was the start of this day's event.

TANKING

At 0815 hours all aircraft were on state, but as the exercise developed in answer to the incoming threat, the neat rows of Lightnings from Nos.11 and 5 Squadrons gradually depleted as aircraft were scrambled or sent to the Operational Readiness Platform (ORP). Pilots could be on thirty-minute state, then brought up to ten-minute or five-minute states; for the latter the aircraft had to be on the ORP at the end of the runway as it takes five minutes to taxi from dispersal to that point. At cockpit readiness a pilot can start up and scramble a Lightning in under two minutes flat, but this was not a requirement demanded that day.

'Our turn to get into the action came just before 1400 hours. As it was impossible for me to 'scramble' in any shape or form, I was strapped into the right-hand seat of Lightning T.5 XS451 'X-ray' and made 'live' (the safety pins pulled out of the ejector seat). A last run through the ejection procedures, which I had done earlier that day together with a dinghy drill and at cockpit readiness we awaited instructions.

'Over the tele-line comes another Lightning alert and 'Mission 36' – our call sign – is given by Binbrook Station HQ in reply. 'Roger 36,' from Boulmer, "vector 045, flight level 230, CAP Fox XX". But however much I strain my ears, it is impossible to follow this unfamiliar jargon on the R/T, so I leave my pilot to unscramble his scramble instructions and settle back to savour my first Lightning flight.

'Five minutes' taxiing to the end of runway 21 where four Lightnings are waiting on ORP and with throttles fully open we roar off past them down the runway in answer to this invasion threat.

'For Wing Commander Ted Nance, CO of 11 Squadron, our take-off was another line to add to the movement board in the Operations Room of his squadron. Connected by tele-line to SOC Boulmer and the Mission Control H.Q. at Binbrook, from which both Lightning squadrons were being directed, he filled in on his wall chart the take-off and landing times of all 11 Squadron's pilots so that he could control how long they had been airborne and avoid any unnecessary fatigue.

'On the other side of a glass partition Squadron Leader G. L. Perry, 11 Squadron's Senior Engineering Officer, knew exactly where each aircraft was deployed by checking the magnetic board which indicated the number of aircraft in the air, those on dispersal and those on ORP. His airmen on first line have got the turn-round time of their Lightnings down to a fine art. As aircraft after aircraft taxied in either to be re-scrambled, stood down or sent to ORP, three crews of five men each refuelled, rearmed (i.e., changed the camera film), checked oil, brakes and tyres and refitted brake chutes in the space of ten minutes. If a pilot taxied past Squadron HQ with air brakes out, this was the signal that he had a snag to report and for the servicing boys to run out and be ready to go to work when the aircraft came to a halt.

'Our Lightning, or 'Mission 36', was hardly airborne before it hit the low cloud over Lincolnshire that day, but heading north-east over the North Sea with the altimeter winding round the thousands of feet in seconds, we burst through into sunshine that soon stretched all the way down to the sea. Once on CAP between base and the expected direction of attack, our task was the immediate interception of 'enemy' aircraft when their position was either defined by our controller or by ourselves using the Lightning's search radar.

'Spread over that afternoon alone more than ninety aircraft both from the UK and the Continent were due to attack the UK in waves. But even so, our first CAP produced no 'trade' and we saw nothing more exciting than a friendly Shackleton AEW aircraft from 8 Squadron, Lossiemouth, cross-telling targets to the SOC. Perhaps our invaders had changed course as an evasive action? If they were still in the Boulmer sector of operations, then no doubt another Lightning or a Phantom from Coningsby would have been told to intercept.

'For our T.5 it was time to refuel. 'Happiness is a tanker-ship' – a joke amongst pilots but if it had not been for the tanker we would have had to return to base. With a tanker up the Lightnings can extend their area of operation and/or endurance.

'At 25,000 feet Victor K.1A XH649 from 57 Squadron, Marham, was patrolling a set course enabling pilots to rendezvous without any R/T contact being made. This cuts down R/T chatter and the possibility of jamming, so Paul took up position alongside the port nose of the tanker to let the captain know we wished to refuel. As another Lightning was refuelling on the No. 1 starboard hose, we dropped astern and crept up on the port hose.

'My pilot made contact first time, confirmed by an amber light at the rear of the tanker's refuelling pod. As he brought the T.5 a little closer, the hose reeled in and amber changed to green to show that fuel was flowing into our tanks.

'Inside the tanker the only member of the crew who could see the Lightning throughout the whole operation was the Nav. Radar and Refuelling Operator, Flight Lieutenant 'Tommy' Thomson. A rearward-facing periscope enabled him to give a running commentary on our progress to the Captain, Flight Lieutenant Barry Hunt and co-pilot, Flight Lieutenant Phil Marsh. They had their CO, Wing Commander Alistair Sutherland, on board that day as navigator; he and the Air Electronics Officer, Flight Lieutenant Tom Keeley, could look through two small sideways-facing windows but had no vision of what was going on at the rear.

'For approximately seven minutes the Lightning had to be held in position until all tanks were full – even the small flap tanks. Then the green light flashed to indicate that we could drop back and clear. Up to the front again to show the Victor captain that all was well and with a friendly thumbs-up sign we broke away.

'The unanimous opinion of all Lightning pilots is that it is a superb aircraft to fly. For sheer acceleration and manoeuvrability it can out-fly all its contemporaries and on the last tactical evaluation on its mission effectiveness, judged by a mixture of NATO officers, the Lightning earned a 'One'.

'The next stage of our mission confirmed some of these facts. On a course of 210 degrees to our next CAP I tentatively suggested a loop. It did not seem quite cricket to be doing this in the middle of a NATO exercise, but then this was also supposed to be a demonstration flight! My pilot obligingly put the throttles into reheat and soared straight upwards at around 300 feet/second using up 7,000 feet of sky.

'These radar controllers don't miss much, I thought, as we were asked to confirm our height at 7,000 feet, but as we were by then on our way down again it was not too much of a lie to confirm. That was really great!

'I was just on the point of suggesting another manoeuvre when everything seemed to happen at once. 'Bogies'! At last... We hurtled off in the direction indicated by the radar controller. At 620 knots we soon reached the position of our target and with air brakes out and throttles back we came to a juddering slow down. Here we joined up with another 11 Squadron Lightning flown by Squadron Leader Stuart Rance and together in battle formation carried out a square search.

'Bogies to our left.' This time from our pilot on his southbound beat and diving down to come round below and behind them I could swear the altimeter read 300 feet. First time we were too close so over we barrelled, came round again pulling 5g and levelled out behind our targets – four Buccaneers flying westwards at around 500 feet.

'I would never have believed that a Lightning could carry out such tight manoeuvres, but it was only seconds from first spotting the invaders to the moment the Lightning's radar had locked on to the nearest of the four Buccaneers and the Red Top missile had been armed and fired. Only a camera shot, of course, not a real live missile!

'I was sorry to leave the scene of action, but with one 'kill' to our credit it was time to return to base. The Lightning's radar picked up Spurn Head and the Humber Estuary quite clearly and as we flew in over the Grimsby Fish Docks, Binbrook lay ahead. Grimsby has conferred on RAF Binbrook the Freedom of that Borough; very noble of them when you consider that most Lightnings use Spurn Head and the Grimsby Fish Docks as a landmark when returning to base.

'The Lightning today has four roles to perform: UK air defence, fleet air defence, overseas reinforcement and IAF (Interceptor Alert Force). It says much for the original Warton-inspired design – that of a fast, high-level interceptor – that in the hands of the RAF's highly qualified pilots the Lightning is still a most effective fighter in the front-line.

'Armed with Red Top or Firestreak missiles, both radar- and computer-launched, the Red Top tends to be favoured as it has a collision-course capability and a more powerful, longer-burning motor than the Firestreak.

'Three Lightning squadrons are fully operational in the UK, Nos.11 and 5 at Binbrook and 56 at Wattisham, but while the Lightnings at Wattisham are being phased out and replaced by Phantoms, the Binbrook Lightnings will remain in service until the early 1980s. A decision welcomed in RAF circles as it adds two squadrons of fighters to the UK air defences which they would not otherwise have had. A decision welcomed at Binbrook, too, as it enables them to continue to fly and maintain an aircraft of which they are proud.

"We only take top quality pilots," Wing Commander Nance, No.11's CO, said "and Training Command knows this now and send us only the best." That pretty well sums up the pilots, but on the servicing side it is much the same. Together they represent a high level of expertise with enthusiasm to match.

'Squadron Leader Perry, the Senior Engineering Officer, has to be able to get 70 per cent of No.11's aircraft on the flight line at twelve hours' notice, but this did not seem to concern him in any way. "The Lightning has now been modified to the extent where it is very reliable," he maintained. "It has been serviced so long that we know what to expect and the spare stock level is just right."

'The squadron has been established for 120 ground crew, although it is slightly over that figure at the present time. Thirty of the men are on first line, fifteen during the day and fifteen at night, as night flying training is carried out all the year round. In the hangar, three teams of twenty men work two shifts per day and one at night. The night shift normally finishes at 0400 hours, but if important work has to be done it is not uncommon for the day shift to find everybody still at work when they arrive at 0800.

'All servicing and rectification, each Check 1 at 75 hours and Check 2 at 225 hours, is carried out at squadron level. The major checks and overhauls (Check 3 at 500 hours and Check 4 at 1800 hours) are done by the Aircraft Servicing Flight for both squadrons. While this has the advantage of streamlining the major servicing, it removes the incentive the squadron has to get its own aircraft back on the line.

'In addition to looking after No.11's mixture of F.6s, F.3s and one T.5, Squadron Leader Perry maintains the three T.5s of the Lightning Training Flight, which is attached to the squadron but will shortly branch out on its own.

'Two Lightnings at Binbrook are on a permanent state of alert. Armed in earnest with Red Top missiles and guns loaded, they sit poised for flight in a hangar behind power-operated doors. At any moment a Lightning could be called upon to investigate a violation of national air space or an unidentified dot on the radar screen and it is a comforting thought that, once rolling, a Lightning can reach a height of 36,000 feet in 2½ minutes.

'Nos. 11 and 5 Squadrons share this duty, each squadron for two weeks. While the pilots – on a permanent ten-minute state of alert – take it in turns to eat and sleep in the IAF hangar, the ground crew of six airmen and one sergeant remain there a whole week.

'For about another decade Lightnings will intercept invaders, patrol our north-eastern approaches and defend British ships and even after that there will be some life in them yet.'[17]

An anonymous Lightning pilot wrote about another Combat Air Patrol in an exercise overseas with the Royal Navy:[18] 'I was allocated an aircraft and a wingman at ground readiness. After an hour or so, we were brought up to cockpit readiness, for the Combat Air Patrols (CAPs) had detected a low-level raid and there appeared to be a running battle in progress about eighty miles south of us. The two-seater squadron had formed a quorum, back-tracked along the enemy's attack path and were shooting up the ship and anything trying to take off from it. Our own CAPs were mixed up with the enemy strike, which was progressing, via move and counter-move, towards the airfield. We checked in on telebrief and in response the SOC crackled into life:

'Alert 2 Lightnings.'

'49 Alpha and Bravo,' from Base Ops. This was it; those were our call signs: '49 Alpha and Bravo, vector 270, make angels one zero, call stud 52.

Six plus Fakers heading north fast and low. 240 – 40 miles from you and mixed up with chicks.

'Your mission to intercept and exercise destroy. Gate, gate, scramble – acknowledge.'

'Scramble start, check Bravo's canopy coming down, wave off the marshaller and watch him scuttling for the slit trenches. Pre-take-off checks complete, take the far side of the runway and we're off. A check in the mirror and there is Bravo about too yards behind and left. After take-off, check right for ten seconds and reverse – there's Bravo in battle formation on the left.

'Weapons and cameras! Stud 52 go.'

'"Bravo," as he checked in.

'Loud and clear. Mission 49 – two chicks, gated angels ten. Tiger fast twenty.'

'From the SOC: "Roger left 250, your target's track 773, 11 o'clock twenty – heading North – reported line abreast one mile with escort 5 miles astern in a mix-up with chicks. I'll bring you in from the south, out of sun."'

'Good planning! I hope we have plenty of overtake speed. Perhaps that's why we are at 10,000. Then, from my wingman:

'Bravo – I hold 2 – ten left 52 miles, low, line abreast.'

'Roger – I hold them – going down – call visual and watch for the escort.'

'Then I saw them, two dark-grey banana shapes, intermittently merging with the sea:

'Tally ho – twelve o'clock 6 – only two, in on the left one.' 'Bravo out – tail clear.'

'Alpha – they've seen us and are going right.'

'Their smoke trail was now visible and thickened as they accelerated to avoid us. Then, again, from my number two: "Bravo, your tail clear. Can I take the other one?" 'Something stirred in the recesses of my mind: "Negative, stay together, look for the escort."'

'Copied – no contact – your tail clear – watt one, two escorts three miles astern no threat yet, but closing in the turn.' I checked behind number two and called:

'OK Bravo, engage the escort and keep them off me. Your tail clear. Splash on my first target, going for the other.'

'Then silence for about a minute – too long. The second missile saw and fired on the second target.

'Splash on both. North of you about four miles, 5,000 feet. Joining you in a right turn. Bravo – report.'

TANKING

'I yo-yoed out right, craning my neck for sight of the escort and my number two. Then I saw them: two different dark-grey shapes in my 9 o'clock low, turning right underneath me. Bravo's g-strained voice huffed something about having the escorts tied up in a turning fight and my memory stirred again. Where is he? Forget the escorts for a moment. There he is! Filling my right windscreen. Break! Phew, too damned close. I was shaken and felt that enough was enough.

'Bravo, haul-off east, cover me.'

'He feinted at the opposition, who countered and ran off to the north, presumably I to join their two charges. Realistic tactics, I suppose – we could argue their demise at the debrief. Breathing heavily, I advised SOC of the two that got away and they reassured me that they were now SAM targets.

'Bravo and I reformed into defensive battle formation and went looking for the rest I of the excitement. It was then that my mind started to clear and yielded up its stored memory. "It's the one that you don't see that gets you."'

Following a subsequent Whitehall defence review, all 56 Squadron's Lightnings had gone by the end of January 1975 and only the SAR helicopters of 84 Squadron remained on the troubled island. However, Lightnings did return to Cyprus again, albeit on five-week detachments, when its importance as an Armament Practice Camp was fully realized. Each pilot would fly a series of cine-camera work-up flights against a banner towed by a Canberra. When the pilot was considered safe, he would fly nine live gun firings on the banner. Scoring was completed by tipping the head of each 30mm round in a special semi-drying paint, which, when it hit the banner, left a stain around the hole that left no room for doubt. To avoid confusion on multiple sorties, each pilot's bullets would be tipped with different colour paint. An anonymous Lightning pilot described his APC in Cyprus.[19]

'It was a lovely summer's day in Cyprus, tailor-made for flying the Lightning – dark and dirty North Sea nights were a million miles away and who needs a radar when you can see 100 miles anyway? We were engaged in an Armament Practice Camp, firing air-to-air against a towed banner: this was in the days of the straight banner tow, so the Canberra trundled backwards and forwards just south of Akrotiri, which was always visible. I'd been doing quite well, thank you, and was determined to maintain my position as leading shot, so I set out on this sortie determined to be very pedantic about my firing parameters and really annihilate the flag. I was very disciplined – pass after pass I refused to fire because the pipper wasn't quite on the front of the spreader bar, or the speed was ten knots fast, or whatever. My No. 2 fired out and departed for RTB and I'd still only fired about half my rounds. In time, the fuel started to run down a bit, but - no sweat - I looked over my shoulder and there was Akrotiri, so close you could almost touch it, so in we go again ... Another twenty or so rounds later and the fuel was getting decidedly down. But I still had at least another couple of passes to go and - quick look - yes, Akrotiri was still a short glide away; OK another couple of passes should do it. However, the fuel pucker factor was obviously affecting my ice-cold judgement a bit, 'cos the tracking on the next two passes was a bit dismal, so no fire and try them again. Look over the shoulder again. Still OK. No hassle to get home. Pull up and idle/fast idle cruise descent back onto finals. No problem: I won't make minimum landing fuel on the downwind leg, but pulling up and starting recovery with minimum landing fuel is showing willing and besides, fighter pilots are always ace at running the fuel just right. Now I'll just get these last two passes sorted...

'The guns were finally "fired out" and I pulled up, turned round and pointed at the island.

'Gata Radar, 44 complete for recover'. 'Roger 44, pigeons 060 55 miles'.

'55 miles! Bloody hell. It got suddenly cold in the cockpit, in spite of the sunshine. Next mistake, I failed to climb to a sensible recovery height – a cringing animal at controls convinced that he couldn't afford the fuel to climb. Next mistake, I failed to transfer remaining fuel/shut down No. 2 engine – more worried about reputation and landing on one than on saving petrol, even at that stage. In a remarkably calm voice, I told Air Traffic that I would be joining downwind to land, precautionary (first smart thing I had said/done for about three hours).

'Some long time before reaching the circuit, both pumps captions came on steady – inevitable really, you can't expect transfer pumps to keep pumping fuel to the collectors when they're not surrounded by fuel. I slid onto the high downwind, only breathing once every ten minutes and flew a sort of glide approach – I don't really know why, I suppose it seemed familiar from JPs and Hunters, although it wouldn't be a lot of use with sixteen tons of ominously silent aluminium. Halfway round finals, both FUEL captions came on (for the unlucky who haven't flown the Lightning, it means the collector boxes are empty: every other time I've seen it, the associated engine flames out shortly afterwards). I didn't twitch at all: I'd frozen completely at that stage. To my amazement, the mighty Avon thrustmasters kept pushing me along and after a couple of life times. I touched down at about the right speed and place. Drag bag, brakes and adrenaline and I managed to exit at the first turn off, 3,000 feet in – who said the Lightning needs long runways? I didn't dare shut one engine down, 'cos I didn't know which one was going to stop first, so I taxied in very fast, jammed the brakes on hard on the chocks (to make the fuel gauges plus-up). The fuel gauges still didn't read anything remotely respectable, but it made me feel marginally better.

'I managed to climb out without falling down the ladder and signed-in in a shaky hand; "It's a fighter pilot's 800lb-a-side, Flight Sergeant," I said, giving him a knowing wink. He gave me a lugubrious look back. Afterwards, whilst I was into my second mug of coffee (I'd spilt most of the first), he phoned up to tell me how much fuel he'd put in: I knew then that he was having me on, because everyone knows the Lightning doesn't hold that much.

'Plenty of morals in this little tale: find 'em yourself. For me, I've run short of fuel on occasions again since then, for much better reasons, but I've never run as short as that and I've always reacted better – climbed, shut down engines, diverted and so on. I'm grateful that on this occasion I started my recovery from the western end of the area, with the standard Akrotiri 25-knot wind to help me along, as well as help me stop quickly on landing. It was a hard way to learn, but since then I've always been fuel/distance/time conscious and I doubt that there're many Lightning pilots who haven't learnt in similar ways.

'And after all that, I only got half my previous score on the banner: there's another moral in there somewhere!'

'Each squadron left Binbrook once a year for RAF Akrotiri in Cyprus for live gun firing,' recalls Glen Johnson, an armourer.[20] 'Each pilot would fly a series of cine camera work-up flights against a banner towed by a 100 Squadron Canberra. Then, when the pilot was considered safe on the cine sorties, he would fly a total of nine live firings on the banner. Canberras normally fly either two or three two-hour sorties each day, thirty minutes of which occupied by transiting and finding a clear area over the sea. The pilot of the Canberra tug serves as a range safety officer, keeping a look out for boats that are in the range area. The Canberra usually flies at about 180 knots; a speed limitation imposed by the breaking strain of the 300 yard cable towing the 24 foot by 6 foot banner. Usually after about 116 hours the banner starts to rip and tear, so every effort is made to minimise the flight time of the banner. With one fighter on the banner the Canberra follows a triple race track pattern, but with two aircraft on the banner a figure of eight is adopted, Also, as a safety factor, the Canberra assumes a 30 degree angle of bank once the fighter has positioned itself and the latter must not come within 300 yards and a 12 degree angle-off. Having flown in a Canberra target towing, it is rather a sobering sound hearing the gun belching away in the background and hoping the jockey's wearing his glasses. Once he has flown his live shoots he may be Ace qualified. The Ace qualification is a percentage score and the standard is laid down by SHAPE (Supreme HQ Allied Powers Europe). Obviously there are things that are outside the pilot's control, such as gun bounce, let spread and velocity Jump. These factors mean there is a less than 50% chance of the rounds fired hitting the banner and this clearly makes the pilots' task very difficult indeed. The scoring is done by tipping each bullet head in a paint called 'tipping paint'. The paint semi-dries, so if you rubbed the head with a cloth it would leave a mark on it. To get over the fusion of more than one pilot on the same banner each pilot would have his own individual colour, so that with three aircraft flying a/c one would have yellow, a/c two would have green and a/c three would have red. The banner gets dropped over the aircraft; a hole's a hole, a colour's a colour, there's little room for argument. Near the end of the APC, we as armourers could have a bit of fun and load an aircraft with a bow load. This means that in one aircraft each round was tipped with a different colour; this caused confusion looking at the banner after the shoot.'

The APCs continued right up until 1987, tanked there and back, as always by the ubiquitous Victors, who were always on time and on target![21]

Chapter 7

Quick Reaction Alert

Suddenly the telephone would ring and it would be one of the radar controllers from around the UK ordering you to scramble immediately. And so you would run to the aeroplane, jump in. They [Soviet aircraft] were just monitoring, listening, recording everything that went on. So you would get up alongside and normally they would wave, quite often there would be a little white face at every window. They knew we were there just to watch them. One I intercepted when he violated the airspace and I was trying to get him to land but it was scary. He just wanted to get out of there, he was out of Dodge as fast as he could go, he didn't want to mix it with me.

RAF Lightning pilot John Ward.

The Lightning's most demanding role was to intercept, supersonically, enemy aircraft penetrating NATO airspace at altitude and, if called upon, shoot them down with air-to-air missiles and cannon. If the deterrent was to work effectively, RAF Fighter (later Strike) Command had to station Lightnings and later Lightnings and Phantoms, on immediate readiness, twenty-four hours a day, 365 days a year. Quick Reaction Alert (QRA), as it was called was just that, with intercepts possible at 40,000 feet just minutes after a re-heat take-off. It was all very well having the world's most advanced supersonic interceptor with this capability, but if sorties were to be successful, then pilots needed to apply completely new techniques vis-a-vis radar and weaponry. Initially, the missile and radar systems were beset with teething problems and it fell to pilots like Bruce Hopkins at the AFDS at Coltishall to carry out trials work on the Lightning's radar and fire control systems.

'At the start, in 1960, we had problems with the fire control computer,' he recalls. 'Once the radar was locked on we had a very simple analogue computerized steering programme to do the intercept. The theory was that we tracked the dot on the scope to obtain the optimum pursuit path for firing. The trouble was, it was bloody useless! You could do a manual intercept far better. So, we threw the steering programme away and developed a system of intercept using the basic 'B' radarscope display. This became the basis of all Lightning AI work. Unless you had a high closing speed, the intercept bracket was about two miles from the target. The skill came in making the intercept at subsonic speed. If you got it wrong, you had to go to re-heat to make up the distance.

'We did a hell of a lot of work on intercepts, high-level then low-level, where the radar did not perform too well due to ground clutter. (Although the AI pulse radar at this time had a maximum range at height of twenty-five miles, at sea level it sees less than five miles.) Once we had got what we thought were the basic techniques, we started fixing the supersonic intercept mission. Now we really had fuel problems! It meant that there was less time to get the radar intercept right. Our radar scanned horizontally at 45 degrees with a beam width of two to three degrees, so we had to search vertically for the target by use of a scanner elevation control. As we moved the elevation lever the radar dish looked up and down. This is known as the 'elevation search'. Of course, supersonically, we had less time to search for the 'blip'. Then we had to lock on to the target using the trigger switch and we went into the intercept with it locked on.

'From February 1961 onwards we started missile firing trials at Boscombe Down. At first we used telemetry-fitted Firestreaks with the explosive removed, against pilotless, remotely-controlled Meteor targets. Then, in March, on the Aberporth ranges in Wales, I fired at Australian-built Jindiviks.[1] Major Bill Cato, our American exchange pilot, Jim Reynolds and I carried out a whole series of Firestreak firings during 1961. Jim Reynolds and I would fly a Javelin FAW.8 to Boscombe Down on the Monday (which we also used to go back and forth to Coltishall for spares etc.) and fly back to Coltishall on the Friday after a week of missile firing exercises. We must have been the most expensive commuters in the world. We had competitions to see who could transit between Coltishall and Boscombe the fastest. The ground rules were, you were not allowed to break any airframe limits or air traffic rules. After take-off from [runway] 22 SW, you would cruise in re-heat at about Mach 0.94 and make a straight-in approach at Boscombe. Jim Reynolds finally got the time down to eighteen minutes, seven seconds!

'We fired a total of five Firestreaks. This all proved very successful. Then we did quite a bit of gun firing, which wasn't so successful! All we proved was that the pilot attack gunsight was very basic. It was OK if we did approaches from behind, but it was not so good under G conditions using lots of angle. In fact, it was only any good from line astern. Still, guns were a very useful weapon to have, the basic philosophy being missiles for long range (one mile minimum) and guns for within a mile of a target. I was always a member of the "let's keep the gun" lobby. The Lightning, though, was never a good aircraft for gun fighting. All our air-to-air gunnery was done on the 'flag', i.e. the quarter attack. With a couple of hundred rounds you were lucky to get twenty per cent of the rounds on target in a Lightning; this compared with 40 to 50 per cent on Hunters.'

Bruce Hopkins left AFDS in September 1962, being posted as a Weapons Instructor on T.4s to the Lightning Conversion Squadron at Middleton St. George. Promoted to squadron leader, he left 226 OCU (the LCU had expanded) at the end of January 1964 on a posting to the Air Ministry. In 1989 Bruce Hopkins became one of the Lightning specialists at the Empire Test Pilots' School (ETPS) the British training school for test pilots and flight test engineers of fixed-wing and rotary-wing aircraft at Boscombe Down in Wiltshire that was established in 1943, the first of its type. The school moved to RAF Cranfield in October 1945 and to Royal Aircraft Establishment, Farnborough in July 1947 before returning to Boscombe Down in Wiltshire on 29 January 1968. Bruce Hopkins, himself a graduate of the school in 1961, had done a tour with Farnborough's IEE during which he was principally involved with electric controls on the Avro 707C and head-up displays in the Hunter Mk.12[2] followed by attachment to BAC Warton where he built up Lightning test experience. By 1969 he was back at ETPS as one of the Lightning specialists, flying T.4 XL629, the second prototype two-seater, which was used for all the supersonic exercises at the school. Late that year Bruce Hopkins flew aviation author J. D. R. Rawlings whose article about his flight in the Lightning appeared in the November issue of *Air Pictorial* magazine: 'Recently the school granted me the great privilege of taking part, as a sort of pseudo-student, in one of the test exercises to experience for myself the type of flying in which a student would be involved. On the day of my visit there was fortunately a suitable slot in the afternoon's Lightning flying programme. Bruce briefed me for the sortie and together we rolled ourselves into immersion suits and then I clambered up the long blue ladder to reach the right-hand seat of XL629. There followed a prolonged period of strapping in, ceremonial removing of the 'bang' – seat pins and then my tutor signed out and we were ready to go.

'I soon realised that I was not to be a passive member of this sortie as the engine starting buttons were my side. I did as I was told in the correct sequence and all seemed to be humming satisfactorily, judging by the hands on the ears of the bystanders. With all instruments reading as they should, I was told to taxi out to the threshold of Runway 24 and so off we set, a little drunkenly at first until I had got the feel of handbrake and toe pedals. My tutor must have reckoned that driving this potent beast would take up most of my time, so he graciously undertook communications with the outside world.

'Having obtained take-off clearance, he told me to taxi out and line up, then open up to full power cold, release the brakes and go. Obedient as ever I gingerly moved out on to Boscombe's oh-so-long Runway 24, brakes on, opened up, all dials looking healthy, no warning lights on, so brakes off. First few seconds were involved with brake and rudder as I had not lined the nose wheel up straight, but this was soon remedied and the concrete was roaring by underneath – 135 knots and a steady pull brought the nose wheel off, 155 knots fully rotate.

'Bruce Hopkins cleaned up the undercarriage and said: "Push through to full reheat and hold 450 knots indicated." This I did and received a hefty kick up the back, managing to keep the speed down to 450 knots by pulling back, back, back on the stick until I was almost lying horizontally on my back. Puff and we were through a layer of scattered fair-weather cumulus and now, for the first time ever, I witnessed the whole earth just falling away behind me, almost unbelievable. All the instruments were steady except the altimeter which was frantically winding up – the VSI was off the clock.

'Just under two minutes from wheels off and I pushed over as we passed through 35,000 feet to level off at 36,000 indicated. We were given a course to steer out Channelwards and having set course I started to survey the world outside again. It was possible to trace the coastline way out westwards by the edges of the cumulus layer; to the east and below was the back end of the front that had gone through that morning.

'"Watch your airspeed" came over the intercom, to disturb my gazing and I looked to see the needle passing Mach 0.95 upwards. I eased back on the stick for there was plenty of Dorset still below and a 'bang' would not have been a good idea. I trimmed back to 0.8 and we surged out over Portland Bill. We were now under Southern Radar's control and a feminine voice – which I was assured was Hilda Robinson, a WRAF controller – eventually found us a clear course for our test run, which involved a straight and level acceleration from Mach 0.8 to 1.6 followed by a constant rate turn to decelerate to 0.8 again.

'"Steer 120 and advise when supersonic," said Hilda. I turned on to 120 and pushed through to full reheat. The success of this part of the exercise rested on keeping level. Due to position error, it was necessary to use the VSI as a primary instrument not the altimeter, which slowly unwound 2,000 feet on the run. We came up to Mach 1 and all that marked it was the flicking of the pressure instruments as the pressure head adjusted to the shock wave and Bruce's voice telling Southern Radar that we were supersonic. Acceleration now was slow, it being a warm day, until Mach 1.2 was reached when the centre of pressure movement aft induced longitudinal instability and pitch down, but this was easily held with the stick.

'Acceleration was now quicker and then we were there, at Mach 1.6, the magical 'ten-ton', 36,000 feet below the earth and clouds moved slowly aft at much the same speed as if we were flying at 250 knots at half the height. Bruce now took over and established us in a steep (70-75°) turn to starboard at a constant 3g which brought us steadily back to Mach 0.8; as we came back through Mach 1 slight buffeting commenced and continued until he levelled out – XL629 was then handed back to me.

'Our TACAN told us we were 75 miles from Boscombe. We were given a northerly heading to steer, so I eased the throttles back, as told, to 250 knots and with a trickle of power we began coasting earthwards. The Isle of Wight was beneath us and I suggested that we might be able to see the Royal Review at Spithead so Bruce half-rolled and we looked upwards through the canopy, but of course a patch of cumulus obscured it so he went on round the roll and handed back to me. Hilda had now handed us back to Boscombe who brought us down through the cumulus to break cloud north of the airfield.

'We had been given 1,500 feet, so this I held while my tutor switched in the autopilot and locked it on to the ILS; we then had the absurd situation of two pilots sitting with their arms folded while the Lightning flew itself back on to the centreline of Runway 24 and began the descent. This was unlocked and the aircraft given back to me for a couple of circuits. As we reached the threshold I was told to overshoot, so I put on power and as we surged forward pulled round in a steep turn, nicely as I thought, on to the downwind leg. "Circuit height is 1,000 feet, not 2,000 feet," came over the intercom, so I eased down again and when told to do so, swung round on finals, much to my surprise lining up nicely.

'"Keep a steady 175 knots downhill, pulling back to 155 at the threshold and then a firm flare and she'll settle." It sounded all right, I thought and surprisingly enough so it turned out – a steady descent, with no trace of Dutch roll, a flare at the right moment just over the white lines, a steady thump and we were on. "Nose wheel down and then pull the drag chute." I eased the stick forward and just when I was beginning to think that the nose wheel couldn't be down, it touched. I moved my left hand on to the stick and pulled the drag chute with my right – a reassuring pressure on my shoulder straps told me it had deployed. "Now ease over to the right of the runway and turn off by that fire tender," came the command and as I came up to the fire tender the chute was chopped, I turned off and motored gently back to 'A' Squadron hangar where I diffidently suggested that my tutor should park the Lightning, otherwise we might end up in, rather than by, Harrier XV281.

'After clambering out and reverting to normal attire, I learned what would be required of me as a pukka student. While we were flying the exercise three 12-channel recorders had been hard at work monitoring the 'vital statistics' of the flight. I would have to get the traces from these recorders, mark off lines at the vital points of the flight and using these figures, establish an actual 'G' value from a calibration chart. I would then plot the change in tailplane position between the acceleration and the subsequent decelerating turn and using the actual 'G' value already established in ground school, calculate the longitudinal manoeuvrability. Having gone all through this exercise, I would then have to repeat it at a forward CG position (our sortie having been flown at an aft CG) and by plotting aft and forward CG values on a graph, the manoeuvring stability could be determined. This, Bruce told me, would involve about ten hours' work for the average student – to me ten days would not be long enough!'

On leaving the ETPS Bruce Hopkins began a two-year exchange tour with the US Navy on the F-4J Phantom and he did not return to the Lightning force until 1972, when he was given command of 23 Squadron at Leuchars. 23 Squadron was a key element in Britain's air defence. The front-line squadrons were backed up by a first-class ground-controlled defence system. No.11 Group's Air Defence Ground Environment (ADGE), with its headquarters and operations centre at Bentley Priory, near London, provided early warning of Soviet aircraft and missile threats. Tu-95 'Bears', Tu-16 'Badgers' and occasionally M-4 'Bisons' and Il-18 'Coots' of the Soviet Long-Range Air Force and Naval Air Force, flying reconnaissance missions around the North Cape of Norway and on towards the central

QUICK REACTION ALERT

Atlantic and the British Isles, would be investigated in the UK Air Defence Region by 11 Group using QRA interceptors. Usually the Soviet aircraft practised their war roles of maritime surveillance, anti-shipping and anti-submarine warfare and simulated strikes on mainland Britain.

The UK ADR, contained entirely within NATO Early Warning Area 12, forms part of a unified air defence system under SACEUR (Supreme Allied Commander Europe), which extends to cover three other NATO air defence regions. Three Master Radar Stations (from 1975, key Sector Operations Centres (SOCs)), with control and reporting facilities, were grouped around radar units at Boulmer, Buchan, Scotland and Neatishead, Norfolk. These were fed with data from six NATO Air Defence Ground Environment (NADGE) stations via digital link with the Air Defence Data Centre at West Drayton and the Air Defence Operations Centre at Strike Command HQ, High Wycombe, forty miles west of London. Here sat the Air Officer C-in-C Strike Command, who also wore the NATO 'hat' of COMUKADR (Commander UKADR). Further long-range, low-level radar coverage was provided by twelve Shackleton AEW.2 Airborne Early Warning aircraft. From 1975 onwards, data was also fed into the system from the control and reporting post at Benbecula on North Uist and from the reporting site at Saxa Vord. The Ballistic Missile Early Warning System (BMEWS) station at Fylingdales in Yorkshire provided additional links.

At the 'sharp end' four armed Lightnings (from September 1969, Lightnings and Phantoms) sat in a 'shed' near the end of the runway. Two fighters were at Leuchars in the Northern QRA all year round, the other two at alternately Wattisham and Binbrook (later, Coningsby's Phantoms were also used) in the Southern QRA. In Germany in September 1965 19 Squadron's Lightning F.2s began performing a QRA role at Gütersloh and in December that year 92 Squadron's F.2s at Geilenkirchen joined them in the role. In January 1968 92 Squadron moved to Gütersloh and together with 19 Squadron carried out interceptor duties until replaced by Phantoms, in December 1976 and March 1977 respectively.

On QRA seven ground crew, one or two from each trade and a SNCO (Senior NCO), would attend each pair of Lightning interceptors in charge. Two pilots dressed in full flying kit, minus their life preservers and helmets, but including their immersion suits during the winter, were at ten minutes' readiness. This meant that an aircraft had to be airborne within ten minutes of the 'scramble' order. (In keeping with the Second World War fighter spirit, 'scramble' signalled a take-off, while that other popular term, 'buster', which originally meant 'through the gate', was used to describe re-heat.

Targets were known as 'trade', another throwback to the war.) At nights, it was relaxed to thirty minutes. Even then they had to don their flying kit.

Brian Carroll recalls: 'Hunting bears for most folk generates visions of big brown beasties or even the polar variety in off-white; but for us, the pilots who manned the Northern Quick Reaction Alert Force, the vision was quite different. We knew precisely what to expect, something in silver with a wingspan of 167.7 feet, 162.4 feet in length, 39.75 feet high and weighing in at around 185 tons, all propelled by four turboprops, each producing 14,795 ehp and the whole capable of moving along at 525 mph (456 knots). They were bristling with a number of mean-looking cannon which at times were pointed our way, quite un-nerving as they attempted to track us as we flew around the 'Bear' examining it for any new equipment or changes from the current information.

'Northern QRA was a vital part of the defence of the UK. Over the years we spent many hours on standby, either relaxed at a thirty-minute state or in the cockpit, ready to start engines and be airborne within two minutes. At night we slept next to our steeds, having earlier carried out a full pre-flight, including setting the cockpit switches for a fast get away. It was surprising just how quickly one could move from being asleep to being airborne; less than five minutes was the norm. Let me then take you through a sortie from, say, a thirty-minute state of readiness all the way to a successful interception and a recovery back to home ground.

'We usually operated in pairs and would be dressed and ready to move at a moment's notice. Our immersion suits would be on but unzipped as they were on the warm side while sitting around, though essential should one be unlucky enough to come down in the North Sea. The QRA pilots would, at the thirty-minute state, be in the crew room along with the rest of the squadron, often carrying out one or another of their secondary duties or simply relaxing with a good book. The phone rings; northern radar has requested two aircraft to he brought up to a ten-minute state. We are at most only five minutes' stroll from our aircraft, both of which have been checked over and are ready to go. We take another look around them and chat with the ground crew who are also on standby in the alert dispersal.

'At this stage the alert may come to nothing; the 'intruders' are known to play cat and mouse with us, flying close enough to wake us up and then turn away before we scramble. This time we are brought to cockpit readiness and a few moments later instructions are passed to scramble. The usual information is passed, giving a vector to fly, height to climb to, whether they wish us to make a re-heat or standard climb out and the range of the target.

QUICK REACTION ALERT

'Four Avons thunder into life, all systems are 'go'. Almost as one, both aircraft roll from the alert hangar, air traffic automatically clearing us for an immediate take-off. Entering the 'active', both aircraft smoothly apply full cold power and surge down the runway. A glance across at my No. 2, all is OK, a nod of the head and we both engage full re-heat. Airborne, clean up and turn onto the climb out vector, my No. 2 moving automatically into battle formation as soon as we are clear of any cloud. From now on there will be little if any R/T communication between the aircraft or the ground; silent procedure is the name of the game. Standard battle formation is established as we fly north.

'The intruder (at this stage we are not aware of its identity) is over 400 miles away, so for the next forty-five minutes or so there is little to do but fly the required track and monitor our on-board systems. The occasional visual signal is passed between us, confirming that all is OK. We already know that a tanker aircraft has been scrambled ahead of us and that shortly we will achieve a RV (rendezvous) allowing us to top up our tanks. This, too, is a well-rehearsed procedure; no chat between us and the tanker, the aim being not to let the target know until the last possible moment that we are on our way.

'It is now thirty minutes or so since take-off and we have contact with our mobile fuel store. As lead, I take us both into a stern position then, leaving my No. 2 there, fly up alongside the tanker's cockpit to let them know we have arrived (they saw us coming anyway). Again, a visual OK from the tanker captain that we are clear to top up. Dropping back, I wave my No. 2 onto the port hose whilst I take the starboard one. Full tanks and we are on our way, now flying a closer tactical formation to allow hand signals to be passed between us. A wave to the tanker crew as we accelerate away, they will follow us for a while and then set up a loiter pattern allowing us to meet up later for more fuel should we need it and right now, being so far from home, we certainly will.

'Range from base is now approaching 430 miles and the silence is suddenly broken by a cryptic message from ground radar. Our target is fifty miles dead ahead and coming our way – if he holds that heading we should be right with him in just over three minutes. But no, he has already started turning away; not, we discover later, because of us, simply a routine turn to keep him 430 to 500 miles from our base. This is going to be a long chase if we maintain our present cruise speed, so with tanks still nearly full we crack the burners and accelerate. We both check our weapons, missiles and cannon; one never knows if they will be needed. Cameras, including the hand-carried 35mm, are re-checked and ready for use.

'Still nothing more from the ground, so (briefly) I activate my airborne radar and there is a nice fat blip, not too far away and closing nicely. Radar back to stand-by again, just in case they realise that they are being scanned. Conditions are ideal to surprise our Russian friends. The Bear (as it turns out to be) is flying just above a thin cloud layer only some 1,000 feet thick, so we close in from below, preventing his rear lookout from seeing us. Another quick look into the radarscope confirms that we are approaching 2,000 yards. I signal my No. 2 to maintain his position at 2,000 while I close to 500 yards before popping up through the dud layer. The effect is dramatic. Ivan in the rear blister obviously reports my presence and the captain immediately throttles back, slowing the Bear very quickly.

'A brief flip of speed brakes and a tight high G roll bleeds off enough speed to remain astern. I'm now very much aware of the twin cannon in the tail that are starting to track me as I close in. The adrenaline tends to flow a little faster at this stage! This particular interception was, in fact, the most northern intercept that had been made at that time; they hadn't realised we were using tankers, so thought that they were out of our operating range. Time now for a little fun and games with their rear gunner/photographer.

'As I close alongside the rear fuselage I can see him clearly in the side blisters, manhandling a somewhat cumbersome camera mounted on a tripod. He's hoping for some pictures of our Lightnings and with luck he won't get any. My 35mm camera is somewhat easier to manage as I switch easily from side to side, rolling over and under the Bear, taking pictures all the time. Meanwhile, I manage to keep my would-be 'happy snapper' nicely out of phase; no sooner has he positioned his camera on the port side than I am on the starboard. This continues for a while as I collect a comprehensive number of photographs to add to our ever-increasing library. Meanwhile, Ivan is looking somewhat knackered; still, I saved him a fortune in film!

'Time now to bid farewell to my budding Russian cameraman. I give him a wave and receive one back (a friendly wave, too, not what you might think!). Calling my No. 2 to rejoin, we break away, taking up a heading for a rendezvous with our tanker. No need now to keep R/T silence. We are in fact 540 miles from home and the Lightnings are feeling thirsty and in need of another drink. The tanker is 100-plus miles south of us, so I give him a call to head our way for a while to save a little time to the refuel point. Allowing for turning manoeuvres, we should be ready to make contact with the hoses in about fifteen minutes.

'After a while I obtain a good radar contact on the tanker and call him to reverse his direction so that we can roll in astern at a mile. Closing, we are cleared to make contact. As we did on the outbound leg, my No. 2 takes the port hose while I load up from the starboard. We don't need full tanks this time, so with base and diversion weather good and with no on-board problems we only partially refuel. A few words of thanks to our tanker friends and we wing our way back to base for a routine approach landing. We had been airborne for around three hours, the sortie was text book and all concerned feel that another job has been well done.

'Of course, not all QRA missions are carried out in such ideal conditions. Poor weather certainly puts added strains on the pilots. At night it can get very interesting trying to identify an unknown target, usually without any lights and quite liable to pull odd manoeuvres just to add interest to the whole exercise.

'Back at home base, time for a coffee or two and a debrief. The film meanwhile has been rushed away for processing – it turned out to be a regular, standard issue 'Bear D'. Nothing new had been added, but then no news is, as they say, good news. While we were away, other pilots had been standing QRA duty, another pair of Lightnings ready, as we had been to launch at a moment's notice. And so it went on round the clock; a lot of waiting around, but exciting when things moved and very satisfying to successfully make a good interception and let the Ruskies now that we were on to them all the time.'[3]

Pete Nash, a ground crewman occasionally on QRA at Wattisham, recalls: 'Sometimes a klaxon, just like those World War Two submarine diving alarms, would rend the air, meaning that a scramble was imminent and cockpit readiness was required. The pilots would let us ground crew rush out first, punching a button that opened the front and rear doors. First out would hit the button, even if his aircraft was the second and furthest away. Beforehand, all jobs were allocated so each knew what he had to do. One would start the Houchin (ground power set) and press the power buttons. The second would go round the other side and remove the Master Armament Safety Brake, then stand clear, while the third would help the pilot strap in. If a launch was ordered, then the pilot only waited long enough for a thumbs up from the ground crew to indicate that the 'fireman' had extinguished any flames from the starter exhausts, before he released his brakes and taxied out. The power lines and telebrief [through which the pilot was given his orders] were anchored to the floor so, as the aircraft moved forward, they were disconnected. As he left the 'Q-shed', the pilot lowered his flaps and trusted air traffic to clear the runway for him because he didn't stop. On to the runway he then engaged double re-heat and away he went. A QRA scramble had priority over all other local traffic. Meantime, 'Q2' would sit at cockpit readiness until 'Q1' was well on his way and declared that his aircraft was serviceable. Only then would he stand down to ten minutes.

'For the ground crews, QRA was a rest. We did a week continuous, sleeping in the accommodation next to the aircraft shed, doing the flight servicings when required, an engine run every so often and watching telly, playing board-games, or fixing our cars. It was the easiest job on the squadron! If an aircraft went unserviceable then it either had to be fixed or replaced; half an hour ago, if not now!

'Before the flight servicings could start we had to contact the fighter controllers for permission to take the aircraft 'off state' and then we were only allowed one hour to fix it otherwise we had to change aircraft. Another aircraft had to be armed and ready; usually on the flight line with a pilot close by, while the 'Q' aircraft was fixed. When it came to meal times we went to the head of the queue and our Land Rover was parked right outside the mess doors, ready for an instant call back for a scramble. Wattisham shared the Southern QRA with Binbrook. Leuchars was always on Northern QRA.'

Flight Lieutenant Bob Offord was posted from 56 Squadron to become the A Flight Commander on 23 Squadron at Leuchars in September 1964, a move that meant transition to the F.3: 'The F.3 was a different aircraft in many ways. It had a totally different instrument layout; the engines were bigger and it had a faster autopilot that worked. It had height and heading hold and could be used for turning. It also had a priority for automatic ILS, although it was set up for 3 degrees (the Lightning liked 2½ degrees), so it was very rarely used. Our preferred approach was GCA, which would be 2½ degrees and in some cases, manual ILS. The autopilot was like having another pilot and it let the aircraft look after itself more while you looked after the radar. The AI.23B doubled the range and V-bombers now appeared on screen much sooner. I could also now carry Red Top.

'At Leuchars, 23 Squadron had sixteen pilots. Flight Lieutenant Ian Thompson, the 'B' Flight Commander and me did not operate as separate flights. We would chop and change and took it in turns to do the day and night shifts. We operated a pair of Lightnings on QRA, 8am to 8pm. It was intensive, especially for the 'plumbers', though in the summer we gave up night flying, because, flying at the heights we flew, it does not get dark enough. Normal take-offs were carried out on cold power, at 150 knots IAS and you became airborne at 165-170 IAS. (The front wheel would not retract above 165-170 IAS.) Then it would be a 10-degree climb out at 450 knots, pitching up to 22 degrees on the Initial Altitude Indicator, invariably to 36,000 feet (at the tropopause, the height at which the stratosphere begins), where we did most of our work. QRA used re-heat take-offs, so getting the gear up was more critical. So too was fuel, but from October 1965 onwards we used Victor tankers. (The Lightning was short of fuel the moment you started the engines!) Acceleration and the rate of climb were phenomenal – from brake release to 36,000 feet took just two and a half minutes. And you did it at a 47-degrees angle. Also, the seat was angled at 23 degrees, so the combination of the two made you feel that you were lying on your back!

'On head-on supersonic interceptions (with another Lightning) we tried a closing speed of Mach 3-4. Head-on attacks were very exciting and set-up had to be very good! For a successful 'shoot-down' to happen, three parameters were needed. First, the trigger had to be pulled (first, because we had to do this up to fifteen miles' range, then hold it until the interception), when the missile saw the target, in range and 'fired'. There was no audible sound that the missile had 'locked-on' but a circle in the sight, which collapsed once you were in range, indicated that you were in range (the Red Top would normally see the target before it was in range). I carried out head-on attacks in daylight, never seeing the target visually. After the attack we rolled down and went home. During my time on the squadron no Russian aircraft were intercepted, but from 1966 onwards they started in a big way, right around the clock.'[4]

One of the 23 Squadron pilots on QRA at Leuchars at this time was Flight Lieutenant Tony Aldridge, a former Black Arrows and Blue Diamonds Hunter aerobatic pilot, who hailed from Edinburgh. He recalls:

'The normal briefing for a rotation take-off was: after rotating the aircraft off the ground, level off and retract the undercarriage as soon as possible. Fly level until reaching approximately 220 knots and then pull back sharply on the stick, pulling approximately 3g in the process – 3-5g being the maximum. At around 60-degrees, climb, maintain speed in the order of 180 knots until chosen altitude is reached – usually around 2,000 feet – then ease forward or wing-over and resume normal climb.'

During the weekend of 26 March 1966 a long-range QRA exercise was held involving two Victors of 55 squadron and two Lightnings. All crews were held at thirty minutes' readiness to attempt the interception of Soviet reconnaissance aircraft passing between the Faroes-Shetland gap. No operational scrambles were called but the aircraft were scrambled in order to practice the planned procedures. On 30 March Flight Lieutenant Tony

Aldridge and his No. 2 Paul Reynolds took off, flew the sortie and then made their supersonic tactical recovery. During the supersonic descent both pilots were looking straight down into the centre of St. Andrews as Tony Aldridge recalls:

'We (the operational pilots) were trying to work out a descent to the airfield that would allow the maximum time at altitude for the sortie followed by the shortest time back to base and on the ground. My idea was to do the descent at supersonic speed, followed by a break into the circuit for landing. To this end I started a vertical descent a few miles from the airfield, aiming a couple of miles short of the runway. Speed built up rapidly to something in the order of 1.5 M and then power was eased off. The descent was continued at about 80 degrees nose down. Mach number decreased as we got lower until it was time to pull out. I ended up over the end of the runway at about 1,000 feet and 600 knots, before breaking into the circuit and landing – an extremely quick way to get from altitude and onto the ground, which is what we were trying to achieve. However, the shock waves created when going supersonic don't go exactly where the aircraft is pointed, as I had hoped, but beyond it. Therefore, if you want to drop a bang on a place you aim short of it, exactly as I had done – unintentionally. We dropped a bang on the airfield and also on the Ancient and Modern [sic] golf course at St. Andrews, which is a very sensitive establishment. The golf club's head person was straight on the phone to our station commander, who called the OC Flying who in turn called our boss. Squadron Leader John McLeod called me and we had a fairly one-sided discussion about the situation.'[5]

Squadron Leader (later Group Captain) Ed Durham flew QRA at Leuchars as a flight commander in 23 Squadron during 1968-70. 'It was one of the loneliest feelings there was,' he recalls, 'being 600 miles north of Lossiemouth and looking for a tanker to refuel from.' (As many as six in-flight refuellings could be required on a long-range QRA sortie.) It could sometimes be quite hectic too, although in a given period, not all flights were QRA sorties. On 25 February 1970, Squadron Leader Durham intercepted two 'Bear-Ds' on a night QRA. He had already flown four sorties the day before and three more followed on the 26th and the same number two days after that.

John Bentley of *Flight International* visited Wattisham and 29 Squadron in April 1970 and wrote about QRA.[6]

'Wherever you are, whatever you are doing as you read this article you can be sure that an element of 29 Squadron, part of the RAF's Strike Command, is alert, waiting for the word at Wattisham, the squadron operates Lightning

QUICK REACTION ALERT

3s as part of the 'Quick Reaction Alert' (QRA) force. Two aircraft stand on a special 'ready' pan, armed and ready to go at ten minutes' notice, 24 hours a day, with air and ground crew of 29 Squadron, waiting in their ready rooms at the same notice.

'Once an alert is sounded – a strident hooter has replaced the wartime gong – the two pilots belt for their transport and drive across to the pan, where, strapped in, they are ready to be airborne within two minutes. Ground crew supply external power to the aircraft during these waiting periods and the pilots get their briefing via a plug-in telebrief direct from the relevant operations room. Their job is to maintain the integrity of UK airspace in the southern half of England (the northern sector is served by aircraft from Leuchars). The Lightnings are a 'known armed presence', who can be seen to intercept any aircraft approaching the UK without a flight plan or who crossed into the air defence zone without warning.

'Many of the alerts are practices – intruders simulated by Canberras from RAF Germany – but there are 'quite a few' visitors from Russia. Some are long-range maritime flights from the far north which fly past Norway and turn over the Shetlands. Some visitors are clearly testing the readiness of the QRA force. Others listen for the signatures of current NATO ECM devices and there are the electronic-intelligence gatherers, which fly around listening to radio and radar frequencies. There are even some practice bombing runs. Whatever they are doing the Lightnings intercept, identify and accompany them out of the area, armed with cameras and live missiles. Nobody has yet refused to go.

'The squadron is also on call to reinforce certain overseas theatres both inside and outside NATO, including Germany, the Near East Air Force and the Far East Air Force and annually visits Malta and Cyprus on alternating years as part of this commitment. The object is to train the squadron personnel in both the physical job of rapid deployment and in integrating with a different theatre of operations. The job which would be required in the eastern Mediterranean would be somewhat different from that in the conventional NATO environment.

'NATO bases in other countries are also visited by 29 Squadron regularly in order to exercise the squadron ground crew in servicing the aircraft of other air forces and vice versa. The visits are also an opportunity for the pilots to gain an insight into the air defence environment of different parts of Europe and to exchange experience. The countries taking part include the Benelux group, plus Germany, Norway, Denmark and, surprisingly, France which, although outside NATO, still participates in the exchanges.

'Tom Hamill and I met 29 Squadron earlier this year in Cyprus where they were on a month-long detachment which seemed to us to be one long exercise from dawn until well into the night. The fact that we were in Cyprus was largely irrelevant; it could have been anywhere and there were few days when we didn't hear the QRA hooter.

'The twelve aircraft had been flown out from Wattisham direct to Cyprus in 5 hour, air-to-air refuelled by Victor tankers from Marham. The trip could also be done in stages, but the refuelling exercise is well worth the trouble and has the advantage that if a transport aircraft is sent along at the same time the squadron's ground crew can arrive at almost the same time as their Lightnings. The whole squadron can be operational within hours of arrival at the new base.

'As part of the mobility concept the squadron always has to keep a proportion of its aircraft serviceable and has a 'fly-away' pack-up of spares and equipment permanently available. The exact number of aircraft which must be serviceable is determined by Strike Command, as is the state of alert at any given time. If the alert state is raised to a level above that of aircraft readiness the engineer officer has to mobilise all his ground crew to make ready the necessary number of aircraft in the shortest time. All flying has to stop until the required number is on the line.

'The fifteen pilots carry out a minimum of twenty hours flying each month, training in the various roles in which they have to be proficient during daytime and at night. The squadron has a typical range of ages and experience (unlike the Phantom squadrons, whose pilots seem to have a higher average age) from the CO Wing Commander Brian Carroll and his flight commanders Squadron Leader Dave Kuun and Squadron Leader 'Dick' Bell, down to the junior pilots, somewhat more excitable and not long out of Sleaford Tech.

'A new pilot receives a six-month intensive training course on both the aircraft and its weapons systems. If he is up to scratch at the end of that period he is made 'combat-ready' – capable of leading a flight of two aircraft on any of the squadron's flight profiles, day or night. As he progresses and gains more experience he is given more responsibility and will eventually be allowed to lead a four-aircraft flight.

'Each of the more experienced pilots also has a second specialisation, which he uses to instruct the other pilots in the squadron. One of the most important of these is the interception weapons instructor, whose responsibility is to see that each pilot gets a really thorough training on all the tasks which the squadron does. Others specialise in airframes, engines, electronics, navigation and aircraft recognition. There is no point in sending a Lightning pilot up to intercept something if he is not going to recognise it when he arrives.

'Flying training itself is varied but strictly governed by mandatory requirements for specific tasks to be done on a certain number of occasions each month. In the UK most of the training concentrates on interceptions, but when on deployment the squadron makes use of the different environments and aircraft available to practise combat missions against different aircraft and at varying speeds.

'Visual identification of strange targets is practised by making an approach to an intruder from behind and at some 300 yards' range identifying him visually. At night this has to be done in whatever light is available. On all occasions a radar lock-on has to be achieved. The aircraft, which are put up against the QRA force, include Canberras, Phantoms, Buccaneers and Sea Vixens. All fighter pilots have an intensive aircraft recognition course at OTU and when they come to the squadron they are kept in practice by continuous refresher training both simulated and live.

'Normally the squadron operates with the local air-defence radar network, which will vector the interceptors on to a target until the Ferranti Airpass radar has picked it up. Once this has been done the Lightning can be flown into its tail position to identify without itself being seen. The Lightning, although it has been around for some time, is still able to climb to height quicker and accelerate to supersonic speeds faster than its new stable mate the Phantom and is therefore ideal for the QRA role. Its greatest attribute is said to be its handling qualities; particularly in the transonic bands it is highly manoeuvrable.

'It is also praised as a very effective missile vehicle, carrying Red Top or Firestreak. The Ferranti Airpass AI.23B radar is a pilot-interpreted system, which means that the pilot must position himself within brackets which are displayed in order to make an effective missile firing. To do this he can fly a computed flight path, also displayed, or position himself manually. The technique in an attack is to approach a target either very high or very low so that the attacker cannot easily be seen. For very high-level attacks the technique is to accelerate to supersonic speed near the tropopause and then climb at attack speed to the height required.

'While mock attacks on other Lightnings, or whatever is put up against them, are carried out on deployment overseas, live missile firings are made at RAF Valley, Anglesey. At the missile practice camps the usual deployment techniques are exercised for the benefit of the ground crew, while some six pilots at a time are given at least one live missile firing against a magnesium flare target which is towed behind a drone from Llanbedr. Said one pilot: "It's quite exciting. You can hear the rocket motor igniting even over the noise of your own aircraft and you can feel the reaction."

'The engineers of the squadron have changed probably more than any other branch since the war. On 29 Squadron they practise what is known as 'opportunity servicing'. In effect this means that every component has a latitude band of flying hours instead of a fixed limit. Every job that has to be done has a card on which is listed the number of other jobs on the aircraft which can conveniently be carried out at the same time if the components concerned have reached their servicing latitude band.

'It is done in this way mainly because of access problems on the tightly packed tube known as the Lightning. There are few external access panels; most are in the engine and jet-pipe bays. The servicing schedule for the squadron is so complicated that two men spend their time doing nothing else but planning it. On top of this routine servicing are the periodic check system and the never-ending programme of modifications and mandatory instructions.

'If possible before it goes on a detachment the squadron carries out progressive servicing on all the aircraft so that all will set off from Wattisham with a clear number of flying hours ahead of them in which no routine servicing needs to be done. Once it arrives at its destination the squadron's problems are mainly concerned with the backing available at the station. If there is a Lightning squadron based there, as there is at Akrotiri, an arrangement is made to borrow any special gear required – even down to such mundane items as steps and tail parachutes. If no Lightning squadrons are resident it takes eight C-130s to hump all the gear which is needed, plus many second-line servicing personnel from Wattisham. Much of the heavy gear is peculiar to the Lightning: Lox trolleys, slings, wheels, ventral tank trolleys, etc. With only nine landings per tyre, quite a few of these are needed too.

'The supply organisation was highly praised by the SEO Squadron Leader Peter Babler. He said that the priority demand system worked very well. Stores are listed in a central computer at Hendon and can be called up by signal. The computer sorts out which is the nearest available replacement component and routes it to the squadron by priority air movement and the 'Earlybird' network of road movement in the UK.

'The squadron has started a scheme known as the 'welfare group' which has aroused interest in other squadrons. It is similar in outline, although not as formal, to the naval system of divisional officers. On 29 Squadron each pilot is responsible for the general off or on-duty welfare of a number of airmen, about twelve per pilot. One of the problems of a mobile squadron is that personal problems tend to be magnified because the men are often away from home base for a long time. So far the scheme which has been in operation for eight months seems to have gone some way to ameliorate the problems.

'Flying the Lightning is regarded as being not too difficult because the aircraft is said to have no vices. It had always seemed to me to be a hair-raising aircraft, particularly in those stream landings, which used to be made at the SBAC show. "We shan't be pulling much more than 3g at altitude, so you shouldn't have any trouble," was the line. The squadron's champion Kockinelli-taker strapped me in the right-hand seat while the pilots of our four-aircraft flight were completing their self-briefing.

'"Have you ever flown before?" asked my pilot Squadron Leader 'Dick' Bell (well it was a change from "Are you all right?" and there were a lot of TV camera teams in Akrotiri that week). He seemed reassured: "Oh, well you can do it all then, can't you?" Actually, to save him stretching too far there were a few things I was able to do, such as starting the first Avon, having two wet starts on the second and then finally starting that one.

'I hadn't flown in formation for a number of years and the old regime of formation starts and canopy closures, R/T checks and taxiing began to bring back that once-familiar slight apprehensive stomach-tightening tension which always used to accompany me along the taxi track and into the air until the formation closed up and I was too busy to worry.

'But it was not my responsibility in the T.5 and I was able to relax as we trundled along, the last of four, at 30 knots to the runway end. We lined up four abreast, nicely positioned in echelon port and for one stimulating moment I thought we were about to do a formation take-off. That would have been quite a run, as my pilot was on the dead side. "We shall be doing a stream take-off at five second intervals; full re-heat followed by a max rate rotation climb as soon as possible after getting airborne," said Squadron Leader Bell. "You've probably seen them at Farnborough. The thing is to unstick the aircraft and let it accelerate to the appropriate speed then just pull hard back on the stick to rotate the aircraft to about a 70-degree climb angle. She'll climb at that angle at a steady speed, no trouble."

'"Leader rolling," came the call. A loud rumble, quickly followed by the even louder crackle of twin Avons on re-heat, came from our right. "Two, three, four, five..." Dick, the senior man in the flight, was counting his young pilots out as a check on their own efficiency. Another burst of noise as number two surged forward. The leader was already airborne, wheels tucking in nicely. "Come on number three," growled Dick under his breath, then, as three rolled forward, he began the countdown for us. Full re-heat in a Lightning feels just as it sounds – a smart kick in the back. Once I had accustomed myself to the rate of acceleration I looked for the others. Three was airborne, just rotating into the climb, a split-second transformation from rear profile to planform, but where were the first two ...?

'Hell's bells. I couldn't see the leader but two looked to be going up literally like an arrow at about 10,000 feet in the clear sky above Akrotiri. Then we were airborne at about 160 knots, wheels coming up; Dick held it at about 200 feet while the horizontal tape ASI slid along until the cursor showed 240 knots. Then a hard pull-back on the stick and we were pointing what appeared to be vertically upwards. "We lose about ten knots on the rotation, you'll notice, but she'll hold 230 knots all the way up." Sure enough she did and once the rotation was complete the ride was unexceptional, if you are used to being launched in a rocket. The feeling of lying on my back and being propelled by two crackling afterburners straight up to the troposphere is something I shall remember for quite a while.

'Once we were in the climb the three aircraft ahead came into view. We seemed to be number four in an elongated tail chase pushing upwards at the rush, with the noise of the pressurisation competing with that of the afterburners. At about 30,000 feet, some 70 seconds after rolling, the leader peeled off left and levelled off, shutting down his burners and setting course for our exercise area. His three followers turned inside him and joined up in battle formation before splitting into two pairs for the mock attacks which we were about to practice.

'When Squadron Leader Bell had positioned us 400 yards behind number three he gave me control of the stick and told me to hold the same relative position. Wisely, I left control of the throttle in his hands. We soon began yo-yo manoeuvres, diving through the transonic speeds just below the tropopause then pulling quickly up in a surging climb still at supersonic speed in a simulated zoom attack.

'After a couple of these we split into two pairs, numbers one and two being vectored away by radar in preparation for an attack on us. It was not long before number three started jinking ahead of me. From my left came relaxed comments to close up, go more to the left and most of all, to pull harder. The Lightning really is a delightful aircraft to fly between Mach 0.9 and Mach 1.3, the range in which we were operating. I had no trouble in keeping lateral position by quick applications of aileron followed by opposite aileron to counter the drift. As soon as I saw number three bank I could follow him quite easily.

'But when we began pulling G in turns or in climbs the leader tended to creep up the windscreen while I craned my neck watching him through the canopy and pulling hard back on the stick. In the thin air some long-forgotten reflex was telling me not to pull too hard in case I developed a g-stall. "Pull harder", came the voice, this time somewhat more concerned in case we lost number three altogether. Dick took over and repositioned us, before handing back to me.

'Chat on the R/T warned number three that our attackers were somewhat close, on my side it seemed, but I saw nothing until Dick pointed out two arrows far below us. "They are just preparing to zoom up on us," he said. "Watch for number three taking avoiding action."

'Then we began another series of twists, turns, climbs and descents. I shall never know whether we did evade our attackers – I was too busy trying to keep number three in the centre of my half of the windscreen. When the turns became really tight Dick pushed in the re-heat, felt, as well as heard and we wound round even tighter. In the end, just as it was our turn to make an attack, somebody had a radar failure and someone else was low on fuel. So we met our targets head-on and turned in behind them in a tight upward supersonic arc until we were all four strung out in a descending tail-chase. At least, downwards was the general direction. Number one took the four of us through a downward and seemingly never-ending corkscrew. Sea, clouds and sky reared themselves continuously across the screen. I had forgotten what it was like to be at the back of a tail-chase, watching the three in front making their moves to follow the man ahead. And then, as the three began to drift as a group from their position on the screen, remembering that I too would have to do something before they disappeared entirely.

'It was during one of these lazy moments in the descent that I absentmindedly allowed us to drift upwards through the wash of number three, 300 yards ahead. The buffet was so startling and strong that I really thought we had hit something. It didn't worry Dick though and we pressed on downwards towards Akrotiri.

'Dick took over again as we closed up for a line-astern formation before our final run-in. There is something about line-astern flying, especially in a group of four or more, which is quite fascinating to watch. The twin jet pipes of number three are five feet forward and above the canopy. Above him are two more pairs of jet pipes. A movement of the leader is repeated and magnified by number two, who is followed by number three, by which time the leader has settled down again. Number four, if he is lucky and experienced, can watch the two ahead of him snaking about, while he retains his position relative to the leader and damps out the oscillations. If he doesn't he can find himself having a somewhat undulating ride.

'We tightened up considerably in the short echelon starboard run-in to Akrotiri for the two-second break. When it came it was less stress making than I had anticipated and the approach and landing which followed was very smooth.

'Afterwards at the debriefing it was interesting to listen to the four analysing what had gone on and being mildly critical of themselves and of each other. For the leading three it had been a working flight and for Squadron Leader Bell it had been a check-ride as wing man to a young section leader. Those readers who remember the fighter squadrons of wartime days and the stories afterwards in the crew room, with hands and fingers expressively used to demonstrate who has done what to whom, will be pleased to know that little has changed. The youngest pilots still discuss their tactics in hurried, strident tones while their elders listen and say little. The senior pilots still worry about aircraft availability and whether so-and-so will be able to complete his programme of flying exercises.[7]

'Plus ça change'

Wing Commander Bruce Hopkins, CO of 23 Squadron since May 1972 sometimes took part in his squadron's QRA[8] commitment at Leuchars, as he recalls:

'At one time all my pilots had done at least two intercepts against Soviet aircraft. Eric Houston did twenty-four scrambles that resulted in intercepts, 1972-75. The QRA shed was at the end of the runway and we would go there for twenty-four hours at a time and sit and wait. We'd sit in the crew room, kitted up and sleep there in proper beds in our underclothes. Our immersion suit, g-suit and Mae Wests were laid out. We would get a build-up – in other words, a recognized air picture. A typical scramble would begin with one of the Norwegian radars plotting a Soviet aircraft transiting the Northern Cape and on into the North Sea. It could be a training flight. 'Bears' were always going to Cuba via the Faroes-Scotland-Iceland gap – or an intelligence-gathering sortie. Every time we had a naval exercise in the area you could always guarantee Soviet aircraft would monitor it. Sometimes we would go weeks without any Soviet aircraft, then get a dozen in a four-day period. The plot would be picked up by Saxa Vord, who would 'tell in' to Strike Command at High Wycombe, who would organize resources.

QUICK REACTION ALERT

Tankers would usually be called in to support us. You therefore knew well in advance when you would be scrambled and if and when you would get a tanker. First we were brought up to cockpit readiness. The ground controller would relay all relevant information, together with your call sign and that of the tanker. The type of call depended on the circumstances. The aircraft was always fully armed. We would carry a hand-held camera in the cockpit.

'Usually, one aircraft could be scrambled, but both pilots would be in their cockpits in case of a problem. Once airborne, we would first get to a tanker and then stay with him and refuel until the actual intercept. (A typical sortie would be five to six hours and involve several rankings, or brackets.) Once the intercept was set up, we would cast off from the tanker and head for the target. We would intercept, investigate and shadow, take photos and feed information on new aerials aboard an aircraft etc., back for intelligence gathering. Flying a Lightning and taking photos of a manoeuvring Bear was not the easiest job in the world and we developed a technique. First we would fly under the 'Bear', or the 'Badger', etc. and take photos from all angles. Sometimes, to make life even more difficult, they would trim in to you or away from you. Sometimes the guy at the back would wave. At night they shone lights at you to find out who you were. Although international airspace reached to within twelve miles of the coast of Britain, usually, the Soviet aircraft never came within 100 miles.'

Squadron Leader Dave Seward was also asked to take photos of Soviet bombers from the cockpit while on QRA intercepts. 'I think that the Lightning cockpit was built around Roly Beamont, a 4 feet 8 inch monster who had hands like meat plates and not for six-foot-tall chaps like me! Trying to turn around in the cockpit when your head is almost touching each side and wearing an immersion suit and oxygen mask etc. to take a photo with your Vivitar was, shall we say 'difficult'? Taking photos whilst flying the Lightning 1A, whose early autopilot was an AFCS giving just heading and attitude hold, was even worse. At that time QRA was a lot of sitting around on the ground. At Wattisham, whenever we were used 56 Squadron reinforced the Northern QRA. On Christmas Day 1962 the Russians put lip a stream of 'Bears' and the odd 'Bison' round the North Cape and we were up and down and landed at Leuchars. The Russians could be sheer bloody-minded. Commanding officers did not do normal QRA but generally speaking, we did Christmas Day and Boxing Day duty.'

In December 1973 the 23 Squadron CO, Wing Commander Bruce Hopkins, leading from the front and volunteering for it, did a Christmas and Boxing Day stint, from 0900 hours on Christmas morning to 0900 hours on Boxing Day. All was quiet until 0400 hours on Boxing Day morning when he was scrambled to investigate a plot over the North Sea. As usual, he expected to first make a rendezvous with a tanker. (Tankers were usually available at a high readiness state, in order to keep the interceptors airborne for as long as required – sometimes up to seven or eight hours.) 'However,' he recalls, 'there was no tanker available and so I did not have enough fuel to get to the intercept point. It was a 'Bear' making the Cuba run. I flew out for forty minutes in the hope that I would get a look at it but the target profile probably turned away. A year later on 17 September 1974 I intercepted two 'Badgers' flying together, going north. The training and probing flights continued and each time we would send Lightnings up to investigate. Sometimes they were one of 'ours'. Sometimes they weren't. It was hard work but I enjoyed it, Comparing the Lightning with the Phantom was like comparing a sports car with a ten-ton truck. The Lightning handled beautifully and had a responsive feel to it, whereas the Phantom did not have that preciseness of control.'

Bruce Hopkins left 23 Squadron in April 1975. Seven months later, in November 1975 Group Captain Ed Durham arrived at Gütersloh having forsaken ('not reluctantly') a desk in MoD London earlier that year to take command of 92 Squadron. Group Captain Durham recalls: 'I had spent some months refresher flying and was looking forward to taking my first command of a fighter squadron. All my time in the RAF had been spent in air defence in the United Kingdom and I had already flown three tours on the Lightning. To return to flying after an absence of six years was a tremendous thrill in itself but to be given a famous fighter squadron to lead and at an overseas location was real icing on the cake.

'In the UK the threat we faced was largely a long-range bomber one, at medium to high level and at some distance from the UK mainland. In Germany it was a totally different matter. The threat was at low altitude, had a substantial self-defence capability and could well be dedicated to defensive counter air; in other words we, the fighters, were their prime target. Generally speaking we were heavily outnumbered as well. Such considerations tended to concentrate the minds of 2 and 4 ATAF fighter crews and the impetus was skill though realistic training. Ground Control was a bonus and we spent much of our time in the low-level combat air patrol patterns although we talked to 'Backwash' and 'Crabtree' [GCI stations in Germany] occasionally.

'Lightning Alley' was some obstacle fir the ATAF fighter-bombers to penetrate and affiliation training was achieved regularly under the 'Dial a

Lightning' concept. All we needed was a 'phone call from some base like Laarbruch or Brüggen to say that so many Jaguars would be south of Soest at 1200 and there would be at least two Lightnings on visual patrol ready to do battle.

'There is no doubt in my mind that my flying at Gütersloh was some of the best I have done in my air force career. Low-altitude operations are exciting and stimulating in themselves but to add to these the extra bonus of air combat not only increased the flow of adrenaline but also revealed the sense of responsibility innate in our young fighter pilots of the day. Mostly they were given free rein to do the job and with very few exceptions they responded in an effective and mature way. I was very proud of all my men on 92, aircrew and ground crew alike and I felt very privileged to be their commanding officer. We met every challenge, such as tactical evaluation, which came our way. I would also pay tribute to the other squadrons on the base for their contribution to the outstanding combat capability of the base and also for the friendly rivalry that helped to make life as good as it was.'

In 1972 an article appeared detailing QRA in RAF Germany.[9] 'On every station, some personnel will have been on duty throughout the night – in the Ops Room, the guardroom and so on. But at Gütersloh, just eighty miles from the East German border, the centre of quiet activity is a warmly-lit, miniature hangar a few yards from the runway threshold. Inside, behind heavy steel doors that open electrically at the touch of a button, sit two silver Lightnings – fuelled, armed and ready to go. In a small annexe two pilots, dressed in bulky rubber immersion suits, pressure vests and all the other paraphernalia of a modern jet fighter pilot, have probably been playing cards all night; a few feet away in another room, the ground crew doing the same thing. This tiny world is the Battle Flight, RAF Germany's first line of defence and the scene is much the same 24 hours a day, 365 days a year, be it Christmas, Easter or April Fools' Day.

'While the rest of the station begins its daily tasks, life in the hangar continues along the same lines. Across the airfield, the pilots' colleagues are beginning their day's work by attending the daily weather briefing and the long-suffering met man is enduring his daily dose of ribbing from the crews. (With the possible exception of the NAAFI, the met men are the pilots' favourite Aunt Sallies.) Within the hour, the first wave of Lightnings is roaring into the sky and the day's training programme is under way. In pairs or singly, the Lightnings accelerate down the long runway with an ear-splitting roar, twin jets of flame from their re-heated engines scorching the concrete as the wheels leave the ground, some heading for special areas where, at great heights, they are allowed to go supersonic. Then they will chase each other around the sky on practice interceptions, guided by the disembodied voice of a man sitting miles away in a darkened room, watching the green blips that are the Lightnings on his radar set. The days when fighter pilots depended on the evidence of their own eyes are long past; with two Lightnings approaching head-on at supersonic speed, by the time the pilots spot each other it would be too late to avoid a collision. Others will be practising similar interceptions at a much lower level, while still more could be heading for a rendezvous with a converted Victor V-bomber from Britain, its bomb-bays now heavy with fuel. Once in contact, the Victor streams three long hoses, each with an inverted cone at the tip and the thirsty Lightnings nose in, their pilots carefully juggling the controls in order to spear the cone with their refuelling probes. Once 'plugged in', the fighters guzzle fuel at a fantastic rate and within a remarkably short time, gorged, they pull back and swing off to continue their exercise. The Victor, much, much lighter, turns for home, reeling in its hoses as it does so.

'Meanwhile, away to the east, a small civilian aircraft, carrying businessmen from Southern Germany to a conference in Lübeck on the Baltic, is creeping slowly eastwards away from its planned route; the pilot's radio navigation instruments are giving him a false reading. Eventually the aircraft crosses an invisible border in the sky and inadvertently enters the Air Defence Identification Zone, within which aircraft must not fly without special authority: its purpose is to prevent just such an occurrence from turning into a border incident. In another darkened room, another man at another radio set has been monitoring the aircraft for some minutes. Attempts to contact it by radio have failed and as it enters the ADIZ the controller reacts. An alarm bell rings loudly in the miniature hangar near Gütersloh's runway and cards and magazines fly in all directions as pilots and ground crew sprint for their aircraft. The heavy steel doors are already rolling back as the pilots leap up the ladders to the cockpit. Less than a minute has passed since the bell sounded and already the engines of one of the Lightnings are winding up. Around the second, the frantic activity ceases; this one will be held at immediate readiness in case No.1 needs assistance.

'As his engines come to life and his instruments come on line, the pilot of No. 1 is receiving, through his earphones, essential instructions – which controller to contact, initial heading, climb rate, altitude and so on. The flow of information comes to an abrupt halt as the aircraft, ready to go, rolls forward and disconnects from the telephone line plugged into its side.

QUICK REACTION ALERT

From here on, communication is by radio. The Lightning rolls swiftly to the runway and swings on to it. While still in the turn, the noise from the engines increases to an ear-splitting crescendo and as the aircraft straightens, twin tongues of flame shoot from the jet pipe. The gleaming fighter screams down the runway, lifts off and within seconds dwindles to a tiny dot in the sky. A little more than two minutes have passed since the bell sounded. Three minutes later, the pilot of the civilian aircraft gets the shock of his life as the Lightning thunders across his nose, swings round and closes up to formate on his right wing-tip and his stomach muscles contract as the awful realisation of his error dawns. He swings away westwards. Ahead, after landing, lies a highly embarrassing interview with an official from the aviation authorities; but for the Lightning, he would have been heading for a far more uncomfortable time on the other side of the border!'

19 and 92 Squadrons carried out Lightning interceptor duties from Gütersloh until replacement by Phantom FGR.2s, 19 Squadron disbanding first, on 31 December 1976 and reforming at Wildenrath on 1 January 1977 on the Phantom. On the eve of disbandment Group Captain 'Ed' Durham led a 92 Squadron twelve-ship formation over the snow covered fields at Gütersloh. Three months later when 92 Squadron disbanded, on 31 March, Group Captain Durham was determined to mark the passing of the Lightning in RAF Germany in a manner befitting the occasion but this time he had to content himself with just two aircraft for a flypast. Shortly before midnight on 31 March he and Simon Morris took off from Gütersloh on a 55-minute sortie, during which time the CO called up each GCI station and one by one bid them farewell. 'We landed,' he says 'back at Gütersloh and were then asked by the tower to stop for five minutes. There were no lights on at all; not even on the ASP [Aircraft Servicing Pan]. Then we got the "Clear to taxi in" call and suddenly, all the lights came on at once. The ASP was filled with people! We were carried shoulder high to the hangar and a big 'hoolie' followed. It really was a wonderful moment.'

In January 1977 92 (Designate) Squadron began training as a Phantom air defence unit at RAF Wildenrath and on 1 April this unit formally adopted the 92 numberplate. By the end of 1977 only 5 and 11 Squadrons were equipped with Lightnings. Sergeant David R. Bishop was based at RAF Binbrook from August 1986 to July 1988 and is well qualified to write about being on QRA from an Air Traffic point of view.

'On Q with Air Traffic was similar for each squadron involved and those techies detailed to do it, except we only did it once during the two-week stint. On the Wednesday going onto Q the usual panic started within Air Traffic of getting the confidential codes sorted out. The night shift working that week started off Q. When normal night flying was finished for the evening, one Local (Visual Control Room) qualified controller and one assistant remained behind, with one approach/director qualified controller on call for when the aircraft recovered. I never did a night on Q. I always seemed to pull a Saturday duty, 24 hours stuck in the tower, so let's concentrate on this and give you an insight to the only time the USSR had the damn cheek to penetrate UK airspace when I was working.

'The shift started at 0800 and relieving the off-going controller, he or she would give me two briefings, one on the state of the airfield and the other being the state of Q and what readiness they were on. Up to the local and sign on as having taken over the watch and then back down for the 0800 briefing over the secure communication lines. Briefing over, it was time to pop down to the Met Office for the weather brief along with some of the pilots who were on Q for the next 24 hours. I was only really interested in the forecast wind, one to choose the duty runway and two, was it safe for 03 departures? Briefing over I collect the Rover keys and ask the assistant to man local while I am out and about doing the airfield inspection, slightly different inspection this morning as I stop on the 26 threshold piano keys. I ask the assistant to raise and lower the barrier, even though I know ground equipment technicians will be out later to do their little bit. I need to confirm its operation. Down the active instead of turning off and onto the taxiway back to Air Traffic, I turn right and have a look at the Q taxiway to ensure that everything is OK down there and pop into the pilots' crew room to say 'hello' and to let them know that me and Flight Lieutenant so-and-so are on duty today and ask if they have any particular scramble requirements should they go. All done and back up to local to start my VCR checks and all appears to be serviceable, as we are on Q; a double check of the Very pistols; all complete and I add that information in my airfield log book. Then downstairs to check the radar, but as Ground Radar are doing their DI's, I ask them if it is all OK. They would like to do some maintenance today on various bits and I ask them to call me before starting, just in case Q gets scrambled! Then, with all the frequencies patched through to the Switchboard Room, I join the assistant and confirm that the Radar controller has checked in and we discuss what videos we have to watch and when. We decide to watch *Weird Science* in the afternoon and *Highlander* during our loosely termed dinner.

'In the afternoon we start to get some updates from Boulmer of possible activity later. That would be nice for a change as when it has been my turn for being on standby for Q these last eighteen months, I never had a scramble once. I had been up to cockpit readiness but no scramble. Now it is evening and pitch black outside and time for me to do another airfield inspection; this time the Night Inspection, which consists mainly of checking the airfield lights. Back in the tower and it's up to local for me to check airfield light settings etc. The only lights I leave on are the taxiway lights from the Q shed to 03 threshold for the Q aircraft if needed for a scramble. I then stick little cardboard disks over the equipment. I have a switch to turn on if we get a scramble. That way I cannot make any mistakes.

'Watching *Match of the Day* we get a scramble. It is the fastest you will ever see a controller move! Up to the Local I go, main lights for the VCR are switched on so I can see what I am doing. Then I remove the numbered disks in order. First the runway lights switched on, obstruction lights on and that is that for the lights. Visual check of the runway. I can hardly see anything anyway but habits cannot be changed. Then remove the disks for the barrier and raise the 26 threshold barrier. I then check the surface wind and crosswind resolver and everything is within limits. Hive of activity down the Q sheds. Buzz through to Waddington approach to see if they have any conflicting traffic; nothing at all to conflict. Traffic lights on red; no one is one the airfield. Buzz down to the fire section to inform them Q is being scrambled; just over three minutes from scramble. The Lightning is fast taxiing out. Seconds under four minutes and airborne. Not bad as they have to get airborne in five minutes from a standing or sleeping start. Buzz down to the assistant that Q is airborne and make a log entry of the departure time in the movements log and my own log. All departures are silent. I switch off the bi-directional lights leaving the omni-directional lights on for the next fifteen minutes. Switching frequencies hear Q1 has declared himself serviceable and 2 is stood down to ten minute readiness. Going downstairs I confirm with Rudy that the radar controller is on her way in. A couple of hours later Q1 is recovering for Runway 21 and up to Local again. I switch on the approach lights and the runway lights for 21. I slowly move the intensity of all the lights up to max and slowly back down again. The aircraft saw the lights at a range of sixty miles. With Q1 calling finals to land, up with the binoculars to see if I can pick up a good 'chute and I call it. As the aircraft calls clear of the active he reports 'one on the can' which we know as he has intercepted a 'zombie' and the information is passed around. Needless to say, on hearing the aircraft touch down, my lovely approach controller left the tower quicker than I made it up to Local. When the aircraft has safely shut down I then switch all the airfield lights off bar the obstructions lights, as someone was forgetful in leaving them off.'[10]

THE MEN WHO FLEW THE ENGLISH ELECTRIC LIGHTNING

By the end of 1977 only 5 and 11 Squadrons remained equipped with the Lightning. The rest of 11 Group's interceptor force had converted from the Lightning to the F-4M Phantom FGR.2. 5 and 11 squadrons at Binbrook remained equipped with the Lightning, serving until 31 October 1987 and 30 April 1988, respectively, when they were replaced with Tornado F.3 aircraft. Binbrook remained equipped with the Lightning and these served until 31 October 1987 and 30 April 1988, respectively, when they were replaced with Tornado F.3 aircraft.

Chapter 8

Tigers Fly East

1963 saw my departure from the Squadron and from Lightnings. 74 Squadron moved to Leuchars and then to Singapore soon after I left. That was where the incident occurred when a python wrapped itself around Ian McBride's main wheel u/c leg after he taxied in; it nearly gave a heart attack to the man who went to put in the ground lock. Great days on a great squadron; how I wish I had stayed with them.'

Dave Betts. In a four-month period, May-August 1970, 74 Squadron at Tengah lost three Lightnings, two of the crashes proving fatal. On the night of 26 May Flying Officer John C. Webster (flying XR767) was killed when he crashed into the sea after becoming disorientated during low-level practice intercepts over the Malacca Straits.

Perhaps the most spectacular item in the Lightning repertoire was the rotation takeoff. The seemingly almost vertical climb with the aircraft supported on two invisible but ear shattering columns of thrust was an unforgettable sight. This manoeuvre obviously intrigued 25-year-old Flight Lieutenant Frank Whitehouse on 74 Squadron at Tengah, because on 27 July 1970 when he and Flying Officer Roger Pope were briefed for a sortie Whitehouse wanted to make his rotation take-off as spectacular as possible and arranged for a cameraman to be stationed at the end of the runway to capture his rapid climb to 20,000 feet on film. The two pilots briefed for the sortie. Pope was to be the leader of the pair, but as he had not done a rotation take-off for about a year the brief for this seemingly almost vertical climb to height was left to Whitehouse. The minimum speed for rotation was 260 knots with a maximum pull of 3g. However, both pilots agreed that the more normal speed of 290 knots was preferable, although they would observe the 3g limitation. Having entered a climb of around 60 degrees the recovery would be effected by a wingover to port. The brief over, the two pilots went out to their aircraft. As they separated to go to their own particular machine Whitehouse turned to Pope and laughingly said 'Don't overstress it.'

While they strapped in, the photographer who was to film the take-off came to the foot of the aircraft ladder and asked Whitehouse where the rotation would take place.

'Anywhere between here and the barrier,' was the reply. Clearly he was in a happy, light-hearted mood.

The two Lightnings entered the runway and lined up in echelon port ready for the off. Pope released his brakes and accelerated down the runway. At the far end of the runway, with the briefed 290 knots indicated, he rotated. Unfortunately, possibly because of his lack of experience, he overdid it a little and clocked 4g. However, he was safely airborne and gaining height like the proverbial homesick angel. He waited for a call from Whitehouse in XS930, which took off just five seconds behind but nothing came so Pope transmitted to the tower and informed ATC that both aircraft were airborne and changing to the Approach frequency. 'Standby, your No. 2 has crashed on take-off,' was the chilling reply.

Whitehouse had held the aircraft down low picking up speed rapidly. While still 300 feet short of the runway barrier, rotation took place. Spectators saw the Lightning snap into an almost vertical climb and then start to roll left. In doing so he probably pulled 5g or more. Onlookers reported that it was the fastest rotation they had ever seen. XS930 appeared to have entered a spin. Pilot's Notes for the Lightning F.6 provided information on the effects of rapid, harsh application of G. They warned that the aircraft would pass rapidly through the pre-stall buffet zone into a flick manoeuvre with the aircraft rolling and yawing to either left or right. This seems to be exactly what happened in the accident. Having reached a height of about 600 feet XS930 started down again and after what looked like an attempt at recovery it disappeared behind some trees where the Lightning crashed into a Malay village and exploded. A pall of black smoke confirmed the crash in which Whitehouse and a Chinese farmer, Cheong Say Wai, lost their lives. Two villagers were injured and 100 buildings were destroyed. Whitehouse was well thought of by his superiors and had an assessment of high to above average. However, his enthusiasm had at times to be tempered with fairly close supervision. On his final flight he allowed his eagerness to get the better of him. With a cameraman poised to film the take-off one can imagine the determination of the pilot to ensure that he provided a rotation to remember and one worthy of being projected on the screen. Quite simply he tried too hard and paid the penalty.

Dave Roome watched the whole incident: 'Following a fire on start to XS928[1] in April, caused by a sticky overwing vent valve, we had adopted the policy – agreed by BAC Warton – of selecting the flight refuel switch to flight refuel until after take-off. This prevented the ventral tank fuel pump from starting up on the ground, which normally occurred after 120-160lb of fuel had been burnt after the start and which had pumped the fuel out through the vent valve. Unfortunately, no one had realized that burning fuel from the wings and not from the ventral had the effect of moving the aircraft's CG aft and Frank had had a long wait on the ground and a long taxi to the take-off point. By the time he got airborne his CG was outside the aft handling limits, which had the effect of reducing markedly the stick force per G on the control column. When he 'snatched' the stick, as we used to for a good 'rote' the aircraft over-rotated and stalled. He should have ejected immediately but, with the aircraft virtually at the vertical, it staggered up to 400-500 feet purely under the influence of two Rolls-Royce Avons before autorotating and falling out of control. Frank ejected too late and was killed on impact with the ground.'[2]

74 Squadron had been posted overseas in June 1967 to Tengah, Singapore to replace the Javelins of 64 Squadron. Operation 'Hydraulic', as it was known, the longest and largest in-flight refuelling operation hitherto flown, began on 4 June when the CO, Wing Commander Ken Goodwin, led six Lightnings off from Leuchars. Five more departed the next day and the last two flew out on the 6th.[3] All thirteen Lightnings reached Tengah safely, staging through Akrotiri, Masirah and Gan and using seventeen Victor tankers from Marham, for what turned out to be a four-year tour of duty in the tropics.[4] A Lightning fatality occurred on 12 September 1968 when 24-year-old Flying Officer Pete Thompson was approaching Tengah in XS896 on the downwind leg and was heard to call, 'Three greens,' then, 're-heat light on shutting down No. 1'. The F.6 was seen to pitch tip, then roll twice and enter a spin. The No. 1 in the formation told Thompson to eject. The aircraft was now at low level and in the airfield circuit. Thompson's canopy was seen to leave the doomed aircraft but the unfortunate pilot was later found dead twenty feet from the seat, which landed in a mangrove swamp north of Tengah. To discover the cause of the crash, Group Captain Antony Barwood of the Institute of Aviation Medicine at Farnborough and Brian Limbrey of Martin-Baker Ltd were despatched by RAF VC-10 to Singapore. Antony John Barwood was born at Norwich on 1 April 1915 and

educated at Oundle. He had seen his first crash, a Vickers Vimy that fell near his prep school at Aldburgh in 1926. In 1935 he went to St. Bartholomew's Hospital Medical School, graduating five years later. It was during the first months of the war that he came to the attention of the RAF. He was cycling home when a Hampden bomber crashed in a nearby field. The crew escaped the burning bomber, but the rear gunner was trapped by his foot. Barwood entered the aircraft and removed the gunner's boot with a medical scalpel. They had just escaped when the bomber blew up. He joined the RAF in 1941. He recalls: 'There were several witnesses to the Lightning accident. Some of them aircrew on the ground and in the air, but the key witness was a corporal's wife who was hanging out her washing. She told us what she saw, not what she thought she thought we wanted her to tell us. (The best witnesses to aircraft accidents are schoolboys!) She saw the aircraft invert and the pilot eject downwards. All the seat systems had functioned correctly until the seat hit a mangrove tree and slithered to the ground with the pilot just detaching from it. He had a technical problem and presumably hoped to land the aircraft, but had left it too late.'[5]

Flight Lieutenant Dave Roome was posted to the 'Tigers' that same year. He relates: 'By the time I came to the Lightning in September 1967, the F.6 was already in production for the squadrons, though only thirty-nine were built in all (a further fourteen were converted from the 3ER [extended range]). The OCU course was conducted initially on the F.1A and T.4, flying the conversion phase with 1 Squadron on 226 OCU and the basic radar phase on 2 Squadron. It was during the latter phase that we received our postings, for those destined for Germany would remain on 2 Squadron, as 19 and 92 squadrons then flew the F.2, later the F.2A and only those posted to fly the F.3 or F.6 completed their course on the T.5. The first seven tourists on our course were told that there were four UK postings, all to Leuchars, while three of us would go to Germany. This caused a small problem as five of us wanted Germany. Whilst we might be officers and gentlemen, none of us was going to give up a Germany posting voluntarily. In the end we drew straws and whilst the three lucky ones were celebrating, the two of us who had missed out agreed that the toss of a coin would leave that one with the chance of any 'odd' posting that might come up. The other could be certain that he would go to Leuchars. Some days later, I was asked by my squadron commander to confirm that I had indeed won the toss. I duly did so and received my posting, to 74 Squadron at RAF Tengah in Singapore!

'During the three-and-a-half years that I was at Tengah many events, both happy and sad, took place. On 23 October 1968 I had the chance to intercept a USAF RB-57F, a highly modified version of the Canberra with a 122 feet span and 42,000lb of thrust. This was in Singapore carrying out high-altitude meteorological trials on turbulence prior to Concorde starting commercial services to Singapore. The abilities of this aircraft in the upper atmosphere were demonstrated graphically when he climbed 15,000 feet, from 65,000 to 80,000 feet, whilst flying a 180-degree turn! He was surprised that the Lightning, which carried out the next intercept, overtook him in a descent through his altitude and advised us that his last run would take some time to set up. This time his altitude was into six figures and he was safe, but it left me with the thought that out in the tropics where the tropopause is in the order of 55,000 feet the Lightning could probably achieve above 85,000 feet. I was determined to try it when I got the chance and some months later, that chance arrived.

'There was a Victor tanker returning from Hong Kong and offering about 17,000lb of fuel to us. I went up the east coast of Malaysia, almost to the Thai border and filled to full. I was now left with a straight run home and the east coast was the area in which we could fly supersonic. Initially I climbed to 50,000 feet, which was the subsonic service ceiling of the aircraft and there I accelerated to 2.0M and started a zoom climb, selecting about 16 degrees of pitch. I levelled off at 65,000 feet and let the aircraft have its head, reaching 2.2M before once again flying the same zoom profile. This time I held the climb attitude, though to do so, required an increasing amount of aft stick as the reduction in downwash over the tail increased. Eventually the stick reached the backstops and I gently topped out, 200 feet short of 88,000 feet. From there, Singapore looked tiny and I convinced myself that I could see from the very southern tip of Vietnam over my left shoulder, past the Borneo coast in my 11 o'clock, to the western coast of Sumatra on my right hand side. The sky was pitch-black above me and all of a sudden I realised that I did not belong here. With idle/idle, I started a glide back down which would have carried me over 150 miles. A marvellous example of the Lightning's sheer performance; though the pressure jerkin, G-suit and normal oxygen mask would not have been sufficient had the pressurisation failed.

'We also took the Lightning to Australia for the first time in June 1969 for an exercise called 'Townhouse', which was mounted in the Northern Territory and we were based at Darwin. This provided some excellent flying as the rules were few – the base commander was quoted by the local Press as saying that, if they were to practise the defence of the area realistically, then the aircrew needed freedom and the town should "expect to get boomed".

Darwin was still used by the major airlines as a staging base and one sight that sticks in my mind is of a 707 taking off whilst being overtaken by an 'attacking' RNZAF Canberra. Giving chase were one RAAF Mirage and one Lightning, which went either side of the 707 as it pulled into its normal, steep, noise-abatement climb. The complaint of the 707 captain was met by the RAAF air traffic controller's statement to the effect that "didn't he know there was a war on?"

'There were many problems with the aircraft during my time on it. By far the worst problem was that of fuel leakage into the fuselage where it had a rather tiresome habit of catching fire. During my time at Tengah I had four fire warnings in flight.

'Also, there was much fun to be had, not least because there was no QRA, very few exercises and several detachments to places such as Butterworth in Malaysia, to Bangkok and across Australia. We had our own tactical air force in the Far East Air Force: Tengah had 20 Squadron with Hunter FGA.9s and three Single Pioneers for FAC work, 45 Squadron flew the Canberra B.15 and 81 Squadron operated in the recce role with the Canberra PR.7. Elsewhere on Singapore there were Hercules, Shackletons, Bristol Freighters Andovers, Meteors, Belvederes and Whirlwinds. North in Malaysia by some 330 nautical miles was Butterworth, which operated two RAAF fighter Squadrons, eventually both with the Mirage III and we used to have a regular exchange, called Tiger Rag.

'There was a long-standing competition for the fastest time from passing the ATC Tower at one base to arriving at the other, which had started way back in the days of Sabres and Meteors. The Hunter had brought the record back to the RAF but the arrival of the Mirage allowed Butterworth to regain the title. Eventually 74 planned an all-out assault, using four Lightnings on their way to start a 'Tiger Rag'. Each took off at five-minute intervals and had several check points on the route north. If the lead passed a checkpoint with more than the planned minimum fuel, those behind left full burner in and so, of course, the back man slowly caught up the lead! Eventually all four passed the tower at approaching 0.999M and the base commander, a somewhat irascible man, took umbrage at this hooliganism and ordered all four aircraft to return to Tengah the next day! They brought back the record though, of 24 minutes for the 330 nautical miles and it was to stay with 74 for the remainder of our time there.

'On 22 October 1970 I was lucky enough to fly one of the two aircraft up to Bangkok for a display there (the boss, Wing Commander Dennis Caldwell, had announced the detachment some time earlier by saying "I don't know

Four of 5 Squadron's F.6s that flew non-stop from RAF Valley to RAF Muharraq in operation 'Gambroon' in May 1968. Hunters on 208 Squadron took photos of the formation approaching Bahrain at the end of the operation.

F.6s on Treble One Squadron. XM188/F first flew on 27 March 1961 and joined 111 Squadron on 31 May that same year. XM188 had a premature end at Coltishall on 21 June 1968 when Squadron Leader Arthur Tilsley taxied this aircraft in with no brakes and crashed it into the side of 1 Hangar at the station. One Avon jammed at about 80% power and a Rolls-Royce technician scrambled underneath to the engine bay and eventually managed to stop the runaway engine. Tilsley, meanwhile, had climbed out of the cockpit onto the roof of the hangar offices. T.4 XM994 first flew on 12 March 1962 and was issued to 19 Squadron at Leconfield on 6 November 1962. After being used to help conversion of both 19 and 92 Squadrons to Lightnings, XM994 was transferred to 226 OCU at Coltishall on 27 June 1963, where it served until 8 May 1974. The aircraft was scrapped in 1977.

5 Squadron on the line at Luqa during exercise 'Nimble', 1-9 August 1968. T.5 XS451/T nearest the camera first flew on 3 June 1965. It ended its days as ZU-BEX with Mike Beachy Head's Thunder City organisation in South Africa, crashing at Bredasdorp in November 2009 during an air display at the annual Overberg Air Force Base fly-in.

On 28 August 1968 F.6 XR725 on 23 Squadron was one of two F.6s, which made the non-stop, air-refuelled, 7 hour 20 minute flight to Goose Bay, Canada to appear in an air show at Toronto. It was flown there and back on 3 September, by Squadron Leader Ed Durham and on its return, was put into store. This Lightning, which was built as an F.3, first flew on 19 February 1965 and was issued to 23 Squadron after conversion to F.6 on 16 August 1967. XR725 then went to 5 Squadron on 8 December 1969 for ferrying out to RAF Tengah to join 74 Squadron.

Prince Faisal bin Bandar Al Saud, son of King Faisal of Saudi Arabia on an advanced training course for pilots at RAF Valley, Anglesey on 26 February 1968. He and Captains Ahmed Behery and Bakry; Prince Turki bin Nasser (Later, Brigadier General, Deputy Defence Minister and Commander of the RSAF); Major Essa Ghimlas (killed in a Lightning F.52 whilst practising single-engine approaches to Khamis Mushayt on 28 November 1968); Major Hamdullah; Captains Abdul Aziz and 'Mo' Algehani; and Ahmed Sudari underwent training on four RSAF T.55s attached to 3 Squadron, 226 OCU at RAF Coltishall, 1968-69. Prior to the first course of Saudi pilots, Captain Turki Bandar Al Thunayan Al Saud was the first RSAF pilot to convert to the Lightning, on 9 June 1967.

T-55 55-711/A, one of the production batch of six two-seaters for the Royal Saudi Air Force at Coltishall on Battle of Britain Day, 14 September 1968. (Tom Trower)

In early 1969 11 Squadron took part in exercise 'Piscador Plus', the largest air-to-air refuelling exercise ever undertaken by the RAF when ten F.6s deployed to Tengah via Muharraq and Gan During 6-11 January on a four-week visit. On 30 January the Squadron performed a 'diamond nine' formation flypast over Singapore Island before beginning the return to RAF Leuchars via Gan on 1 February after completion of the exercise. XR758/J at the back of the formation was left behind at Tengah for 74 'Tiger' Squadron.

Captain William Olin Schaffner, a small, powerfully-built 28-year-old USAF Exchange pilot on 5 Squadron who was killed flying a Lightning on the night of 8 September 1970.

F.6 XS894 on 5 Squadron, which crashed in the sea five miles off Flamborough Head on 8 September 1970. Captain William Olin Schaffner USAF who was on exchange with the squadron was killed.

T.4 XM974 on 226 OCU taxies out during the Battle of Britain Open Day 1970 at RAF Coltishall. This 'T-bird' was abandoned in the North Sea near Happisburgh, Norfolk on 14 December 1972 after an ECU/re-heat fire. Squadron Leader John Spencer and Flying Officer Geoffrey Philip Evans, 226 OCU, ejected safely.

F.6s on 11 Squadron at RAF Leuchars at Luqa in November 1970 during exercise 'Lime-Jug '70' 2-15 November, which practice procedures for co-operation between Royal Navy forces and RAF shore-based aircraft in the Mediterranean. XR723/L crashed into sea 15 miles south of RAF Akrotiri on 18 September 1979 after an engine fire. The pilot, Group Captain Pete Carter, ejected safely and returned to dry land within half an hour. XR763/B crashed on approach to Akrotiri during APC on 1 July 1987 after an engine flame-out following ingestion of part of target banner. Flight Lieutenant D. K. M. 'Charlie' Chan ejected safely. XS934/K crashed two miles off Cyprus on 3 April 1973 following severe vibration and fire caused by disconnected air trunking. Flight Lieutenant Frederick A. Greer ejected safely.

On 14 September 1979 F.6 XS903 was on a test flight prior to being issued to the LTF when its nose wheel failed to lower returning to RAF Binbrook, which was at the time the duty Quick Reaction Alert (QRA) Station. The pilot, Squadron Leader Piper was therefore instructed to divert to Coningsby. After several circuits he positioned for his landing and the combine was instructed to follow the aircraft as soon as its rear wheels touched down but the aircraft suffered a nose wheel collapse and the nose gradually lowered until it was soon scraping along the runway but without catching fire due to an excellent piece of airmanship by the pilot. XS903 was built at Samlesbury and made its maiden flight on 17 August 1966. After retirement from service on 18 May 1988 it was flown to Elvington where it can be seen at the Yorkshire Air Museum sporting a pair of over-wing fuel tanks.

Above: For Quick Reaction Alert (QRA) duty four armed Lightnings (from September 1969, Lightnings and Phantoms) sat in a 'Q-shed' near the end of a runway, two fighters at Leuchars in the Northern QRA all year round and the other two at alternately Wattisham and Binbrook (5 Squadron pictured in a MoD publicity 'scramble' photo) in the Southern QRA. Later, Coningsby's Phantoms were also used.

Right: A Soviet gunner on a Tu-20 (Tu-95) 'Bear C' long-range reconnaissance aircraft over the North Sea waves to a Lightning during QRA.

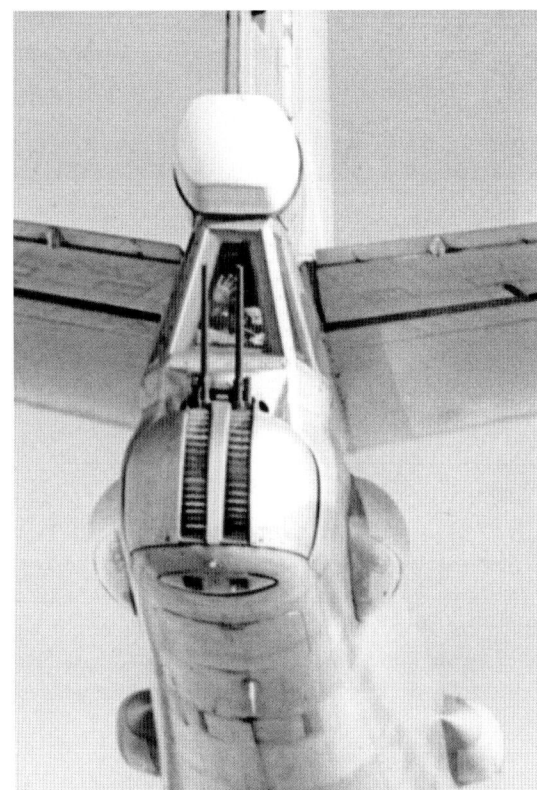

F.3 XP746/K on 56 Squadron. This aircraft first flew on 26 March 1964 and was issued to 56 Squadron on 12 November 1969. It joined 'Treble- One' Squadron on 4 August 1970 and operated for four years before going into store at Wattisham in October 1974. XP746 was SOC in April 1975 and was used as a target (Proof and Experimental Establishment (PEE)) aircraft for gunnery at Shoeburyness in 1976.

T.5. XS416, which first flew on 20 August 1964 was the first T.5 produced, the initial flights being part of the development work for the type. The aircraft then went on to serve on the OCU at Coltishall, 11 Squadron and finally the LTF at Binbrook. XS416 suffered an undercarriage collapse at Binbrook on 19 July 1984. The two occupants, one of whom was the investigating officer returning from the inquest on the crash of XS920 in West Germany, suffered no injuries. It last flew on 21 December 1987 and was sold for scrap but the aircraft was purchased and restored by the NATO Aircraft Museum at Peaks Top Farm, New Waltham, near Grimsby, S. Humberside. When that collection was forced to move, the T.5 ended up at Grainthorpe and in September 2008 moved to New York in Lincolnshire.

T.5 XS420 pictured at Gütersloh in 1974 first flew on 23 January 1965. On the night of 31 January 1973 Captain Gary Catren, a USAF exchange officer attached to 226 OCU, with student pilot Flight Lieutenant George Smith, attempted a take-off for an SCT (Staff Continuation Training) sortie in XS420 from Runway 04 at Coltishall, but the lower reheat failed to ignite. With flaps down (as per a Command directive!), the resultant force of the upper reheat did not allow the nose wheel to be raised. As the T-bird headed for the barrier, Catren, a Texan, shouted *Sheeeeeeeet, George*! Smith, wrongly believing his instructor was calling for the chute, dutifully pulled the brake-chute handle; only for the chute to disintegrate into cinders in the reheat! XS420 took the barrier with it into the overshoot but the T-bird fortunately dug in before it crashed into the railway line and both pilots walked away unhurt. XS420 flew for the last time in May 1983. It is now displayed at the Fenland Aviation Museum in Wisbech.

T.5 XS459 on 226 OCU, which first flew on 18 December 1965, went on to serve with 29 Squadron and the LTF as 'X' at RAF Binbrook. While on the LTF on 21 March 1981 it suffered an undercarriage collapse on approach to Binbrook when Ross Payne and student pilot, Paul Field were the unlucky occupants. XS459 was repaired and made its last flight on 18 March 1987. It is on display at the Fenland and West Norfolk Aviation Museum, West Walton, Wisbech, Cambridgeshire, having previously been displayed in the grounds of the garden centre nearby.

F.6. XS919 which first flew on 28 September 1966 and last flew on 15 March 1988.

Vulcan B.2 XH561 of the Waddington Wing leading four F.6s on 5 Squadron in a formation to mark the formation of RAF Strike Command by amalgamating Bomber and Fighter Commands on 30 April 1968. XS894/F crashed into the sea 5 miles off Flamborough Head on 8 September 1970. Captain William Olin Schaffner USAF attached to 5 Squadron was killed.

Nine of the ten Lightning F.6s on 23 Squadron detached to Luqa for the Malta ADEX 29 April-2 June 1970. Amongst the exercises the squadron engaged in was a one day ADEX on 20 May, in which Canberras from 13, 39, 85 & 360 squadrons, along with Vulcans from Akrotiri posed as hostile forces. 23 Squadron Lightnings flew 24 sorties, claiming 30 interceptions against approximately 56 raid tracks. It was written in the squadron's ORB that the majority of targets were at low level, which would have been engaged by SAMs had they been deployed.

T.5 XS418, which was delivered to 226 OCU on 25 May 1965, photographed on 25 September 1974 during a sortie from RAF Coltishall. XS418 had crashed at RAF Stradishall on 23 August 1968. Flight Lieutenant Henry Ploszek and SAC Lewis were unhurt. The aircraft's last flight was in September 1974 and it served as a surface decoy until being scrapped in September 1987.

XR762/L/K on 11 Squadron, which crashed into the sea off Cyprus on 7 April 1975 after Squadron Leader David Hampton misjudged height above sea during tail chase and he was killed.

Victor K.1 XH621 prepares to receive F.2A XN724/F on 19 Squadron at RAF Gütersloh in 1976. Built as an F.2 and first flown on 11 September 1961, the aircraft went to Boscombe Down on 22 May 19621 and did not see squadron service until after conversion to F.2A, being issued to 19 Squadron on 18 May 1968. It was withdrawn from use on 7 December 1976 and it became a decoy at Laarbruch. (Richard Reeve)

Saudi T.55s 55-713/C (G-27-72 ZF598) RSAF (now at the Midland Air Museum, Coventry Airport); 55-714/D (G-27-73 ZF595) and 55-711/A (G-27-70 ZF597) in formation. The Lightning retired from Saudi service in 1986. Of the 47 delivered, not counting two that had been lost before delivery, 18 had been lost in Saudi service, 22 returned to the UK for a hoped-for re-sale to the Danish Air Force and those which remained in Saudi Arabia were retained as gate guardians and for static display.

F.6 XR755/BJ on 11 Squadron in 1980. Built as an F.3A, this aircraft first flew on 15 July 1965 and was issued to 5 Squadron. In 1967 it was modified to F.6 standard and went on to enjoy long service with 5 and 11 Squadrons. It flew for the last time in December 1987 and in 1988 was bought by Castle Air in Cornwall.

T.5 XS452/ZU-BBD; the first of four Lightnings owned and operated by Thunder City in South Africa, the other flyable Lightnings being T.5 ZU-BEX (XS451) and F.6s ZU-BEY (XP693) and ZU-BEW (XR773). XS452 first flew on 30 June 1965, joined 226 OCU on 20 September that year and continued to operate from 'Colt' until February 1971 when it was allocated to 'Treble-One' Squadron. After many years' faithful service '452' was SOC. in June 1988. Registered ZU-BBD and painted black overall and marked as 11 Squadron 'BT', flew for the first time in its new guise on 9 March 1999.

Left: F.53 53-691 of the Royal Saudi Air Force in flight.

Below: Line up of Saudi Lightnings at Riyadh with F.53 53-698 (G-27-68) nearest the camera.

Wing Commander (later Group Captain) D. A. 'Andy' Williams, the last 'Boss' of 5 Squadron is presented with the Squadron mascot 'Leafy' from the outgoing 'Boss', Wing Commander Mike 'Stretts' or 'Red Dog' Stretton in front of F.6 XR754/AE at RAF Binbrook. This Lightning had suffered an engine fire at Souda Bay returning from the APC at Akoriri, Cyprus where the Squadron had been for live gunnery practice, on 28 August 1984. It was one of three Lightnings that returned to Binbrook on 17 October with sharks' mouth markings added to their forward fuselage. (XR770/AA, which in 1986 acquired a red fin to commemorate 5 Squadron's 21 years of Lightning operations, was adopted by 'Andy' Williams and XS903/AM, were the others). XR754 went to 11 Squadron on 9 December 1986. 5 Squadron re-equipped with the Tornado F.3 at RAF Coningsby early in 1988, leaving 11 Squadron to soldier on at Binbrook for a few more months with the remaining few Lightnings in RAF service. When 11 Squadron disbanded to also re-equip with the Tornado F.3 at RAF Leeming, the Lightning was withdrawn from service.

Wing Commander Jake Jarron, Commanding Officer of 11 Squadron, 'the last Lightning unit'.

ZU-BEX (XS451) which was lost during an air display at the annual Overberg Air Force Base fly-in at Bredasdorp, South Africa on 14 November 2009 when the Lightning apparently suffered hydraulic problems. While attempting to return to the field and on a long approach to Runway 28, it crashed in a ball of flame starting a veld fire approximately 3km east of the field. The pilot, Dave Stock, apparently reported that he may have to eject on at least two occasions. He then reported that he was ejecting, followed immediately thereafter that there had been an ejection failure. After the crash the air show was stopped and two hours later it was confirmed that the pilot had died in the accident and that his body had been recovered some distance away from the downed aircraft. The air show then resumed and the day ended with the SAAF 'Silver Falcons' Aerobatic Display Team flying the missing man formation in tribute to Dave Stock, who had accumulated 15,900 flying hours during an illustrious career, not only as an Air Force test pilot, but also as a commercial pilot.

T.5 XS458/T painted in 1954-2004 Anniversary colours. This T-bird first flew on 3 December 1965 and was issued to 226 OCU in February 1966. It joined 5 Squadron on 12 January 1979 after service with the LTF. Its last flight was on 30 June 1988. Following retirement the T-bird was purchased by Arnold Glass and flown to Cranfield on 29 June 1988 and was later resold, in 1995, to a consortium led by Tony Hulls. In 2001 Russell Carpenter took ownership of the aircraft and today it is unique in the UK in being the only live T.5 and performs regular fast taxi runs at Cranfield.

who else is going".) We landed to find that the squadron commander of one of the Thai F-5 squadrons had been on the same staff college course at Andover and Dennis and he insisted on taking us for 'Thai Tea' which came out of a very large whisky bottle and didn't involve any water! Now one of the Thai customs is that good friends hold hands, regardless of sex and the Thai grabbed hold of Dennis' hand and refused to let it go. I watched the boss trying to look as if his right arm no longer belonged to him and I, as the Squadron Diarist, tried to get my camera out to record the evidence, only to be given an abrupt "There'll be no photographs!" So another marvellous scoop went down the tubes!

'However, it wasn't all fun, for there were tragedies too and in one four-month period in 1970 the squadron lost four aircraft and two pilots, a large percentage of a twelve-aircraft, sixteen-pilot squadron. But we always bounced back, a sure sign of a good squadron. On 26 May Flying Officer John Webster was killed flying XR767 doing low-level practice intercepts over the Malacca Straits. He was, in fact, my No. 2 that night and was on my radar scope until probably only seconds before impact with the water, though I was not aware that he had crashed for some time, as it was not unusual to see and then lose a radar return. The weather was stormy and he had just flown through a fairly bad rain shower although, as he should have been at 1,000 feet above the sea, he should have had no problem. Only a section of overwing tank has ever been found from the aircraft.'

Having witnessed the loss of Flight Lieutenant Frank Whitehouse on 27 July 1970, Dave Roome recalled that a month later, on 12 August, Flying Officer Mike Rigg ejected from XS893/G off Changi when he could not get his port undercarriage leg to lower. 'The leg did not even leave the bay, as could clearly be seen by the taxi light illuminating the bay as Mike overflew Tengah several times (I was OC Night Flying that night). The area into which the aircraft fell, the designated ejection area, turned out to have been used as an ammunition dumping area by the RN and the army for years and no amount of pleading could get any salvage divers to go down! The ejection area, though never used again, was then moved to be Southwest of Tengah by fifteen nautical miles.'

Happily, Rigg ejected safely off Changi and suffered only bruising in the process. Even so, lessons were learned, as Group Captain Barwood explains: 'With plenty of time, the pilot tried everything, high G, hunting and so on, to no effect. He was then vectored out to the ejection area off Changi and ordered to eject. This he did at 12,000 feet and at 300 knots. He was surprised to find himself hanging in his parachute harness, his life preserver hard up under his armpits and nothing, apparently, between his legs. It was dark and he was aware of 'something' flapping around in front of him. He could see the lights of Singapore and of fishing boats and he could feel the quick-release box of his harness high up on his chest compressing his life preserver onto his face. He inflated his life preserver before entering the water and then undid his QRB to get rid of his harness. He inflated his dinghy and got into it and was quite quickly recovered to Changi, as all the rescue services had been alerted. He was uninjured, apart from scuffing on the side of his body where the straps appeared to have pulled up and across his skin. His harness was not recovered.

'I spent about three hours with this pilot, getting a detailed narrative, which he gave very well. Then I questioned him and we had a discussion. He wanted to know what went wrong as much as I did. Next morning I visited the Safety Equipment Section and had a look at an identical harness. From the design of that harness and the way in which the back riser webbing was sewn to the seat loop, it seemed obvious that a load applied at anything but a right angle could overload the corners of the sewn webbing and that it could then peel off. We had no sophisticated method of measuring the load to peel a strap like that. We suspended the pilot with the crutch loops torn and this was exactly the situation he had during his parachute descent. I sent signals to the UK, which were copied to Martin-Baker's factory at Denham, where I went as soon as I got back. A large gathering at all those concerned were waiting. Sir James Martin was livid that I had dared to suggest that one of his harnesses had failed, as he said that it had never happened before, in use or on test. I reminded him that two naval Scimitar pilots had ejected over the sea and were never recovered. "This could be the same thing," I said. Steam was coming out at his ears. "Anyway, we have got a dummy fixed up to drop and to simulate the seam parachute opening load."

'I had a look at the harness where I thought that it had failed. It was just as I thought. It was not at right angles. The dummy was dropped and fell straight through the harness into exactly the position described to me by the Lightning pilot. It was like an H. M. Bateman cartoon – so many mouths dropping open! Sir James had gone back to his office and did not witness the drop. I persuaded them to take photographs of the dummy in the failed harness and of the load areas of webbing stitching failure so that I could send them back to the Board of Inquiry in Singapore. The modification to prevent this recurring was extremely simple, well within the capability of every unit with a fabric workshop sewing machine. I sent copies of the photographs to Tengah, together with some of the drop tests we did at Farnborough. The pilot's mistake was that he opted to eject too high – 12,000 feet – and too fast – 300 knots. The suggested speeds for a controlled ejection at this time were 9,000 feet and 250 knots. The higher altitude and speed produced a much higher parachute opening load, resulting in the damage to his harness. This may have occurred before, but had never been seen, as the navy pilots were not recovered and possibly they fell through their harnesses.'

'Finally,' says Dave Roome, 'the time came to fold up RAF fighter operations in Southeast Asia and we disbanded 74 and left Singapore in early September 1971. Our departure was in dribs and drabs too, for we ferried the aircraft in pairs via Gan to Akrotiri and gave them to 56 Squadron who had been operating the F.3. I decided that I wanted to go out with a bang rather than a whimper and talked over an idea for a final flypast on our departure. The Victor tanker captain was quite content, for he had plenty of spare fuel and both OC Flying and the Station Commander agreed in principle. They attended the brief, at which I mentioned that I would take a line, which would put me "between the Victor on the main pan and the ATC Tower". That is exactly what I did, but the two senior officers were watching from Local, 60 feet above ground level and I was out of sight to them both as I passed! I flew down the pan as low as I dared at about 330 knots and then plugged in the burners over the squadron for the last time and left for Gan, not realising the apoplexy I had left behind! Luckily, OC Flying talked the Station Commander out of his plan to fall in senior flight lieutenants and recall me for a court martial. Instead, my punishment involved removing my authorising status (just prior to my last ever Lightning sortie). I'm still very grateful to Erik Bennett for that generous action.

'So my last single-seat Lightning F.6 sortie, in 'my' aircraft, XR773/F was Gan-Akrotiri with seven 'prods' taking on 36,000lb from the Victors. At the end of it I sat for a moment in the cockpit and thought back over all the good times I had experienced in the Lightning. What a marvellous, beautiful, powerful fighter it was and quietly thanked it for giving me such never-to-be-forgotten experiences ... then it was over and I went off to the Jet Provost 3 to learn to be a QFI!'

Chapter 9

'Linies'

Lingua Franca (the lore of the service) defines a 'Liney' as 'non-flying personnel, those who work on the flight line, preparing the aircraft for flight and recovering them afterwards.' Almost exclusively they were and still are to a great extent, the lowest ranks in the RAF: the LACs and SACs (leading and senior aircraftsmen). As such, they are invariably looked upon as the lowest form of life in a squadron, but they are amongst the hardest working tradesmen on a station.

Peter Hayward was one of the ground technicians on 226 OCU at Coltishall and remembers the Lightning as a 'noisy beast of prey which shattered the peace and tranquillity of certain rural counties in England and Scotland all those years ago. The same Lightning that frightened children, old ladies and all manner of animals also gave pleasure to the pilots who flew it and headaches to the technicians who serviced it. The flight line was the 'sharp end', as Wing Commander Engineering called it. "How are things at the sharp end today?" he would say. The flight line was a busy, noisy hive of industry with pilots and ground crews coming and going, aircraft being marshalled in and out and turn-round, pre-flight and after-flight inspections always going on. Aircraft were refuelled and new brakes installed. Meanwhile, the fog from the LOX (liquid oxygen) trolley crept along the ground like at a latter-day rock festival as oxygen tanks were replenished, followed by the sharp hiss of an AVPIN engine starter and the subsequent acrid smell and eye-watering after-effects of the fumes. This and the ear-shattering blast of the engine starters forms perhaps the most vivid recollections for many Lightning ground crews. The two Avon engines were each started by a small turbine fed by liquid isopropylnitrate (AVPLN). The burnt gases from these two turbines exhausted overboard at high velocity, the No. 1 (lower) engine starter vertically downwards and the No. 2 (upper) engine starter parallel to the ground underneath the port wing. The choking fumes were extremely pungent and irritated the eyes as well. On a calm day they hung in the air until the aircraft taxied out and dispersed them with its jet blast.

'We were almost deafened out of our ear defenders by one of those big silver bullets coming out of nowhere with both re-heats at full chat. The trouble was, they crept up on you. They crept up so fast that you didn't hear them coming until they'd gone. Then you heard them all right, but that ear-shattering roar of two Avons with the re-heat nozzles fully open and enough fire coming from their rear ends to make you realize that hell was closer to earth than you thought. The steely-eyed jockeys who flew them took great pleasure in showing off the awesome power of the engines and incredible rate of climb of the aircraft. Especially in the aerobatic displays. A take-off with full re-heat would be followed by few seconds of level flight a few feet above the runway until the landing gear was tucked away and the aircraft was clean and moving fast. Then up into a near vertical climb until the aircraft was a speck in the sky, for the mere mortals on the ground anyway. An unimaginable din accompanied all this; it was simply shattering.

'For the technicians who serviced them it was a love-hate relationship. The noisy beast of prey was difficult, the systems complex and it seemed that the designers had packed equipment in with hardly a thought as to how to get it out again. Oh, there were plenty of access panels, but it seemed that for even the simplest of jobs one of the engines had to be removed, or the ejection seat, or the radar bullet. "Top hatch off, ventral tank off, bottom hatch off. Fuel leaks, hot air leaks." Then it all had to be put back together again, tested, engines probably run and if you were lucky, if you were really lucky, the aircraft was cleared and handed over to the flight line. A check was carried out on every pre-flight inspection to make sure that the access panels were all properly attached and that no fasteners were missing. On the two-seat versions there were two large hinged access panels just aft of the cockpit. Because they were hinged at the bottom and so opened upwards, they were known as the 'elephant's ears'. These panels hid the fuse and circuit breaker boxes, which had on occasions to be accessed with the engines running and the cockpit occupied by two pilots waiting to leave on a sortie. This required some degree of acrobatic talent from the electrical technicians and they could often be seen hanging on to the cockpit access ladder with one hand and fighting with one of the 'elephant's ears' with the other. An alternative method was to stand precariously on the inboard section of the wing leading edge, grasp one of the antennas on the top of the fuselage and reach forwards to open the panel. This was no less acrobatic than the first method, but a darned sight more entertaining for onlookers, particularly if the wing upper surface was wet with fuel.

'The really hectic times would come during exercises. Aircraft would be serviced for the next flight in record time and from taxiing out, a turnaround inspection could be done in nine minutes. This included completely refuelling the aircraft and instilling a new brake 'chute and a change of crew. The hive of activity continued even when the weather was too bad for flying. 'Clampers' was the term used. It meant bad visibility. The activity, however, was confined to the flight line hut. It consisted of endless games of bridge and other card games, darts, innumerable cups of tea and coffee, erotic books and magazines, sleeping and asking if the squadrons could stand down, as the weather obviously wasn't going to improve, was it?

'Most impressive were re-heat runs at night, for which, at Coltishall anyway, the aircraft would be towed into the old Second World War concrete revetments. The reason for this, I imagine, was to reduce the noise for the civilian population that lived within earshot of the airfield – and that, on a still winter's night, was a good number of miles. Even wearing ear defenders, the noise as re-heat was engaged was awesome. First the engine was taken up to full dry power and then the throttle lever was rocked outboard into the re-heat range. This caused a slight reduction in noise as the re-heat nozzle opened, then the bang as the fuel in the jet pipe lit. As the throttle lever was pushed forwards towards the full re-heat position, the ground shook, the walls of the revetment vibrated and the aircraft compressed its nose landing gear leg and pushed its nose wheel hard into the concrete, fighting on its special chocks and with its brakes fully applied against the power of the engine. The visual effects were no less impressive. The jet blast now consisted of a long pattern of large blue and red diamonds roaring its way for about sixty feet out of the re-heat nozzle.'

Pete Nash joined the RAF in September 1967 and passed out as an LAC Aircraft Mechanic (Weapons) late in March 1968, being posted to RAF Wattisham and then to 29 Squadron on 1 April. He well remembers his introduction to the squadron. As he was led up to the squadron armoury by a sergeant from the station armoury, he looked across the front of Hangar One (29 Squadron's Lightnings were in Hangar Three) to see 29's T-Bird stuck in the grass alongside the runway after bursting a tyre on landing. On a typical squadron the technical personnel would be split into two shifts: one on days, the other on nights. A typical working day for the 'linies' ('about ten or twelve of us'), Pete Nash recalls, 'started at 0700, when we arrived at the hangar. The Line Chief, a chief technician of the airframe ('riggers') or engine ('sooties') trade would have drawn the keys from the guardroom and unlocked the centre fire doors. He would then go to Engineering Control, an office where all hangar servicing and rectification was controlled from and where the Form 700s were kept to find out which aircraft were available for that day's flying. Assisted by his two line corporals, usually from the rigger and scenic trades, he would detail off the towing teams and who was to take out all the ground equipment, etc. The hangar doors would be opened and the aircraft and ground power sets.[1] The towing team would consist of three: a driver, brakeman and chockman.

'The tractor driver had an endorsement on his RAF driving licence stating than he had been examined and found sensible enough to tow aircraft and that his colour perception was safe (CPI), i.e. that he could tell red from green as required by Air Traffic when they changed the traffic lights, or shone a red or green light at him, or, if he was in danger of annoying the Senior Air Traffic Controller (SATCO), a Very light across his bows. The brakeman was certified as having been trained to sit in the cockpit and if the aircraft broke free of the towing arm, to apply the aircraft brakes.

'On the Lightning this was a squeeze lever on the control column. Upon entering the cockpit he had to ensure that there was enough hydraulic pressure to operate the brakes. 1,500 psi had to register on the gauge to operate the brakes at least once. If it was insufficient, then the manual pump handle was removed from the port wheel well and inserted in the pump just in front of and slightly below the port tail plane. Fortunately, it did not take long to pump the reservoir up to the required amount. Sometimes, when a canopy lock had not been used, the canopy would droop down and prevent entrance to the cockpit. When this happened, a small triangular panel behind the cockpit on the port side was opened. Inside was a two-position rocket-switch and handle. The switch was pushed away and the canopy was pumped up using the external hydraulic pump, accompanied by an audible warning. If the canopy was to be closed, then the switch was toggled towards the operator and the canopy would drop under its own weight. The handle was to lock the canopy, by pushing it inboard, inflating the canopy seal at the same time if there was enough air in the system.

'The chockman would connect the towing arm to the towing pintle of the tractor. Then he would pick up the wheel chocks, throw them onto the back of the tractor and walk at the wing tips until the Lightning was clear of the hanger, checking that the aircraft would not hit any obstruction on the way. Outside the hangar he would jump on the tractor and ride out to the line. With the nose wheel on the painted mark on the line, the two chockmen placed the chocks in front of or behind the wheels, depending on the slope of the pans. Then they disconnected the towing arm, lowered the wheels, fitted the earthing lead, jumped back on the tractor with the brakeman and went back for the next aircraft. Meanwhile, more 'linies' would be taking out the Houchins and the brake 'chutes and wheel trolleys and collecting the LOX (Liquid Oxygen) trolley from the LOX bay. Others would be taking out the fire extinguishers and earthing leads stored in and around the 'line hut'. Within half to three-quarters of an hour the once-empty line would get cluttered by all the paraphernalia used to operate Lightnings.

'The line was clearly marked out with lines and rectangles. The lines, in yellow, reached back to the taxiway and indicated the ideal path an aircraft should take to arrive at a square where the nose wheel should stop. At various places, red lines were painted, pointing at an angle to the yellow lines. These were for use when live missiles were fitted and indicated the 'safe heading' where a missile, if accidentally fired, could head off without damaging anything nearby. The rectangles delineated the ground equipment areas, where the Houchin had to be and where we could safely put LOX trolleys and access ladders etc. With two Avon engines sucking through a narrow annular inlet, there was a very real danger of FOD (Foreign Object Debris) ingestion. Also, with the No.1 engine exhaust at about chest level, any loose, light articles were easily blown about.

'While all this was going on, those not otherwise detailed to get the equipment out would start the 'B/F'. This was the Before Flight Inspection, where the Lightning was inspected and any replenishment done to prepare it for flight. The B/F lasted for eight hours and if no other inspection was done in the meantime, another B/F was done.

The riggers would check LOX levels, tyre pressures and the condition of the tyres and check for hydraulic leaks and oil levels etc. The sooties checked fuel states, AVPIN starter fuel and engine oil levels etc. AVPIN was a mono fuel. It created its own oxygen as it burned, so it could be used in a totally enclosed ignition chamber. In its liquid state, it had a distinctive sweet smell. Burnt, it had a distinct, sharp odour, shared only with other select AVPIN-started aircraft. [The fuel was not shock-sensitive and tests showed that armour-piercing ammunition might be fired into tanks containing this fuel without any danger.]

'As one of the armament mechanics, or 'plumbers' as we were known, I ensured that the Master Armament Safety Break (MASB) in the starboard wheel-well was fitted. Initially this was a quick-release electrical multi-pin plug, later modified to be a push-in-and-turn key. It physically open-circuited some of the armament-firing circuits, preventing, along with the undercarriage micro switch, firing of guns or missiles when on the ground. During armament system tests a special tool operated the weight-on-wheels switch and the MASB fitted, or inserted, as required. Next, using a cocking indicator box, I made sure that the manual 4,000lb bomb hook holding the belly tank on was correctly cocked. The missiles were inspected for loose wings and fins. This became a problem with Red Tops later in their life. The wings often became loose on their mountings. This was why in some photos, especially late in the Lightning's career, the wings were missing.

'The infrared seeker head on the Firestreak was cooled using a combination of Stannag air and anhydrous ammonia. If the Lightning was fitted with Firestreak the missile-pack air bottle pressure was checked and topped up if required and the ammonia bottle fitted. Air pressure was read off a small gauge just in front of the cooling intakes on the right-hand side of the missile pack. Upper and lower limits were 2,500 and 1,700 psi respectively. The ammonia bottle formed the rear position of the launch shoe. It was screwed in by a worm drive engaging a thread on the bottle valve. Red Tops were cooled by a replaceable pure air bottle, fitted and removed using an in-built winch through a panel at the front of the pack. The pressure in the bottle was read off a cockpit gauge. Both Red Top and Firestreak missile packs had a misfire indicator viewed through a small round window below the stub pylon. It consisted of a solenoid and plunger that operated when the pilot squeezed the trigger, but the missile failed to launch. The plunger was re-set by turning a cam. Checking it was required on the B/F because the hangar people would often forget to do it if they had been testing the pack. Also on the missiles, the shear bolts were checked for proper engagement.

'The Lightning always flew with two missile bodies fitted: a weighted drill round on the port side and an acquisition on the starboard. It was always that way round to protect the glass seeker head from being damaged by the access ladder being fitted and removed. Sometimes, a metal cover was fitted over the glass to protect it when the aircraft was going to be used for in-flight refuelling. It was rather expensive to replace the seeker when a flailing refuelling hose smashed it if it got on the wrong side. The pilots also preferred to have the missiles fitted. The aircraft was better balanced. Both the Red Top and Firestreak were launched forwards from launch shoes, the electrical services being provided by spring-loaded pins onto corresponding flush connectors. To stop the missiles sliding off they were held in position by a bolt between the missile body and the launch shoe.

On rocket motor ignition the bolt was sheared when enough thrust had built up and the missile was launched. On one occasion a catalogue of errors and omissions occurred which allowed a shear bolt to be incorrectly fitted to a Firestreak drill missile fitted to XP755 'E' on 29 Squadron. A pilot reported feeling a jolt and a bang. He looked out of his cockpit and found the port missile missing. The inevitable board of inquiry was convened. It 'cogitated' and 'deliberated' and came out with its findings. One of its results was that torque wrenches in the RAF were inspected and calibrated on a more frequent basis. I didn't hear any more about the incident so I assumed that, as the last plumber to sign the flight certificate, I escaped by the skin of my teeth. The damage done to the aircraft was minor: a few cut wires in the external cable duct and a few dents in the belly tank. The aircraft was soon repaired and back flying again.

'After doing my external checks it was into the cockpit for the seat checks. Fitting the cockpit access ladder was not entirely without risk. On the F.3, 5 and 6 the cockpit access ladders were held in position by four balls on stalks engaging four elongated slots in the fuselage. Often, because of damage, the balls needed a little encouragement to engage the slots. In difficult cases it was accepted practice to jump up, grab the stalk or cross bar and our weight would pull the ladder into the slot. This had tragic consequences for one liney. We were all told of the dangers of wearing wedding rings. One liney had a rather ornate one with crinkled edges. He leapt up to grab the cross hat and his ring caught. He was left hanging, screaming in agony. We got him off and into a Land Rover to take him to sick quarters, where they had to cut the ring off before treating him. When we saw him a few days later he wasn't happy with his wife: she was more annoyed with the damage done to his wedding ring than the injury to his hand!

'Once in the cockpit it was a quick look under the seat for loose articles (any found were by consensus claimed by the finder unless it had been reported beforehand). This is how I came to be the owner of an aircrew torch. Captain Ed Jordan, a USAF officer on an exchange tour, left it on top of the seat. The seat inspection started with a look underneath to ensure that the leg restraint lines were anchored to the floor. This was followed by a look up the left side to make sure that all the pipes and connections were made, then across and down the tight side, before removing the seat safety pins from the guillotine and the canopy jettison and seat firing sears. These were then placed in the stowage on the cockpit coaming port side.

'Then it was turn around, sit down and flick the battery 'on', if there was no external power running (third switch down on the outboard bank of switches by your right leg). Next, check the air pressure for the Red Top pure air bottle and give a quick burst of up and down on the seat raises and lowering actuator. Pure air pressure was read off a gauge on the right console by the knee. It had a red sector reading from 0-2,500 psi and green up to 3,300 psi. Below 2,500 psi the bottle was to be replaced. However, if the system was operating before it went into the red, it was sufficient for the air to liquefy and continue to keep the head cooled. If the electrician wasn't about, or external power was on, I would take the seat pan down to its lowest limit and back up again to make sure that there were no obstructions. If a rigger were about, we'd call out the LOX contents. Below five-eighths would mean replenishment. Finally, I would stand up, turn around and re-tie the shoulder straps over the seat head box. Climbing out of the cockpit I would descend the ladder face first until I could grab hold of the refuelling probe and swing myself down to the ground, before going off to the line hut, sign up and back out to do the next Lightning.

'As the aircraft became available, flying started. A two-man starter crew comprising a marshaller and a fireman, both detailed by the line corporals, was required. While the marshaller followed the pilot on his walk round, stowing the MASB, the fireman removed the intake blank, started and ran up the Houchin and fetched a CO_2 fire extinguisher and asbestos glove. Walk-round completed, the marshaller would follow the pilot up the ladder and assist him strapping in, handing him his shoulder straps and pulling up the kidney pad to sit in his lumbar region. His final act before climbing down was to remove the face screen safety pin and place it in its stowage. The ladder was removed and placed within the ground equipment area. Removing it entailed lifting it about half an inch and swinging it out and down clear of the refuelling probe. Being top-heavy it was hard to control, so it usually hit the concrete bending the arms at the balls. All was then ready for engine start. The pilot raising and waggling an index finger signalled No. 1 engine start. The AVPIN pumps whined and a pitched scream assaulted the eardrums as the AVPIN ignited and spun the engine up to speed kit ignition. After about five seconds the starter kicked out and the engine ignited and became self-sustaining. The starter exhausted through the bottom hatch, any residual flames being extinguished by the fireman placing an asbestos glove over the exhaust port. The same procedure was followed for No. 2 engine, its exhaust coming out just above the cable duct on the port side. The starter frequently failed to ignite. Three failed attempts and the mission was scrubbed, as a half-hour wait was required for the starter system to cool down. Sometimes it would start on the second try and igniting any fuel from the previous attempt.

'With both engines running, two hydraulic system checks were then carried out. Facing the aircraft the marshaller raised both hands, palms together, above his head, opening his arms as the airbrakes were opened and closed. Next, he turned sideways on with arms horizontal, one over the other, lowering his bottom arm to indicate that the flaps were operating. (Only once did I come across an occasion when the flaps operated differentially and the sortie was abandoned.) Checks over, there was a wave from the pilot, repeated by the marshaller, which indicated the time for the fireman to remove the power leads and chocks. Most would then have a final check on the line of seat safety pins in the stowage, making sure that all five pins were in the stowage. The one usually missing was the seat-pan pin. A reminder to the pilot was usually in order before allowing him to go any further. The marshaller then walked out to the other side of the pan centre line and would wait for a flash on the taxi lights to marshal the aircraft out.

'On average, an F.3 sortie lasted forty-five minutes, unless air-to-air refuelling was involved, with a take-off about every fifteen minutes, so the line was a busy place. When an aircraft returned, it was subject to a run-around inspection (T/R). Like the B/F, it also lasted eight hours. If it didn't fly again, we had to do a B/F before it did. When it returned, the Lightning was taxied back onto the line, marshalled for the final turn and up to the nose-wheel mark. At first it was a frightening experience marshalling fifteen tons of metal travelling at about 20 mph, especially if your only experience was a Chipmunk or Jet Provost at training school. About eighteen inches from the final stop point the aircraft was stopped and the tread on the main wheels inspected for bald spots, cuts and depth. Once completed, the aircraft was marshalled forward for the final stop. Two stops were required because the part in contact with the concrete could not be checked.

'Good tyres were important; at fifteen tons the Lightning landed at about 140 knots on tyres about six inches wide and inflated to 345 psi. They only lasted for seven landings, on average many times less than that. For this reason, the Lightning never did a 'roller' touch-and-go landing. The only time a Lightning took off again after touching down was on the rare occasions that the 'chute 'candled'. (The procedure for a 'chute that partially opened was to jettison it and take off again. Then wait for the recovery vehicle to retrieve it and then land again as close to the start of the runway and be followed by the fire section in case either the brakes caught fire or a barrier engagement was inevitable.) One day we were talking to one of the more experienced pilots about the way they slammed the aircraft onto the runway, so he taught us a lesson. On a later trip he eased it onto the runway. When he got to the end he called air traffic for a party to be sent out to inspect the wheels. The word came back to send the men and equipment to the end of the runway to do a double wheel change. When he took off the tyres were in good condition; they were bald when he stopped at the runway end. The lesson he taught us was that by slamming the aircraft onto the runway, the wheels got up to speed practically instantly. By creasing it onto the runway, the wheels took longer to get up to speed and wore the tread off the tyres!

'While the wheel checks were being done, the MASB was fitted, or removed if it was a pre-key MASB. Soon after engine shutdown the bowser pulled up behind the aircraft. Mostly, these were driven by civilian drivers and such was the relaxed, ready-to-help atmosphere at the time, anyone would help the driver reel out and connect the hose to the refuelling point on the fuselage under the port wing. The sooty would replenish the AVPIN tank in the spine and the brake under the tail would be replaced. The plumber would straighten out the seat straps and carry out an inspection similar to the B/F. If it needed LOX-ing, the rigger donned a facemask and leather gloves and connected the LOX trolley to the charging point in the nose-wheel bay. Clouds of condensation would form on a warm day as the LOX in the aircraft tank was first vented out. The pipes and ranks were flushed and finally, when it was down to the proper temperature, liquid oxygen started to flow into the tank and it filled with LOX.

'Sometimes we would get sprayed with fuel from the wing upper surface when the overwing vents failed to shut off. A shout of *Oi*! to the bowser driver would get the fuel shut off. Above the refuelling point was a rectangular panel with a Perspex insert covering seven lamps. These lamps were the tank indicators; one for each main, flap and belly rank. When the tanks were full, the lamps extinguished. If the wing tanks vented and the light was out, then judicious and skilful application with a General Service (GS) screwdriver handle to the vent shroud followed, to ensure that the valve would slant off. The belly tank shut-off valve also suffered from the same fault. Again, hitting or kicking it ensured that it operated properly. The remaining two lamps were the indicators for the overwing ferry tanks. These were rarely fitted to the F.6 and never on the F.3.

'Another, potentially more serious, problem with a returning aircraft was a leaking ammonia bottle on Firestreak-equipped Lightnings. It wasn't hard to detect a leaking bottle. It stank, like 2,000 wet nappies put into a bin and opened two weeks later! The type used was anhydrous ammonia, a particularly nasty form, with a high affinity for water. It sucked up any moisture, including that of human flesh, if you stood near enough to it. To remove a leaking bottle we were provided with a fireman's breathing apparatus, complete with full facemask and cape over the head and shoulders and a pair of full-length rubber gloves. Another accoutrement of the armourers was a two-wheeled barrow to keep Red Top wing and fin covers. This came in handy for changing ammonia bottles. It was the right height for standing in. So, wearing breathing apparatus and gloves, pushing the trolley, I would approach the leaking bottle, remove it and carry it, hissing and spluttering like an angry cobra, to the grass area behind the line. Along the back of the line and at each squadron line hut was a 45-gallon oil drum with the top cut off and filled with water. If anyone got a burst of ammonia in the face they were meant to be dunked headfirst into the barrel. Fortunately, in five-and-a-half years, I never saw them having to be used.

'Once all the consumables had been replenished and all trades signed their boxes on the flight-servicing certificate, the Lightning was ready for another flight. However, if it was unserviceable and had to go into the hangar for rectification, then an After Flight (A/F) inspection was carried out. This inspection was valid for seventy-two hours and once it was completed, the aircraft required a B/F before it could fly. If it didn't, then another A/F had to be done. It wasn't unusual for an aircraft that had been in the hangar for a long time, say four days, to require an A/F and B/F before it could fly. This was because the last A/F was over seventy-two hours old and therefore invalid. It had to be done again. In practice the differences between the two servicings was small. For instance, on the A/F the armourers did not have to straighten the seat straps, or ensure that the missile was above limits. So what tended to happen was that one inspection was carried out by each tradesman covering both A/F and B/F inspections. After which he would sign the certificate and start on the next aircraft. Personally, I used the one inspection to cover all three servicings, except on an A/F the ejection seat safety pins were fitted to all five places required to make the seat 'safe for servicing' i.e. seat pan and face blind firing handles, main gun, canopy jettison and guillotine sears. For the other servicings on the face screen and seat-pan, safety pins were fitted. In the line hut were the servicing schedules. We were each meant to have a copy and follow them every time, but there were insufficient copies to go round, so each inspection was memorized.

'One day [29 October 1971] I finished a turn-round and standing at the top of the cockpit access ladder I watched a 'Tremblers' (111 Squadron)

Lightning take off, retract his undercarriage and sink back down, dragging his backside along Runway 23. Tongues of flame and billowing smoke followed as the contents of his 360-gallon belly tank burned off. I later learned that it was XR711 and the pilot was Flight Lieutenant Eric Steenson.[2] [Dennis Brooks, who was directly behind Steenson for this nine-ship, two-second stream departure flew right through the fire undamaged and diverted to Coltishall.] On 7 August the following year, XP700/K on 29 Squadron I did exactly the same thing, but this time the pilot successfully clawed his way into the air. Unfortunately, the resulting fire destroyed all tailplane control and the pilot abandoned the aircraft. I didn't witness this event; I was on leave.[3]

'So flying continued throughout the day. Wheels were changed and brakes were replaced. On one particular day we were flying hard and by mid-afternoon, things were getting a bit frayed between the flight sergeant in Engineering Control and us on the flight line. D-Delta required a double wheel change and was delayed for its next sortie. The squawk box buzzed. The flight sergeant, irascible and irate, called, "What's going on with Delta?" "Wheels" was the cryptic reply from a harassed line corporal before he switched the box off.

'After the landing run, these were jettisoned at the end of the runway, picked up and bundled into the back of a Land Rover operated by the brake section. They were taken back and hung for a period to straighten out and dry, then re-packed into their curved, metal-backed containers and re-issued. Sometimes, they would fail to release and be dragged back to the line by the Lightning. The container was fitted under No. 1 exhaust and two wires led, one either side of the jet nozzles, to a socket at the base of the rudder.

'Wattisham was meant to be the inspiration for one of the exercises (called 'Little Snoring', after a Second World War airfield in North Norfolk) held one time at the RAF School of Personnel Management at RAF Newton. The exercise was about packing brakes with random chance selected by cards. Apparently, the Wattisham brake section was having a hard time meeting its commitment so a time and motion team was sent in. They arrived at about 12 o'clock as everybody was leaving. When asked where they were all going, they received the reply that it was lunchtime! This did not please the time and motion team, who quickly came up with the answer that, "if they had time to shut down for lunch, then there was no point in them being there to help them with their problem." Whether this was true or not, I do not know, but it was a strong rumour from 'rumour control' when I did my management course.

'On days our shift ended officially at 1700 hours (five o'clock), but the night shift started at 1630 hours, so we were away soon after they arrived. Night shift was just a continuation of days with one exception – *Magic Roundabout*. Somehow, it became a tradition that all line work, including see-offs and seeing aircraft in, ceased, so that we could see the *Magic Roundabout*. Eventually, even the pilots joined in and watched with us. On the few occasions they got their timings wrong they would wait for us, engines running round the back of the line hut for it to end before we would go out and marshal them in. Oh! Halcyon days of ground crew power!

'Finally, flying for the day ended. Noise restrictions meant that flying finished at about 2330 hours. One night [10 December 1972] we on 29 Squadron had finished flying. The last A/Fs were being done and some of us were sitting in the line hut waiting to row the aircraft into the hangar when we saw a blue flash light up the north sky, rapidly followed by the crash alarm sounding over the Tannoy system. We rushed to the windows and saw a Lightning sliding on its belly along the runway and a shower of yellow sparks.[4] Some of us on 29 shared a block with people from Air Traffic and 'rumour junction' was soon alive with the 'gen'. Apparently, the pilot had done one practice approach, overshot, retracted his undercarriage, gone around again and on his final approach, had called 'Finals, three greens' and plunked his belly on the runway. Normally, at night, the pilots could switch on their taxi lights, which were on the main undercarriage legs, but not all did this. So when the pilot called 'three greens' telling everybody that all three undercarriage legs were extended and locked, the runway controller in his caravan thought that the pilot had left his taxi lights off, so did nothing. After every incident there is, usually, a procedure change and so it was in this case. Pilots were now to switch their taxi lights on when landing and the runway controller was instructed to fire off a red Very light if he didn't see them. At least this is what 'rumour control' said was to happen.

'As the aircraft landed from their last sorties they were given the final flight servicing. Any landing sooner and turned round were also A/Pd. Unserviceable aircraft were put into the hangar as soon as possible while the serviceable ones were left for last so that they were down the centre of the hangar and were first to be pulled out in the morning. At about 0100 or 0130 hours, with all the aircraft put away for the night, we 'linies' would go home. We left the hangar night shift to work on for another couple of hours before they too packed up, locked up and went home also. Towards the mid-seventies NATO started to increase its alert and exercise status, calling 'no-notice' exercises. I remember that on one of the first we were involved in, the 'Directing Staff' (Di-staff) put a cardboard sign on a Houchin that was being used in the hangar to supply power to an aircraft. It read 'Fire!' The Di-staff approached a tired, harassed, tradesman with the query, "What are you going to do about that?" The tradesman took one look at the sign, picked up a piece of paper and wrote 'Foam', placing it over the 'Fire' sign and walked away!

'In March 1974 I left the Lightnings to go on Jaguars with 54 Squadron to form at Lossiemouth and come south to Coltishall, just as 226 OCU was winding up in July-August 1974. By this time practically all of the Lightnings had gone, the few that were left going to fire dumps. Years later, when on 56 Squadron, we were detached from Wattisham to RAF Leuchars for Red Flag build up. I drove a Sherpa north. One of my refuelling stops was at RAF Boulmer, near Alnwick in Northumberland. Arriving at the main gate I was surprised and delighted to see XP745 still in 29 Squadron markings; an 'H' standing guard over one of the fighter control stations that had, no doubt, controlled it in earlier years. I remarked to my passenger that I wished I'd had a pound for every time I'd serviced it. He brought me back down to earth by sarcastically remarking that I must be old if I'd worked on a gate guard!'

Chapter 10

Lightning Strikes

'I have visual contact, repeat visual contact. Over.'

'Can you identify aircraft type?'

'Negative, nothing recognisable, no clear outlines. There is...bluish light. Hell, that's bright...very bright... I'm alongside it now; maybe 600 feet off my...It's a conical shape. Jeez, it's bright, it hurts my eyes to look at it for more than a few seconds... Hey wait...there's something else. It's like a large soccer ball... like it's made of glass. It's bobbing up and down and going from side to side slowly. It may be the power source. There's no sign of ballistics... There's a haze of light. Yellow... it's within that haze. Wait a second, its turning... coming right for me...shit...am taking evasive action...'

'Come in 94. Foxtrot 94, are you receiving? Over. Come in 94. Over.'

Two and a half minutes after the single blip on the radar screen came to a halt it started to move again, accelerating rapidly to 600 mph and climbing to 9,000 feet, heading south back towards Staxton. Shortly afterwards the single blip separated into two, one maintaining its southerly heading, somewhat erratically at between 600 and 630 mph and descending slowly, the other turning through 180 degrees to head north westerly and vanishing at a speed later calculated to be around 20,400 mph.

Extract of the supposedly official transcript of the conversation which took place between a Lightning pilot and the radar station at Staxton Wold on the night of 8 September 1970.

In the period autumn 1970 to spring 1971 UFOs were seen over the Lincolnshire coast around Cleethorpes. At RAF Donna Nook, a 180 foot long UFO was seen hovering for many hours by RAF personnel and was accompanied by 'glass ball' objects. On the night of 8 September 1970 a couple and their daughter were walking their dog along the coastal path at Alnmouth Bay, Northumberland when they heard a very high pitched humming noise. Their dog kept cocking her head to one side and growling. It seemed impossible to tell from which direction the noise was coming; it seemed everywhere. It lasted for maybe ten to fifteen seconds. About five minutes later the eastern sky lit up rather like sheet lightning, only it took about ten seconds to die down again. Over the following three minutes this happened many times, but the 'lightning' was only visible for a second or two at a time. It appeared very similar to the northern lights. The whole spectacle was completely silent. After two or three minutes there was another flare-up of 'sheet lightning' which lasted about the same time as the first. This was followed by that awful shrill sensation, only this time it was worse. 'You could actually feel your ears ringing,' the family said later. They called in at the local police station to report what they had seen and heard. Theirs was one of many similar reports that night to both the police and the RAF at nearby Boulmer. The time and the location fit in exactly with events unfolding sixty miles south at Staxton Wold, which stands on high ground overlooking Scarborough and they could have been watching some kind of natural phenomena. Or there could be another explanation.

In an isolated building on the Shetland Islands at Saxa Vord, one of the chain of radar stations whose task it was to spot unidentified aircraft approaching the North Sea or the sensitive 'Iceland gap' a radar operator picked up the blip of an unidentified aircraft over the North Sea halfway between the Shetlands and Ålesund in Norway. The contact was monitored for several minutes at a steady speed of 630 mph at 37,000 feet, holding altitude and on a south-westerly heading. Then Saxa Vord noted the contact was turning through 30 degrees to head due south. It increased speed to 900 mph (Mach 1.25) and climbed to 44,000 feet. Following laid-down procedures, radar controllers at Saxa Vord flashed a scramble message to the Quick Reaction Alert Flight at the nearest NATO airfield, RAF Leuchars on the east coast of Scotland, not far from Dundee. There, two Lightning Interceptors, which had been ready on the flight line for just such an alert, were scrambled and within minutes were airborne and heading out over the North Sea. After checking the position of their tanker, a Victor K.1A, the two fighters were guided north by Saxa Vord.

So far it was a routine scramble for what was then assumed to be a Russian 'Bear' or 'Badger', the long-range reconnaissance aircraft used to test the nerves of the Royal Air Force. But it was then that the radar plotters on the Shetland Islands saw something on their screens which they found impossible to believe. The contact they had been tracking at speeds and altitudes consistent with modern Russian warplanes turned through 180 degrees on a due north heading and within seconds disappeared off their screens.

With the contact now gone, the Lightnings were vectored south to rendezvous with the tanker and remained airborne on Combat Air Patrol. During the next hour the mystery contact reappeared several times, approaching from the north. Each time the Lightnings were sent north to intercept, it turned and disappeared again. By now two F-4 Phantoms of the US Air Force had been scrambled from the American base at Keflavik in Iceland. They had much more sophisticated radar then the Lightnings and were able to pick up the mystery contact themselves. But when they, too, tried to get close enough to identify what was by now beginning to cause some alarm to NATO commanders, they found they were just as impotent as the Lightnings.

The alert had reached such a level that the contact was being monitored by the Ballistic Missile Early Warning System at Fylingdales Moor near Whitby along with a second BMEWS in Greenland. The information they were collecting was relayed to the North American Air Defence Command at Cheyenne Mountain and the US Detection and Tracking Centre at Colorado Springs. In the meantime, the cat and mouse game over the North Sea between the Lightnings and Phantoms and the mystery contact was still going on. Then at 2105, after the fighters had made yet another abortive attempt to get close, the contact vanished off the radar screens.

The Lightnings were ordered to return to Leuchars while the Phantoms were instructed to carry out a Combat Air Patrol to the east of Iceland. Then, at 2139, radar controllers picked up the contact again. This time its speed was decelerating to 1,300 mph – almost the limit of both the Lightnings and Phantoms – at a holding altitude of 18,000 feet. It was on a south-westerly heading coming from the direction of the Skagerrak, off the northern tip of Denmark. Two more Lightnings were scrambled from Leuchars and were ordered to rendezvous with a Victor tanker and then maintain a CAP on a fifty-mile east-west front, 200 miles north-east of Aberdeen. As a precaution, two further Lightnings were ordered into the air from Coltishall in Norfolk and with another tanker, to form a CAP 170 miles east of Great Yarmouth. The contact was somewhere between these two lines of supersonic fighters.

LIGHTNING STRIKES

At around 2145 four Lightnings, two Phantoms and three tankers were already airborne and they were joined by a Shackleton MR.3 from Kinloss, which was ordered to patrol on a north-south heading at 3,000 feet, ten miles out from the east coast. Binbrook's QRA Lightnings were being held in reserve, but it was decided to send out a single aircraft from Binbrook in North Lincolnshire where 5 Squadron was participating in a TACEVAL. The evaluation involved 5 Squadron's pilots identifying and shadowing simulated Soviet bombers, closing up behind them in all weathers to a range of 200 yards at any altitude.

Captain William Olin Schaffner, a small, powerfully-built 28-year-old USAF Exchange pilot who loved to fly the single-seat Lightnings, so different from the new generation of sophisticated aircraft then starting to come into service in the USAF was both day and night current and qualified to sit quick reaction alert duties. Born in Wadsworth, Ohio in September 1941 Schaffner had earned a Reserve Officer Training Corps scholarship in 1959. Four years later he graduated from Ohio State University with a degree in International Studies and he received his officer's commission. After completing pilot training at Webb AFB Texas and Advanced Combat Crew Training on Convair F-102 Delta Daggers at Perrin AFB, by August 1965 Schaffner was on his way to Clark in the Philippines to begin his first combat tour in Southeast Asia. At the end of his second tour, having flown 209 combat missions on the F-102 and a promotion to captain, he was assigned once more to Perrin AFB where he served as an F-102 Delta Dagger instructor pilot with the 4781st Combat Crew Training Squadron. In October 1969 he was selected for the USAF-RAF Exchange Programme. On 31 October Major Charles B. Neel, the exchange pilot Schaffner was to replace on 5 Squadron wrote: *'Welcome to the RAF. Come prepared to enjoy yourself and fly a really hot ship. Once you get used to the cockpit and controls, you'll find the Lightning to be a great ship that will outperform and outmanoeuvre anything you may have previously flown. We will need the F-15 to take it in air combat. Range and armament are its only limitation.'* On 22 September 1969 Major Neel abandoned XS926 fifty-one miles east of Flamborough Head after he failed to recover from spinning during ACT. Neel, who had previously ejected into the sea in an F-100 Super Sabre in November 1967, ejected from the F.6 safely and clambered into his dinghy after just four seconds in the water! He was picked up and whisked back to base in a helicopter with nothing worse than two grazed fingers.

Bill Schaffner was initially sent to 229 OCU at Chivenor, Devon to fly the Hawker Hunter and was then selected in February 1970 to convert to the Lightning at 226 OCU at Coltishall. He completed the five statutory sorties in the T.4 and soloed on F.1A XM189 on 25 February. In June he completed OCU and headed north to Binbrook with his wife and new born son Michael to join 5 Squadron. He had accumulated 121 hours on the Lightning, of which 18 were at night. He had been declared limited Combat Ready after only eight weeks on the squadron, this unusually short period of time being based on his previous operational status as well as his performance this far on the Lightning. Schaffner was qualified in two of the three phases of 'visident', which meant that he would be capable of carrying out shadowing and shepherding tasks only if he was in visual contact with the target.

On the night of 8 September Schaffner was sitting in the crew room at Binbrook overlooking the apron where a line of all-metal-finish Lightnings stood, illuminated by the high-intensity sodium lighting. The crew room itself was sparsely furnished with ageing chairs which had seen better days, a bar which dispensed nothing stronger than black Nescafe and walls adorned with plaques and photographs donated by visiting RAF and overseas air force units. The American exchange pilot was still in his flying suit after returning earlier that evening from a training sortie. He had already flown two sorties, one in XS903 against a Canberra and another in XS894 for a total of about 3 ½ hours' of flying. 'Normally,' recalls Ian Black, 'pilots who were not combat-ready were stood down at the start of an exercise and given other duties. However, 5 Squadron was running light on aircrew and holding QRA it was all hands to the deck.'

During a TACEVAL exercise, all missions would start following a scramble call, either by telebrief connected to the local radar station or via a radio call to the aircraft. Anyone able to listen in to such transmissions would think that World War Three had started. Spurious information relating to raids in other sectors would be broadcast to 'flesh out' events in the local sector and thereby make the atmosphere before scramble more realistic. When the call came, Schaffner was helped into the remainder of his flying gear by other 5 Squadron air crew, went out through the door, turned right and raced across the apron to XS894/F which was carrying two dummy acquisition missiles. He climbed the steep ladder, hauled himself into the cockpit, strapped in and started the engines. Weather conditions had deteriorated – his previous one-hour sortie had been spent with twenty minutes in cloud and his recovery to Binbrook had been by an instrument approach. Schaffner was scrambled at 1947, taxiing out as quickly as possible, but the sortie was cancelled before he could get airborne and he returned to dispersal for a refuelling top up. A second scramble was ordered for 2025 and his call sign was 'CPM 45'. In an effort to get airborne as quickly as possible, Schaffner ordered the ground crew to stop the turn-round and began starting engines. The clipboard that detailed the servicing schedule was later found near the runway; in his haste it had not been removed from the wing. One of the men on the ground crew at the time was Brian Mann of Grimsby, who was driving one the fuel bowsers. He remembers XS894 being refuelled at a rate of 150 gallons a minute when suddenly the engines started. 'The windows on the tanker almost went in. I panicked, took the hoses off and got out of the way,' he was to say later. Mr Mann remembers Schaffner disregarding the grounder marshaller, who was the eyes and ears of the pilot on the ground, as he swung the Lightning round. 'His actions were unorthodox to say the least,' he said. At 2206 XS894 blasted off from Binbrook's main runway into the night sky. Those on the ground saw it disappear with a sheet of flame from its twin tail pipes as Schaffner used reheat. It turned over the Wolds and the last they saw was its navigation lights heading out towards the North Sea.

At RAF Boulmer SACA Yates, the controller's assistant for the sortie, recalls. 'What kept it in mind for me was that I had met and spoken to Major Schaffner at length the day previous, when pilots on 5 Squadron had paid us a liaison visit. Major Schaffner approached me while I was on duty in the Master Control Room, asking questions about my duties, the equipment etc. He was far more casual and friendly than the average RAF senior officer, a major being equal to squadron leader in rank. That night there was a queue of aircraft waiting to intercept a simulated 'intelligence gatherer' (in this case an Airborne Early Warning (AEW) Avro Shackleton on 8 Squadron at Lossiemouth flying at 160 knots at the minimum authorized height of 1,500 feet) during a period of rising tension. We, Boulmer, were talking to it on one frequency, while my controller and I had another frequency for the fighters, as their turn came they were handed over to our position for the intercept. The Shackleton was at 1,500 feet AGL and in our 'clutter' (ground returns) but we could still see it. Major Schaffner checked in on our frequency, giving his call sign, fuel state and exercise weapons fit and asked for target information. After we gave him this he called 'Judy', meaning he could handle the intercept himself and closed for a 'Visident' as briefed, but didn't respond to any further calls. We later guessed that he had got too close to the considerable turbulence created by the Shackleton's contra-rotating propellers; at that altitude he would not have had time to pull out. After the sortie my logbook was impounded, which was standard practice. It was one of the sadder moments of my Service career. *Per Ardua Ad Astra.*'

The 'intruder' entered the UK airspace during daylight and remained on station through dusk and into darkness. The contact was flying parallel to the east coast 90 miles east of Whitby at 530 mph at 6,100 feet – an ideal course for an interception by a Binbrook Lightning. One by one, the 5 Squadron pilots were scrambled to identify the 'intruder'. Each subsequently completed the task before returning to Binbrook. The TACEVAL continued as darkness fell, by which time it became the turn of Captain Schaffner. He climbed to 10,000 feet and was handed over to GCI. He was then given a shadowing task against a Shackleton at 1,500 feet. At night, or in poor weather conditions, this involved flying the Lightning as slowly as was practically possible whilst maintaining radar contact. The procedure was to fly a series of 'S-turns', weaving behind the target in an attempt to keep the radar blip on the screen. The Lightning's monopulse radar had a particularly poor performance at low level and flying very low and slow whilst maintaining radar contact at night was a very demanding exercise. At a range of 28 nautical miles he was told to accelerate to Mach 0.95 in order to expedite the takeover from another Lightning. Schaffner called that he was in contact with the lights, but would have to manoeuvre to slow down. His voice sounded strained, as though he was being affected by G. XS894 was seen by the other Lightning pilot and appeared to be about 2,000 yards astern and 500-1,000 feet above the Shackleton, in a port turn. The Shackleton crew then saw Schaffner's Lightning; apparently very low.

The rules covering this type of exercise in 1970 were that the target should not fly below 300 feet and the fighter should not fly below 500 feet. This meant that the interceptor would always have the problem of distinguishing the target on radar against the clutter caused by the sea and the pilot would have the extra workload in an already highly loaded situation of increasing and decreasing the gain on his screen to focus on the Shackleton. On the other hand, if the fighter dropped below the level the target aircraft and looked up, the radar picture would be free from clutter and the target easily seen.

Did the pilot lose his radar contact and dip below the level of the Shackleton to give himself better chance of reacquiring the target? We shall obviously never know. However, it is a fact that, following this and two similar accidents which all occurred around the same time, the minimum altitudes allowed in this type of exercise were changed to 1,500 feet for the target and 2,000 feet for the fighter.

Schaffner failed to acknowledge instructions and emergency procedures were initiated. He crashed into the sea five miles off Flamborough Head. XS894 impacted right wing slightly low. Schaffner survived the crash and vacated the cockpit prior to the aircraft sinking. It would have been almost impossible for him to extricate himself and his life raft from the aircraft in this situation. Evidence from the recovered wreckage suggested that he unstrapped and stepped over the side. A cold North Sea at night without protection from the elements afforded by the life raft would have presented him with little hope of survival at the best of times. Denied the aids contained in the dinghy and the time already taken to get out of the cockpit would have meant that his hopes of maintaining consciousness and activating his SARBE (Search and Rescue Beacon) with numb fingers were virtually nil.

The search and rescue Whirlwind from nearby Leconfield arrived on the scene and began a systematic search of the ditching area. The aircraft were shortly joined by lifeboats from Bridlington, Flamborough and Filey as the weather began to deteriorate. The search continued well into the next day but there were no transmissions from the beacons carried by the aircraft and the official reports say no distress flares were seen. The following day flares were seen about ten miles offshore and the Grimsby trawler *Ross Kestrel* which was passing through the Flamborough area and had gone to investigate but, even though more flares were seen, she found nothing. A search by the Shackleton and a further ASR search failed to find any trace of the F.6 or its pilot.

Two months later Bill Schaffner's Lightning was located five miles off Flamborough Head. When divers from HMS *Keddleston*, a Royal Navy minesweeper, inspected the Lightning. It was on the seabed at a depth of 190 feet, almost completely intact with the canopy closed. The cockpit though, was empty, but the seat was still in the aircraft, the harness release box undone and the harness still in position. The ASI read 176 knots. A team from Farnborough arrived one wet winter's day at Binbrook in the belief that they were about to start a detailed Investigation which, in turn, would lead to the preparation of a report on the incident to the Ministry of Defence, the report being used as the basis for an eventual inquiry into the loss of Lightning XS894. Group Captain Barwood, who was involved in the investigation into the accident, tells what happened next: 'When the aircraft was raised it was established that the seat-firing mechanism had been initiated but that the cockpit jettison mechanism had failed to fire The cockpit area was completely undamaged, but the visor attachment track on the pilot's flying helmet had contacted the instrument panel. This probably had no effect on the pilot. He had accidentally flown into, or onto, the sea and the very large belly fuel tank with which the aircraft was fitted acted as a boat hull to take most of the impact load. [During salvage the ventral tank and the belly of the aircraft were found to be ripped open and there was under-tail damage.]

'The pilot had attempted to eject, but the canopy mechanism would not fire as the firing mechanism had been incorrectly assembled. (The breech-firing mechanism of the cockpit canopy jettison system had been clamped in a vice, partially flattening the threads, so that when assembled, it was not screwed completely home, so that the firing plunger did not contact the percussion cap with sufficient energy to fire it.) He then opened his cockpit canopy manually using the ordinary post-flight opening mechanism, which is hydraulically operated. He still could not eject, as the interdictor wire had not armed his seat firing mechanism. He undid his combined harness quick release box and climbed out of the cockpit. His dinghy lanyard was still connected and as he separated from the cockpit this extended – fully. At full extension it would check his upward movement, so he released it.

'The pilot's body was never recovered. The cockpit canopy hydraulic pressure system slowly decayed so that the canopy closed, trapping the extended dinghy lanyard line. We did find some broken visor transparency on the cockpit floor. This would have broken when the pilot's Mk.3 helmet had hit the coaming beneath the in-flight refuelling panel and it is possible that a sharp edge cut his life preserver. We shall never know.

'Altogether, night visidents were responsible for the loss of three Lightnings and Keith Murty had a narrow escape when he hit a twin-engined Cessna which had entered UK airspace and was unknown to the air defence network. Neither pilot realized that there had been a collision until the Cessna pilot saw the damage to his wing on landing and associated this with the hump he had felt in flight.'

The year 1971 proved the worst on record with no fewer than ten Lightnings lost. The first, involving Captain William 'Bill' R. Povilus, a USAF exchange officer, occurred on 25 January during a head-on night intercept in XP756. Povilus, who had flown 373 combat missions as a forward air controller in Vietnam, had been attached to 29 Squadron at

LIGHTNING STRIKES

Wattisham since 1969. He recalls: 'It was a normal pairs take-off, climb-out and positioning, about sixty miles off the coast of East Anglia. Bawdsey CCI control was the radar agency overseeing the mission. [As an interesting note, another American exchange officer, Major Bud Manazir USMC was on duty with Bawdsey that evening.] After a thirty-mile split to obtain separation, Bawdsey turned both aircraft toward each other and ordered acceleration. I pushed both engines into re-heat and accelerated through the Mach. After what was probably only a minute or two, a No. 1 engine fire warning illuminated and I instantly pulled both engines out of re-heat. (I had been checked out as a test pilot in the Lightning and had two previous instances of fire warnings – both had been false). In any event, all other indications appeared normal, but the fire light stayed on and I proceeded through the appropriate drills, shutting down No. 1 engine and then jettisoning the belly tank. The light stayed on; so in short order I informed Bawdsey of the problem, turned westerly and asked my wingman to try and catch up. The first indication that I might have real problems was an erratic hydraulic gauge that finally went to zero. Then the machometer motored ever so slowly also to zero – I had no airspeed!

'I kept a hot microphone open to Bawdsey and kept them informed about what was happening. My wingman finally called to say he saw flames at the rear of my craft and recommended ejection. I guess the water temperature that January night motivated me to stay with XP756 as long as possible. As other gauges and indicators also began to fail I knew ejection was inevitable; then I became aware that the rudder pedals had gone totally slack, as if disconnected! Shortly thereafter the aircraft nosed over slowly and I was unable to change its course. A British exchange officer in the States had once told me that, 'Fail all else, you can always place your faith in God, Mother and Martin-Baker.' I left XP756 to determine its own fate. [The F.3 crashed off Great Yarmouth.]

'I found that my preparations came automatically and without hesitation. I called 'Bailing out', locked my knees as I forced against the rudder pedals and I pulled the seat-pan firing handle with both hands as I stiffened to receive the howitzer shell that was about to fire into my butt. The decisions I had made long before that night surely helped save my life. I have long legs and knew I must press as hard as possible against the seat in order to escape with my knee caps still attached – hence the locked knees. I had also long ago decided that the bottom handle was the only one for me regardless of the situation. I always used it in simulator practices and virtually forgot that the top handle even existed.

THE MEN WHO FLEW THE ENGLISH ELECTRIC LIGHTNING

'As I pulled the seat-pan handle I heard a swoosh of air as the canopy left the aircraft. [The American ejected at 25,000 feet and at 30 knots.] Everything from then on appeared to happen in slow motion. I felt my hands able to pull just a bit more on the handle (double pull seat) and then I started rising slowly amidst a shower of sparks that were coming from alongside and below me. I can remember glancing at various instruments as I started up and the last I saw of my ship was the windscreen brace as it passed in front of my face. There was no sensation of wind blast as I left, only a feeling of flipping over backwards, then everything happened in 'real time' again and I found myself spinning violently in a very unstable fashion. I tried desperately to focus my eyes on the lights that I knew to be the East Anglian coast but was unable to do so due to the spinning and tumbling. It is hard to describe the experience – it was almost intolerably unpleasant, my whole existence consisting of blackness interrupted by brief flashes of light that continually changed position as they streaked by. A dull greyness I interpreted as being a cloud layer. I knew such cloud existed at about 5,000 feet and I decided that as I approached it I would pull the manual separation lever; I even felt for the lever to make sure it was still there. Then I felt myself losing control of the situation – losing consciousness – and I made a last-ditch effort to stop the spinning and tumbling by forcing my arms straight out. The motion slowed and then suddenly lurched the other way. A bang occurred behind me and then the opening shock of the parachute suddenly brought me into a completely different environment.

'I was stable and could clearly see the village lights on the coast and the greyish cloud below. In contrast to the trauma of only seconds ago I was quite comfortable now, mentally and physically. The opening shock of the chute had pulled my feet out of the boots and up to the leg restrainers in the immersion suit. I corrected this and proceeded pre-landing drills. The mask disconnected quite easily and I threw it away. I then checked the PSP connection (several times) and tried to locate the release connections. I had waterproof gloves on and just couldn't get hold of those releases. After trying many times I almost got panicky for fear of going into the water with the pack still strapped to my butt. I decided to take off each glove in turn and find the release mechanism. I had no trouble at all with my bare hands, but was very careful not to drop my gloves and quickly the PSP was deployed.

'Next was the Mae West inflation and then followed what seemed to me the next logical step. I pulled up the life raft lanyard, found the T-handle and inflated the dinghy. Again a decision I had made a long time ago; a decision that was reinforced by troubles other chaps had had with the dinghy T-handle once in the water. (American exchange officers flying the Lightning had speculated about inflating the life raft in the air on the way down and having it ready for use once splashdown occurred. I followed this alternative procedure and it was a likely factor in my survival. Interestingly about a year after my incident, the RAF adopted automatically inflating life rafts.)

'I tucked that dinghy under my left arm with the large end facing rearward. I entered cloud, rotated the quick-release box, grabbed it with my right hand and prepared to enter water. I remember coming out of the warm moistness of the cloud but could see nothing – total darkness all around. Hitting the water was a complete surprise and certainly the worst shock of the evening. My left arm rested over the side of the dinghy so I merely swung around and pulled myself inside. Total time in the water couldn't have been more than thirty seconds.

'After about fifteen minutes a red flashing light appeared on the horizon and progressed toward me. I became somewhat elated and knew I must fire some flares for him [an RAF Whirlwind from Coltishall] to find me. That was when I started having trouble getting the pen gun to engage the flares in the kit. I just couldn't seem I to screw the gun into the flares. A certain sense of urgency developed as the chopper came closer and closer. I managed to fire off about four flares as the chopper swung around within about a half-mile of me and then headed toward the horizon again. As he left he fired a green flare, but by now he had caused me to foolishly waste half my mini-flares and I was mad at him. As I tried to screw another flare into the gun (just to have one ready) the pen gun came apart in my hand and the parts fell. I 'battened down the hatches' for a long night, pulling my head down into the dinghy and doing up the Velcro all the way to the top.

'I spent a good hour inside my little self-created womb and did little things like trying and arranging items in the raft – by feel of course. I knew it fatal to start thinking about my predicament so I kept busy by doing little mundane tasks over and over again. The SARBE antenna was blowing over in the strong wind. I could hear it whipping against the dinghy canopy. I detached the beacon from my Mae West, listened to the reassuring beep-beep and then fixed it down between my legs. I ran the antenna tip through a small hole in the Velcro and thus had about 2 feet of straight vertical length for transmitting. A squall came up and the rain pelted my back and the waves broke over me more often. Suddenly I found myself going over into the water. I lunged in the opposite direction and managed to right the dinghy again. I became very afraid of tipping over and crouched down in my dinghy even more.

'I first heard a noise that wasn't the wind and stuck out my head for a look around. Immediately I saw a great number of red flashing lights far off and then saw a large aircraft through breaks in the cloud. Several white flares were dropped about five meters away and my sense of elation was almost overwhelming. I knew it had to be the rescue chaps from RAF Woodbridge with the Hercules and Jolly Green Giants. One flare fired by me quickly brought the search pattern closer. Another flare and another until one chopper headed right at me. I fired off my day/night flare but the helicopter drifted away again. Finally the Hercules dropped a batch of white illumination flares right overhead and a Jolly Green Giant came right alongside. I fired my next to last mini-flare vowing to shoot the last one right into his cockpit if he moved away. A basket was lowered and the chopper pilot kept trying to get it near me. For the first time I realised how rough the seas were – 10-12 feet waves and a whole lot of spray and white water.

'I thought about getting out of my raft (standard USAF procedure) but was so entangled in the cords and lanyards that I couldn't get free. When the basket came within about three feet I lunged for it, literally falling inside with the life raft still strapped to my back. Talk about happy – you have no idea. Up I went and let them pull me inside just like the book says. An NCO took out his knife and cut me free from the dinghy and I was able to stand up though on somewhat wobbly legs. I almost kissed the NCO. We got my immersion suit off (there was about half an inch of water in the boots and my seat was damp) and I wrapped up in a batch of blankets. While laying there for the half-hour trip home I got the shakes – partly from the transition of warming up – but mostly I think from the fears that were finally catching up with me. As I lay there I kept on thanking God and Martin-Baker over and over and over.

'What caused the fire? From the sequencing and timing of events as recorded by Bawdsey that night, the engineering staffs were able to locate quite precisely the source of the fire and the resultant loss of control. The fire originated in the proximity of an elbow in the main fuel line in the firewall between Nos. 1 and 2 engines. All F.3s were X-rayed for cracks in the fuel line elbow and I was told several were found to be close to imminent failure. Hydraulic, pitot, static and control cables also ran through the same fire-walled area and as they melted or were burned the respective instrument or control surface failed. I was told that ultimately the tail section probably burned off.'[1]

At Gütersloh three days later, on 28 January, Flying Officer Pete Hitchcock and Jim Watson on 92 briefed for a 2 v 1 combat against Rich Rhodes. Chris Tuckley, the airman who strapped Pete into aircraft 'November' (XN772), told the pilot that it was his twenty-first birthday. Pete replied that they would 'sort out something' when he returned. When Chris Tuckley had finished strapping Pete in he started to descend the ladder then remembered that he had not removed the safety pin from the ejection seat face blind firing handle. Forty five minutes later Pete and his aircraft entered a spin at 32,000 feet, not a recommended manoeuvre in a swept wing aircraft. Pete recovered by using his Martin-Baker ejection seat (he had some difficulty as his head was high in the canopy, but eventually he got his right hand to the blind handle and then his left) but his aircraft, after recovering from the spin by 14,500 feet, flew into the ground to cause a little disturbance just to the North East of a lake called the Dummer See, near a town appropriately known as Diepholtz. Pete was quickly taken to hospital after landing in a thorny hedge but was soon out and about. The German Water Authorities were onto the Squadron even quicker as they claimed the aircraft was spilling oil and kerosene in a Wasserschutzgebiet (Water protection area) and had to be removed immediately. Rich Rhodes claimed, but was not granted, five points for the first 'confirmed' combat kill. Pete Hitchcock was kept grounded by the 'docs' for a few months until his 'Martin-Baker Back' had cured but soon he had some company as Vic Lockwood broke his leg on the Winter Survival course.[2]

On 28 April Flying Officer Alastair Cameron 'Harry' MacLean on 23 Squadron in XS938 suffered a re-heat fire in the No. 1 engine shortly after take-off from Leuchars. He turned back and then received a second fire warning. MacLean put out a mayday and said he was ejecting, making a face blind initiation at 4,000 feet and 250 knots, slightly nose-up. There were no problems but after separation from his seat one side of the PSP support was undone. He lowered it gently but it increased in oscillation, so he pulled it up again and inflated his life preserver. Then he lowered the PSP again; this time there was no oscillation and he was able to clamber into the dinghy. He was picked up shortly afterwards, twenty-eight minutes after his Mayday signal. The F.6 meanwhile, had crashed into the River Tay.

In Cyprus on 10 May Flight Lieutenant Robert D. Cole on 56 Squadron abandoned F.3 XP744 shortly after take-off from Akrotiri after he received a zonal fire warning. Cole ejected safely and he was picked up uninjured by a helicopter after thirty minutes. His aircraft crashed eight miles southeast of Akrotiri. Flight Lieutenant A. J. N. 'Tony' Alcock had a narrow escape on 20 May, during an 11 Squadron detachment to Colmar in France when XP752 was involved in a collision near the base with a French Air Force Mirage IIIE. The French jet hit the starboard side of the cockpit canopy and nose of the F.3 as they broke formation in cloud. The Lightning's pitot head was bent in the collision, which also jettisoned the canopy. Alcock, who received a blow on the right side of his helmet, decided it was time to eject, but he did not pull his seat-panhandle hard enough and the seat refused to budge. Obligingly, the Mirage pilot formated on Alcock's damaged Lightning and led him in to land without further incident. XP752 was later written off. On 26 May Flight Lieutenant Alastair J. MacKay RCAF, who was attached to 5 Squadron at Binbrook, ejected safely from XS902 near Grimsby following Fire Warning 1 after take-off followed by Reheat Warnings 1 and 2. The F.6 crashed nine miles east of Spurn Head. MacKay's was a routine ejection and the Canadian was recovered by helicopter within the hour and treated for neck abrasions and bruising of the shoulder and crotch.

Then, during a 29 Squadron detachment to Cyprus on 8 July Flight Lieutenant Graham Clarke safely abandoned XP705 near Akrotiri after a Reheat Fire Warning 1 followed by Reheat Fire Warning 2. His ejection was copybook straight and level at 230 knots at 13,000 feet – and Clarke was picked up with only a bruised front shoulder. He was flying again ten days later. The F.3 crashed in the Mediterranean.

On 22 September 1971 Flying Officer Phil Mottershead, a 29 Squadron pilot, crashed into the sea thirty miles off Lowestoft. During a climb at Mach 1.3 to 35,000 feet to intercept 'Playmate' at three miles, Mottershead's 'Mayday! Mayday! Mayday!' had been rapid and panicky before his F.3 (XP736) fell away to port and spiralled into the sea.

Group Captain Antony Barwood recalls: 'Nothing more was heard. About half an hour later a searching Phantom crew saw an empty, deflated dinghy floating on the sea. This was recovered by the ASR launch and sent to the IAM [Institute of Aviation Medicine] Accident Laboratory at Farnborough. The dinghy pack had obviously been hit very hard with displacement of the CO_2 cylinder under and obvious scuffing and some paint transfers. It looked as though it might have hit the outside of the aircraft. The Radar Unit at Warren reported that they had a plot of the aircraft and that one only left the aircraft when the pilot ejected. They had a plot from an earlier ejection in almost the same spot and that normal ejection showed quite clearly two items leaving the aircraft: the cockpit canopy first, followed briefly by the seat. It seemed likely that this young pilot's ejection seat had failed to fire. The Lightning cockpit canopy was a purely metallic structure, which must be jettisoned before ejection can proceed. The jettison system is operated by ejection initiation which unlocks the canopy locking mechanism by withdrawing two lock or shoot bolts, operated by explosive cartridges. Explosively operated jacks then lift the canopy from the fuselage sill and the aerodynamic load takes it well clear of the aircraft. As the cockpit canopy separates, it removes the interdictor, which prevents the ejection seat from firing into the partly solid canopy. We had to assume that the interdiction had failed to operate, so that the ejection seat could not fire.

'The pilot may have attempted manual abandonment. To do this he would operate his manual override handle, unlocking his seat restraint harness from the seat structure. His dinghy pack would remain attached to him. This would considerably hamper his efforts to get clear of the cockpit in a high air-blast situation. We assumed that he had disconnected it from both sides and from the dropping lanyard and that he pushed it out of the cockpit and that it picked up its paint markings as it contacted with the outside of the fuselage. I went to Warton with the board of inquiry to see the plots for myself and then went on to Coltishall with the pilot's damaged dinghy and with an identical dinghy. They found me an identical aircraft with exactly the same paint finishes as the lost aircraft. By bashing the dinghy with a wooden mallet onto various parts of the side of the aircraft rear side of the cockpit and the on the inner edge of the wing leading edge, I was able to show that the paint transfers were identical.

'About a month later, the pilot's bone-dome was recovered by a Danish fishing-vessel and returned to Farnborough. The break rivet on the chinstrap had broken, so we assumed that it had been torn off by exposure to air blast. The remains of the aircraft were located on the sea bed and showed that the ejection seat was still in the aircraft at impact, but the seat systems had totally disintegrated and no evidence of a misfire or other malfunction could be found. Six months later, his cockpit canopy was dredged up. It was sent straight to the lab at Farnborough. It was immediately obvious that the interdictor cable had broken. This cable is made of twenty-eight strands of stainless steel wire twisted into four smaller cables which are twisted together to form the interdictor wire. The ends of the cable are swaged onto a steel sleeve (the wire being inserted into a sleeve and then subjected to high, all round pressure, a well-established method of securing a steel cable into a connector). The broken end of each individual outer cable, six forming the outside with one in the middle, had cracked, producing a six-sided facet. This cracking had occurred at the cable end of a swage and as this end was covered with a rubber sleeve; it was therefore not visible for routine inspection. Every time the cockpit canopy is opened, this cable is flexed slightly. Many repetitive flexings had produced the cracking of the outer six wires forming the strand, leaving one intact central wire in one of the four sub-cables – only one intact wire out of twenty-eight. This single strand of wire failed in extension when the interdictor wire tried to pull the interdictor catch off the seat firing mechanism.

'We were able to reproduce this wire failure by clamping the swaged end so that it was firmly fixed and flexing the cable through 30 degrees, each side. It only required thirty-five flexions to reproduce the identical failure. This was one of the occasions when I went straight to the Director of Flight Safety to get him to ground all Lightnings until their interdictor wires had been tested under load. The interdictor wires were replaced and subsequently redesigned.'

In Cyprus on 30 September Flight Lieutenant Richard 'Dick' Bealer on 56 Squadron was forced to abandon XR764 near Akrotiri after take-off on full re-heat. At 22,000 feet Bealer received a Reheat Fire 1 Warning and he throttled back and turned toward base. His controls stiffened and the Reheat Warning Light illuminated. Bealer called 'Mayday! Mayday! Mayday!' as the warning lights refused to go out despite his completing the fire drills. He ejected at 22,000 feet and 220 knots and tumbled in his seat to such an extent that he believed his drogues had failed. Thankfully, however, the seat separated perfectly normally at 10,000 feet and he entered the water with his PSP under his arm. A helicopter picked him up from a choppy, but warm (65-70°) sea twenty minutes later. The F.6, meanwhile, had crashed into Limassol Bay southeast of Akrotiri.

Despite the Fire Integrity Programme, most of the losses in 1971 had been due to fuel leak-related fires and so the RAF redoubled its efforts to stamp out the problem. None of the Lightnings lost during 1972 were due to fuel-related fires and the first casualty on 16 February was the result of a collision during a 29 Squadron night supersonic interception exercise from Wattisham. XP747, flown by Flight Lieutenant Paul Reynolds, had slowed to Mach 0.9 at 35,000 feet, turning onto 350 homing to Wattisham. As he descended and forty miles southeast of Harwich, Reynolds experienced a bump and pitched nose down but felt that he was being pushed upwards (XP747 and XP698, flown by Flight Lieutenant Paul Cooper, who was killed, had collided). Reynolds' tail controls were lost and he was diving at 45 degrees so he put out a Mayday signal. At 31,000 feet he put one hand to his face blind and pulled. Just fifteen seconds later, XP747 crashed. Dry and warm in his immersion suit, Reynolds was picked up by a fishing boat and a USAF Jolly Green Giant helicopter arrived to hoist him aboard, but the RAF pilot declined as he was sick and did not know how to use the Kaman winch used by the USAF. (Two T.5S of 226 OCU were lost, on 6 September and 14 December and brought the year's Lightning losses to five.)

In early 1972 Roger Levy had the opportunity of flying in a Lightning at Wattisham. His affinity with the Lightning had begun ten years earlier when he watched an early Mark 1 take off just before dusk from Waddington's long runway, make a distant and apparently leisurely circuit of the field, before returning silently in a low-level pass, suddenly pulling up steeply into the golden evening sky in a shattering vertical climb at almost the speed of sound. He was impressed! Levy was even more impressed after he had the privilege of flying on 111 Squadron in a Lightning T.5 (XS422) piloted by Flight Lieutenant 'Tony' Alcock from Wattisham and his article appeared in the February 1972 issue of *Air Pictorial*.

'After being briefed on ejection procedure and the use of survival equipment, there followed the business of kitting-out: woollen vest, long johns, anti-G suit, immersion suit (inspired by Houdini but very necessary as the North Sea can be rather chilly), Mae West, gloves, oxygen mask and bone dome, by which time one feels much better equipped to go deep-sea diving than flying. We were ready to go.

'I mutely followed Tony's instructions to start-up (the relevant buttons being on my side of the cockpit), only the initial hiss being audible as each Avon was separately ignited.

'Taxiing at 20 mph the forward visibility was superb. We turned on to the runway, wound up the Avons to 85 per cent power, released the brakes, applied full cold power and 'Charlie 84' was off, surging forward, gathering speed quickly until after less than twenty seconds, with 140 knots on the horizontal strip ASI, the nose was lifted and a few seconds later we unstuck at 170 knots so smoothly that it was impossible to feel the precise instant.

'The next few seconds provided the most fantastic sensation of acceleration, with absolutely no illusion of forward progress as we sliced through the warm air of a perfect English summer morning and saw rural Suffolk rolling away a few hundred feet below us.

'We kept low until we had 450 knots on the clock, then pulled the stick hard back and climbed to port on our heading out over the sea, causing fields and clouds to tilt wildly and the G-suit to squeeze tightly as we pulled a mere 3Gs in the process.

'In no time at all we were over-flying a Vulcan contrailing at 34,000 feet. Soon afterwards Eastern Radar warned us of traffic on a reciprocal course at about our height, twelve miles distant and closing fast. Tony flicked on our AI and immediately picked up the offending blip (although the display was quite unintelligible to me); then pointed to a black speck at 11 o'clock which zipped past us about a mile to port. 'Another Lightning'.

'We positioned ourselves for a supersonic run, received clearance from Eastern Radar and began a shallow dive, cut in reheat with a definite 'thump' and watched the ASI record our progress past Mach 1.0 (without so much as a quiver) until it indicated just over 1.7. We then banked away from the distant East Anglian coastline and began a steady climb, keeping a close check on our fuel and on other traffic, which included another Lightning which curved overhead about 2,000 feet above us leaving a non-persistent contrail. A few moments later we levelled out at 60,000 feet at which height everything seemed more silent than ever. After this Tony throttled back out of reheat, producing an effect like throwing out an anchor so great was the deceleration.

'On one side of us the English coastline stretching from Lincolnshire to Sussex was clearly visible, while on the other the Continent was spread out in the distance. From this height the earth appeared an arid, yellowish-brown, while the sky above us had darkened to a blackish-indigo. Altogether an unforgettable view.

'The tranquillity was suddenly broken by a tremor which rippled through the airframe – clear air turbulence.

'We turned for home, about 100 miles away, pushing the nose down and producing the strange sensation of negative G for a few seconds. As we reached the coast we practised a tactical recovery, descending from 30,000 feet to 2,000 feet in a horizontal distance of only ten miles. With throttles back and airbrakes out the Lightning drops like a brick!

'This was followed by an approach and overshoot. The horizon straightened as we crossed the hedge at 190 knots and let the tyre-blackened runway drift beneath us for a few seconds before pushing the throttles through the gate into reheat, whipping up the gear and blasting round the circuit for a final landing. The effect was dramatic, even though only one burner had worked, with the world outside in a 3G twirl.

'Landing in a Lightning is not nearly as hair-raising as it seems when viewed from the edge of the runway. A very smooth touchdown was accomplished at about 160 knots. Because of local R/T chatter I did not hear Tony's first command 'Chute!' as the nose wheel was lowered on to the runway. He repeated the instruction a little more anxiously as the runway's end was fast approaching, whereupon I yanked the appropriate tiger-striped handle from my side of the dash and after a momentary delay we felt the reassuring pressure on our seat straps which indicated that the tail braking chute had deployed and our speed trickled down almost to walking pace.

The canopy was opened as we taxied back to dispersal and gratefully we loosened our masks and breathed in the fragrance of the countryside. We remained strapped in while our aircraft was readied for a second sortie, this time a rendezvous with a Victor tanker and three more 'Treble One' Lightnings which were practising air-to-air refuelling about ninety miles out to sea, in Wattisham's 'patch'.

'Twenty minutes later we were airborne again, this time after a semi-rotation takeoff with both burners working. The Lightning leapt off the runway at about 40 degrees and maintained this angle of climb until we had passed 20,000 feet – my stomach was still at least 10,000 feet behind. We eased out of the climb at 30,000 feet, a mere 2½ minutes after take-off, crossed the coast and were vectored by Bawdsey radar on to the tanker formation. This we discovered was only at 24,000 feet, so we half-rolled down to the appropriate altitude, pulling the by now customary number of Gs in the process. We picked up the formation on our AI long before visual contact was made. The Victor was visible as a black dot from several miles away, but the 'three chicks' remained invisible until the sunlight transformed their banking wings into three brilliant white lights in the sky.

'We called the Victor captain, informed him of our presence and obtained clearance to join the quartet. Two Lightnings were 'in tow', while the third held off to starboard, all flicking their airbrakes in and out to maintain station. Tony brought us close into the port side for a good look, then did a quarter roll so that I could get a downward view of the formation.

'Although we were not fitted with a probe we made several practice approaches to the Victor's starboard drogue, which was bouncing airily in the rather turbulent conditions. The Lightning's closing speed is only one or two knots higher than that of the tanker, positioning being aided by aligning the fighter with a series of dayglo and black stripes painted beneath the tanker's wing. Once the probe has made contact with the drogue, the hose is wound in a short distance before fuel transfer begins. The Victor is equipped with an elaborate lighting system which permits night air refuellings and the Lightning has a light fitted to its probe which illuminates the nozzle.

'Our own fuel situation soon obliged us to break away from the formation and return to base, where another smooth landing brought to an end a brief but exhilarating experience which for me added a new dimension to flying. It also left me with a great respect for the Lightning and a profound admiration for the professionalism of the young pilots who fly it.'³

The first Lightning loss in 1973 occurred on 3 April when XS934 was abandoned near Akrotiri, Cyprus, after an ECU fire during a general handling sortie. Flight Lieutenant Fred Greer on 56 Squadron throttled back at 11,000 feet and increased power on one engine. The fire went out but then recurred again and Greer experienced some stiffening of the controls. After pointing the F.6 towards the sea, he called 'Ejecting!' and left the aircraft safely. Another Lightning was abandoned before the year was out and two more, F.6 XR719 and F.3 XP738 on 11 Squadron, were declared 'Cat.5' after belly landing on 5 June at Coltishall and 10 December at Wattisham respectively.

The fire prevention measures taken in the early '70s now began to pay dividends, for after 1973 fire-related accidents were halved, although XR715, the first of three Lightnings which crashed in 1974, on 13 February was lost to 'Lightning Fire Syndrome'. Flight Lieutenant Terence 'Taff' A. Butcher, one of a pair on 29 Squadron at Wattisham exercising at 7,000 feet, experienced some difficulty in locating his face blind with his left hand. Butcher finally ejected at 8,000 feet and 270 knots. The Southwold lifeboat was alerted in case the Lightning came down in the sea. But it clipped two willow trees in a paddock at Mells near Halesworth in Suffolk and ploughed a 200-yard furrow before ending up in three main sections across a barbed wire fence, just 100 yards from Watermill Farm. Butcher, who landed in a field near the Norwich road, was flown to the RAF Hospital, Ely, where X-rays revealed that there were effectively no injuries and he was flying again the next day.

On 24 June Flying Officer Kevin Mason on 111 Squadron took off from Wattisham in XR748 and did a slow roll over the station at 8,000 feet, when both hydraulic warning lights illuminated and remained on. Mason commenced a slow climb towards the coast, tightening his lap, shoulder outer and negative G straps, but after twelve minutes control was lost and Mason ejected near Coltishall at 18,000 feet and 380 knots. The F.3 crashed in the North Sea off Great Yarmouth and Mason also dropped into the sea, having separated from his ejection seat automatically at 10,000 feet. Mason could not release his QRB or inflate his life preserver and he was dragged along for about fifteen seconds. He finally clambered into his dinghy but his harness pulled him out again. A Whirlwind arrived and the winchman managed to release Mason from his harness and pull him aboard the helicopter. On 29 October XR768 had to be abandoned by Flight Lieutenant

LIGHTNING STRIKES

T. W. 'Tex' Jones on 5 Squadron near Saltfleet, Lincolnshire, after his top engine flamed out off the Lincolnshire coast during banner firing. It refused to relight, but after a fire warning on No. 2 was followed by a fire warning on No.1, it re-lit spontaneously. Jones, who had previously ejected from a Gnat on 23 May 1966 after flying into high-tension cables, ejected at 3,500 feet and 260 knots. During his descent he dropped his PSP and he was a non-swimmer. Once in the sea, Jones was in his dinghy in ten seconds flat! The F.6 crashed three miles off Mablethorpe.

Lightning losses, thankfully, now began to tail off. In 1975 two were lost and in 1976 and 1977 only one a year was lost, although the first of these, in Cyprus on 7 April 1975, proved fatal. Squadron Leader Dave 'Quingle' Hampton, a very experienced pilot on 11 Squadron, took off from Akrotiri in XR762 on an AI exercise with another Lightning. Hampton climbed up to 40,000 feet and carried out a tail chase down but then lost contact in a barrel roll. Hampton recovered but later lost it again. His No.1 saw him spinning through 12-10,000 feet and called, 'Eject, eject, you are below 12!' No. 1 thought he saw Hampton recover and pull out but the F.6 hit the sea with one large and two smaller splashes. It hit at a shallow angle and the seawater rushed up through the air intake and burst through the cockpit floor, forcing the seat upwards and firing the canopy jettison system. No. 1 called 'Mayday' and alerted the Akrotiri helicopter, which arrived at the scene in fifteen minutes. There was no sign of the aircraft but Hampton's body was seen floating face down, his PSP up but without any sign of a parachute canopy. The crewman turned the body over, inflated his life preserver and undid the QRB and tried to resuscitate the unfortunate squadron leader, but to no avail.

In June 1975 T.4 XM991 was written off after a ground fire at Gütersloh. In 1976 on 29 July F.6 XS937 piloted by Flying Officer Simon Manning on 11 Squadron at Binbrook suffered an undercarriage failure overhead Leconfield. Eighteen minutes later, off Flamborough Head, he ejected at 7,000 feet and 300 knots. A SAR helicopter in the descent area picked up Manning ten minutes after he entered the sea. Manning got his feet tangled in his rigging lines and took a minute to free himself. Apart from some low lumbar pain, Manning suffered no lasting injuries. In 1977, on 24 February, Squadron Leader Michael Lawrance on 92 Squadron at Gütersloh was giving Lightning experience to Squadron Leader Christopher 'Hoppy' Glanville-White, the 4 Squadron Harrier operations officer at Gütersloh in T.4 XM968 when, at the end of the trip, while breaking into the circuit to land, the aircraft suffered a services hydraulic failure and the undercarriage would not lower. This was shortly followed by a failure of one of the flying controls hydraulic systems, so the undercarriage emergency lowering system was also lost. The aircraft was already doomed and running very low on fuel when Lawrance shut down the No. 2 engine to save the little fuel that remained. He applied positive G to try to shake the wheels down, but to no avail. There was just enough pressure in the hydraulic system to power the controls while the pilot pulled out of a dive about three miles short of the runway. Then the controls seized and Glanville-White and then Lawrance ejected after the canopy jettisoned. The aircraft continued to pitch nose up until it was pointing vertically upwards then described an aerobatic manoeuvre known as a stall turn. The manoeuvre, not thought to be possible in a Lightning, worked perfectly on this occasion and the aircraft accelerated vertically downwards. As the speed increased the pilotless aircraft started to pull out of the dive, pointing straight at the married quarters. Had the aircraft started its final climb at a slightly greater height or if the controls had seized at a different angle, the aircraft might have pulled out of the dive and flown right into the houses. Instead it crashed at a shallow angle in a field and its wreckage was scattered over a wide area and no one was hurt. The aircraft crash was witnessed by many observers on the ground including the pilot's wife Jan who, knowing that her husband was flying the two seater that day, fainted. The Harrier pilot sustained crush fractures and Lawrance spinal injuries and spent a few weeks in hospital.[4]

No Lightnings were lost in 1978, the first clean sheet since 1958. In 1979, though three were lost. The first occurred on 25 May when Flight Lieutenant 'Pete' Coker on 5 Squadron abandoned XS931 near Flamborough Head after a control restriction caused by FOD and the F.6 crashed off Hornsea. 'Pete' Coker recalls:[5] 'I was leading a pair on my squadron combat-ready work-up training with Neil Matheson on my wing. I recall the take-off time was about 0830 and the ejection took place fifteen minutes later. Due to a control restriction I was unable to gain much height and spent the time trying to establish the cause of the restriction whilst flying at low level. I do believe I passed quite close to the cranes at Hull before easing the aircraft right towards the sea, but making the turn caused even greater height loss. I do recall passing very low over a town, which I subsequently discovered was Hornsea. After passing over the town, the sea appeared and with no further hope of recovering the aircraft, I ejected. Unfortunately, my first pull of the handle was too light; it requires up to 75lb force to pull! I left the aircraft at an estimated 200 feet and 350 knots with a fair amount of nose down. I was not in the parachute long and did not have time to release the

PSP. For some reason, I also broke my leg in two places, which made it even more difficult when I was in the water to undo my PSP. Although I inflated the dinghy, I never managed to get into it! The weather was a beautiful spring day and the sea was calm, although there was apparently about a 500 feet deep bank of fog in the area of my ejection. The helicopter arrived some ten minutes later and took me to Hull Royal Infirmary. I am sure that if I had had the time I would have been able to see the coastline and Hornsea in the background, as it was only a mile or so off the coast.'

On 17 August Flying Officer Raymond Knowles on 5 Squadron, a short, breezy Irishman from Belfast who after getting three A levels, spent eight years in the Air Training Corps and then made a good living as an itinerant bricklayer in Europe before returning to the RAF, was on a normal transit flight in XP737 from Binbrook to Valley, where the F.3 was to be part of a ground display for an open day. In the circuit west of the airfield the port undercarriage warning light came on when the gear was operated and the tower confirmed that the port undercarriage was only 20 degrees down. Knowles completed all his emergency drills and attempted to fling the gear down with G, to no avail. Positioned four miles off Anglesey with a 22 Squadron Wessex alerted, Knowles, who had made four previous parachute drops, pulled the SPH and ejected at 9,000 feet and 250 knots over the Irish Sea. His PSP finally dropped at 500 feet and the life preserver inflated at 300 feet. The winchman aboard the Wessex saw Knowles dragged along for fifteen seconds before safely picking him up. Knowles suffered a very minor neck injury and was in a collar for seven days.

On 18 September XR7Z3, a 5 Squadron F.6 which was on detachment to Akrotiri and was piloted by the Station Commander, Group Captain Pete Carter, received fire warnings on both engines followed by aircraft failure. Carter, who had made a previous parachute drop, corrected his posture, tightened his straps, adjusted the seat height and checked arm and leg clearance as he climbed from 4,000 feet to 7,500 feet before pulling the SPH and ejecting at 250 knots over the sea. He suffered back pain as the seat fired but managed to scramble into his dinghy after just twenty seconds and was flown by helicopter to land in minutes. XR723 crashed fifteen miles south of Akrotiri. There were no Lightning crashes in 1980 and just one in 1981. On 23 July XR765 was lost when Flight Lieutenant Jim Wild on 5 Squadron abandoned it over the North Sea after a double re-heat fire. The F.6 crashed fifty miles northeast of Binbrook. Wild ejected safely. The next Lightning to crash occurred on 26 August 1983 when XP753 plunged into the sea off Scarborough during unauthorized aerobatics. Flight Lieutenant Mike

Thompson on the LTF was killed. In 1984 two more Lightnings crashed. Flight Lieutenant Dave Frost on 5 Squadron was killed on 13 July when XS920 was lost near Heuslingen, West Germany after the F.6 hit power cables during air combat manoeuvres.

On the afternoon of 8 November Flight Lieutenant Mike Hale on 5 Squadron took off in XR761 from Binbrook for a routine training sortie. Almost immediately the pitch trimmer, which keeps the control column forces in balance, ceased to operate. As a result Mike Hale had to maintain a constant forward pressure on the control column. He elected to cancel his planned mission and instead, circled to the east of Binbrook and over the sea to reduce the fuel load before landing. After circling for approximately seven minutes he started positioning his aircraft for a landing at Binbrook. However, at about fifteen miles from the airfield, the No. 2 engine fire warning indication illuminated. Mike Hale shut down the No. 2 engine and again flew the Lightning out to sea. Shortly afterwards, a second fire warning, this time for the re-heat zone of No. 1 engine, illuminated. This was followed by a third fire warning indicating that there was also a fire in the No. 2 engine re-heat zone. In addition there were indications that the aircraft generator and other electrical services were not operating correctly. A second Lightning inspected XR761 for damage. Its pilot reported that smoke was issuing from the No. 2 engine jet-pipe and that an orange-coloured fire was burning between the two jet-pipe nozzles. Meanwhile, the pilot of XR761 noticed that the flying controls were becoming stiff to operate and that the warning indicators in the cockpit showed that the two powered flying control systems were no longer functioning correctly. He was unable to control the aircraft and just before the aircraft entered a spiral dive into the sea, he ejected. The ejection and parachute descent were normal. However, once in the sea the pilot was dragged for some distance. The lanyard connecting the pilot to his dinghy became entangled in the parachute risers, exacerbating the problem and making it difficult for the pilot to breathe as he was continually being dragged under water. Mike Hale finally disconnected himself from the parachute but in doing so lost his dinghy. He was in the sea for about twenty-five minutes before being rescued by a RAF helicopter.[6]

Two more crashes in 1985 followed these losses. On 6 March XR772 on 5 Squadron was abandoned by Flying Officer Martin 'Tetley' Ramsey off Spurn Head after a possible structural failure and crashed into the sea, twenty miles northeast of Skegness. Ramsey ejected but he was dead when he was recovered from the sea.

LIGHTNING STRIKES

On 19 September XS921 on 11 Squadron piloted by Flight Lieutenant Craig Penrice crashed approximately thirty miles off Flamborough Head after an uncontrolled spin. Penrice recalled: 'The day started all very normally, this was my second day back at work following a wonderful ten days of leave spent in a cottage on the West coast of Scotland opposite Skye. Well-deserved leave, I might add having just returned from our annual six-week detachment to Akrotiri, Cyprus for the squadron's APC (Armament Practice Camp). It was just before 5 pm when I took off as number two of a pair of F-6s on our way to undertake our normal bread and butter training sortie of medium level P.Is (Practice Intercepts). We would each take it in turn to act as Target (bad guy) and Fighter (good guy). The fighter controller on the ground at RAF Boulmer would vector us apart by about 40 miles then turn us towards each other, the fighter would then have to use his AI.23 radar to first detect the bad guy and then, through some nifty mental gymnastics work out the target heading and altitude before making corrections to his own course to achieve the correct point in space from which to start a turn to end up in a missile firing cone behind the target.

'The sortie all went as we had planned it. We were almost down to recovery fuel and I was acting as the target. Once the flight leader had completed his turn to end up behind me and was closing to finish his attack I started a gentle turn to the left so that we were heading back more directly to Binbrook. Things went downhill from here.

'Having moved the control column to the left to roll the aircraft into the turn, the aircraft thought it would be a jolly good wheeze if it kept moving the stick of its own accord. Despite my best efforts the stick continued to move all the way to full deflection left and the aircraft duly did as it was told and kept rolling left. As the aircraft passed the inverted position the nose started to drop and very quickly I found myself in a near vertical spiral dive (not a spin). The ailerons had gone to full deflection (normally they were limited to half deflection with the gear up) so the aircraft was rotating very quickly and as I was going downhill the speed was also increasing rapidly.

'At this point I did a number of things. The first was to make a call on the radio in which I said "I've got a very bad control restriction." At the same time I swapped hands on trying to move the stick and used my right hand to switch off the auto-stabs in the hope that they were the source of my problems. (The auto-stabs effectively had the job of smoothing out the ride for the pilot at high speed around the transonic region, where, if it were not for the auto-stabs the aircraft would exhibit a pronounced nodding tendency.)

'After what seemed like an eternity, but was actually in the order of 3 seconds, the flight leader came on the radio and asked 'Is it better now?' I answered 'No' – about 4 octaves higher than my normal voice. Immediately after that I ejected; there was no thinking about it or time to prepare, the situation was obvious, the aircraft was rotating rapidly and going downhill like a train.

'I was now in cloud, speed was increasing, my one action that I could think of to make it better had done nothing and answer to the question 'is it better?' was quite definitely NO! So I ejected.

'I can remember pulling the lower ejection handle with my left hand while simultaneously throwing my head and shoulders back against the seat with as much force as I could manage and trying to grab my left wrist with my right hand in order to secure it against the wind blast. As you will see subsequently, this latter action proved somewhat futile. The next proper recollection that I have is sitting facing backwards on the cabin floor of the Wessex just as the side door was being closed and feeling very, very cold, nothing else, just very cold. This was about 50 minutes later. I wish I could fully describe how cold I felt, but in all the times I have recounted this story I have never been able to satisfactorily describe the intense, all encompassing cold that I felt then.

'Some interesting things are worth a mention at this point. This was a Thursday; on the Monday of the same week the entire fleet of Binbrook Lightnings had had a modification embodied to the ejection seat such that the PLB (Personal Locator Beacon) would be activated during the normal ejection sequence at the point when man-seat separation occurs, rather than having to be manually operated. This was considered to be a great improvement: if the pilot were incapacitated the beacon would still be operative. In addition, with the beacon transmitting from 10,000 feet its range could be increased and transmission was more immediate than previously. The PLB was stowed in a pocket in the life jacket we wore all the time and auto-activation was achieved by means of a sticker strap incorporated into the existing lanyard, which attached the dinghy pack to the life jacket. As man separated from the seat the lanyard pulled taut and a cam rotated the power switch of the beacon to 'ON'.

'The only drawback of this arrangement comes under the heading of 'old dogs and new tricks'. Previously there had been no big deal when getting out of the aircraft if you stood up having not disconnected the dinghy lanyard; you simply felt a tug (and a bit of a fool), which reminded you to undo it. The same was not now the case, all the above was true except in addition the PLB was set off and a transmission was going out on the distress frequency, until you scrabbled around and managed to extricate the beacon from its pocket and switch it off. This in turn resulted in three things: some work for the safety equipment fitters who had to rebuild the jacket. The rescue system initiating a scramble for the nearest helicopter unit until they had obtained confirmation through the ATC network that the beacon they had observed near Binbrook was in fact an inadvertent activation; and much embarrassment for the individual pilot concerned.

'In my case, the rescue helicopter unit at Leconfield were in the process of walking out to their aircraft for the umpteenth time in the week, cursing those idiots at Binbrook who were incapable of extracting themselves from an aircraft without alerting the safety coordination system. However, it soon became apparent that the signal from this PLB was much stronger than previously experienced and by the time the rescue crew were in the aircraft and in radio contact with their control centre they were getting the message that this was a real scramble; this probably saved me about 5-7 minutes, time that would become invaluable.'[7]

Almost exactly a year later, on 15 September 1985, Flight Lieutenant Bob Bees on 11 Squadron safely abandoned XR760 after a rear fuselage fire. The F.6 crashed into the North Sea seven miles north of Whitby.

From February 1986 until April 1987 Squadron Leader Clive Rowley was OC LTF. He recalls: 'Flight Lieutenant Barry Lennon on 5 Squadron had been selected as the Lightning display pilot for the 1987 season. On 19 March 1987, he was conducting a 5,000 feet minimum altitude practice over Binbrook airfield in a borrowed LTF F.3 [XP707] when he trialled the effects of a slow feeding ventral and negative G. The resulting manoeuvre, a negative G tuck into an inverted spin, had never before been demonstrated. We were all much relieved that he survived the subsequent ejection and parachute landing on the airfield with nothing worse than a pair of bruised heels to show for it. Within twenty minutes of the accident he telephoned from 5 Squadron and said: "That aircraft is u/s sir; can I have another one?!"'

On 1 July 1987 during the last Lightning APC Flight Lieutenant D. K. M. 'Charlie' Chan on 5 Squadron abandoned XR763 near Akrotiri. He was flying an air-firing sortie on a target banner towed by a Canberra when the upper wheel from the banner spreader bar came off and was ingested by the Lightning's No.2 engine, which promptly seized. Chan shut it down and headed back to Akrotiri with the No. 2 engine now running at abnormally high temperature due to debris damage. At about 2½ miles from the airfield the engine began to lose thrust. When Chan applied full power, the JPT rose to 900°C (the normal maximum allowable JPT being 795°C). XR763 continued to lose speed and at about 250 feet and 150 knots, Chan ejected safely. The F.6 crashed in a vineyard close to some houses and exploded in a fireball. (The fin, later recovered almost intact from the wreckage, was erected in the grounds of a bar used by service personnel.) It was an ignominious end for XR763, which had first flown over twenty-two years earlier. So too had XR769, which was safely abandoned over the North Sea by Flight Lieutenant 'Dick' Coleman RAAF on 11 Squadron on 11 April 1988 after an engine fire during practice air combat with a 74 Squadron Phantom. (The Phantom crew landed and marked up their aircraft with one 'kill'!) XR769 was the eightieth and last RAF Lightning lost to all causes.

Chapter 11

A 'Magic Carpet' Ride

The Royal Saudi Air Force had contracted to buy newer marks of Lightning to replace their earlier marks (Saudi Arabia ordered 34 of the F.53 export variant (twelve were also ordered by Kuwait) and aircraft 53-666, the first Lightning for the Royal Saudi Air Force, flew on 1 December 1966, the first delivery taking place in December 1967. The first Saudi pilot to convert to the Lightning was Lieutenant A. Thunneyan, whom Mick Swiney checked out on a standardization sortie at the conclusion of his conversion phase on 9 June 1967. In an effort to stop Yemeni incursions, the delivery of the Saudi Lightnings was preceded, in June 1966, by the arrival in that country of five ex-RAF F.2s (designated F.52), two ex-RAF T.4s and ex-RAF pilots to fly them. The programme, codenamed 'Magic Carpet', also included Hunters and Thunderbird surface-to-air missiles (SAMs). In 1969 226 OCU was given the Saudi training commitment, with four Saudi T.55s (two more were purchased by Kuwait) being attached to No. 3 Squadron. 'Magic Palm', the second phase of the Saudi delivery programme, had begun in 1968, the year that Kuwait also took delivery of the Lightning. The F.53 was first used in action by the RSAF on ground strikes against border positions in Yemen late in 1969. Kuwait operated the Lightning for seven years, before replacing them with the French Mirage. At Coltishall, the RSAF course was almost double the RAF course. To quote the Koran, 'The lightning all but blinds them'. George Black recalls one memorable incident which involved a Saudi student who somehow managed to align his compass 180 degrees out and instead of heading out over the North Sea, ended up over London at 36,000 feet – much to the consternation of Air Traffic Control. Another aircraft had to be sent up to get him back.

Flight Lieutenant Bob Offord, who completed three years as an instructor on 3 Squadron, 226 OCU in 1969, the year he retired from the RAF, recalls the Saudi pilots: 'During my time, 1968-69, I flew Captain Ahmed Behery, Captain Bakry, Prince Turki bin Nasser (Later, Brigadier General, Deputy Defence Minister and Commander of the RSAF); Major Essa Ghimlas (killed in an F.52 whilst practising single-engine approaches to Khamis Mushayt on 28 November 1968); Major Hamdullah, Captain Aziz and Prince Bandar Faisal, one of the King's sons. Bandar arrived at Coltishall in a Lamborghini; crashed it and bought another. Not to replace it, mind, for when the first one was repaired, he kept both. The Saudis were loaded and well paid, but to them, flying was a hobby rather than a career. Some of them came from Cranwell. Some had flown F-86s. Most of them were quite good, some pretty good; three we would like to have had in our squadron. I went out to Saudi Arabia in 1969 and continued training for Airwork Services. The runways there were longer. Dhahran, for instance, was a former USAF SAC base.

'January 8th 1969 was scheduled for a normal and routine night flying programme and basically that is exactly what it turned out to be,' recalls Brian Carroll, 'but with one small exception. Some days before, our sister Squadron had set forth on a detachment to Singapore, flight re-fuelling all the way with the assistance of a largish proportion of the UK tanker force. We were quite jealous, having hoped that we might be selected to fulfil that task, but it was not to be, so we were left holding the fort at Leuchars, increasing our QRA commitment and reducing any free time that we might otherwise have enjoyed. Night flying had just got under way when we received a call from Command HQ informing us that a couple of spares were urgently needed for two of the Lightnings stranded at Gan. A VC-10 was due out of Brize Norton that evening and we were asked to fly the necessary items down to Brize right away. A slight adjustment to our programme was made and with the spare parts duly located and delivered to our operations room, I prepared to fly the bits down to Brize in one of our Mk 6s, a trip that would only take a leisurely sixty minutes.

'A flight plan was quickly filed, Brize Norton informed of our intentions and away I went. Being overland, the flight had to remain subsonic in spite of the urgency; even so I would get to Brize well before the VC-10's ETD.

A 'MAGIC CARPET' RIDE

A cruise at around FL 340 at 0.9 Mach soon covered the ground and with weather conditions favourable, a routine descent for a GCA approach and landing was duly carried out. Brize were not quite tuned in for our somewhat faster approach speeds, but even so the controller gave me an excellent talk down, even if he had to speak a little faster than he was normally accustomed. Safely down, I was handed over to local control for taxi in instructions. In fact, they very kindly sent a 'Follow Me' truck to lead me into the designated dispersal, probably thinking that without a navigator a mere fighter jock couldn't find the way!

'Engines shut down and I climbed out of the cockpit to hand over the package for its flight to Gan. The VC-10 was due to depart thirty minutes later, so all was well. I briefed the ground crew on the turnaround procedure. Fortunately the surface wind was fairly brisk and with the Brize runway being one of the longer ones in the country, 3050 metres (slightly over 10,000 feet), I had not needed to use my brake chute. Had I done so I would have had the doubtful pleasure of re-packing and installing it, a job that was not one of the more popular ones amongst Lightning pilots. (Laying on one's back attempting to get 4 cubic feet of chute into a 3.5 cubic feet space is not a pastime that I would recommend.)

'That done it was off to the nearest crew room for a coffee and a chat before returning to Leuchars. Not having used the chute, I intended to take a little longer than normal before attempting to start and taxi out. This was in order to give the brakes more time to cool down, though as I recall they were not especially hot; gentle braking and a long runway had taken most of the sting out of the landing.

'Coffee break over and it was time to fly back to Leuchars. First, though, a visit to air traffic control and the Met office to confirm my departure time and to ensure that the Scottish weather hadn't gone sour on me. All looked OK, so I made my way back to the crew room to root out the ground control to see me off.

'I was soon strapped in and ready to start engines. Both fired up on cue, systems all on line and I was ready to move out, this time declining the use of a 'Follow Me'. The R/T chatter from this point on went something along the following lines:

'Brize Norton Tower, this is Eagle Red One, request taxi clearance.'

'Eagle Red One – Brize, you are cleared to taxi for Runway 26, the QNH is 1021, follow the centre line lights from your present position past the large hangar on your left.'

'Brize Norton Tower, Red One R/W 26, 1021 set, moving out.'

'I continued to taxi for the duty runway, carrying out the vital actions prior to take off – all was well. Approaching the runway and another call to the tower. "Brize Norton Tower, Eagle Red One request line up and take off."'

'Eagle Red One – Brize, are you familiar with our standard departure procedure?'

'Brize Norton Tower – Eagle Red One – negative.'

'Eagle Red One – Brize Norton Tower are you ready to copy?'

'Eagle Red One, affirmative.'

'Roger, after take-off climb to and maintain 2,300 feet on runway heading at 240 knots for two minutes, then carry out a rate one turn left onto 130°. When steady on heading, climb to 5,000 feet maintaining 240 knots and advise. You will then be cleared to turn left again onto 060° and continue the climb to 10,000 feet. We will then advise when you are clear to climb to your required flight level of 350. Eagle Red One read back.

'Brize Norton Tower – Eagle Red One I regret to inform you that I do not have sufficient fuel for such a protracted departure, request a straight climb out on runway heading to FL 350 and then a right turn onto track for my base.'

'Eagle Red One – Brize Norton Tower, not possible, we have an Airway 23 miles from the end of the runway extending to FL 245.'

'Brize Norton Tower – Eagle Red One, that's OK, I will clear FL 245 before reaching the airway.' Long pause from ATC.

'Eagle Red One – Brize Norton Tower, if you are certain, you are cleared for a straight climb out. Call our departure frequency on 239.6 once airborne.'

'The clock was now running! Nose wheel off, unstick, clean up, undercarriage locked, all lights out, flaps up, radar TX on, scanning for any conflicting traffic. IFF TX on and a change to departure frequency. (Time elapsed from wheels roll approx. 25-30 seconds.)

'Brize – Eagle Red One airborne maintaining runway heading and climbing to FL 350. have contact with one dead ahead range two three miles.'

'Eagle Red One – Brize, that is a civilian in the airway crossing you from right to left, confirm you are still contact.'

'Red One affirmative, I still have positive contact and am well clear.'

'Brize – Eagle Red One advise passing FL 100.'

'Red One – Brize I am through 100.'

'Roger, Red One advise through FL 150.'

'Red One is through FL150.'

A 'MAGIC CARPET' RIDE

'Roger, Red One, advise through 200.'

'Roger, Red One is through 200 and I am now levelling at FL 350.'

'Pregnant pause from ATC followed by something along the lines of "Oh S H one T".'

'Have a good flight, you are clear onto your recovery heading, call radar on 296.8 – goodnight.'

'The Lightning's time to height in full re-heat was very respectable, somewhere in the region of 2.5 to 3.0 minutes depending upon the ALJW and the ambient temperature, so for a controller only used to dealing with Air Support Command aircraft my climb rate was to say the very least surprising, hence the fact that the R/T calls never did catch up with the climb rate.

'The return to Leuchars was just another routine trip (for me), the skies were clear and empty of traffic apart from the one civilian aircraft seen during the climb out from Brize. Closer to base there were a few pairs of squadron aircraft operating. The weather was excellent, clear of cloud and good visibility so I elected for a free let down for a visual rejoin to the circuit. Touchdown was 55 minutes after departing Brize. Time then for another coffee before retiring to the mess for one of their famed 'night flying suppers'.

'There is a deal of truth in many of the well worn and used sayings such as 'one door never closes without another one opening' and 'you never know what is around the next corner'. So it was for me on the afternoon of Thursday 6 August 1973. I had flown a couple of single-seat sorties that morning in two of the Mk.1As (182 and 214) on 65 Squadron. That afternoon, I was in the operations chair running the programme and planning the flying schedule for the following day. The phone rang (again). A long-standing friend and associate from BAC at Warton was on the line with an intriguing offer, or rather a potential offer. After some small talk, he asked whether I would be interested in a job. Not really, I said, I have one already. Well, he said, we (British Aircraft Corporation Ltd) are seeking a Chief Flying Instructor to set up and run our new training programme for the Royal Saudi Air force at Dhahran and we wondered if you might be interested. I am not sure of exactly what I said. I did, however, ask whether I might think it over and call him back the following day. This was agreed and I now had to do some serious thinking. Having been in the RAF for a little over 22 years, the cold outside world looked more than a little alien to me. However, the offer was too good to ignore, so on the Friday I called back and said I would like to talk some more. The upshot of this was an invitation to visit Warton on the Monday for a briefing and a formal interview with Roland 'Bee' Beamont (who else?).

'My boss at the time agreed that I could go on the Monday and that, in the interests of navigation training, could borrow a Lightning for that purpose. Came the day and I set off in a Mk.1A (215) for Warton, a mere thirty minute hop across the country, for the promised briefing and the interview with 'Bee'. The day progressed well and having spent thirty minutes or so with the great man himself, he informed me that the job was mine if I so wished. However, as there was considerable urgency to have their new CFI in post, I had to make a swift decision and persuade the RAF to expedite my release in quick time. As things turned out, I was in Saudi and flew my first sortie in a T.55 (714) on 14 October 1973, which was good going by any standards.

'Back to the day of the interview: 'Bee', having asked the questions and received all the answers he needed, now wondered if I would like to stay for lunch. Of course, I accepted the offer. He said "Fine, I will see you at lunch." About to depart his office, he called me back and said, "By the way, go and see our accounts people and they will refund your travelling costs. We pay first class rail fare, which should cover your petrol expenses."

'Well,' I said, "that wouldn't quite cover them."'

'"Sorry about that," he said, 'but that is all we pay. How come it's not enough?'

'If you care to look out of your window,' I said, 'you will see my transport parked a few hundred yards away'. And there was my Lightning, all bright and shiny, just waiting for me to fire it up again.

'"Very amusing," he said.

'"Well," I quipped, "I had to prove to you that I could fly them."'

'"This we already knew," he said.

'Tell you what, we will refuel it and say no more about the train fare.'

'I thought that was a very reasonable solution! I don't suppose that many people have gone for a job interview in a Lightning, but it sure beats the motorways and knocks BR into a cocked hat.

'The rest is all water under the bridge; ten years of excellent flying with some great guys in Saudi, all of which came to an end far too soon.'[1]

On arrival in Saudi Arabia, Charles 'Slim' Wightman, Don Creswick and Pete Hay had found Dick Ingham, a Kiwi who had served on 19, 29 and 92 Squadrons, as chief pilot. 'So he, Don, Pete and I,' recalls 'Slim' Wightman, 'made up the Lightning team, complemented by a similar number of ex-RAF/RN Hunter pilots who flew the Hunter Mk.6s which went with the 'Magic Carpet' contract. Our role was mostly flag waving and escorting the royal flight in and out of Riyadh. During this time we had frequent visits by Roland Beamont, who thrilled us with his antics around the circuit in a Lightning. Eventually came the time when we had to adopt a more operational stance and our numbers were swelled by the arrival of Don Brown, 'Vorn' Radford and Bob Driscoll, all ex-RAF pilots. After moving to Khamis Mushayt, this number was added to by Tony Porrier, an ex-RN pilot who had been flying the Hunters in Riyadh and who went back to Coltishall for the full treatment and somebody Williams, an Airwork stalwart who did a conversion at Warton including a landing during which the undercarriage broke off, breaking his leg. Other than the landing, how did you enjoy your flight Mr Williams?

'When the two year 'Magic Carpet' contract finished, the RSAF offered Thomas Vaughan 'Vorn' Radford and me direct contracts. 'Vorn' was a most astonishing, talented, versatile and entertaining personality. There can be few people associated with Lightnings, at least of the old school, who have not heard of him. He used to do the illustrations and cartoons for the Fighter Command *Flight Safety* magazine and was a founder member of the team of new Lightning pilots on 74 Squadron, the first to be equipped with that aeroplane. Dick Ingham returned to England and served with BAC at Warton doing production test flying and ferry duties until he returned to NZ, where he saw out his working life with an airline. He retired in Auckland. We lived cheek by jowl in adjacent married quarters at Khamis Mushayt for a number of years, although to be honest we had very little time at home. Most of our life was spent on standby at the end of the runway in a tent. The longest time without a break was period of 150 consecutive days in which we didn't see our houses in daylight. Can the modern 'elf and safety' brigade even begin to comprehend what that was like? Five months without even half a day off? Our furniture in the tent consisted of two beds and rickety table and upright chairs. Mostly we lay on the beds with our boots off, reading or sleeping, but this was interspersed with some picture painting by 'Vorn' or typing of procedures on an old style typewriter.

'Occasionally we would get a training flight or air test, but it was barely enough to keep current. In seven years I accumulated the grand total of 500 hours. But we became proficient at leaping into the air in a hurry when a radar target appeared down at the radar station. My fastest time from asleep on the bed to wheels in the well was three and a half minutes though usually it was a bit longer than that because the straps don't always go into the quick release box so readily and the PEC doesn't always mate up with the seat under the guidance of the trembling hand. In all those years I only ever intercepted one stray aeroplane, an AN 12 [Antonov An-12 four-engined turboprop transport aircraft] from a neighbouring country which had the words 'Air Force' hastily and clumsily painted over with 'Airways'. It was bristling with guns at all the turrets. The pilot initially ignored my signals to follow me but it was amusing to see the speed at which his wheels came out after a quick burst of 30mm cannon past his windscreen.

'On 2 May 1970 'Vorn' and I were tasked with staging a demonstration high level interception for a visiting dignitary. My assignment was to lurch off into the distance and return on a heading for the airfield, to be picked up by the radar unit. 'Vorn' was to be scrambled and the ensuing interception would be witnessed by the visitor from the radar room. After take-off, one of the checks is to make sure the ventral tank fuel is flowing into the wings. On this occasion it wasn't; which likely meant a sticking fuel/no air valve. This malfunction could normally be cured readily by application of a bit of positive and negative G, but on this occasion the initial result was that the 'Hyd 1' warning lit up on the AWP, followed shortly by 'Hyd 2' and 'Hyd' on the SWP complete with bells and clangers.

'I continued the climb with minimum use of controls to gain some distance from the ground, but the elevator accumulator gave out almost straight away. It was relatively easy to maintain pitch control using differential engine power settings. However when the aileron accumulator exhausted at 26,000 feet the aircraft slowly rolled over and pointed at the ground. Faced with a supersonic vertical descent and no control, I issued a hasty Mayday and pulled the face blind handle. A hiss of air and sudden decompression was followed by what seemed an age before a severe kick in the pants sent me into the 460 knot airstream. Discarding the face blind, I noticed the seat and I were doing about 120 RPM in an uncontrollable spin. No amount of arm and leg waving made the slightest difference and as I felt like vomiting. I started mentally going through the manual separation procedure, when suddenly the chute opened with a jerk and I was left dangling at 16,500 feet with a lovely view over the desert. Making a note of the time, I started to prepare mentally for the landing which would occur exactly ten minutes later at a height of 7,000 feet AMSL. This area to the east of Khamis Mushayt is made up of gentle hills with no visible vegetation, but covered with sharp, spiky rocks six feet or more in height like a Martian landscape. On this day the surface wind was twenty knots which, combined with the 10,000 foot density altitude, filled me with some misgivings about the landing, particularly in view of the rocks. Needless to say I was swinging like a pendulum in about an 80 degree arc despite my best efforts at pulling on the shroud lines and hit the ground right at the bottom of the arc ensuring maximum downward speed. But my luck was in because I landed smack in the middle of a smooth, hard goat trail between the rocks.

'It was a bad landing, legs astride, knees up around the ears and with my face planted firmly in the dirt, giving me a bloody nose, a manoeuvre I have not been able to replicate since and which no doubt was the cause of one rib to break off at the spine. Right in front of me on the path was a shepherdess and her raggedy flock. With my strange costume and bloody face she probably thought it was the second coming of a prophet or a visitation from another planet because she shrieked, threw her arms into the air and sped off up the path followed by her sheep. She must have told her experience to her husband or father because in no time a red Ford pickup truck came bouncing across the desert in a cloud of dust with a friendly man who asked if I needed help. I explained that it wouldn't be long before my friends arrived with a helicopter to pick me up and sent him on his way, an action which I nearly came to rue very badly because my SARBE was set to a training frequency and nobody picked up the signal. It was only by luck that I was spotted some hours later by a helicopter.

'After taking leave of the truck driver, I spread out the parachute under a circle of stones and struggled up a small hill to plant the SARBE as high as possible, intending to return later for the survival pack so that I could play with the heliograph and eat the goodies. But by the time I reached the top of the hill I couldn't walk and realised that both ankles were sprained. So there I sat, watching Saudi Airlines, Air Force C-130s and other aircraft all obviously doing a search. How easy it would have been with the SARBE working or even if I had had the heliograph. As I was pondering my folly of not keeping in touch with the truck driver, I heard the thrumming of an Augusta Bell 212 and to my great relief it plopped down next to the parachute. From there I was able to hail the pilot, my friend Farouk and his crewman who carried me down the hill. Strange to relate, the aircraft remained airborne for fifteen minutes after the ejection, five minutes longer than I was on the end of the parachute and it landed the right way up in a very shallow descent so that it was sufficiently undamaged to discover at least one of the control hydraulic systems was still full of hydraulic fluid. So, it looks as though if I had stayed with the aircraft I would have been able to make a relatively normal recovery to base. If only – I would have been spared a sore back. Anyway in exactly a fortnight I was back in the air and life went on.

'Vorn's wife had their first daughter during our time there. My wife and I already had three small children. It was tough with no school or medical services of the sort we were accustomed to, so when my wife became pregnant again in 1973, we had to move on. But it had been a most interesting period in our lives, flying with some very talented people, ex-RAF and Saudis.'

On 10 August 1977 Brian Carroll and a student Lightning pilot flew a trip in a Mk.53. 'Weather conditions were reasonable, though not good enough to launch a full programme. Selected student pilots who were well into the conversion course were briefed and authorised to fly certain instrument flying sorties. By late morning I was airborne on a weather recce, some twenty minutes ahead of one solo student. Horizontal visibility was poor at around 2,000 yards in dust and blowing sand, while look-down visibility was good from 30,000 feet. The effect of this was that from altitude it was impossible to see ground features other those directly below and then only by entering a steep turn, bearing in mind that one sand dune looks pretty much like any other. The student involved had been well briefed and should have been flying in an area some fifty to eighty miles to the south of the base. The student, having been airborne for nearly forty minutes, made a call on the R/T to the effect that he was lost. Ground radar were unable to locate him, his TACAN would not lock and he could see nothing of the ground.

'At this time I attempted to obtain a bearing on him, assuming that he was approximately in the area to which he had been designated, but repeated attempts to get a bearing failed. I instructed him to head east in an attempt to pick up the coast and to use his airborne radar as an aid. This he did and managed to glimpse parts of the coastline, though nothing that he could recognise. Again, assuming that he had to be south of the base I suggested that he make a northerly heading, keeping the coastline in sight if at all possible. By now I was short of fuel and had little option but to recover and land. By the time I had landed and reached our operations centre it was fairly certain that our 'lost' student had to be on the ground one way or another. He either had to have landed (!), bailed out or crashed, since his fuel would by this time have been used up. A full rescue operation had been put into effect. This included an American-manned C-130 that was now on its way to us in preparation for a co-ordinated search pattern to be set up.

'Ninety minutes after the student had taken off the phone rang in our operations room. On the other end was our lost pilot. He had landed at an airfield, the name of which was unknown to me and indeed, to everyone else in the room. He was able to give us its approximate location and plans were made to fly in a recovery team in the C-130 to pick him up and to see whether it was possible to fly the Lightning out. I say possible, because the landing strip that he had found was only 3,300 feet long and made of soft tarmacadam. They had never heard of the term LCN. With all the kit we had on board, even the C-130 pilot got quite excited at the prospect of making a landing on so short a strip.

'The Lightning was parked, or perhaps 'planted' is a better word, at one end of the strip, the main wheels nearly buried in the tarmac. Otherwise it looked OK. When I asked the student how he had managed to stop on so short a runway, he told me that for a brief few moments, i.e. as he was touching down, a surface wind of 70 knots was recorded, straight down the runway heading. Prior to and immediately following his arrival there was no wind at all! Hence my opening remarks!! It makes you think, or it did me.

'Recovery was the next concern. We had taken some PSP with us and managed to get the aircraft sitting safely on it prior to a thorough check out and a refuel. An examination of the landing strip by courtesy of the local Emir's large limousine showed that the strip was rather uneven, definitely softish and was indeed slightly over 0.6 of a mile in length, somewhat shortish for a Lightning. The aircraft proved to be OK and refuelling was commenced by hand. This took several hours, by which time the ground crew were knackered.

'I made the decision that recovery of the aircraft was just feasible given cool conditions early the following morning, some sort of breeze along the strip and only internal fuel. We did, in fact, put approximately 500lbs into the ventral. This would allow just enough fuel to get back to base but keep the weight low enough to get airborne. Finally, I directed that the aircraft be positioned at the extreme end of the strip, overhanging the landing surface and on a section of PSP, thereby giving the maximum possible take off run.

'The following morning conditions were as good as we could have hoped for, though the breeze was only about two knots. The C-130 positioned at the far end of the strip and the Lightning was fed to the start of the strip. All the local dignitaries were in attendance and all our goading to keep further away from the aircraft (they were within five feet of the wingtips) fell on deaf ears, or at least they were about to be deaf once engines were running and the re-lit engaged; ground starter failed to function and a start was successfully made on internal batteries. I calculated that I needed

3,000 feet to unstick and should I fail, that I would eject. The C-130 crew nearly had kittens as I lifted off with a few feet to spare. As for the Emir and his entourage, well, they nearly lost their robes, head-dresses and everything else as the re-heats re-engaged prior to rolling and the Lightning disappeared in a miniature dust storm of its own, only to re-appear like a phoenix a couple of miles away.

'Journey back was OK apart from a main instrument and a services pressure failure. This, combined with the weather state going to RED while I was some ten minutes out with visibility restricted to 1,000 yards, made it a very interesting couple of days. We never found out why or how the student found himself north of his briefed area and as for the 70 knot wind, that remains very much an unknown.[2]

'In Saudi Arabia in June 1981 I was privileged to hold the post of Chief Flying Instructor at Dhahran, where we operated F.53 and T.55 Lightnings. The weather was fairly standard for Saudi, very hot (100 degrees in the shade), clear skies and a moderate wind. The aircraft involved was a T.55 (1316). A new course of Saudi students had nearly completed their school training and were looking forward to their first taste of the real thing. This particular sortie was always known as the 'Instructors' Benefit Ride', since the student was assigned to the RHS and simply had to sit back and enjoy the ride while the instructor demonstrated the flight envelope of the aircraft.

'The briefing covered a re-heat take off and climb to 36,000 feet; turn performance in cold and hot power; a supersonic dash to around 1.5 Mach; high rate descent to 2,000 feet; speed handling, i.e. below 200 knots with the undercarriage lowered; level acceleration at 2,000 feet to 600 knots pulling into a re-heat, near vertical climb, aiming to level at followed by a standard recovery to base for a couple of circuits and a landing.

'Initially, all went to plan, the student being duly impressed. We had just entered vertical climb following the maximum rate low level acceleration when the 'Re-Heat 1' fire warning light came on; red lights flashing and the 'clangers' ringing out loud and clear. Both re-heats were immediately cancelled and No 1 engine closed down with No. 2 at idle as we levelled at about 22,000 feet. Full emergency drills were completed and a Mayday Dhahran was acknowledged, including the fact that we were eighty miles SSW of base. During the preceding few minutes, my student had calmly opened his emergency flip card and asked if all the necessary actions had been taken. We then went through them again sure that nothing had been omitted. Needless to say, nothing had. The student then asked what we should do. My response was 'Do Not Panic'.

A 'MAGIC CARPET' RIDE

'Our recovery continued towards Dhahran in a slow glide maintaining sufficient power to keep the AC supplies on line. At around 8,000 feet the Re-Heat warning light was still on and a bail out was looking ever more likely. Nine minutes later (it seemed more like nine hours) it finally went out. We were now over the Gulf on a straight in approach with 45 miles to go to touch down. The flying controls continued to function normally and I therefore decided that a landing was possible, though we would both eject should the controls show any sign of stiffening. A high approach path was set up to give a little more height advantage should the situation deteriorate. With eight miles still to go, I lowered the undercarriage and started the final approach. At this moment, the main flight instruments began to fail; not a good sign. AC power was lost and we were close to flying on the proverbial wing and a prayer. At three miles, the standby instruments also started to fail and just before touchdown all the electrics had quit. We vacated the aircraft at the end of the runway with the assistance of the ground crew and fire department.

'On inspection, the rear end of the aircraft was still burning, molten metal dripping onto the hardstanding. The plane was declared Cat 3+. Some 182 days later I flew 1316 (713) again on an Air Test following a near total rebuild. Two sorties, a total of one hour thirty minutes proved the aircraft to be fully serviceable again, a credit to our engineers.

'My student, who by now was operational on Lightnings at another Saudi air base, had a repeat experience in a F.53, a 'Re-Heat 1' fire plus all the rest. He landed successfully and when I spoke to him over the phone and asked him about it he said 'Sir, I Did Not Panic'.

'Looking back, I guess the actual emergency only lasted twenty minutes, but it seemed like a month. As for my student, I think he learned his lesson well.'[3]

Brian Carroll[4]

The Lightnings of the Royal Saudi Air Force returned to the United Kingdom in January 1986. In all, 22 aircraft were scheduled for return in five waves of four aircraft and one wave of four. They were all air tested in January by Tony Winship of BAC and were duly declared ready for the seven hour return flight to this country. It was planned for the operation to be carried out in two parts with each wave of aircraft initially accompanied by a VC-10 tanker. Latterly, air-to-air refuelling support was provided by four Victor tankers that had been deployed to Palermo in Sicily for the task. Prior to the recovery operation, the Lightnings were cleaned and polished and their national markings erased. UK national markings and specially allocated serials were then applied by BAC together with refuelling probes provided from the spares held at RAF Binbrook. This was the first time the Saudi Lightnings had carried air-to-air refuelling probes since their delivery flights eighteen years earlier. Four VC-10 aircraft were deployed to Tabuk on 11 January 1986 taking with them fourteen Lightning pilots (two were 'spare') from both of Binbrook's resident Lightning squadrons. On the same day the four Victors flew to Palermo/Punta Raisi. The return flights were scheduled to take seven hours and to that end seven air-to-air fuel transfers were planned. On each occasion approximately 4,000lbs of fuel was to be transferred to the Lightnings. All of the Lightnings made successful and relatively uneventful return flights. One particular pilot, having reached the top of the climb, arranged the contents of his 'doggy' bag on the combing above the instrument panel and planned the way he would sustain himself over the seven hour flight. On arrival in England all 22 Lightnings were immediately placed into open storage[5] and over the next four years corroded in the salty air of Warton airfield.

Chapter 12

Last of the Lightnings

The Lightning was an exceptional aircraft in every respect, but XR749 was one of the best of the best. It is probably the best aircraft that I will ever have had the privilege to fly. Because of her tail code 'BM', she was known as 'Big Mother', although the tail code changed to BO for her last few months on 11 before joining the LTF in January 1985. She was a very hot ship, even for a Lightning. She remained my aircraft for all her time on 11 Squadron despite my being entitled to an F.6 as I moved up the squadron pecking order. I invariably asked for her to be allocated to me for the major exercises such as 'Mallet Blow', 'Osex' and 'Elder Forest' despite her being a short range F.3 – there were invariably plenty of tankers about!

In April 1984, during a squadron exchange at Binbrook, XR749 participated in unofficial time-to-height and acceleration trials against F-104 Starfighters from Aalborg. The Lightnings won all races easily, with the exception of the low level supersonic acceleration, which was a dead-heat. This is not surprising when the records show that the year before on one sortie XR749 accelerated to Mach 2.3 (1,500 mph) in September 1983. It was also in 1984, during a major NATO exercise that he intercepted an American U-2 at 66,000 feet; a height which they had previously considered safe from interception. Shortly before this intercept, he flew a zoom climb to 88,000 feet and later that year he was able to sustain FL550 while flying subsonic. Life was not entirely without problems, however, as in a three month period his No. 2 engine seized in flight and its replacement failed during a take-off when intake panelling on the inside of the aircraft became detached and was sucked into the engine.

In April 1985, British Airways were trialling a Concorde up and down the North Sea. When they offered it as a target to NATO fighters, Mike spent the night in the hangar polishing XR749 which he borrowed from the LTF for the occasion and the next day overhauled Concorde at 57,000 feet, travelling at Mach 2.2 by flying a stern conversion intercept. Everyone had a bash – F-15s, F-16s, F-14s, Mirage, F-104s – but only the Lightning managed to overhaul Concorde from behind.

The official ceiling for a Lightning was 60,000+ feet, although it was well known within the RAF to be capable of much greater heights. The late Brian Carroll reported taking an F.53 Lightning up to 87,300 feet at which level 'Earth curvature was visible and the sky was quite dark'. Flight Lieutenant Mike Hale flew 80 sorties in XR749 after the aircraft was allocated to 11 Squadron at Binbrook.[1] Mike Hale also participated in time-to-height and acceleration trials against F-104 Starfighters from Aalborg. The Lightnings won all races easily, with the exception of the low level supersonic acceleration, which was a dead-heat.[2]

'The original concept of the Lightning,' recalled Flight Lieutenant Iain Small, formerly on XI Squadron,[3] 'was for a very quick reaction interceptor that excelled at high altitude and high supersonic speed. The envisaged targets in the early days were the high altitude and sometimes supersonic Soviet bombers. Well, the Lightning certainly did excel in that environment, but with the introduction of the F.2 to Germany in 1964 and later the F.2A, the aircraft was to encounter new threats. Gütersloh, being very close to the East German border, meant that quick reaction and high speed were still important, but in the event of hostilities the targets would not be the high altitude bomber but the fighter bomber with a MiG fighter escort. The Lightning became a very potent dog fighter and the second-to-none reputation of the Gütersloh squadrons is legend.

'With the realisation of a possible fighter threat to the UK, with longer range Soviet fighters with tanker support and also more recently aircraft carriers, the UK squadrons also carried out Air Combat Training. The squadrons could also be deployed world-wide where they might be up against fighters.

'Air Combat Training on XI Squadron in the 1980s initially took place mostly in the Lightning F.3. The F.6 by this time was a good way through its fatigue life and the remaining fatigue had to be looked after very carefully. The F.3 had a better power to weight ratio than the F.6, as it was considerably lighter and the handling was slightly different due to the different wing plan form. The down side of the F.3 was a lot less fuel. With about 5,000lbs of combat fuel available after takeoff and with a burn rate of 1,000lbs per minute, it was not unknown for a total flight time of ten minutes which included only five minutes of combat training ten miles away from base. It doesn't sound much, but it was a very exciting ten minutes and a lot could be learnt. Later, when some of the F.6s were given modifications to extend their fatigue life, we could stay in combat much longer.

'The incredible aerodynamic performance and excellent handling qualities of the Lightning meant that it was a very good performer in the air combat arena. It would always do extremely well against all RAF adversaries and indeed most of NATO. Only when up against aircraft such as the F-15 and F-16 would we lose the performance advantage – that's where tactics came into play.

'Generally in air combat, the maximum speeds achieved were about Mach 1.1 to M 1.2, but for most of the fight it would be much less than that. With its superb power to weight ratio, the Lightning would accelerate very quickly at around 25 knots per second at low level. In a turning fight, a very respectable turn rate of 12° per second could be sustained in maximum reheat, pulling 6G at around 450 to 480 knots. Slightly higher instantaneous rates of around 14° could be achieved at 400 knots, this being very useful to avoid a missile for example.

'One particularly impressive aspect of the Lightning was its performance in the vertical plane. The aircraft had an initial climb rate of around 50,000 feet per minute and in a turning fight at low level could sustain a 5G turn and still climb at 18,000 feet per minute. Clearly, if other aircraft were struggling to sustain 5-6G in a level turn at low level, the Lightning would be able to climb as well as turn, thus allowing more freedom of manoeuvre.

'The problem area for the Lightning in combat was without doubt its weapons system and radar. Optimised for medium to high altitude intercepts against bomber targets, the system left a certain amount to be desired. Against a fighter, the AI.23, being a pulse radar, had a very limited range of about 15-20 miles looking up and looking down suffered from ground clutter which reduced the pickup range considerably. In its favour was the fact that its high sweep rate and ease of handling were ideal for air combat, where the targets would be manoeuvring wildly both in direction and altitude.

'In air combat the radar would be used on the run-in to the fight to try and get the target visual. Once visual the radar would largely be redundant unless the target was lost, possibly flying through cloud or towards the sun. Without a Head Up Display giving target information, the most difficult aspect of the fight would sometimes be trying to convert a blip on the radar to a visual target outside. The missiles, both Firestreak and Red Top, had to be fired within a narrow cone of the target's jet pipe and could be used if the targets were not evading too hard. Once in a hard turning fight, the guns were the primary weapon.

'Lightning tactics on XI Squadron in the 1980s involved primarily a pair of aircraft and most of our training involved fighting against dissimilar types. Typically, a fight would be a 2 v 2, but other options such as 2 v 1, 1 v 2 and 2 v 4 would also be practised. Transits to the combat patrol area would be at a fuel-economical 360 knots. Once on the combat patrol, 400 knots would provide reasonable economy but with good instantaneous turning ability if bounced. When engaged in a combat, ideally the speed would be about 450-480 knots for best turning performance. This is a good speed to fight in a high threat environment with lots of targets, as it leaves many options available. Once engaged in the proverbial 'knife fight in a telephone box' against a single target at slow speed, it is very easy to be shot by another unseen hostile aircraft. In a 2 v 2, the ideal situation would be for a pair of Lightnings to kill one target, giving each other support and then go on to kill the other. More often, the fight would degenerate into two 1 v 1 combats, probably close enough for an element of support to be given.

'In February 1985, Sea Harriers from Yeovilton and Hawks from Chivenor had been invited up to Binbrook for a week of combat and tactics discussions, normally held in the Blacksmith's Arms at Rothwell. On 6 February I flew XS904 on a 1 v 2 v 2 combat against Sea Harriers and Hawks; a very hostile environment. The Hawk is a very small agile fighter with good missiles and is very difficult to pick up. The Sea Harrier is not quite so agile, but has a very good weapons system. The plan was to fly the combat over the North Sea just to the south of Flamborough Head with the help of one of the east coast Air Defence Radar sites. The Lightning Wing at Binbrook had a very close liaison with the controllers (I actually married one!) who were very adept at the type of control we needed.

'The fight started with the three elements split by 20 miles on each corner of an imaginary triangle. Running in from my start point just subsonic at 0.95M the controller started giving me information on the other two formations. I decided to aim at the Hawk formation. As they were without radar I had a chance of a quick kill without being seen. If we got tangled up with the Hawks for any length of time the Sea Harriers would come in and kill everyone.

'As the controller called the Hawks at eight miles and at slightly higher level, I picked them up on the radar. At this stage the Red Tops had been armed, but the guns were elected for firing. The selector to change from missiles to guns was on the right hand console. This was not a terrific place for it, especially when pulling 6G with your right hand on the control column. By keeping guns selected, they would always be live for a guns kill or a lucky snap shot and if a missile shot did present itself it was then not a problem to make the selection. Approaching the merge I managed to get visual with one of the Hawks, but not the other. I had the throttles back at idle to give a low heat picture to their Sidewinder 9L missiles. As it would be suicidal to turn in on one Hawk, I selected full reheat and accelerated straight through. The controller called that the Hawks had not turned in on me but were heading for the Sea Harriers.

'When ten miles clear, I turned back in and was immediately given a vector by the controller. The Hawks and Sea Harriers were now fighting each other and had split into two 1 v 1 fights separated by five miles or so. I ran in towards one of the fights and picked them both up at about five miles. A change to missiles and with the sight now on the jet pipe of the Hawk, the Red Top acquired. I gave the call "Fox 2, Hawk left hand turn at 8,000 feet." The Sea Harrier quickly turned into me to try for a shot. I again put the throttles to idle to counter the Sidewinder and passed him head to head very close. Another maximum reheat acceleration took me clear of the Sea Harrier and towards the south-west and home, as usual with no spare fuel remaining.

'A thirty minute flight, ten minutes of combat, with one kill achieved and no claim against. Not a bad result, but what it could have been with a pair of Sidewinder 9Ls!'[4]

Group Captain John Spencer describes a combat scenario: 'The Mission is a 2 v 2 air combat training sortie against two American F-5E 'Tigers' from the Aggressor Squadron at RAF Alconbury.[5] Your call signs are '25' and '26' and your opponents are '51' and '52'. After a comprehensive briefing by your leader, which includes the comparative advantages and disadvantages of each type, you sign the authorisation sheet and the aircraft servicing document and climb aboard. A check around the cockpit reveals all is well and you start the engines in response to your leader's order. Dial flickers into life, warning lights go out and as everything looks OK you close the canopy and taxi out behind the leader. Pre-take off vital actions are completed, the radar is set up and you line up in echelon starboard. A final check as you run up the engines, then the leader nods his head and away you go. Another nod and you select reheat and juggle the throttles to maintain position as you accelerate down the runway at something better than ten knots a second. Lift off, retract the undercarriage and flaps and you widen into battle formation. In line abreast, you climb swiftly and easily to 15,000 feet making sure everything is still working as it should and changing radio frequencies from local to departure control. Level now, with the other Lightning a mile and a half away on your starboard beam and the weather is perfect.

'Just a few flecks of high cirrus cloud and excellent visibility, Grimsby is sliding under your port wing, Spurn Point is ahead. North, you can see the pointing finger of Flamborough Head and south, the curve of The Wash, is visible as you head out north-easterly at eight miles a minute to your operating area. Departure tells you that your control agency, the radar station at Staxton Wold, has you in contact and you change frequency to call them.[6] "Staxton, 25 and 26 coasting out heading 050 at flight level 150."

'Roger 21, 51 and 52 are 45 miles ahead and we have thirty miles to run to the area.'

'OK, you think, time to relax a little and make sure everything's ready for the combat: Fuel, engines, radar, sight system all look good. Seat adjusted to give the best look out, a quick mental recap of the game plan and you are all set.

'From Staxton: "You are now entering the area, Vector 010, 51 and 52 are turning left onto a southerly heading, fight's on"'.

'A last check of the switches, missiles selected and armed, radar searching in long range and nothing wrong in the cockpit as you hit the stop watch. In accordance with your plan, the leader increases power and starts a descent to 5,000 feet and you slip into trail behind him, trusting to Staxton to guard your vulnerable stern area.

'"Targets right, range 30, close pair at 28,000 feet," from Staxton.

'Speed now 540 knots indicated, 0.95 Mach and the leader is two to three miles ahead. You're closing with the targets at twenty miles a minute as you search intently with the radar to pick them up.

'Range now 25, still slightly right, still high but widening to two or three miles.'

'The controller is giving just the right amount of information and seems reassuringly on the ball.

'Your leader chips in: "Two contacts, dead ahead and five right, range 23, 10 high". You look hard into the radar; ah yes, there they are, splitting even wider now, five miles apart: The westerly man five degrees left at twenty miles and the other 10 degrees right, same range. Maybe they're trying a pincer or maybe a drag, soon know now.

'From Staxton: "Easterly man descending through 20 and turning towards, westerly man heading 240 and still high."'

'Looks like a drag you think, as your leader turns hard to the northwest to try and put both opponents onto the same side.

'Range 15 on the westerly man, 17 on the other who is still descending.

'From your leader: "Going for the one on the left"'.

'Select reheat, climbing hard now towards the high man.

'From Staxton: Easterly man, still heading south, now north east, 15 miles'.

'The question is whether you can engage and kill one target before the other threatens you.

'From your leader: "Eight miles 10 right, high"'.

'You look away from the radar scope and concentrate on a visual search for the small target, using the leaders prompting: Nothing yet.

'From your leader: "Five miles dead ahead but no tally"'.

'From Staxton: "Easterly man coming back west ten miles"'.

'The trap is beginning to spring. Search, search, search; still nothing. From the leader: "Tally, my 11 o'clock high, turning hard left"'.

'Where the hell is he, you mutter, horribly aware of the other one now behind you and therefore dangerous.

'Got him! The small darting shape is in your 11 o'clock slightly high turning hard left and diving gently. Your leader is also turning hard left in pursuit but is almost 180 degrees out in relation to the F-5.

'Has the F-5 seen you? You pull up steeply, trying to hide in the impartial glare of the sun in your 6 o'clock, watching intently. The F-5 is still turning hard left and now you can see his pale underside, as he slips under your nose at less than a mile range. He hasn't seen you and the advantage is yours. You roll right, picking him up again one o'clock low. But now, either seeing you or warned by his friend, he reverses into a hard right turn. You notice your leader turning back towards you and transmit a quick 'Tally one and visual' to tell him that you can see him and one of the enemy. You spiral down in pursuit of the F-5, the G forces pulling you down in your seat, tunnelling your vision as the blood drains from your brain.

'From Staxton: "Easterly man range five and closing"'.

'Your F-5 has reacted in time and is now trying to drag you across and ahead of the other one. No you don't, you mutter and transmitting: "Coming off left"'.

'You reverse to face the second F-5. Where is he?'

'From your leader: 'I'm in your left eight o'clock high'. And you look there and see the solid shape of the Lightning.

'"Roger, visual but no tally", you call.

'OK, we'll bug out on east for separation'.

'Good idea you think, but then: "Tally one, your four o'clock low, turning in."'

'You break hard right, searching frantically. There he is, your leader's call had been just in time and the roundabout starts again. The F-5 is now in your three o'clock about 1,500 yards trying to pull his nose onto you.

'Keep turning', your leader calls and now it is you trying to drag the F-5 in front of your leader. But the F-5 realises the danger and flicks away to pass beak-to-beak with '25'. You continue.

'Turning right to keep him in sight but what about the other one? Right on cue, Staxton comes back with: "Merged, with one out to the west four miles, heading back."'

'By dint of hard, painful lookout you've kept contact now in your three o'clock low two miles away, turning left through a northerly heading and again fortune has put you up sun as you continue your hard right turn towards him.

'The westerly F-5 now flashes through the middle of the fur ball pulling up and turning right as your leader calls:

'Tally two and visual'.

'Good, you think as you concentrate on your F-5. You're now in his eight o'clock and at this height, 12,000 feet; the Lightning's greater power has kept your speed higher than that of your opponent. But he is still dangerous as he turns towards you and the angle-off builds up. No chance of a shot, so you roll off and pull up into a yo-yo. The F-5 slices past below you and reverses nose high to counter your manoeuvre. But you have the speed he hasn't.

'You keep your nose high, passing over the top of him then barrel-roll hard into him, kicking lots of top rudder to speed the roll and stop the nose from dropping.

'It works and you slide into his six o'clock, turning after him some 500-600 yards behind.

'From the radio you are aware that '25' and the other F-5 are sparring with each other above you somewhere, but your entire world and all your conscious attention is now focussed solely on the F-5 dancing in front of you. You are too close for a missile shot so you select guns and try to pull the pipper onto him. It's not easy. Like any good fighter pilot, he is not giving up. He breaks into a steep descending right-hand spiral, gaining speed and piling on the G.

'You follow trying to pull enough lead and close the range. One moment you are 6,000 feet 500 knots right on the G limit: The next the F-5 has pulled up steeply, feathers of condensation trailing from his wings, as he aims to lose you in the hard brilliance of the sun. You squint frantically, blinking rapidly to stop the sweat stinging in your eyes. You manoeuvre hard to avoid losing sight of him and you just spot his cunning turn reversal.

'The next moment you are both topping out at 26,000 feet, the speed dropping dangerously as you both try desperately to avoid letting the nose drop, which would give the other the advantage. Gently, gently on the controls, small delicate movements to avoid stalling as you both hang there.

'Once again though, the Lightning's superior power gives you the edge and almost lazily, the F-5's nose falls.

'You roll gently inverted and drop onto him. The speed and G build up again; high G reversals, violent jinks, negative G, rapid rolls; he uses all of them to fight you off and only by total concentration and anticipation do you manage to achieve even fleeting opportunities to fire.

'Eventually though, luck throws the 'dice your way and had you been firing bullets rather than taking cine pictures, he would have been destroyed.

'You transmit 'Fox 3 kill' and rather thankfully, pull away from him.

'Now is the greatest danger, because all your efforts have been needed to win the fight, you have lost virtually any idea of what else has been going on: your situational awareness is close to zero and until you pick up the threads, you are totally vulnerable. Luckily your leader, whilst fighting off the other F-5 has kept his situational awareness and tells you what to do: "Come right onto 210, I'm in your five o'clock high two miles with the other one."

'You look for him and see him and call visual as he comes into your 12 o'clock high.

'"Passing beak-to-beak and bugging out now," he calls.

'He and the F-5 pass head-on and the Lightning drops its nose into a shallow dive to pick up speed and disengage.

'You do the same, descending to 5,000 feet, watching the F-5. You call a turn away from the F-5 sufficient to bring you into line abreast with your leader and regain defensive battle formation. Fuel, always a problem, is now down to little above the minimum for recovery. In the eight minutes since you started the stopwatch, you have used over 600 gallons. You use what little reserve you have to leave the area and the F-5 at high speed.

'Your leader tells Staxton that: 25 and 26 are now RTB through the slot; will free call Binbrook'.

'Staxton acknowledges and you change to Binbrook direction. 'Frequently, climbing to 16,000 feet to transit through the slot in the Bravo One airway.

'"Binbrook 25 and 26 recovering via Alpha".

'Roger 25, Binbrook is blue, no restrictions, Waddington is crash, what sort of recovery?'

'"Visual, will call you going stud one".

'You cruise back, tired but very satisfied. You muster-up enough concentration for the approach, circuit and landing and taxi-in. It's good to open the canopy and savour the coolness, it's good to drop the oxygen mask from your face and breathe in the fresh air. You reflect on the sortie. Today the luck was on your side, tomorrow it may not be. It was hard work, physically and mentally, but there is nowhere you would rather be, no job you would rather do and nobody in the world whose lot you envy.'[7]

'The most lasting impression gained by anyone who has ever flown a Lightning,' recalled Wing Commander Jake Jarron, Commanding Officer of 11 Squadron, the last Lightning unit, 'is the sheer brute power and manoeuvrability of the machine. From its very inception as the English Electric PI, the aircraft has had incredible power, unlike the Buccaneer, Hunter and others which entered service low on power and which were gradually developed to take more powerful engines. Of course the Lightning has had its share of development but this was concerned more with the avionics, weapons systems and airframe rather than the engines.

'The early marks, namely the F.1/A, F.2 and T.4, bore the Ferranti AI.23 radar, could only carry Firestreak missiles and had more basic avionics than the later marks, the F.3, T.5 and F.6. These later marks initially had the improved AI.23B radar which has since evolved into AI.23D and which has many refinements and extensions over the original model. These aircraft also had a completely redesigned cockpit bearing improved avionics including a very capable autopilot, radar altimeter and an integrated flight information system. The late marks were also capable of carrying the Red Top missile which gave the aircraft a limited head-on capability and the F.6 regained the two Aden cannons of the earlier marks but this time installed in the ventral fuel tank instead of in the front of the cockpit in the F.1 and F.2/A. The most significant airframe development was the introduction of the cambered wing and large ventral tank of the F.2A and F.6. This wing gave better low speed handling and of course the larger tank eased the Lightning's Achilles heel, its dreadful shortage of fuel.

'But, back to flying.

'Before take-off the brakes are checked at 92 per cent, power and then brakes are released and the throttles advanced to full reheat. The aircraft accelerates quickly and reaches the unstick speed of 175 knots in about eighteen seconds. Once airborne, with the undercarriage and flaps retracted the light, responsive nature of the aeroplane becomes obvious. Throughout the flight envelope, the aircraft is light and pleasant to fly and despite its rather unconventional wing shape it has remarkably few vices.

'The Lightning's main weakness is its short range and a question often asked is "How long is the average sortie?"

'At high level on a subsonic sortie the aircraft is at its most economical and an F.6 will be able to complete a sortie of about 75 minutes. A gentle sortie at low level will last about 55 minutes but an aggressive low level sortie can be as low as thirty minutes and a full blooded combat can use up fuel so quickly that the sortie can be over twelve minutes. At the lower altitudes around 5,000 feet in full reheat the engines are using around 90 gallons a minute – yes, a minute!

'When you consider that the aircraft takes off with only 1,200 gallons and must land with 200 gallons simple arithmetic shows that such a sortie will not last long. It does, however, provide excellent training for the pilots and is extremely demanding, exhausting but thoroughly enjoyable and it is on the type of combat sortie that the full magic of flying the Lightning is realised. One instant answer to the fuel problem is provided by air-to-air refuelling (AAR) and Lightning pilots quickly become very adept at this technique which not only keeps them in practice but which also very effectively extends sorties allowing much more training to be carried out.

'AAR is often likened to riding a bicycle; once you can do it, it presents no problem but the first few attempts can be hair-raising! It is a common fallacy that the tanker's hose has a magnet in it to help it connect to the receiving aircraft's refuelling probe. This is not so and AAR is a pure formation flying exercise where smoothness and careful trimming of the aircraft are necessary. Eventually pilots are able to refuel at any altitude, day or night, straight or turning and even with no radio communication with the tanker.

'A typical flight profile after refuelling might be a high flyer interception which again demonstrates one of the Lightning's strong points. The Lightning can operate at around 50,000 feet subsonic and supersonic up to 60,000 feet plus, which is infinitely better than the Phantom or even many newer aircraft.

'Its supersonic performance is also impressive and the F.6 can still reach Mach 2; indeed each time a Lightning is taken up for an engine air test following work on the engines, part of the required flight profile is to accelerate to Mach 1.8 so, although old, it is an extremely fast fighter.

'At the bottom end of the speed range the Lightning is also remarkably manoeuvrable, unlike many aircraft with a high wing sweep. In combat it can be flown aggressively down to speeds as low as 180 knots (officially!) but the pilot does have to exercise care. Badly handled at such speeds the aircraft will spin; however, she is a kindly old girl and will normally give sufficient warning which allows the pilot to take the necessary action to stop the spin developing. If the spin does develop then conventional spin recovery actions are effective but the aircraft loses a great deal of height very quickly.

'Of course at the end of any sortie there has to be a landing and landing the Lightning can have its interesting moments. The touchdown speed is 165 knots and there is little margin for error. Land too fast and there is a danger of a drag chute failure and subsequent stopping problems; land too slow and you can scrape the tail which in turn can also lead to a drag chute failure etc!

'Crosswind landings are particularly interesting. The one-up, one-down arrangement of the engines and big angular fin give the aircraft a large side area which, together with the high wing sweep, the differential braking system for steering and the weather-cocking effect of the drag chute, combine to produce a rapidly changing set of forces which the pilot must counter quickly and accurately if he is to keep the aircraft on the runway. Let's just say that landing at night, in rain, on a wet runway in a high crosswind was one of the Lightning's less attractive features!

'For all her foibles though there is no doubt that for all the pilots who have flown and operated the Lightning, that wonderful aircraft will have a special place in their heart, whatever else they might fly.

'She was a true thoroughbred, the last of a great line of British single-seat fighters.

'She may be gone but she will not be forgotten.'[8]

LAST OF THE LIGHTNINGS

The last Lightnings flying anywhere in the world were Mike 'Beachy' Head's Lightnings in his family of seven Hunters, three Buccaneers, four English Electric Lightnings and one Strikemaster in the Thunder City operation at Cape Town International Airport in South Africa. On 14 November 2009 Dave Stock, 46, of Hermanus was flying solo in Lightning T5 ZU-BEX, (XS451) during a display at the annual Overberg Air Show in Bredasdorp when the aircraft's ejection seat failed. Stock tried to eject, but according to a transcript included in the report of the crash, his last words were: 'Ejection seat failure, ejection seat failure, tell her I love her very much.' Scores of spectators saw the aircraft plunge to the ground. On 22 August 2011 the three remaining Lightnings, three Buccaneers and four Hunters were listed as 'for sale by private treaty' when Thunder City shut down the operation blaming the financial climate and inconsistencies in how the South African CAA applied their regulations.

Bruntingthorpe airfield, Leicestershire, is now the only place in Britain where one can see a Lightning fire up its Avons. The Lightning Preservation Group has been fortunate in acquiring the former Wattisham QRA shed to house its pair of Lightnings. The Q Shed is one of only three in the UK, the other two being at Leuchars and Binbrook. The Q Shed was donated by Trafalgar House Construction, who also paid for its dismantling at Wattisham.

Appendix

Lightning Units

5 Squadron

Motto: *Frangas non flectas* ('Thou mayst break, but shall not bend me').

Command Assignments: Fighter Command Interceptor Alert Force; UK Air Defence Region (Southern) Aircraft: F.6 (12.65-12.87); F.1A (6.70-9.72); F.3 (10.72-9.87) Station: Binbrook (12.65-1.5.88).

History: Disbanded at Geilenkirchen, RAF Germany (Javelin FAW.9), on 7.10.65, reforming the next day at RAF Binbrook to begin re-equipment on the Lightning. T.5 XS451/T arrived first, on 19.11.65, followed on 10.12.65 by XR755/A and XR756/B, the first (interim) F.6s, so becoming the first RAF squadron to operate the type. Last of twelve interim F.6s arrived on 8.3.66, the squadron becoming fully operational late that year. XS894/F, first full F.6 standard aircraft, arrived on 3.1.67, the full complement being completed by spring 1967. Took part in 'Adex 67', being based at Luqa, Malta from 6 to 26 October. In May 1968 four F.6s flew non-stop from Binbrook-Bahrain in eight hours, refuelled along the 4,000-mile route by Victor tankers from RAF Marham. Won the Dacre Trophy (awarded to the top UK fighter squadron in weapons proficiency) in 1968 and 1969. Ten F.6s flew to RAF Tengah, Singapore in December 1969 for joint air-defence exercises with other Lightnings and RAAF Mirages there. Participated in local defence exercises in Singapore in 1970, exchanging and returning with some Lightnings from 74 Squadron which were in need of major overhaul. Won the Huddleston Trophy (best interceptor squadron in NATO) in the AFCENT Air Defence Competition, 1970 and 1971. 5 Squadron proved the longest operator on the Lightning, finally disbanding at Binbrook on 31.12.87, reforming as a Tornado F.3 unit at Coningsby, 1.5.88.

11 Squadron

Motto: *Ociores acrioresque aquilis* ('Swifter and keener than eagles').

Command Assignments: Fighter Command Interceptor Alert Force; UK Air Defence Region (Northern) Aircraft: F.6 (4.67-5.88); F.3 (10.72-5.86) Stations: Leuchars (4.67-1972); Binbrook (1972-5.88).

History: Disbanded at Geilenkirchen, end of 1965, reforming at Leuchars, 1.4.67, when re-equipped on the Lightning F.6, the third RAF squadron to operate the type. With the move by 74 Squadron to Singapore, became the main air defence squadron at Leuchars on 15.5.67. With 23 Squadron formed the Leuchars Lightning Wing, part of the Interceptor Alert Force (IAF) or Quick Reaction Alert (QRA); the long-range interception of Soviet aircraft in the Northern UK Air Defence Region. One day, in April 1970, no less than forty interceptions were carried out on 'Badgers' and 'Bears'. Meanwhile, in-flight refuelling was practised. Flight Lieutenant Eggleton established a record on 29.11.67 of eight hours' flying, refuelling five times and flying 5,000 miles. Took part in the biggest air-refuelling exercise so far mounted by the RAF on 6.1.69, when ten F.6s, refuelled by Victor tankers, deployed to Tengah, Singapore, (staging through Muharraq and Gan) and back, a distance of 18,500 miles. F.6s retrofitted 1970 with twin 30mm Aden cannon in the front section of the ventral fuel tank. Replaced at Leuchars on 22.3.72 by Phantom FG.1s on 43 Squadron, moving to Binbrook, 22.6.72, following the departure of 85 Squadron to West Raynham, to continue in the IAF role. Deployed to Akrotiri, Cyprus, in June 1972 for one-month detachment, relieving 56 Squadron, which completed APC at Valley. Six F.6s sent to Cyprus, in January 1974 following the Turkish invasion. Began receiving additional Lightnings from 226 OCU in mid-1974, following its closure and from other F.3 squadrons, which began re-equipping on the Phantom FGR.2. 'C Flight assumed the training task of Lightning Conversion in 1974, the Lightning Training Flight taking over at Binbrook, October 1975.

11 Squadron finally disbanded on 30.4.88 (reforming as a Tornado F.3 Squadron at Leeming, 1.11.88). Squadron Leader Aldington had the distinction of making the final RAF Lightning flight when he delivered one of three aircraft to Cranfield, 30.6.88.

19 Squadron

Motto: *Possunt quia posse videntur* ('They can because they think they can').

Command Assignments: Fighter Command Interceptor Alert Force; UK Air Defence Region (Southern) (1962-9.65); RAF Germany (23.9.65-31.12.76).

Aircraft: F.2 (12.62-10.69); F.2A (1.68-12.76).

Stations: Leconfield (12.62-1.68); Gütersloh (1.68-12.76).

History: Began conversion from the Hunter F.6 to the Lightning F.2 at Leconfield, October 1962, the first RAF unit so to do. T.4 XM988 first aircraft to arrive, 29.10.62. First F.2 (XN755/D) received 17.12.62. Became operational as an all-weather unit, March 1963 with twelve F.2s and one T.4. Took part, July 1965 in in-flight refuelling trials with the new Victor K.1 tankers, winning, that same year, for the second time, the Dacre Trophy (awarded to the top UK fighter squadron in weapons proficiency). Transferred from Fighter Command, 23.9.65, to Second Tactical Air Force, RAF Germany at Gütersloh (less than 100 miles from East Germany), becoming fully operational in 1966. F.2A Lightnings, able to carry four 30mm Aden cannon or twin Firestreak AAMs, or (more usually) twin Aden and two Firestreaks, began arriving February 1968, the F.2s being progressively returned to BAC Warton, 1968-69, for modification to F.2A standard and re-issue to RAF Germany. Disbanded 31.12.70 at Gütersloh. Reformed Wildenrath 1.1.77 on the Phantom FGR.2.

23 Squadron

Motto: *Semper agressus* ('Always on the attack').

Command Assignments: Fighter Command Interceptor Alert Force; UK Air Defence Region (Northern) Aircraft: F.3 (8.64-11.67); F.6 (5.67-10.75) Stations: Leuchars (8.64-31.10.75).

History: Re-equipped from the Javelin to the Lightning F.3 at Leuchars in August 1964. XP707 and XP708 first to arrive on 18.8.64. Full squadron complement reached, end of October 1964. Became operational early in 1965, when in-flight refuelling exercises with USAF KC-135 tankers took place. Replacement on the (interim) F.6, from May 1967, followed by full production-standard F.6s. Won Dacre Trophy that same year (and again, 1969 and 1975, also winning the Aberporth Trophy, 1970 and 1971). F.6 SX938, the last Lightning to be built for the RAF, was flown from Warton to Leuchars on 28.8.67. Squadron fully equipped on F.6 by beginning of 1968. XR725/A and XS936/B flew non-stop to Toronto, Canada, in 7 hours 20 minutes in August 1968 using in-flight refuelling, returning to Leuchars on 3.9.68. Became operational with Red Top missile that same month. Detachments flown to Beauvechain, Belgium in July 1969; Malta, April 1970; Sweden, 1971; and to Cyprus, February 1971 – this to take part in practice air defence of Cyprus and ACM. First successful trial of twin 30mm Aden gun packs on 26.3.71. Replaced in the QRA role at Leuchars by Phantom FGR.2s on 11 Squadron and disbanded 31.10.75, before reforming as a Phantom FGR.2 squadron at Coningsby, 1.11.75, moving to RAF Wattisham, 25.2.76.

29 Squadron

Motto: *Impiger et acer* ('Energetic and keen').

Command Assignments: Fighter Command Interceptor Alert Force; UK Air Defence Region (Southern) Aircraft: F.3 (5.67-12.74). Stations: Wattisham (5.67-12.74).

History: Equipped with Javelins, was relieved of air-defence duties on Cyprus in May 1967 by 56 Squadron's Lightning F.1s, which had arrived from RAF Wattisham that April. Returning to England, 29 Squadron reformed at Wattisham on 1.5.67 to become the last RAF unit to equip on the Lightning. The first aircraft (XV328, a T.5) was taken on charge on 10.5.67 followed, 8.66-5.67, by F.3s, mostly 'hand-me-downs' from 74 and 23 Squadrons at Leuchars, then beginning conversion to the F.6. Fully operational by September 1967. Awarded Dacre Trophy on 19.7.74. Disbanded on 31.12.74 at Wattisham, reforming as a Phantom FGR.2 squadron at Coningsby, 1.1.75.

56 (Punjab) Squadron

Motto: *Quid si coelum mat* ('What if Heaven falls?').

Command Assignments: Fighter Command Interceptor Alert Force; UK Air Defence Region (Southern); and to Cyprus (1975).

Aircraft: F.1 (12.60-4.65); F.1A (1961); F.3 (3.65-12.71); F.6 (9.71-6.76) Stations: Wattisham (12.60-28.6.76); Akrotiri (5.67-12.74); Wattisham (1975-28.6.76) History: Conversion to the Lightning F.1 began in December 1960, to become only the second Lightning squadron in the RAF and the first to receive the F.1A (XM172 being the first to arrive, December 1960). Workup to operational status took place at Wattisham, then, while the runways were resurfaced, continued at Coltishall. Full complement of F.1As received by March 1961. Undertook intensive in-flight refuelling trials in 1962, first using USAFE F-100Cs tanking from KC-50s, then with their Lightning F.1As with Valiants. Two F.1As flew non-stop to Cyprus on 23.7.62 in 4 hours 22 minutes, refuelled from two Valiants on 90 and 214 Squadrons. Became the official Fighter Command aerobatic team, 1963, being named the 'Firebirds'. First AAR detachment to Cyprus, 'Forthright One', took place in 2.64. F-3s began arriving at Wattisham in 2.65, the F.1As being transferred to 226 OCU at Coltishall. Took part in Unison 65 in September 1965 and a year later in the Malta air defence exercise Adex 66. Moved to Akrotiri, Cyprus, in April 1967, replacing 29 Squadron's Javelins, a posting which lasted seven years (5.67-9.74). Meanwhile, F.6s had been acquired from 74 Squadron, which disbanded at Tengah, Singapore in 8.71. Following the Turkish invasion of Cyprus in 1974, 200 operational sorties were flown to protect the Sovereign Base Area airspace. Finally returned to Wattisham, the first of thirteen F.6s (and the Squadron's three Canberra TTs) arriving there on 21.1.75. Awarded Dacre Trophy in 6.75, 56 (Designate) Squadron formed on the Phantom FGR.2 on 22.3.76, the actual squadron disbanding, 28.6.76 at Wattisham, being reformed the next day at Coningsby.

74 (Trinidad) Squadron
Motto: *I Fear No Man*

Command Assignments: Fighter Command Interceptor Alert Force; UK Air Defence Region (Southern and Northern) (1960-5.67); FEAF Air Defence (6.67-25.8.71).

Aircraft: F.1 (6.60-4.64); F.3 (4.64-9.67); F.6 (9.66-8.71).

Stations: Coltishall (6.60-4.64); Leuchars (2.6.64-5.67); Tengah (6.67-1.9.71).

History: Became the first RAF squadron to introduce the Lightning into service. XM165 (the first F.1) taken on charge at Coltishall on 29.6.60. In September 1960 Squadron Leader John F. G. Howe led formation flypasts of four aircraft at the Farnborough Air Show. A nine-ship formation was flown at Farnborough 1961, when the first public demonstration of nine Lightnings rolling in tight formation took place. In 1962 the 'Tigers' became the official Fighter Command aerobatic team. Moved to Leuchars on 28.2.64 and then in April became the first operational RAF squadron to operate the F.3, XP700 being the first to arrive, on 14.4.64. From 1965 onwards shared the northern IAF defensive duties at Leuchars with 23 Squadron's F.3s. Air-to-air tanking became a feature of these interception missions, operational range and endurance being improved from August 1966 by the introduction of the Lightning F.6, XR768/A being the first. From August 1966 full production F.6s, the first to reach an operational squadron, were received. In June 1967 thirteen Lightnings transferred to Tengah, Singapore, in operation 'Hydraulic', the longest and largest in-flight refuelling operation hitherto flown, staging through Akrotiri, Masirah and Gan and using seventeen Victor tankers from Marham, for a four-year

LIGHTNING UNITS

tour of duty in the tropics. During this time, three 2,000-mile deployments were made to Australia non-stop using Victor tankers, the major one being exercise 'Town House' (16.6-26.6.69). Also participated in 'Bersatu Padu' ('Complete Unity'), a five-nation exercise in Western Malaya and Singapore in July 1969. Regular exchanges were also flown with RAAF Mirages at Butterworth, Malaysia and two Lightnings were flown to Thailand for a static display in Bangkok. Squadron finally disbanded, Tengah on 25.8.71. All remaining Lightnings were flown on the 6,000-mile, 13-hour trip to Akrotiri, Cyprus from 2.9.71, staging through Gan and Muharraq and completing seven in-flight refuellings with Victor tankers for transfer to 56 Squadron. Reformed as a Phantom F-4J squadron at Wattisham on 19.10.84.

92 (East India) Squadron

Motto: *Aut pugna aut morere* ('Either fight or die').

Command Assignments: Fighter Command Interceptor Alert Force; UK Air Defence Region (Southern) (1963-65); RAF Germany (29.12.65-31.3.77) Aircraft: F.2 (4.63-7.71); F.2A (8.68-3.77).

Stations: Leconfield (4.63-12.65); Geilenkirchen (29.12.65-12.67); Gütersloh (24.1.68-31.3.77).

History: Late in 1962 began equipping on the Lightning F.2, the first (XN783/A) arriving on the squadron on 17.4.63. Declared fully operational that summer; a team of F.2s displayed at Farnborough that September. Movement to Geilenkirchen, Germany, began in December 1965, replaced 11 Squadron's Javelins. Moved to Gütersloh in February 1968 to join 19 Squadron. Re-equipment on the F.2A followed and was concluded in 1969. Disbanded on 31.3.77, reforming as an FGR.2 Phantom squadron at Wildenrath, 1.4.77.

111 Squadron

Motto: *Adstantes'* ('Standing by').

Command Assignments: Fighter Command Interceptor Alert Force; UK Air Defence Region (Northern).

Aircraft: F.1A (4.61-2.65); F.3 (12.64-9.74); F.6 (5.74-9.74) Stations: Wattisham, (4.61-30.9.74).

History: Re-equipment on the Lightning F.1A began on 6.3.61 with delivery of XM185. XM216, the last F.1A built, was delivered in August. Re-equipment on the F.3 began in late 1964. In 1.65, formed the leading box in a formation of sixteen aircraft for a final salute and flypast over the funeral barge of Sir Winston Churchill. In 1965 formed a formation aerobatics team of twelve Lightnings. USAF U-2 reconnaissance aircraft from Lakenheath, previously thought immune to fighter interception, were successfully intercepted late that summer. F.3s continued to be used until disbandment at Wattisham on 30.9.74, 11 Squadron (designate) forming on the Phantom FGR.2 at Coningsby in July 1974. Full squadron complement followed on 1.10.74.

AFDS (Air Fighting Development Squadron)/CFE (Central Fighter Establishment)

Command Assignments: CFE (Central Fighter Establishment) Aircraft: F.1/F.1A/F.2/F.3/T.4.

Stations: Coltishall (8.59-9.62); Binbrook (10.62-1.2.66).

History: Formed on 1.9.59 under the command of Wing Commander Jimmy Dell after moving from West Raynham, whose runways were unsuitable for Lightning operations. Its role was to carry out tactical and operational trials of all new fighter aircraft types and to investigate all equipment and aircraft systems. First F.1 aircraft, 335 and 336, delivered December 1959. XG334 lost 5.3.60. Four more F.1s were delivered in May 1960 and used in Exercise Yeoman that same month while on detachment to Leconfield. Moved to Binbrook in 1962 with the CFE. First F.2 (XN771) delivered in November 1962, followed by three more (XN726, 729 and 777 (lost 21.12.62). XP695 (first F.3 to enter service) arrived on 1.1.64. First interim version F.6 (XR753) arrived on 16.11.65. CFE disbanded on 1.2.66, AFDS becoming the FCTU (Fighter Command Trials Unit).

FCTU (Fighter Command Trials Unit)

Command Assignments: Fighter/Strike Command Aircraft: F.2/F.3/T.4.

Stations: Binbrook (1.2.66-30.6.67).

History: Renamed from the disbanded AFDS on 1.2.66. Developed the concept of supersonic targets for the front-line Lightning squadrons. Continued to operate from Binbrook until disbandment on 30.6.67, all aircraft going to the Binbrook Station Target Facility Flight.

LCS (Lightning Conversion Squadron)
Aircraft: F.1A/F.3/T.4/T.5.
Stations: Middleton St. George (20.6.62-31.5.63).

LIGHTNING UNITS

History: Formed on 29.6.62 using initially a few single-seat Lightnings from 56, 74 and 11 Squadrons on a daily-return basis. The first Lightning T.4 (XM970) arrived on 29.6.62 and the LCS had equipped with nine more by late 1962. Became 226 OCU on 1.6.63.

LCU (Lightning Conversion Unit)/LTF (Lightning Training Flight)
Aircraft: F.3/T.5/F.6.

Stations: Binbrook (10.74-3.76); Coningsby (3.76-1977); Binbrook (1977-1.8.87) History: LCU formed from 'C' Flight, 11 Squadron, in September 1974 becoming the LTF in the beginning of October 1974. Using initially four F.3s and four T.5s (from 1979 F.6 was added for target facilities purposes with a radar reflector usually carried in place of AI.23 radar), directed to provide conversion training for new pilots arriving from Tactical Weapons Units with fast-jet experience on Hawks, for onward posting to front-line Lightning squadrons. A T.5 flight was followed by two weeks of ground school, including approximately fourteen 'flights' in a simulator, followed by five flights in T.5, before first solo in the F.3. First phase of conversion training involved concentrated flying up to IRS (Instrument Rating Standard), followed by a series of exercises, including battle formation flying, culminating in a handling test on the T.5. A weapons phase, involving air combat training with Red Top acquisition rounds, followed, before a final check ride, normally with the CO. After about forty-two Lightning flying hours the new pilot was assigned to either 5 or 11 Squadron. In addition to conversion training, shorter, refresher courses for lapsed Lightning pilots were run. Flight Lieutenant Ian Black, a former Phantom navigator, became the last pilot to he trained to fly the Lightning before the Flight disbanded on 1.8.87. 5 Squadron and 11 Squadron operated some of the aircraft for some months after.

226 OCU (Operational Conversion Unit)
Motto: *We Sustain Command Assignments*: CFE Aircraft: F.1A7F.3/T.4/F.5.

Stations: Coltishall (4.1.60-8.61); Middleton St. George (8.61-12.4.64); Coltishall (4.64-17.6.74); Leconfield (1966) and Binbrook (1972) used during runway repairs at Coltishall.

History: Formed at Coltishall on 4.1.60 under the aegis of CFE with the task of training Lightning pilots, aircraft being borrowed from 74 Squadron. Moved to Middleton St. George in 8.61 to become miscellaneous Lightning Conversion Squadron (LCS) using mainly Lightnings from 56 and

11 Squadrons. First T.4 (XM970) received on 27.6.62, followed by seven more before the end of 10.62. Re-titled 226 OCU on 1.6.63, receiving seven ex-74 Squadron F.1 aircraft shortly thereafter. Now took designation 145 (Shadow) Squadron (disbanded in 5.71; 65 [Shadow] Squadron being formed in its place). 226 OCU moved to Coltishall on 13.4.64. First T.5 (XS419) arrived on 20.4.65, being followed by fourteen more. Became last unit in the RAF to receive the F.3 (XP696, XP737, XR716 and XR718), on 6.7.80. Formed within 226 OCU (4.5.71) were No.1 (Conversion) Squadron on T.4/F.1A (adopting markings of 65 Squadron); No.2 (Weapons) Squadron using T.4S/F.1A/T.5 (also adopting 65 Squadron markings) and No.3 (Advanced) Squadron on F.3/T.5 in No.2T Squadron markings. 226 OCU disbanded on 17.6.74 and replaced by the LTF. Reactivated late 1974 at Lossiemouth as the Jaguar Conversion Unit.

Binbrook TFF (Target Facility Flight)
Command Assignments: FCTIJ Aircraft: F.1 Stations: Binbrook.

History: Formed in 1966 on disbandment of the FCTU. Two F.1s (XM164 and XM137) were delivered (22.2.66 and 15.3.66 respectively). Disbanded in December 1973.

Wattisham TFF (Target Facility Flight)
Command Assignments: FCTU.

Aircraft:F.1/F.1A.

Stations: Wattisham.

History: Formed in April 1966. Complement of three Lightnings, two pilots, one engineering officer and fifty ground crew. Disbanded in December 1973.

Leuchars TFF (Target Facility Flight)
Command Assignments: FCTU Aircraft: F.1/F.1A Stations: Leuchars.

History: Formed in April 1966. Complement of three Lightnings, two pilots, one engineering officer and fifty ground crew. Absorbed by 23 Squadron in 1970. Disbanded in December 1973.

60 MU Leconfield
Command Assignments: Aircraft: All marks Stations: Leconfield.

History: Carried out all major servicing at all marks of Lightning.

LIGHTNING UNITS

Akrotiri Station Flight
Command Assignments: Aircraft: T.5.

Stations: Akrotiri, Cyprus.

History: Formed from 'C' Flight, 11 Squadron in 1974.

Lightning Conversion Unit (RSAF)
Command Assignments: Saudi Arabia Aircraft: T.5.

Stations: Khamis Mushayt Air Base.

History: Operated as the Lightning Conversion Unit for the RSAF.

2 Squadron RSAF
Command Assignments: Saudi Arabia (Eastern and North-western Sectors) Aircraft: F.53, T.55. Stations: Tabuk Air Base (1969-?); King Ahd al-Aziz Air Base, Dhahran (?-1976); King Feisal Air Base (8.76-1986).

History: Formed mid-1969 from a small number of pilots trained at 22.6 OCU Coltishall in 1968. These were supplemented by officers who had graduated from miscellaneous transitional training course. F.53s delivered by RAF and BAC pilots began to arrive on 1.7.68. A Canberra was used to tow targets for firing practice. Joint exercises aimed at the air defence of the Eastern Sector were carried out. Last RSAF squadron to operate the Lightning, up until 22.1.86.

6 Squadron RSAF
Command Assignments: Saudi Arabia (Southern Zone) Aircraft: F.52/F.53.

Stations: King Abd al-Aziz Air Base, Dhahran (1967-1978).

History: Formed in 1967 from a group of Hunters and F.52 Lightnings. Used in air defence until the arrival of F.53 Lightnings. Lightning Flight declared operational on 13.11.66. From January 1967 onwards, used its air defence along the Yemeni border area. Role changed to attack and defence in 1969, taking part in miscellaneous defence of the Southern Zone until the other types were withdrawn in 1974. With the arrival of F.53 Lightnings, carried out the entire defence of the Southern Zone during 1974-78, by which time the Lightnings were redistributed between 13 Squadron and 2 Squadron.

13 Squadron RSAF
Command Assignments: Saudi Arabia (Fastens Zone and North-West Sector) Aircraft: F.5, F.53, T.55.

Stations: King Abd al-Aziz Air Base, Dhahran (1978-1982); King Feisal Air Base (March 1982-)

History: Formed in 1978 at the King Abd al-Aziz Air Base at Dhahran from the transitional Lightning training unit and part of 6 Squadron. Using F.53 and T.55 Lightnings, along with the F.5, shared in training and joint exercises in the defence of sectors of the Eastern Zone of Saudi Arabia. With the arrival of F-15 Eagles in 1981, Lightning operations began to diminish and transfer to the King Feisal Air Base in the North-West Sector took place during 1981-3.82.

Kuwait Air Force

Command Assignments: Kuwait Aircraft: T.55K/F.55K.

Stations: Kuwait International Airport, Ahmed al Jaber and Jakra.

History: Deliveries of miscellaneous first of twelve F.53 fighters begun December 1968. Operated Lightnings until 1977, when replaced by Mirage F.1Ks.

Endnotes

Preface: Tiger Or 'Pussycat'? – The English Electric Lightning
1. Brian Carroll, *The Lightning Review*.
2. The Lightning's initial rate of climb was 50,000 feet per minute. The Mirage IIIE climbed initially at 30,000 feet/minute, the MiG-21 managed 36,090 feet/minute and the Tornado F-3 43,000 feet/minute.
3. Brian Carroll, *The Lightning Review*.

Chapter 1: Flash of Fire - The First Fighters
1. This and all the quotes from Dave Seward, are from interviews/correspondence with the author.
2. XG307-313 and XG325-337.
3. XA847, XA853 and XA856.
4. The first 'Firestreak' missile was successfully flight-tested at Larkhill on 17 January 1953 and the first air launch of a fully guided and controlled round took place at Aberporth, when a Firestreak fired from a Venom, destroyed an unmanned radio-controlled Firefly. The first Mk.I production versions entered service with FAA Sea Venom squadrons in 1958. The infrared guidance system consisted of a cassegrain IR telescope with 15-degree squint angle located behind an eight-faceted all-glass nose-cone. Cooling of the seeker head and onboard electronics was carried out by nitrogen in the launch aircraft. Target lock-on (rear only attack) was effected by two rings of sensors behind the main seeker head. The 50lb warhead was wrapped around the motor tube just forward of the fins.
5. The Tigers' second South African CO, A.G. 'Sailor' Malan, having been the first (August 1940-March 1941). Born in East London, John Howe went on to attend the Military College at Robert's Heights (subsequently Voortrekkerhoogte, now Thaba Tschwane) and in 1950 he joined the South African Air Force. In 1951 he flew as an F-51 pilot in 2 'Cheetah' Squadron SAAF in Korea, later becoming a flying instructor before coming to Britain and joining the RAF in 1954. His first job was instructing on Vampires and in 1956 he moved over to the Hunter on 222. Squadron. That same year he did a four-month detachment for the Suez crisis, landing on the beach with Royal Marine Commandos to direct air strikes on the port. In 1959 he went on the day-fighter combat leader course. A short spell of instructing followed before he took over the 'Tigers'.

THE MEN WHO FLEW THE ENGLISH ELECTRIC LIGHTNING

6. This and all the quotes from Bruce Hopkins, are from interviews/correspondence with the author.
7. The Belgian Air Force lost 39 Starfighters, the Dutch Air Force 44 and by late 1982 the Luftwaffe had lost 252.
8. Forty-four Lightnings were built as F.2s, thirty-one of them later being modified to F.2A standard with cranked and cambered wing leading edges, a large angular vertical tail; and a 610-gallon ventral tank which was part of the fuselage and thus could not be jettisoned, in place of the earlier 250-gallon jettisonable tank.
9. Originally designated the 'Firestreak' Mk.IV, this collision-course missile, fitted with a new, more rounded seeker head, could lock onto the heat generated by the target aircraft's engines and also the friction hot spots created by its flight path. An improved rocket motor gave a top speed of Mach 3 + with an in-control range of 7 miles. The warhead carried 68lb of explosive. The first 'Red Top' entered RAF service in 1964 with Lightning F.6s of 74 Squadron.
10. The T.5 prototype was produced by converting T.4 XM967, from which it differed externally in having a squared-top fin. Internally, longer cable ducting was used. Jimmy Dell first flew XM967 in its new T.5 configuration on 29 March 1962 at Filton, Bristol. XS417, the first production T.5, flew on 17 July 1964. Twenty-two production T.5 aircraft were built, the first entering service on 226 OCU at Coltishall in April 1965.
11. On 3 August 1955 during air combat training Flying Officer Hedley Molland on 263 Squadron while flying Hunter F.Mk.5 WN989 made a cine attack on his target and followed it into a dive from 37,000 feet. At 31,000 feet the dive steepened uncontrollably, the aircraft diving vertically into the sea seven miles east of Bawdsey, Suffolk. Molland survived the supersonic ejection at 25,000 feet, Mach 1.1 – his left arm was broken on ejection as he only used his left hand to initiate ejection. He also suffered two black eyes and a fractured pelvis. His crash helmet, watch, gloves and one shoe were blown off during ejection. The parachute opened automatically at about 10,000 feet and speed of descent was normal. He is thought to be the second man ever to have bailed out successfully at such a speed.
12. During the 1960s Pakistan investigated the possibility of buying as many as forty English Electric Lightnings; however, Britain was not enthusiastic about the potential sales opportunity because of the damage it would do to its relations with India, which at the time was still awaiting the delivery of large numbers of Hawker Hunters.

Chapter 2: 'Tiger' Tales

1. Squadron Leader John Howe first flew this aircraft on 14 July.
2. XG334, XG335 and XG336. On 5 March Flight Lieutenant Ron Harding on the CFE was forced to abandon XG334, which John Nicholls had delivered on 23 December, after hydraulic failure. On selecting the undercarriage down for landing, the port leg would not lower beyond 30 degrees. Harding initiated

ENDNOTES

the emergency system without success and after a series of slow fly-bys over the airfield to allow engineering staff to access the situation as best they could XG334 was abandoned off the Norfolk coast near Wells-next-the-Sea. It was only the second Lightning loss so far recorded. Harding ejected safely but suffered spinal injuries and was picked up by helicopter from the sea.

3. XM135, XM136, XM137, XM138 and XM165, which was delivered by Wing Commander Roly Beamont, late in the afternoon of 29 June 1960.
4. By 22 July 1960 all of the 74 Squadron pilots had completed conversion training. In addition, Wing Commander Evans, OC Flying, had flown at least one sortie.
5. *Never In Anger*. F.1A XM185 was the only Lightning casualty that year.
6. On 26 April 1963 Burns was forced to abandon XM142 B after hydraulic power loss, off the Norfolk coast, whilst on an air test following a 400-hour servicing. He ejected safely, missing 33,000-volt electricity cables by just thirty yards as he landed.
7. *RAF Coltishall Fighter Station: A Station History* by Mick Jennings MBE. (Old Forge, 2007).
8. He was awarded the AFC on 2 June 1962. Promoted to Wing Commander in January 1966 his developing career took him to a staff posting at Headquarters RAF Fighter Command, a senior instructor posting at Royal Air Force College Cranwell and later as a senior staff officer at the Joint Warfare School. After a 1965 exchange tour posting to the United States where he flew most of the Century Series Fighters and the Phantom he returned to the UK as Officer Commanding 229 Operational Conversion Unit RAF at RAF Chivenor and later 228 Operational Conversion Unit RAF at RAF Coningsby where he oversaw the introduction of the Phantom FGR2 into operational service with the RAF. In 1969 on promotion to Acting Group Captain he moved to two staff postings, firstly as Staff Officer Central Tactics and Trials and later as Deputy Director Operational Research 1. After his rank as a Group Captain was made substantive, in 1973 he was appointed Officer Commanding RAF Gütersloh on the front-line of the Cold War Iron Curtain operations. On his return from Germany in 1975 he attended the Royal College of Defence Studies for ten months and was posted to RAF Bentley Priory as Operations Staff Officer (Training) at Headquarters 11 Group, Strike Command.
9. Inter-squadron rivalry being what it is, out of earshot 74 'Tiger' Squadron was referred to as the 'Ginger Toms', while it was said that when things get hot, 56 'chicken out' – a reference to its badge of the phoenix, rising from the ashes! 'Treble One' was universally known as the 'Tremblers', the 'Trembling First' or, if you really wanted to upset them, 'One, Double-One'. 92 Squadron was simply known as 'Ninety-Blue', a reference to their aircraft colour scheme.
10. *The First Three Years – Memories Of 74 Squadron, 1960-63* by Dave Betts writing in *Lightning Review*.
11. Correspondence with Bob Cossey.

Chapter 3: 'Firebirds', 'T-Birds' and 'Tremblers'
1. Fighter Command first introduced the in-flight refuelling technique in June 1960, when 23 and 64 squadrons, operating the Javelin FAW.Mk.9, began receiver training. In August a 23 Squadron Javelin was flown to Akrotiri non-stop, refuelled and escorted by Valiant BK.1 tankers.
2. This and all the quotes from 'Bob' Offord are from interviews/correspondence with the author.
3. 'Terry' Thompson joined the air force in 1951 following a very brief career with Bank of Nova Scotia. Trained as a radar technician he was employed at a variety of radar stations in Ontario before his selection for officer and pilot training. Awarded his wings at RCAF Station Pehold Alberta in 1954 and on completion of his advanced flying training and gunnery school in southern Manitoba, he was posted to the All Weather Fighter operational training unit in North Bay Ontario. Postings to RCAF Station Cold Lake and later to 409 Squadron at RCAF Station Comox completed his operational flying in Canada. He began his three year exchange tour on 56 Squadron at Wattisham in late 1960 where he converted onto the Hunter followed by the Lightning. During his tour he participated in numerous flight refuelling exercises to the Middle East and during his last year on the squadron he flew with the Firebirds. Returning to Canada in late 1963 Thompson served as a staff officer at the Department of National Defence Headquarters in Ottawa until 1968 when he was posted to staff college in Kingston Ontario. Following graduation in 1969 he was posted to Canadian Forces Base Moose Jaw where he served in a variety of senior flying positions. In 1974 he returned to NDHQ where he held several senior staff appointments until his retirement in 1981 in the rank of Lieutenant Colonel.
4. This and all the quotes from Anthony Barwood are from an interview with the author.
5. On 27 July 1966 F.3 XR714 on 111 Squadron sank back on to the runway at RAF Akrotiri after being caught in jet blast during formation take-off. On 24 August Flight Lieutenant Al Turley on 23 Squadron was forced to eject after F.3 XP760 developed ECU failure, to crash into the North Sea 35 nautical miles off Seahouses in Northumberland. In 1967 another six Lightnings were abandoned including, on 3 March, F.3 XP699, Flying Officer Stuart Pearse on 56 Squadron ejecting near Wethersfield, Suffolk, after a fuel line failure had started a fire. The aircraft crashed at Finchingfield in Essex. Four days later, on 7 March, T.55 55-710 of BAC crashed on landing at Warton in a strong crosswind. On 7 September Squadron Leader Ron Blackburn on 23 Squadron abandoned XR766 near Leuchars, after an uncontrollable spin. Blackburn ejected safely, the F.6 crashing in the North Sea, twenty miles east of Montrose.

Chapter 4: Ab Initio
1. Group Captain Roger Topp continued in the post until 3 June 1966, when Group Captain Mike Hobson took over.

ENDNOTES

2. 'I joined the RAF as an apprentice in 1943, from where I gained a cadetship to university. At the university I read mechanical engineering and learnt to fly on Tiger Moths, with the University Air Squadron. On graduation, I was given the option to continue with an engineering career or to follow a General Duties (Flying) career. I chose the former path and the Air Ministry at that time, considered that there was merit in allowing me to qualify to 'wings' standard as a pilot, in the belief that an engineering officer with a pilot qualification could more easily see the pilots point of view in aircraft maintenance matters. I too, thought this was a very good idea. I qualified on Harvards, but my early engineering duties only allowed me to keep in flying practice on Chipmunks. Whilst I was at Kinloss, I managed to get checked out on Oxfords and on occasions assisted a qualified test pilot, to air test twin engine Neptunes. My only jet aircraft experience was as a passenger in the second seat of a Javelin T.3 and again in the 'rumble' seat of a Canberra. In my service, one of my postings took me to 33MU Lyneham where I had Canberra, Meteor and Lightning types, which were gradually being prepared for despatch to various flying unit tasks. When the Meteor and Canberra types had been cleared, the powers that be, decided that the MU should close after the last Lightning's had been despatched. Up until the last Canberra, I had a qualified and current test pilot on my staff for those aircraft, but he was not a current Lightning pilot. When a Lightning needed test flying, I had to call for any available pilot with a current test pilot rating. Most times I would find one who could be spared within a 24 or 36 hour period.'
3. This and all the quotes from Alex Reed are from interviews/correspondence with the author.
4. Inspection of the aircraft revealed that a small fire had occurred on the starboard side of No.1 engine in zone 2. The fire was caused by engine oil which had leaked from a defective joint coupling on the overboard vent pipe for the No.1 engine wheelcase breather. The accumulation of oil spilled into the No.1 engine hatch during the climb and ignited when it came into contact with the jet pipe. Because of the concealed position of the seal normal servicing procedures did not reveal the defect. When the aircraft rejoined the circuit it was seen to be streaming fuel from the underside of the aircraft. This was caused by the ventral tank/aircraft fuel connection seal remaining fouled in the self-sealing coupling after the ventral was jettisoned. Fuel vented overboard only 12 inches from the scene of the fire thus considerably increasing the hazard to the aircraft. The seal was probably displaced during assembly of the ventral tank to the aircraft and would have eventually caused a ventral feed failure. This is a well-known defect as a result of poor design. Steps are being taken to introduce a modification to position the seal correctly during assembly.
5. Later ACM Sir Michael Graydon GCB CBE ADC FRAeS, Chief of Air Staff.
6. 'Sadly, the Phantom, with Spey engines, was a pig to fly! With a radar operator in the back, the workload was laughably low for the pilot, who became little more

than an aerial chauffeur! (There were no radar controls in the front cockpit). Worst of all, I clashed with my superiors over the unrealistic training, peacetime mentality and poor operational standards achieved. I decided to exercise my option to leave the service, at my eight-year option point and became a civilian.'
7. This and all the quotes from Peter Hayward are from correspondence.
8. 'Sadly, Gil Pink, who had got me to the right place at the right time, was killed on 22 June when the SAR Whirlwind he was riding in on a training exercise lost a rotor blade and crashed into the sea, killing everyone on board.'
9. The Hind is now displayed at the RAF Museum, Hendon.
10. At the disbandment parade at Bentley Priory on 25 April, the fly-past was by Lightnings on 5, 23 and 29 Squadrons and 226 OCU.
11. Squadron Leader Dave 'Quingle' Hampton was killed on 7 April 1975 during an AI exercise in Cyprus.
12. Ed was killed flying his own home-built aircraft in 1975, aged 34, when he hit a tree at Seeley Lake, Montana.
13. Derek Furz Lloyd, *The Lightning Review*.
14. Writing in *Lightning Review*, March 1993 and September 1994.
15. *The Lightning Review*.
16. This involved digging out the existing runway to 12ft and replacing it.
17. Before the move, on 6 September, 226 OCU lost a T.5 flying from Binbrook when Squadron Leader Timothy John Lund Gauvain took Lieutenant 'Danny' Verbiest of the Belgian Air Force on a familiarization trip in XS455. Fifteen minutes after takeoff, near Spurn Head, Gauvain was alerted by both hydraulic captions illuminating on his instrument panel. The T.5 had suffered a double hydraulic failure! Four minutes later, Gauvain sent a 'Mayday' and said he and his Belgian passenger were both ejecting. Gauvain landed in a cornfield, suffering four crush fractures of the thoracic and lumbar vertebrae. Verbiest landed hard near houses and twisted his right knee. The aircraft crashed in the North Sea off Withensea.
18. *'TEN TON TARGET – My Ambition To Fly At 1,000 in a Lightning'* by Brian E. Stiff, writing in *Lightning Review*, September 1992.
19. Despite all the problems, RAF Coltishall also won the 1973 Stainforth Trophy for the 'most efficient station and flying efficiency'.

Chapter 5: The 'Fast Jet Fraternity'
1. This and all the quotes from Clive Rowley are from interviews/correspondence with the author.

Chapter 6: Tanking
1. Brian Carroll writing in *Lightning Review*, March 1993.
2. *Lightning On The Loose* by Brian Carroll, writing in *The Lightning Review* Vol. 2, No. 4 June 1993.
3. XH667 and XH620.

ENDNOTES

4. XH602 and XH648.
5. Bob Offord himself went home at the end of 1965 and in 1966 was posted to 226 OCU as an instructor.
6. In fact the first of six, XA937 did not arrive until 14 February 1966. On 1 July the third and final Victor squadron, 214, formed at Marham and by the end of the year was equipped with seven K.1/1A three-point tankers.
7. Writing in *Lightning Review*, June 1993.
8. By now a further twenty-four Victor K.1A three-point tanker conversions were in RAF service and in 1968 twenty-seven B.2 and SR.2 versions were converted as K.2 tankers to replace the K.1 tankers at Marham.
9. This and all the quotes from Ed Durham are from interviews/correspondence with the author.
10. *The Lightning Review*.
11. Correspondence with the author.
12. *'Exercise Ultimacy: A Lightning Pilot's Eye View' Air Clues*, April 1970.
13. *WIWOL – When I Worked On Lightnings* by Mick Cameron, writing in *Lightning Review* Vol. 4 No.1 September 1994. Correspondence with the author.
14. This and all the quotes from Clive Rowley are from interviews/correspondence with the author.
15. Writing in the *Lightning Review* January 1995.
16. Derek Furz Lloyd, *The Lightning Review*.
17. *Lightning Pilot* by Dagmar Heller *Flying With The RAF Today No.4 Air Pictorial* February 1976.
18. *'I Learnt About Flying From That', Air Clues*, September 1976.
19. *'I Learnt About Flying From That', Air Clues,* June 1988.
20. *Lightning Review* Vol. 2 No. 2 December 1992.
21. Correspondence with the author.

Chapter 7: Quick Reaction Alert

1. The GAF Jindivik is a target drone produced by the Australian Government Aircraft Factory. The name is from an Aboriginal Australian word meaning the hunted one.
2. One two-seat Hunter, XE531, was ordered by the Ministry of Supply on behalf of the RAE Farnborough to be converted from F.Mk.6 standard to feature two-seat cockpit with head-up display and vertical nose-camera. It crashed on takeoff at Farnborough on 17 March 1982 after the engine exploded due to the 11th stage compressor disc disintegrating. Flight Lieutenant Rod Sears and Mr. John Leng ejected but suffered major injuries.
3. Writing in *The Lightning Review*, June 1993.
4. Correspondence with the author.
5. Interview/correspondence with the author.
6. *'Have Lightning, Will Travel. When The Hooter Blares, Everybody Moves – 29 Squadron's Mobile Quick Reaction Capacity.' Flight International*, 28 April 1970.

7. *The Lightning Review.*
8. On 1 April 1971 the term 'QRA' was replaced with Interceptor Alert Force (IAF).
9. *RAF Germany Today,* RAF Souvenir Book 1972.
10. Correspondence with the author.

Chapter 8: 'Tigers' Fly East
1. XS928 had to be airlifted to BAe Warton by a Short Belfast for repair after suffering damage caused by a ground fire at Tengah when fuel vented onto the wing. New wings were subsequently fitted and XS928 operated later with 23 and 56 Squadrons before it joined 5 Squadron as 'K' in September 1976. XS928 served with 5 Squadron until it disbanded in December 1987.
2. This and all the quotes from Dave Roome are from correspondence with the author.
3. XS416, the T.5 trainer which did not have overwing tanks, remained behind at Leuchars, while another, XV329, went by sea from Sydenham, Belfast. XV329 returned by sea to the UK in August 1971 and had to be written off in December when it was discovered that acid spillage from the batteries had corroded the airframe.
4. During their tour in the Far East 74 Squadron made three 2,000-mile deployments to Australia non-stop using Victor tankers, the major one being exercise 'Town House', 16-26 June 1969. The Lightnings also participated in 'Bersatu Padu' ('Complete Unity'), a five-nation exercise held in Western Malaya and Singapore in July 1969. Regular exchanges were also flown with RAAF Mirages at Butterworth, Malaysia and two Lightnings were flown to Thailand for a static display in Bangkok.
5. F.6 XS900, which was abandoned on 24 January, was the first of five Lightning losses in 1968. Flight Lieutenant Miller on 5 Squadron experienced trouble after take-off from Lossiemouth when his controls were jammed by FOD, which caused a total loss of power. He ejected safely. F-53 53-690, which was destined for the RSAF, caught fire at 400 feet on its first test-flight on 4 September 1968. The BAC test pilot, John Cockburn, climbed to 4,000 feet, intending to ditch the aircraft in Morecambe Bay, when he lost elevator control and had to eject. Cockburn was uninjured but Bill Lawrenson of Stakepool, Pilling, 12 miles north of Warton, who was inspecting the newly laid concrete drive to his cottage, had a lucky escape when 53-690 plunged vertically through his nearby greenhouse! The explosion created a crater 35 feet deep and hurled Mr. Lawrenson into the air. His wife, who had been working in the kitchen, was thrown into a corner when the wall blew in. The Lawrensons were taken to hospital and treated for shock and lacerations. Obviously believing that lightning does not strike twice in the same place, the Lawrensons still resided in the same cottage thirty years later!

On 29 November 1968 F.1A XM174, flown by 43-year-old Flight Lieutenant Edward Rawcliffe on the Leuchars TFF and a simulator instructor, was abandoned after the pilot received a series of fire warnings. These were as a result of a hydraulic fire caused by leaking fluid, which then burned through the controls. As the Lightning pitched downwards, Rawcliffe, who had ejected from a Javelin FAW.4 two years earlier, tried, but failed, to pull the face blind. However, he managed to use his seat-panhandle, which he activated at 1,000 feet while the F.1A was doing 190 knots in a 40- to 60-degree nose-down attitude and in a 30-degree bank to port. Both wheels and the flaps were down and the dive brakes out. The ejection seat rotated once, then separated and the deployed. Rawcliffe landed in a hilly scrub fifty yards from the Lightning, which crashed into a quarry at Bulmullo, near Leuchars. A rescue helicopter arrived within five minutes and airlifted the downed pilot to Leuchars, where his only injury was a bitten tongue.

The fire integrity programme begun in 1968, to fit 'Fire Integrity Package' modifications to Lightnings and which went hand in glove with improvements in servicing procedures and engineer and ground crew training, seemed to have an immediate effect, for in 1969 only one Lightning was lost but in the next twelve months eight Lightnings were lost. 31-year-old Flying Officer Tony Doidge on 11 Squadron abandoned XS918 over the North Sea on 4 March 1970 after a jet-pipe fire overhead Leuchars. Doidge climbed the F.6 to 12,000 feet and his No.2 confirmed an aircraft fire. Doidge called, 'Ejecting'. His No.2 saw the canopy go and pilot and seat leave the aircraft, which crashed in the Firth of Forth. The pilot's PSP (Personal Survival Pack) was recovered five hours later floating in the sea, but the lanyard had not extended and Doidge's body was recovered soon after. The weather at this time was very cold indeed and Doidge was wearing no underclothing or other insulation beneath his Mk.10 immersion suit.

On 2 May a RSAF Lightning piloted by 'Slim' Wightman, who was uninjured, was lost. Five days later F.3 XP742 was abandoned over the North Sea off Great Yarmouth, Norfolk, after an uncontrolled ECU fire during a pair's supersonic attack at 28,000 feet. Flying Officer 'Stu' Tulloch on 11 Squadron had just made a climbing turn to starboard at Mach 1.3 in full re-heat when both re-heat fire warnings illuminated. Tulloch pulled back the throttles, called, 'Mayday! Mayday! Mayday! Double re-heat fire – ejecting!' and pulled the seat-panhandle. The oxygen hose to his mask was broken and his helmet blew away in the ejection but Tulloch, who next remembered being in his dinghy, had nothing worse than a bruised forehead and bruising on the back of his shins and tight ankle.

Chapter 9: 'Linies'

1. 'Houchins' - so called from the name of the makers in Ashford, Kent.
2. Who later managed the Red Arrows.
3. Flight Lieutenant George Fenton on 29 Squadron was taking part in a formation rotation take-off when he scraped the belly of XP700 on the runway and set the ventral tank on fire. He climbed to 3,000 feet at 250 knots when the controls began to stiffen, but which were still operative when he ejected using the SPH.

There was some tearing of the pilot chute and main canopy and Fenton, who had done a parachuting course in 1967, landed heavily in a cornfield and suffered crush fractures. He had not tightened his harness straps as he felt they were already tight enough for take-off. The F.3 crashed at Great Waldingfield, Suffolk.
4. XP738 on 11 Squadron.

Chapter 10: Lightning Strikes
1. Correspondence with the author.
2. *Cobra In The Sky* by Simon Morris.
3. Squadron Leader A. J. N. 'Tony' Alcock MBE was a nephew of Atlantic pioneer Sir John Alcock who with Arthur Whitten Brown made the first non-stop transatlantic flight in June 1919 flying a modified WW1 Vickers Vimy bomber from St. John's, Newfoundland, to Clifden, Connemara, County Galway, Ireland and on 21 June 1979 'Tony' and Flight Lieutenant W. N. 'Norman' Browne, a former Phantom navigator brought back from his Buccaneer squadron for the occasion, made a five hour 40 minute commemorative flight eastbound from Goose Bay, Newfoundland to the UK in F-4M Phantom XV424, flying subsonically. In-flight refuelling was provided by Victor tankers on 57 Squadron on five occasions during the flight. Alcock and Browne carried the original toy black cat mascot – 'Twinkletoes' – from the 1919 flight.
4. *Cobra In The Sky* by Simon Morris.
5. In a letter to Charles Ross, Editor, *Lightning Review*, December 1993. Correspondence with the author.
6. The aircraft crashed three miles off Donna Nook. Only a small portion of the wreckage was recovered from the seabed. The wreckage, together with the other evidence available, proved insufficient to determine positively the sequence of events leading up to the fire and abandonment. It was concluded that the Lightning had suffered a persistent fire in the rear fuselage, the cause of which was unknown.
7. On the afternoon of Sunday, 1st of June 2003 Penrice had reason to part company with Hunter Mk.6 G-BVVC before he had otherwise intended to. The force of the ejection resulted in a burst fracture of one of his vertebrae. The fragments of bone embedded themselves into his spinal cord. The result of this was to effectively paralyze him from the waist down. The spine was fixed by the introduction of yet more metalwork in the form of a supporting cage around the burst vertebrae. He has been able to regain the use of his legs but is still devoid of feeling and function below the waist. 'My days of flying bang seat equipped aircraft are over, but I guess it was time to grow up and find a proper job. As those of us who fly know all too well, it could have been worse. I'm still here to tell the tale.' Correspondence with the author.

ENDNOTES

Chapter 11: 'A Magic Carpet Ride'
1. *The Only Way To Go*.
2. *Lightning Review* Vol. 2 No.2 December 1992.
3. Brian Carroll writing in *Lightning Review* Vol.1 No.2 October 1991.
4. *The Lightning Review*.
5. A possible re-sale to Austria fell through for political reasons and Austria bought ex-Swedish Drakens instead.

Chapter 12: Last of the Lightnings
1. *Lightning Review Phoenix Edition* Vol.4 No.4 July 1996.
2. Mike Hale, *The Lightning Review*.
3. *Lightning Air Combat* by Ian Small, *The Lightning Review*.
4. *Lightning Review* Vol.4, No.4 July 1996.
5. The F-5E served with the US Air Force from 1975 until 1990, in the 64th Aggressor Squadron and 65th Aggressor Squadron at Nellis Air Force Base in Nevada and with the 527th Aggressor Squadron at RAF Alconbury in the UK and the 26th Aggressor Squadron at Clark Air Force Base in the Philippines. The 527th Aggressor Squadron flew its last F-5E sortie from Alconbury on 22 June 1988 and personnel and equipment moved to RAF Bentwaters.
6. RRH Staxton Wold near Scarborough in North Yorkshire has been used as an early warning station since the 3rd century AD, when it was the site of a warning beacon. It was first used as a radar station in 1937, when it was set up as part of the Chain Home system. It is the only one of the original stations still in use and may thus claim to be the oldest continuously serving radar station. Today it is a Remote Radar Head (RRH) within the United Kingdom Air Surveillance and Control System (UKASACS).
7. Group Captain John Spencer: Saturday 25 June 1988.
8. Wing Commander Jake Jarron, commanding 11 Squadron, the last Lightning unit. *Lincs Newspaper Special Feature 25 June 1988*.

Index

Adams, Flight Lieutenant Paul 130
Adana, Turkey 117
Adex, Exercises 120, 250, 254
AFDS 9, 11, 13, 15, 18-21, 34-35, 39, 141, 143, 256
Aird, George P. 12
Akrotiri 34-36, 114-115, 117, 119-120, 122, 124-125, 137-139, 159-162, 173, 179, 207-208, 210, 214-215, 217, 219, 221, 251, 253-255, 259, 280
Alcock, Flight Lieutenant A. J. N. 'Tony' 207-208, 211, 285
Alconbury, RAF 241
Aldington, Squadron Leader John 251
Aldridge, Flight Lieutenant 'Tony' 153-154
Allan, Flying Officer 'Chris' 100-101
Allchin, Flight Lieutenant Brian 44
'Antler', Exercise 124
Ark Royal HMS 80
Avro 720 4
Aylward, Wing Commander Douglas 71, 100, 280
Aziz, Captain 224

Babler, Squadron Leader Peter 158
Bakry, Captain 224
Barnato-Walker, Diana 83
Barwood, Group Captain Antony J. 49-50, 173-174, 177-179, 201-202, 208-210
Bealer, Flight Lieutenant Richard 210
Beamont, Wing Commander Roland P. 'Bee' 6-7, 29, 163, 228-229, 279, 282
Bedford, 'Bill' 49
Bee, Flight Lieutenant Martin 25
Bees, Flight Lieutenant 'Bob' 221
Behery, Captain Ahmed 224
Bell X-1 3
Bell, Squadron Leader 'Dick' 156, 159-162
Benbecula 147
Bendell, Anthony 'Bugs' 21-23, 36-40
Bentley Priory, RAF 18, 26, 146, 154, 279
Bentley, John 154-167
Bentwaters, RAF 49, 286
'Bersatu Padu'(Complete Unity') Exercise 283
Betts, Dave 29-30, 171, 279
Biggin Hill, RAF 26, 37, 48-49, 102
'Billy-Boy', Operation 117-118

INDEX

Binbrook, RAF 13, 15, 93, 98-99, 104, 106, 109, 113, 120-121, 123-124, 130-131, 134-135, 139, 147, 152, 167, 170, 197-198, 200-201, 208, 215, 217-221, 236-238, 240, 246, 249-251, 256-258, 282
Bird-Wilson, Group Captain 'Birdy' 18
Black Arrows 40, 153
Black, George P. AVM 25, 83, 85-86, 118
Blackburn, Squadron Leader Ron 280
Blue Diamonds 44
Bond, Squadron Leader 'Terry' 70
Boscombe Down 6, 10, 32, 71-72, 142-143, 145,
Botterill, Squadron Leader Peter G. 26
Boulmer, RAF 130-132, 147, 168, 193, 195, 199, 219
Brindle, Flight Lieutenant Geoff 121
Brize Norton, RAF 224-226,
Brooks, Dennis 191
Broom, AM Sir Ivor 89
Brown, Jeremy E. 25
Browne, Flight Lieutenant W. N. 'Norman' 285
Bruce, Wing Commander 'Chris' 97-98
Brüggen 165
Bruntingthorpe 249
Buchan, RAF 16-17, 128, 147
Burns, Flight Lieutenant 'Finless Jim' 25, 31, 279
Butcher, Flight Lieutenant Terence 'Taff' 89, 214
Butterworth, RAAF 124, 176, 255, 283

Caldwell, Wing Commander Dennis 176
Cameron, 'Mick' 125-126, 282
Carlton, Squadron Leader Terry 80
Carroll, Squadron Leader Brian ix-xvi, 90-92, 114-117, 121, 148-151, 156, 224-238
Carter, Edwin 47
Carter, Group Captain 'Pete' 217
Cato, Major Bill USAF 142
Catren, Captain Gary USAF 97
Champion, Squadron Leader 'Mike' 101
Chan, Flight Lieutenant D. K. M. 'Charlie' 221-222
Changi 177-178
Chapman, 'Pete' ('Chappie') 88
Cheater, Flight Lieutenant Brian J. 41
Chivenor, RAF 69, 90, 197, 240, 279
Clarke, Flight Lieutenant Graham H. 208
Cloke, Flight Lieutenant Richard 'Dick' 41
Cockburn, John 284
Cohu, Flight Lieutenant 'Jerry' J. R 25, 35, 40, 45
Coker, Flight Lieutenant 'Pete' 216-217
'Cold Fire', Exercise 130
Cole, Flight Lieutenant Robert D. 207
Colebrook, Flying Officer Roger J. 77-80
Coleman, Flight Lieutenant 'Dick' RAAF 222
Collins, Flight Lieutenant Peter 19
Coltishall, RAF xiii, xvi, 1, 9-11, 15, 18-23, 26, 29-31, 34, 36, 51,

69-70, 76, 78, 80-90, 93-96, 98, 103, 107, 113, 120, 141-142, 180, 182, 191, 193, 196, 198, 205, 209, 214, 223-224, 229, 253-254, 256-259, 278-279, 282

'Complete Unity' 'Bersatu Padu', Exercise 283

Coningsby, RAF 112, 132, 250, 253-254, 256-257

Cooke, Flight Lieutenant Mike S. 26, 40, 45-46

Cooke, Patsy 46

Cooper, Flight Lieutenant Paul 'Chile' 210

Cosford, RAF 94

Coville, Flight Lieutenant Christopher 95-96

Cranwell, RAF 26, 46, 102, 113, 224, 279

Crumbie, Flight Lieutenant 'Gerry' 70

Crump, Captain 'Ed' USAF 89, 281

Curry, Flight Lieutenant John M. 40, 42-43, 48

Davie, Flight Lieutenant George 120

Davis, Les 70

Dell, Jimmy 14, 256, 278

Derry, John 3-4

Dhahran xiv, 224, 227, 234-235, 259-260

Dodd, Michael J. 25

Doidge, Flying Officer 'Tony' 284

Doleman, Flight Lieutenant 'Dick' 51, 88

Donaldson-Davidson, 'D D' 28

Donna Nook, RAF 194

'Donovan', Operation 120

Downes, Rory 89

Doyle, Flight Lieutenant 'Tony' 14

Duckett, Squadron Leader Dickie 71, 89

Durham, Group Captain 'Ed' 121-122, 154, 164, 167

Duxford, RAF 23

Eagle HMS 79

Eggleton, Flight Lieutenant 121, 251

Elkington, Graham 14

Evans, Flying Officer 'Geoff' 96-97

Faisal, Prince Bandar 224

Farnborough 6-7, 9-10, 23, 26-27, 30-31, 37, 49, 143, 159, 173, 179, 201, 208-209, 254-255, 283

Farrer, Squadron Leader Brian 83

Fenton, Flight Lieutenant George 285

Fish, Flying Officer 'Geoff' 77

'Forthright One' 35, 253

'Forthright 22/23' 119

'Forthright 59/60' 120

Frost, Flight Lieutenant 'Dave' ('Jack') 89, 218

Fuller, Flight Lieutenant Brian 86-87

Fylingdales, BMEWS station 147, 196

Gan 122-123, 125, 173, 179, 224-225, 251, 254-255

Garside, Flight Lieutenant Alan 39-40, 44, 47-48

Gauvain, Squadron Leader Timothy John Lund 282

Geilenkirchen, RAF 114, 147, 250-251, 255

Ghimlas, Major Essa 224

INDEX

Gibbs, Wing Commander G.M. 69
Gilbert, Group Captain 'Joe' 88
Ginger, Flying Officer 'Pete' 22
Glamorgan, HMS 127
Glanville-White, Squadron Leader Christopher 'Hoppy' 215-216
Goodwin, Air Commodore 'Ken' 19-20, 26, 28, 36, 69, 84, 93, 173
Gosling, 'Stu' ('Thumbs') 89, 100-101
Gough, Flight Lieutenant 'Joey' 126
Graydon, Flight Lieutenant 'Mike' 80-81, 281
Greer, Flight Lieutenant 'Fred' 214
Groombridge, 'Rick' 89
Gross, Flight Lieutenant 'Tony' 80
Gunner, Flight Lieutenant 'Steve' 101
Gütersloh, RAF xiii, 13, 32, 108, 110-112, 126-127, 147, 164-166, 167, 207, 215, 238, 252, 255, 279
Guttmann, Professor Sir Ludwig 'Poppa' CBE FRS 46

Hale, Flight Lieutenant 'Mike' 218, 238
Hamdullah, Major 224
Hamill, 'Tom' 156
Hampton, 'Dave' ('Quingle') 89, 126, 215, 282
Harding, Flight Lieutenant 'Ron' 19, 278,
Hargreaves, Squadron Leader 'Les' 114
Hatfield 12
Hayward, Peter 81, 85-86, 180
Head, Mike 'Beachy' 249
Heller, Dagmar 130-135
Hermes, HMS 127

High Wycombe, RAF 147, 162
Hitchcock, Flying Officer 'Pete' 207
Hobley, Wing Commander Paul 76, 88, 93
Hobson, Group Captain 'Mike' CBE 82, 84, 280
Hodgson, Flight Lieutenant 'Pete' ('Hodge') 102
Holden, Wing Commander Walter 'Taffy' 71-76
Holmes, Paul 'Humpty' 70
Honington, RAF 93, 117
Hopkins, Wing Commander Bruce 11, 19, 86, 141, 143-146, 162-164
Horsham St. Faith RAF 25
Houston, Eric 162
Howard, Michael 87-88
Howard, Wing Commander Bernard H. 41
Howe, Squadron Leader John F.G. 9-10, 23-26, 254, 277-278

Ingham, 'Dick' 228-229

Jackson, Flight Lieutenant 'Roly' 28, 69, 163,
Jarron, Wing Commander Jake 246-248
Jewell, Flight Lieutenant Peter M. 'Jimmy' 41, 77, 89
Jones, 'Dave' 25
Jones, David Maxwell 25
Jones, Flight Lieutenant Ernie E. 41
Jones, Flight Lieutenant Lee 49
Jones, Flight Lieutenant T. W. 'Tex' 214-215
Jones, Flying Officer Laurie 32
Jordan, Captain 'Ed' 186

Keddleston HMS 201
Kendrick, 'Jonx' 89
Khamis Mushayt 224, 229-230, 259
Khan, Colonel Akbar 84
Kinloss, RAF 197, 281
Knowles, Flying Officer Raymond 217
Kuun, Wing Commander 'Dave' 156
Kuwait Air Force 223, 260,

Lakenheath, RAF 31, 256
Laughton, Wing Commander Charles 69
Law, Flying Officer Derek 49-50
Lawrance, Squadron Leader Michael 215-216
Leconfield, RAF 13, 19-20, 26, 114, 119, 121, 201, 215, 221, 252, 255-258
Leeming, RAF 102-103, 108-109, 112, 251
Leuchars, RAF xiv, xv, 10, 13, 15-17, 30-31, 69, 80, 119, 121, 127, 146-147, 152-155, 162-163, 171, 173-174, 193, 195-196, 207, 224-225, 227, 249, 251-254, 258, 280, 283-284
Limbrey, Brian 173
Little Rissington, RAF 23, 127-128
Llanbedr 158
Lloyd, Derek 'Furze' xiii, 88, 127-130
Lossiemouth, RAF xvi, 117, 132, 154, 193, 199, 258, 284
Lucas, 'Sam' 47,
Luqa, Malta 114, 250
Lyneham, 33 MU 71, 73-75, 281

MacDermid, Wing Commander Murdo 88, 93
MacEwen, Flight Lieutenant 'Noddy' 40
MacFadyen, Ian 70
MacKay, Flight Lieutenant Alastair J. RCAF 208
MacLean, Flying Officer Alastair Cameron 'Harry' 207
'Magic Carpet' 223-236, 286
'Magic Palm' 223
Malan, 'Sailor' 277
Manning, Flight Lieutenant Robert J. 41, 48-49,
Manning, Flying Officer Simon 'Much' 215
Marham, RAF 90, 93, 113, 117-118, 120-122, 124, 132, 156, 173, 250, 254, 282
Martin, Sir James 46, 178
Martin-Baker 46, 173, 178, 203, 206-207
Masirah 122-124, 173, 254
Mason, Flying Officer Kevin 214
Matheson, Neil 216
McDonald-Bennett, Trevor 'McDoogle-Boogle' 89
McLeod, Wing Commander John 89, 92, 118, 154
Mermagen, Flight Lieutenant 'Tim' F.H. 41
Middleton St. George RAF 28, 51, 69, 143, 256-257
Miles M.52 3
Molland, Flight Lieutenant Hedley 14, 278
Moore, Flight Lieutenant Malcolm J. 'Mo' 41, 45, 47
Moore, Major Al USAF 19
Morgan, 'Al' 70

INDEX

Morris, AM Sir Desmond 'Zulu' 49
Morris, Simon 167, 285
Mottershead, Flying Officer
    'Phil' 208
Muharraq 122, 125, 251, 255
Murty, Keith 202

NADGE 147
Nance, Flying Officer Edward J.
    'Ted' 25, 131
Nance, Wing Commander Stewart
    'Stu' 113, 134
Nash, 'Pete' 151-152, 182-183
Nasser, Brigadier General Prince
    Turki bin 224
Neatishead, RAF 20, 84, 99, 147
Neel, Major Charles B. USAF 197
Nelson, Flight Lieutenant
    'Tim' 23, 25
Newton, RAF 191
Nicholls, Sir John KCB CBE DFC
    AFC 18, 278
Norris, Geoffrey 42-44
North Luffenham, RAF 28, 94

Offord, Flight Lieutenant R. E.
    'Bob' 35, 40, 42-44, 80-81, 118,
    120, 152, 224, 282
Owen, Flight Lieutenant G. M.
    'Glyn' 31

Page, Sir F.W. 'Freddie' 5
Paris Air Show 21, 25, 48-49
Paxton, Squadron Leader 'Tony'
    ('Pax') 101-112
Peacock-Edwards, 'Rick' 89
Penrice, Flight Lieutenant Craig
    219-221, 286
Perry, Squadron Leader G. L. 131
Peterson, Captain 'Al' 76

Petter, W. E. W. 'Teddy' 2, 4-5
Phillips, Peter J. 25
Pink, Flight Lieutenant
    'Gil' 83, 281
'Piscator', Exercise 122
Ploszek, Flight Lieutenant Henry
    R. 40-41, 81
Pope, Flight Lieutenant
    Roger 171-172
Porter, AM Sir Kenneth 75
Povilus, Captain William 'Bill' R.
    USAF 202-206
Price, Wing Commander Nigel 85

QRA xiv, xv, 99-102, 141-170, 249

Rackham, Lieutenant Colonel 'Ed'
    USAF 25
Radford, Thomas Vaughan 'Vorn'
    25, 229-230
RAF Germany xiii, 13, 15, 70, 97,
    155, 165, 167, 250-252, 255
Ramsey, Flying Officer Martin
    'Tetley' 218
Rawcliffe, Flight Lieutenant
    Edward 284
Rawlings, J. D. R. 143-146
Red Arrows 41, 49, 71, 285
Reed, Squadron Leader Alex 76,
    80, 83
Reynolds, Flight Lieutenant
    'Jim' 142
Reynolds, Flight Lieutenant Paul
    154, 210
Rigg, Flying Officer
    'Mike' 177-178
Robertson, Squadron Leader 20
Robinson, Hilda
    WRAF 144-145
Rogers, Squadron Leader John 36

Roome, Flight Lieutenant 'Dave' 173-174, 177, 179
Rothwell, Group Captain 'Freddie' 69
Royal Saudi Air Force Lightnings 223

Sandys, Duncan 7
Sanford, Ian 89
SARBE 201, 205, 231
Saudi Arabia xiv-xvi, 223-236, 259-260
Saxa Vord 147, 162, 195
Schaffner, Major William 'Bill' Olin USAF 197-201
Seward, Group Captain 'Dave' AFC 2, 5, 12-13, 15, 33-35, 40-42, 44-45, 47-48, 50, 69-70, 88, 92-93, 96-97, 119, 163
Shaw, Flight Lieutenant 'Mike' J. F. CBE 27-29
Short S.B.5 4
Simmonds, Group Captain David C. H. 18-19, 39
Sims, Flight Lieutenant John 86-87
Singapore 122-125, 171, 173-176, 178-179, 224, 250-251, 254-255, 283
Small, Flight Lieutenant Iain 238-241
Smith, Flight Lieutenant George 97
Sneddon, Flight Lieutenant 'Jock' 80
Spencer, Squadron Leader John 89, 96-97, 241-248, 286
Squier, John W.C. 7-9,
Staxton Wold 194-195, 242-246, 286
Steenson, Flight Lieutenant Eric 191
Steggall, 'Geoff' 69
Steggall, Flight Lieutenant 'Pete' 28
Stiff, Brian 94-96
Stock, Dave 249
Stoke Mandeville 46
Stradishall, RAF 23
Swart, 'Les' 36
Swiney, Wing Commander 'Mick' 71, 77, 82, 223
Symes, Flight Lieutenant Peter 46-47

'Tambour', Exercise 35
Tehran 120
'Ten Ton Club' 96
Tengah, RAF 122, 171-173, 250-251, 254
Thompson, Flight Lieutenant Ian 152
Thompson, Flight Lieutenant 'Mike' 217-218
Thompson, Flying Officer 'Pete' 173
Thompson, Flight Lieutenant 'Terry' R. RCAF 41, 280
'Thunder City' 249
Topp, Group Captain Roger 70, 280
Tulloch, Flying Officer 'Stu' 285
Turbin, 'Bob' 89
Turley, Flight Lieutenant 'Al' 69, 280

'Ultimacy', Exercise 122-123, 282
Upper Heyford, RAF 117
Upwood, RAF 20, 27

Valley, RAF 89, 103, 125, 157, 217, 251
Van Gucci, Group Captain Peter 77
Verbiest, Lieutenant 'Danny' 282

INDEX

Waddington, RAF 106-107, 169, 246

Ward, John 71, 141

Warton airfield xiv, 4, 7, 9, 14, 18, 29, 32, 117, 127, 134, 143, 173, 209, 227-229, 236, 252, 280, 283-284

Wattisham, RAF 1, 12, 14-15, 21, 33-34, 37, 40, 42, 45-46, 80, 86, 93, 118-119, 134, 147, 151-152, 154, 156, 158, 163, 182, 191, 193, 203, 210-211, 214, 249, 253-256, 258, 280

Webb, Group Captain P. T. G. 'Duk' OBE DL 89

Webster, Flying Officer John C. 171, 177

West Drayton 147

Wethersfield, RAF 34-35, 280

Whitehouse, Flight Lieutenant 'Frank' 171-172, 177

Whittaker, Squadron Leader J. 14

Whittle, Sir Frank 2

Whyer, Pilot Officer Vivian 84

Wightman, 'Slim' 228, 285

Wild, Flight Lieutenant J.G. 'Oscar' 81, 88, 217

Wildenrath, RAF 167, 252, 255

Williams, Flight Lieutenant Maurice J. 25, 36

Wittering, RAF 47

Woodbridge, RAF 25, 206

Wratten, ACM Sir William 'Bill' 70

Wright, Flight Lieutenant Alan W. A. 'Lefty' 23, 25

Wyton, RAF 37, 85

Yeager, Captain Charles 'Chuck' 3

'Yellowjacks' aerobatic team 49

Yeovilton, RNAS 240